DATE DUE

DEMCO 38-296

~ A JOURNEY WITH ELSA CLOUD ~

A JOURNEY WITH

Elsa Cloud

~

Leila Hadley

BOOKS & CO./TURTLE POINT

NEW YORK

Books & Co. / Turtle Point

ISBN 1-885983-16-6
LIBRARY OF CONGRESS NUMBER 96-083491

Design and composition by Wilsted & Taylor Publishing Services

To heart-dazzling friends

Shri Mulk Raj Anand:
scholar, author, editor of *Marg*, for miles of years
the only art magazine published in India;

And to Shri and Shrimata Mattoo:
Meenakshi Devi, artist, designer, and poet,
and Omkar Nath, builder and engineer.

They embrace, and they embraced me in India,
with love; felicitous beauty; ancient, innocent strengths;
ceaseless intelligences.

Dr. Johnson had for many years given me hopes that we should go together and visit the Hebrides. . . . We might there contemplate a system of life almost totally different from what we had been accustomed to see, and to find simplicity and wildness, and all the circumstances of remote time and place. . . .

[James Boswell, *Journal of a Tour to the Hebrides*]

When you have leisure,
Wander idly through my garden in spring
And let an unknown, hidden flower's scent startle you
Into sudden wondering—
Let that displaced moment be my gift,
Or if, as you peer your way down a shady avenue,
Suddenly spilled
From the thick gathered tresses of evening
A single shivering fleck of sunset-light stops you,
Turns your daydreams to gold,
Let that light be an innocent
Gift.

[Rabindranath Tagore, *Gift*]

Part One

One

My daughter has been lost to me in a world I do not understand. I have been lost to her in a world she has left and has come to scorn. In more than two years, I have not spoken to her. Now I have been awakened by a telephone call, and her voice, sure, cool, is coming through the receiver from a great distance.

". . . And don't worry about your Hindi, Mummy. It's easier than Spanish. I'll meet you twenty days from now in New Delhi. At the airport."

I watch the shifting ladders of reflected light on the ceiling cast from the night traffic moving south on Fifth Avenue. They are scored with flickering ribbons stained the color of pomegranate juice—the bottled grenadine syrup Veronica used to sip for its color, suggestive of myth and mercurochrome. My heart is beating like a drum.

As I forcibly shake myself out of sleep, talking is difficult. "Where are you? How did you get the call through?"

"I'm in a toasty hot telephone booth in Janpath. If I call

collect, I don't have to wait long." Veronica sounds exultant. "What time is it in New York?"

I sit up in bed, click on the reading lamp, and check the Tiffany silver bedside clock with my grandmother's interlaced monogram worn smooth from a century of polishing.

"Almost four in the morning. Tuesday. I can hear the echo of my voice saying 'To *you's* day.'"

Her child-like laughter is an unexpected gift. "It's afternoon here. I've just booked a suite for us in Old Delhi at Oberoi Maiden's. And I've arranged an audience for you in Dharamsala with His Holiness."

"His Holiness? What's the Pope doing in Dharamsala?"

"Not the *Pope*, Mummy, His Holiness, the *Dalai Lama*. I thought you'd like to write about him. I gave him some of the flea medallions you sent for his Lhasa Apso."

"But what could I say? What can I ask him? I hardly even know who he is."

I reach for my notebook and pen. *Dalai Lama*, I scribble, while Veronica replies, "Oh, Mummy, you can ask His Holiness anything. Just ask him whatever comes to mind. He's very wise about everything."

"Well, I'm not," I say as the coils of inadequacy squeeze all relevant intelligence from my mind.

"Sorry, but I thought you'd be pleased if I fixed it all up for you."

From fourteen thousand miles away, I hear Veronica sigh. Impatience. Disappointment. Reproach. The advice of an analyst and entrepreneurs of health, wealth, and happiness to the contrary, Veronica has the power to make me feel foolish, unworthy as a person or a mother. Like an empty stage, Shake-speare's O without a figure.

Veronica goes on relentlessly. "It isn't important whether you believe His Holiness to be an embodiment of compassion. At least you could appreciate the purity of his friendliness, his benevolence and tensionlessness. It could benefit your mind. The Indians call it '*darshan*.'"

"*Darshan?*"

"Yes. *Darshan. Darshan*, you know, what happens to you when you visit illumined people and you receive from them a sort of psychic transmission, which the English word 'blessing' doesn't really convey, although it could, if you wanted it to."

Now that Veronica has explained *darshan*, I have some recol-lection, some thought-speck around which a crystal grows. "Oh, yes." I try to will this drop of comprehension into an instant stalactite. "Yes, yes, I understand. You wrote me about that."

For a moment, we are both silent. Then, dispensing with that part of me which ought to be up to her intelligence and isn't, I am once again lured by Veronica's voice, gentled to the persua-sive and assured sweetness of one asking for a favor certain to be granted.

"Could you possibly bring a few things with you when you come? Sweaters, a dress, things like that? And some of those yummy dried soups and the very dark kind of Swiss chocolate? And some Mediterranean herbs? You don't have to bring them in jars or tins. You can empty them into those plastic things. You know, *Baggies*."

"Baggies. Yes." No *darshan* about plastic. In my mind I am

hearing about decanting thyme, basil, oregano, and tarragon into little sacks, firmly securing their fragrance with elastic bands. Staples might tear and make holes. I tell myself that I am practical, energetic, and organized.

"There's no way to make a *bouquet garni* around Dharamsala," Veronica adds silkily. "My thumb and index finger have taken on an almost permanently green tinge from pinching leaves and holding them to my nose. There's wild basil in Manali but not in Dharamsala."

I try to imagine Dharamsala and Manali. All I see in my mind are snow-capped mountains, saffron-robed monks, and Veronica searching for the scent of Greece in the Himalayas during the heat, the cold, and the monsoon. Could the wild basil in Manali possibly be the heritage of Alexander the Great and his armies?

"And I need some of those fine accountant's pens to draw with," Veronica persists. "And cognac. Maybe a bottle of Remy Martin. Even in Bombay and Delhi, you can't get any decent cognac."

I feel suddenly lifted with the sense of being needed. "Of course, my darling Elsa Cloud. Is there anything else I can bring?"

Darling Elsa Cloud. When Veronica was sixteen, she had said, "I'd like to be the sea, the jungle, or else a cloud." The last words, transformed to Elsa Cloud, became an instant homonymic endearment. *Darling, darling* Elsa Cloud.

I know as I cradle the telephone that this is not the prelude to a simple mother and daughter holiday in India. Veronica has embarked on a quest for peace of mind and self-acceptance. She has steeped herself in Buddhism and, from her letters, she appears to be devoted to the presence and teachings of Geshe-la, her lama guru.

All my journeys start with an anxious pang of doubt. Are paradises only those that poets claim have been lost?

After Veronica rings off, I lie listening to the faint ticking of my grandmother's silver clock and my thoughts regress, associations intertwining like the letters of her monogram. I recall the complete and unalloyed bliss of summer evenings in Scotland when my grandmother read aloud to me in a voice rich enough for grand Shakespearean outbursts, dazzling my imagination with all the sahibs and soldiers and the lama in Kipling's *Kim*. From time to time, she would stop to explain Kipling's descriptions of the surfaces of life, and the world of ideas in India, and remark about kinsmen of ours who had been governors and viceroys. Kinsmen became *Kim's men* in my mind, and early on in my childhood, a link was forged associating irrevocably my grandmother and Scotland—with its heathery hills grazed on by barrel-fat sheep, whose wool, rubbed off on barbed wire fences or caught on bramble bushes, I used to save in shoe boxes—with the glitter of India's bazaars and the wonder of its temples and magic mountains.

My mother's mother was confident in the security of her husband's seigniorial Scottish lineage and the cultivation of her own Bostonian upbringing. She demanded respect. A woman of rock-hard conscience and moral caliber, by nature a disciplinarian and a perfectionist, she had a strong sense of purpose, a surprising natural goodness, and devout Christian and intellectual beliefs. Before I was old enough to be able to formulate her character, I sensed her strength and her individuality. I admired her nature, intuiting that it was authentic and tempered with none of the weaknesses of my parents, and more genuinely good than theirs or mine.

It was important to my parents that I know how to behave properly and was suitably well-dressed. It was important to my grandmother that I should read Shakespeare and the Bible, familiarize myself with family history, and write intelligent letters to her. "You can't expect to write well if you don't read good books," she said. As birthday and Christmas presents, she gave me books and leather-bound diaries with lock-straps and tiny gold keys (which I was too afraid I would lose to make any use of except for that first experimental turn in the keyhole to hear the reassuring locking and unlocking click-click, after which the keys would be saved for decorating packages, making collages, or for the matchboxes I filled with secrets and surprises and gave as offerings to people I loved).

My grandmother was the only member of my family who had a kind word to say about James Boswell, my great-great-great-great-great-grandfather, as she pointed out on the family tree—not a tree at all, to my disappointment, but a long parchment scroll inscribed with what looked like a high wall of bricks dripping names. "You should be proud of your heritage," she told me. "Bozzy had his faults, but he was an excellent journalist. He had a strong sense of family. He was a religious man and saw that his children received a religious education. He believed that truth and honor went hand in hand. He had an almost sacred reverence for his ancestors killed at Flodden Field." She looked at me reflectively, fixing me with her truth-telling gray-blue eyes. "He may have been naughty, indiscreet, and intemperate, but he was an excellent journalist, an *excellent* journalist. Remember that, my treasure."

I came to believe that being a journalist was not only an admirable profession, but excused one of many faults, and would be entirely accommodating to my own temperament and personality.

When I was twenty-five, the same age Veronica is now, I traveled east to discover India for myself and, by writing about it, to make it my own. I saw Bombay and Delhi through the eyes of Kim, an imaginary all-knowing interlocutor at my side. I went to Nagpur and ate its sweet oranges while I watched the dances of an ancient tribe that lives in its province. I saw Ellora and Ajanta, the Elephanta Caves and country villages through the amused and sympathetic eyes of Mulk Raj Anand, an Indian novelist and art scholar. A wonderful middle-aged *Kshatriya* (warrior caste) Krishna-man, he always wore something red, which was for him the color of life, and his rapid conversation spiced with ribald wit lectured me deliciously. I saw India through all my senses in a tumultuous assault of sight and sound and smell and taste and resonating color.

Veronica is experiencing India with a Tibetan lama, meditating, practicing Buddhism, studying Tibetan grammar in a lamas' college in Dehra Dun.

She has written that she is living now at the end of a goat path in the Himalayas in a three-storied house she rents for an infinitesimal monthly sum. Cows are stabled on the ground floor. Corn and hay are stored on the top floor. She is ensconced in a high-ceilinged room on the middle floor, surrounded by a roofed-over balcony from which there are splendid views of snow-peaked mountains, apple orchards, and deodars, a large, dark and regal species of cedar, known as the timber of the gods. Somewhere, hidden from sight, is the village of Manali and a small Indian and Tibetan bazaar where she can buy dried cheese, fish freshly caught from the Beas river, buttermilk, and other provisions.

Her bed is in arm's reach of a cylindrical wood-burning stove, a *tandoor*. In her drawing of it, the *tandoor* has the look of a pure, clean sculpture, with two removable lids on top where she can put pots for cooking, and for heating the water that she fetches in a bucket from the stream close by to her house.

She reads by candlelight or the light of a kerosene lamp. She has no electricity. Veronica finds this nineteenth-century pastoral life agreeable, and regards much of the twentieth century as trivial, mindless, and tacky. She writes about white cherry blossoms, red apples, green pears, about a palm squirrel in Dharamsala, a skittish kitten in Dehra Dun, a puppy that lies warm and furry on her pillow in Manali. She writes that Buddha's answer to life's riddles are the Four Noble Truths. Suffering exists. Suffering is caused by desire. Suffering can be overcome by the elimination of desire. Desire can be eliminated by following the Noble Eightfold Path of moderation and clear thought, a statement of the role of reason in human affairs that addresses itself to the human condition and a concern for all life. She writes that the Buddhist doctrine teaches non-attachment, the sublimation of the ego so that even though there is chaos all around you, you can still maintain detachment and an all-calm inner self, not only freed from worldly attachments to people and things, but also in a state of complete and true self-knowledge. You can achieve this state best, she writes, by the mind-emptying exercise of meditation which allows the mind to open outward and let in life, the way a lotus opens to the sun.

What do they mean, these ascetic, cerebral commentaries of hers? What do they have to do with India, *my* India?

Turning off the light, I hear my grandmother's voice again, quoting Shakespeare. "Out of this nettle danger, we pluck this flower, safety."

Would this be true for me? Was it true for Veronica? Had she managed to pluck a flower of safety from that dangerous nettle-bed of the sixties when it was not the fashion to endure reality in an unaltered state?

Lately, I've had the recurring fantasy that I am Demeter and Veronica is Persephone. Demeter knew her daughter was lost, and she wandered over the earth, searching for her. At first, she simply abandoned herself to her sorrow. Then she consciously entered into it as though entering a temple, enclosing herself in a ritual holy place. She contained in her grief not only the loss of her daughter, but also the loss of the young and carefree part of herself.

Likening myself to Demeter and brooding in my own cave of introversion, I had said to my therapist only a few months before, "Veronica has gone to earth in India. I miss her terribly. I don't know what to do."

"So, why don't you go to India and visit her?" My analyst is Jungian, and is as conversant with mythology as he is with my needs for reassurance and encouragement.

"She hasn't asked me. I don't know how she really feels about me now."

"On the archetypal level, your daughter is an extension of yourself. She carries you back into your past and your own youth and she carries you forward to the promise of your own rebirth into a new personality, into the awareness of the Self." He added, with a smile, "Is that what you were thinking? Is that what makes you feel ambivalent?"

I did not know if this were true or not. It was one of those sessions when I had arrived feeling my sense of self shriveled, the fruits of the earth withering all around.

When I told him how I felt, my analyst said, "That's good. You always feel withered when it is time for a transformation. Everything dries up inwardly and outwardly and life becomes sterile until the conscious mind is forced to recognize the gravity of the situation." He paused, gesturing in the air. "Then you are compelled to accept the validity of the unconscious, the force for renewal."

Ever unflappable, ever optimistic, he has reminded me many times before that growth and development are painful.

I am sure his theories are correct, but what I want to know is when will suffering lead away from neurosis to a new life, to new understanding? Will I, like Demeter, be truly reunited with my daughter? Will she, like Persephone, having eaten the food of Hades and taken the dark pomegranate seeds into herself, give birth to her own new personality? Can we both, like the mythical mother and daughter, pass through death and enter a new spring—an ageless inward renewal? Can we accept the necessity of life in the underworld darkness of our psyches?

My puckish therapist sighed an exaggerated sigh as he always does when I go off on what Veronica calls a blither tangent.

"Well, of course," he said. That was down the road. Just give yourself time. Everything would work out. "Just give yourself time," he repeated, glancing at his watch.

Time has gone by. It is February now, almost spring, and I have received a miraculous telephone call. Soon I shall be with Veronica.

Two

Twenty days until I fly to India. I pack and shop obsessively. Having taken care of Veronica's requests and requirements, I wonder what other comforts for her mind and body I should bring. At first thought, the possibilities seem boundless. On second thought, perhaps anything more would only clutter her airy, precise, and functional environment. Stimulated and cautioned, I try also to anticipate what my own needs and wants will be.

When at last I look at all I have bought and assembled, I feel like a dying Egyptian, berserk in the determination to dispatch all the belongings of this world to the next. Hot and cold weather gear for Veronica and me; blue jeans and T-shirts for her to keep or give away to friends; long-skirted, long-sleeved dresses from Laura Ashley, their slender sashed waists of Kate Greenaway inspiration, with overtones of the innocent, the puritan, the pioneer; cotton underwear; washcloths and wraparound bath towels; Veronica's favorite herbal shampoo; Crabtree and Evelyn soaps; foaming bath oil; creams, perfumes, pots and jars of this and that for face and skin, delectably scented and packaged with artistry; cassette recordings of Mozart, Bach, Beethoven, Haydn, Purcell, Bob Dylan; a thick packet of postcard reproductions of paintings and sculpture I hope she will like; a few art books I could afford and more that I charged recklessly; magazines I thought Veronica would enjoy cutting up for collages; a lightweight collapsible bucket, a thermos, enamel-handled cutlery, flashlights, paintboxes, notebooks, scissors, Scotch tape, elastic bands, paper clips, safety pins, buttons, needles, thread.

I delight in lists and in quantifying, preserving the present, pre-sent and unprecedented, before it dissolves into the past or emerges into the future. The evolutional present. Perhaps this is why sometimes I read words and syllables backwards. That the word *love* is contained in *evolution* makes me smile as I list and sort and quantify. Love spelled backwards. I see that nought (o) except love can save evolution from evil. Evil spelled backwards is *live*, and to live is to fare forward. Relying on the complexities of language to deal with my lonely world, I go on packing. I pick up three felt-tipped pens, those liquid crayon-like markers, for easy scribbling and writing in notebooks. Earth spelled backward is *thrae*, Scottish dialect for *three*. Two pens are a lovely royal blue, the other is bright as a spring leaf. There, there, I say to myself and scribble in a notebook:

Vert, vert. An extravert is extra green. An introvert is green inside, green and growing, that's vers libre. Puns are words in copulation. All words are sexual in origin. In the beginning was the word, the spermatic word. In Roman times, perfume was made from oil of ambergris, a substance vomited by sperm whales, mammals, not fish like Ichthus, Jesus

Christ King of the Jews, to whom the Wise Men brought the fragrance of myrrh and frankincense. My father's name was Frank. Sense in Frank? Sense or nonsense?

I pack soft-tipped pens and hard-nibbed ones for filling in the carbon copy forms that Indians revel in. Flea medallions. Cutter's insect repellent. Binoculars. Barley-sugar. Powdered soup mixes, herbs, Chinese tea, *marrons glacés*. Tins of tissue-wrapped Italian macaroons and elaborate boxes of chocolate wrapped in gold foil, the *Amoretti* and the *Baci* that are Veronica's favorites.

All of this I pack into two black fibreboard sample cases—the kind traveling salesmen use for shipping coats and trousers flat, with lock straps and keys, devices pleasurably reminiscent of the lock-strap diaries I had been given as a child. Veronica's father had called these bags "mummy cases," by which affectionately insulting *mummy/Mummy* wordplay, they had become a family joke, and so called, you could see them lumping up into a pharaoh's head, folded arms, feet. Finally, beside these well-worn, voluminous pieces of luggage, I set aside a Louis Vuitton tote bag to carry my camera, film, and quotidian writing materials on the plane. And suddenly this tote bag, brown, made of something synthetic to look like leather and stamped all over with interlocking Ls and Vs, Ls for Leila, Vs for Veronica, links memory and reality in a seamless web.

My earliest recollections of travel are of watching preparations made to "go abroad," as my mother always said, to stay with my grandmother in London and in Scotland. Louis Vuitton trunks, massive leather cubes with brass corner mountings, and locks stamped with L.V. (separate initials, not interlocking as they are now), would be brought from the attic and opened to have the webbed fabric of their trays and their beige linen interiors dusted before their lavish packing with tissue-paper and scalloped-edged flannel coverlets scented with lavender to divide the layers. Then the trunk lids would be ceremoniously closed and locked, and off the trunks would go to a Cunard steamer, to be stored either in our cabins or in the hold. The ceremony was curiously like my own bedtime ritual, being tucked into bed, the lights turned off, my bedroom door closed with the admonition to have a happy sleep, pleasant dreams, and "to sail away to the land of Nod" as it said in one of the bedtime story books my ever-changing nannies and governesses read to me. When I was older, I was given the job of pasting on the identification stickers and the labels with the picture of a funnelled ship on top and space below for our address.

There, in the guestroom of Northlea, the house I grew up in, the room in which all packing of trunks took place, the room large with yellow walls and the triple mirror of the dressing table catching the light and spinning bright geometrics on the walls, the Persian rugs and the burnished trunks, was the genesis of my pleasure in quantifying, and the sensual thrill for me of textures, of materials folded with rustling tissue-paper, and the pleasure of extending these associations in the memory game called—what else? *I Packed My Grandmother's Trunk* (and in it I put . . .), a game my generation played while motoring.

Games are always important, a symbolic expression of ideas and feelings that are meaningful to us. Names are also important. The Ls on the Louis Vuitton trunks had stood in my child's mind for my grandmother's name, Lilla, and also for my own. The V was just there then, an addition, a mystery. Not wanting to name me Lilla, a name not to her liking, my mother named me Leila, after the heroine, she said, of a novel by Bulwer-Lytton. Father or son, I asked, curious. She put me off, telling me in a voice barely masking irritation and impatience that she had forgotten. Perhaps, in naming me, she unconsciously meant to project her own elusiveness, her own eel-like slipperiness into the eel-like sound of my name.

My grandmother's name, Lilla, is infused in my mind with the fragrance of lilies in the gardens of my childhood and the scent of country churches resonating with hymns. I had thought of Lilla when I was making a list of names to call my first-born daughter, but as a given name, Lilla did not go along at all with our surname. And so I chose Veronica for its Latin form, *Vera iconica,* "having to do with the true image," a reference to the representation of the face of Christ on the handkerchief of the woman who later became known as Saint Veronica. Perhaps I had some dim remembrance that Veronica was a name introduced into our family through Boswell's great-grandmother Veronica, Countess of Kincardine, wife of Alexander, Earl of Kincardine. From him, Boswell had written, "the blood of Bruce flows in my veins. Of such ancestry, who would not be proud?"

Through the selective sieve that is memory, fantasies filter back to me about my own given name. In Byron's *Don Juan,* Leila is a Turkish child, and in the *Giaour,* Leila is a beautiful slave girl who falls in love with a *giaour* (ja-ooooer—I could hear in that word the Turkish contempt for all who were not of the Mussulman faith), flees from the Caliph's seraglio, is captured and hurled into the sea. Although my mother assumed that Leila was an "English" name, Leila means *dark* in Hebrew, *one night* in Arabic. In Iran, which I still think of as Persia, there's a legend about Leila and Majnoun, in which they are transformed into doves and their love honored like that of Psyche and Cupid, or the bride and bridegroom in the Song of Solomon. In Hindi Leila, spelled *lila*, and pronounced leela, as my name is pronounced, means cosmic play.

Veronica had sent me for my last birthday a copy of a traditional Tibetan *thangka* she had painted, an iconographic image of mountains, trees, lotuses, grassy cliffs, leaping fish, and a rainbow, the details so meticulously pictured that they look as if they had been painted with the aid of a magnifying glass and a mouse whisker. The significance, Veronica had written, is that out of the original open space of the mind arises the play (*lila*) of being. . . . The rainbow signifies the arising of form, feelings, perceptions, concepts, and consciousness, and its colors are symbolic of the transformation of defilements into wisdom:

> White is ignorance transformed into panoramic awareness;
> Yellow is pride and stinginess transformed into
>   imperturbability or even-mindedness;
> Red is desire, lust, and craving transformed into
>   discriminating awareness;
> Blue is anger transformed into mirror-like wisdom
>   (evenly receptive and reflective at the same time);
> Green is compulsion and ineptitude transformed into
>   all-accomplishing awareness.

The play of being, the transformation of defilements into wisdom, that rainbow a bridge to the past and the echo of my grandmother's certainty that "Good will always triumph over Evil"—Oh, darling Elsa Cloud, you should see how carefully I have framed your *thangka* and covered it with everything-proof glass to protect and preserve it.

Now, when I finally embark on the plane for India with my Louis Vuitton tote bag on my lap and settle into a world of imprisoned flight, L for luggage and Lilla and Leila, and V for Veronica and verity are as tightly knotted in my mind and memory as the strands of my grandmother's lucent pearls.

In my mind I talk with Veronica, trying like Demeter to understand, to *understand*.

Dearest Veronica, my daughter who wanted to be the sea, the jungle, or else a cloud. Elsa Cloud, Elsa Cloud. When you first began to stir in my pelvic embrace, pushing up a lump first on one side and then on the other, pushing against me so that I was afraid if I coughed or laughed I would wet myself, I felt a tenderness toward you that quickened and softened everything around me. I feel the same way now as I did then, twenty-five years ago, but now I am simply pregnant with my selves as they were, your selves as they were.

Sometimes, Elsa Cloud, you are just like me, a branch from the same tree in a dream forest—seasonally flaming, frosted with glittering ice, stencilled with snow, then leafing green and cool into vaulted chambers. As a child when I was not with my grandmother, it seemed natural for me to talk with trees. No one else was willing to stand still and listen, really *listen*. No one else was around who felt as substantial, except my father, but he never seemed as secure, unmoving, as surely *there* as the trees were. I loved my jolly father, and he loved me, but almost wordlessly. He led me on my Shetland pony at horseshows, told me funny wordplay jokes, showed me how to make imprints of angels in the snow, urged me to share with him the pleasures of outdoor sports and those indoor games like backgammon that make conversation impossible and dull people tolerable. He treated me to Fred Astaire movies and cried when he escorted me up the aisle on my wedding day. "We understand each other, don't we, old top?" he would say, flinging his arm across my shoulders. "You bet," I would reply, borrowing a phrase of his. "You bet your sweet life we do." Did you feel the same way, Veronica, about your Daddoo? Do you remember how he called you his little buttercup and fly, the residual child in him?

Sometimes you are not like me, Elsa Cloud, and sometimes, though not like me, you are the way I thought you would be. Family traits are passed on, adapted, compulsively repeated. The past recurs. Unlike me, you were a child conceived in love. I was the result of a union between an affectionate, demonstrative man and a woman who was not able to love but needed to be loved. You, darling, were your father's and my first-born, the promise of everything your father and I wanted to share—all the beauty and grace and wonder in the world—all of which was very different from my first marriage, and the birth of my first son.

When I told my first husband, Bryce Three, that I thought I must be pregnant because I hadn't had the curse for two months, he snapped at me. "Oh, damn it to hell, return your diaphragm to the factory that made it and tell them to send your three dollars back. And call Dr. Ramsey and find out where you can get an abortion. Just get rid of it."

I didn't, of course. I was thrilled at the thought of becoming a mother, of thus magically freeing myself from that remote, terrifying, unpredictable grandmother of yours, that creature I called Mummy and sometimes Mumsie, in letters and when I was living far away from her. Distanced from my mother at boarding school, distanced from her when I was married or traveling, I could fantasize her as the intimate, playful, smiling, laughing mother I longed for, a mother like the cake-baking, pie-making mothers in the funny papers, with flour up to their elbows. Mumsie. This fantasy apparently pleased her, for she took to the name and often used it herself in letters to me, even in the telegram she sent me announcing the death of my father.

To become a mother myself, to break with the past, to become a new person, another identity, a real Mummy-person—oh, the simple joy of that thought, the wonder! But my young husband hated surprises, and wasn't prepared to be a father. He wanted to be the baby himself, and certainly didn't want to relinquish his place on center stage, at least while he went off to battle in World War II. So all he said was, "Get rid of it. Call Dr. Ramsey."

I must have told you about Dr. Ramsey, the doctor my first husband's mother sent me to to have my hymen broken so her son wouldn't have a painful time penetrating me on his wedding night. That was the reason she gave me, but I'm sure she also wanted to check on my virginity to be certain her son was getting the unsullied seventeen-year-old, good family, old money debutante I appeared to be.

I still remember the flush of embarrassment that made me feel I was the color of a ripe tomato stem-to-stern with my feet up in the stirrups of Dr. Ramsey's examining table, and he with a rubber-gloved hand and an instrument that looked like the kitchen utensil used to tweeze asparagus out of a saucepan moving painfully inside of me. Afterwards, he told me to slip a Kotex inside my panty girdle so I wouldn't "stain" my Best & Co.'s best which I had worn for the occasion of my first visit to a gynecologist's office.

So the first thing Bryce Three said when he came home from the war and saw Bryce Four in my arms was: "Is he house-trained?"

"No," I replied.

"He should be," he said. My mother agreed. She told me I was "perfectly house-trained to go in a teacup" by the time I was only six months old.

Bryce Three spent the next month trying to train his son by sitting on the edge of the bathtub making grunts of defecation while Bryce Four sat next to him, strapped in his Tiny Toidey and smiling mirthlessly, a baby gargoyle, with no teeth showing. For Christmas that year, Bryce gave me a diamond-and-ruby clip, a gold-and-diamond clip, and a vacuum cleaner. He played with the vacuum cleaner as though it were an electric train, pointing out with delight all its attachments and demonstrating how they worked.

Not long after that, I left for Las Vegas, accompanied by a minister who was a friend of the family lawyer. Considered old enough at seventeen to get married, I was evidently considered too young two years later to get divorced without a chaperon.

I was never sure whether I was reveling in my own youthful sense of inviolability or was simply suicidal that summer, for later on, after my divorce was granted, I took trips to the Grand Canyon and other national parks, and played a childish game with myself, trying to see how close to the edge of a canyon rim I could walk. Imagining that I was a Mohawk, territorially displaced but inherently unafraid of heights, I ran along narrow walls at the road's edge, ignoring the precipitous drop to one side of me. Mohawk, gymnast, funambulist, Hermes, I sprinted, feeling the rush of air into my lungs, feeling the joy of it, feeling my sweat dry in the breeze, taking into myself the sky, the red rocks, the pines.

When I returned to New York, my mother told me she was too ashamed to leave the apartment she and my father had just bought as a *pied-à-terre*, because my divorce was the "first in the family on either side" and all her friends would be "horrified" and she would be too "mortified" to face them.

"Nonsense," I retorted with new-found strength. "It's much better to be divorced than miserable."

"But now you can't be presented at Court," she said, obstinate, accusing.

Eight years later, I married Robert, your father. With a background like mine, I explained to him, you grow up complacent, defensive, or insecure about your own identity. "I just need someone who loves me," I said. "Tell me what you want me to be, and I'll be it." I wanted to be loved, cared for, needed. What I also wanted was a new kind of *us*-ness. I was brought up to believe that if you weren't in the *Social Register*—the "stud book," my father called it—or *Debrett's* or *Burke's Peerage*, you were simply N.O.C.D. (Not Our Class, Dear), not top drawer. Whenever I mentioned people I had met, my mother would look in the *Social Register* to see if they were in it. If they weren't listed, she would close the book with its discreet brocade slip-cover, prettier and less slippery to the hand than the leather slip-covers for the telephone books, and dismiss whoever they were by saying, "Well, they're not here. They can't be much."

Sometimes, she didn't even look. She knew, just from the name, that they wouldn't be in it. There were *us*, with our club memberships, and there were *the others*. (There were also the Lower Classes, as my grandmother referred to them, the *"hoi polloi,"* *"the rag-tag and bob-tail,"* as my mother said, people who sat in the cheap public seats at the races and made up the crowds at public events, people my father said smelled "keekee," and my mother said were dirty and could give you germs, and the nurses said might kidnap me if I didn't watch out.) *Us* meant people who either knew your parents or went to school with you. They were on the side of the good. They contributed money to charities. They went to church. They supported the arts. They liked sailing or riding or beagling or duck-shooting or skiing or playing golf, tennis, squash, bridge, gin rummy, or backgammon. Many had swimming pools. Some had billiard rooms and yachts. They all had fresh flowers and very clean houses. They had a special look, a way of behaving, speaking, dressing, a vocabulary of words and gestures and stances that was unmistakable.

I accepted these qualities and characteristics as pleasant and comfortable to be around. As I say this, I hear myself sounding like an anthropologist discussing the beliefs of Fijian cannibals in the mid-nineteenth century, beliefs, aims, rules of another culture, another time, another world, but beliefs which Mummy and Daddy considered fundamental and eternal, and which are only a frail antique veneer of the eighteenth-century hierarchies where they appear to have survived. To give myself credit, I wanted more. I wasn't quite sure what. I felt I was different. How, I wasn't sure. I liked living in my mind. I searched for people with whom I could enjoy an emotional communion, people, as I still tell myself, that I won't have to be a chameleon with, changing my colors to get along.

So when Robert asked me to marry him, saying he wanted to have at least six children, I was not concerned that he did not hail from the *Social Register* set. I thought only how wonderful it was that he had perceived, as no other man had before him, that I was neither the blithe, beautiful, glamorous debutante nor the successful career girl that other people would have me be, but the potentially good wife and mother that was my own image of myself, and the ideal of the fifties.

"I have no money," he said abruptly.

"Don't worry about money," I said. "I have money. What's mine is yours. It will be *our* money."

I felt instantly protective and, at the same time, felt that Robert would provide a perfect shoulder for me to lean on and that we were a good complement to each other's sensibilities. That is, his California-casual life-style, his "education-happy family" as he described them, didn't seem irreconcilable with my Long Island upbringing and my New York ways. There was just the "tiresome paperwork," as my mother would say, of sending letters of recommendation about Robert to the *Social Register*.

"Wouldn't you rather be in *Who's Who* than in the oh, so very *Social Register*?" Robert asked. "Don't you want to do something, accomplish something really worthwhile?"

"There's nothing the matter with being in the stud book, and there's nothing the matter with not being in it," I replied, "but Mummy would be hysterical if we weren't in it, and I don't want to be taken out because then a lot of people would think you weren't as good as Bryce, and they wouldn't be able to look me up in Married Maidens or Dilatory Domiciles to find out what my new married name is or where we are." I was unable to conceive of the possibility of becoming an independent professional woman like Robert's widowed mother, engaged in a serious endeavor, and I already saw the jobs I'd had in journalism, publicity, and public relations the way Robert saw them—as frivolous and inconsequential, so I fell back on the role models of my mother and grandmother. "You be in *Who's Who* so I can admire you," I told him. "I like to be around people whom I can learn from and admire."

"What a sweet attitude, lambie," Robert's mother said with what I hoped was an expression of approval. "I hope you'll teach Robert to dress better. He doesn't even own a proper suit to get married in." Nothing ever seemed to faze Kate. She produced from the cedar closet a suit that had belonged to Robert's father, and with her usual efficiency, managed to get it cleaned, altered to fit, and pressed in time for the wedding. This time around, no lists, no engraved invitations, no registering at Tiffany's for silver and china, just a simple church ceremony with a few friends and members of Robert's family in attendance. Feeling guilty but unrepentant, I telephoned my mother after the service.

"I hope he will take care of you," she said, an expression of concern, I realize now, but at the time, I took it for yet another reminder of my inabilities, dependencies, inadequacies, another instance of the way she had of knocking out any sense of my self-esteem or self-worth, the better to give her power over me, to make me into her image of me.

When you grew too big for me to carry past the term the

doctors predicted, Veronica, your birth was induced. Instead of natural childbirth, I chose the painless, self-indulgent way, which was still the accepted fashion of the early fifties. Anesthetized with sodium pentathol, floating in an ocean thrumming with the sound of a motorboat, I seemed to be steering around bell-ringing buoys, and hardly felt the fierce concentration of my body's forces when you were born.

When you were presented to me a few hours later, swaddled in a flannel blanket, your face as round as a pocket-watch, your duck-down hair caught up in an absurd pink ribbon—probably off a florist's box—I offered you homage, a tribute to your innocence, beauty, and purity. I saw your skin bleached, your features simplified to two nostril dots, two fringed crescents, and one larger crescent, I put the tip of my finger to your nose, your warm eyelids, your mouth. Later, waking up at night, I would breathe in your sweet scent of milk formula, soap, talcum; inhale the ammoniac reek of your wet diapers and the sour, primitive, animal pungency of your "dirty" ones, and say silently, Thank you, God. Oh God, thank you, thank you, thank you. Feeding you with breast and bottle, watching you lying on your back months later in your slatted, screened, sweet-butter-yellow crib, batting at a mobile of vinyl blue jays, cardinals, and canaries with your tiny soft hands, creased and padded with fat, I felt we were alone in the world, the way lovers do, and I talked with you in my mind about all my thoughts and dreams for you and for myself. You sceptered your great-grandmother's ivory rattle with silver bells in a fist so tight that your skin was mottled a painterly gray and mauve. You gurgled with laughter, smiled toothlessly, seldom cried except when you were hungry.

I splurged ecstatically on what I called "your trousseau"—

everything yellow or white sprinkled with yellow roses. Yellow, the color of the sun, symbolic in Renaissance paintings of divinity and truth revealed, the color of the center of a daisy or the day's eye, this was the color I chose for you. Yellow, if you will, for pride—no defilement, to my way of thinking—although stinginess I abhor, and I doubt that even-mindedness is a beatitude; even-mindedness is a bore. But I don't mean to find fault with your *thangka*. I am "loving it so," as Robert used to say to you when he saw you enjoying something. "Are you loving it so, my little buttercup and fly?" he would ask you fondly. "Tell your Daddoo you are loving it so." He would smile at you and you would smile at him and I would be almost dizzy with delight and hear in my mind:

> Three with a new song's measure
> Can trample an empire down.
> For each age is a dream that is dying,
> Or one that is coming to birth.

Who is this by? What *is* his name? I ask myself, and Robert replies. O'Shaughnessy, late nineteenth century. Ode: We Are the Music Makers, We are the dreamers of dreams, and now I can't remember the rest of it.

Robert was one of those people who find in the flaws and imperfections of others reassurance about their own, but you were faultless, even in his eyes. I can't remember his ever being impatient or cross with you. "She looks as though she would shit ice cream," he once said, as he changed your diaper. "But she sure doesn't," he added, as he chucked it, unrinsed, into a waist-high metal container that released an odor like an un-mucked-out stall. The smell of the stable I hung about as a child while my father's polo ponics were being exercised, the smell of Zulu *kraals* and "kaffir beer" in South Africa where we lived while your father was getting his Ph.D. in geology. I like these primitive, natural, un-deodorized smells, and now, breathing the chemically "freshened," odorless, oxygenized essence of an airline's un-birdlike flight, I try without success to recreate them. From time to time, I pull down a tray, put food into my mouth, drink coffee, push the tray back against the seat in front, fasten the catch, totter up the aisle to go to the john, see my face in the fluorescent light, totter back to my seat, close my eyes, and drift off.

You and I, Elsa Cloud, mother and daughter, and your Dad-doo who died at the untimely age of fifty on Epiphany day, six weeks almost to the day before your miraculous telephone call . . . Do you remember the night when we were driving across country from California, where you were born, to New York, where I was born, to board the freighter that would take us to South Africa, and our U-haul trailer was set on fire by a passing truckman's discarded cigarette? No, how could you? You were only six months old. We could all have been killed, you, your Daddoo, and I. I still shiver all over, the way a horse does when it wants to get dry, when I think of that night. You, your father and I alone on that ghostly flat desert, with bats and bouquets of sparks whirling around us while the trailer burned to embers.

The next frame flashes in my memory's viewer. You at the age of three, wearing a robin's egg–blue woolen coat, hat, and leggings, your arms and legs the same simplified shape, standing on a lawn in the garden suburbs of Johannesburg. You are hap-pily reproducing the complex tongue and palate maneuvers of your Xhosa nanny, whose speech is punctuated with phonetic clicks, one like the sound of a drop of water falling into a bucket, another like the cluck of a hen, a third resonant as the clop of a horse's hoofbeat. Your Xhosa nanny turns to me and says, "She's going to grow old, Madam, and walk with a stick, she be so bright and good." Your father was good at languages. He could speak Papuan, Mandarin, Afrikaans, and Spanish. My French is passable, and with a phrase book in hand I can make myself understood in almost any language. But you, Elsa Cloud, your mimetic abilities never cease to astonish me.

Here you are again, you endearing creature, at the age of four, still in South Africa, moving your body and kicking your legs in the fluid, sensual way of our African servants, accompanied by penny-whistles and home-made drums at a native party.

And now, a mite of a child in a white sun-bonnet and yellow sun-dress, you have been transported to Jamaica in the West Indies where we have come to live after Africa. A big, roomy, old-fashioned house with jalousies at all the windows, and hummingbirds flying through the giant tulip tree. A pet goat named Billy the Kid. A cat who was always having kittens. Because she always was, I called her Underfoot. Pet guinea fowl, balls of brown and white fluff with coral-colored legs when they hatched. Sometimes I warmed the ones who weren't strong enough to pip by themselves and had to be rescued from cracked eggs, by tucking them into my bra, and when they cheeped loud enough, I set them down with their hardier brothers and sisters to grow into the speckled gray and white pear-shaped creatures you used to summon by trilling, "Here, giddy flowers! Here, giddy flowers!" Oh, Elsa Cloud, I can hear your voice sweet and clear above the rustling and coughings of the passengers, their mumblings, and the hum of the plane.

In our Jamaican garden, I planted parsley in the shape of an R for your Daddoo, L for me, V for you, S for baby Sam, and later, A for baby Allison and B for your big half-brother Bryce who was away in America at school, and came back to us only during his vacations.

I love my other children. They love me. But it is you now, the prodigy, the prodigal daughter, who has taken over my imagination.

By the time you were six, you could swim with the craft of a young otter. I watched you dive into a friend's swimming pool. You sprang up lightly, then arrowed into the water with your toes pressed back against the sky. You were a glimmer in the water before you surfaced to swim with stupefying ease.

"A girl she don't like swimming and dancing none, she never be able to be making love," your Jamaican nanny said.

Jamaica fades out, and here you are, still with sun-whitened hair, still in a bathing suit that shows off your long legs and your little girl's body like a glimpse of pregnancy. You stand beneath the palm trees on an esplanade in Tangiers, your younger brother and sister on either side, dark-plumed shadows of palm fronds at your feet. We are enjoying a long family vacation in Morocco, all of us together, the last such vacation we are ever to have.

Ominous quarrels with your father about money have caused us to move from the best hotel to a smaller one, further back from the beach. Called the Dante, it turns out to be a boys' brothel, but by the time someone at the Bar Parade tells us what it is, we have settled into two connecting rooms on an upper floor, and I am too lazy to pack everything up and go elsewhere.

Why bother? The particulars of the Dante mean little to me. You are inviolate, immune to evil, cruelty, decadence.

In contrast, I see you in the early 1960s standing in a white-washed village church, somewhere near Marbella in southern Spain, holding an armful of yellow lilies. Your father has gone off on his own to a Philippine jungle in pursuit of yet another romantic business enterprise that promises instant millions, but which in four years will end in financial disaster and our divorce. Our diminished family is living in New York where I have found a job as a magazine editor. You, Sam, Allison, and I have flown to Spain to be photographed for an eight-page fashion spread, ostensibly to promote a book I have written about traveling in Europe with children. I like the image of you in that simple country church as the afternoon light slants in. My baby madonna, aged ten.

I am unaware that Robert has planned to stay away for four years. I expect him to return any week. Standing next to the fashion editor, watching the photographer frame you in the archway of the church narthex, you standing with a wreath of flowers on your head, a group of local children clustered around you, I see you as an angelic creature, almost too perfect, too beautiful to be true. (When the picture is published, however, I am startled by the expression of sadness and resignation in your face.)

"Christ, what a shot," the photographer says. He has recently tattooed the backs of his hands with blue dots and triangles. He is high on pot and constantly on the make for our Spanish driver. I am afraid of corrupting influences. I remember how it was in New York before your Daddoo left us, and I hear myself saying, "Fresh flowers from old gardens; old, beautiful, and beloved houses; people who are kind, good, honest, and who have respect for language, learning, nature, religion, and the arts—these are the touchstones I want us always to have."

"You're lucky that we aren't living in a bomb shelter," your father says.

He is showing you how difficult it is to clasp your hands with an egg between them, with each end touching the center of a palm, and to break the egg by squeezing. The optical axes of his eyes are slightly divergent, giving him the mildly strabismic gaze of a visionary as he looks past me through the living-room window at the trees greening in Central Park.

"The Orphic Egg," he pronounces. "The vast egg-shaped world that is under no obligation to conform to our desires."

If only he had stayed. If only he had been at home during the sixties. We were a good balance, your father and I, but he could never accept the fact that we were living on the money I had inherited instead of money he had earned.

Oh, darling Elsa Cloud, I know you know all this, have heard me say it all before, but hear me out. Bear with me.

Part of you grew up through what I told you was appropriate to feel and do. You went through the motions of what was expected of you, just as I had as a child. Good manners, being nicely dressed, speaking well and correctly, certain that there is a right way and a wrong way of doing everything, attentiveness to a daily pattern in which certain things like homework and brushing your teeth should be done at certain times, and observances of the changing seasonal patterns and rhymes, each with its own rituals, celebrations and pleasures. I think that was mostly what I was brought up to know. Everything else I had to learn for myself.

Your fastidious, meticulous motions and delicacy of movement showed up early in your handwriting, your drawings, and later in the way you embroidered your blue jeans with pansies, captioned *pensées* in white-and-blue-beaded stitchery. You played a guitar long before your friends did, and when they were strumming their chords to accompany their version of *Puff, the Magic Dragon*, you sang about someone with scarlet ribbons in her hair, and made the guitar sound like a harpsichord.

I admired your self-control, your self-containment, never my forte, but which seemed effortlessly to be yours. Yet there were times when I found your rectitude tedious—not smug, not holier-than-thou, just unremitting, and as unreal to me as the goody-goody Elsie Dinsmore, that eponymous heroine of a series of books my mother had given me as a child.

Seeing you on the sofa dressed in your bottle-green velvet party dress with its Irish lace collar—so like one I used to have —your white wool knee stockings covering the sun-bleached down of your brown legs, your ankles precisely crossed so that your black patent leather slippers would not smudge your stockings, hearing you speak in the gentle English accent you acquired in the West Indies, I fondly called you Miss Priss and wondered if you were a paragon of all virtues, or if you were in the process of becoming a pious little prig.

Or was I such a demanding, tyrannical mother that this was the way you supposed I wanted you to be? Was I as insufferable to you in my way as my mother was to me? Did you obey out of fear, adapt yourself to suit my opinion of you to conceal all that might attract anger or disapproval, the way I did myself when I was a child?

Robert's mother, Kate, a child psychologist, speaks to me as clearly now as she did when she was alive. "A mother who is at core emotionally insecure depends for her narcissistic gratification on her child behaving in a particular way, and is able to hide her own insecurity from her child and from everyone else behind an authoritarian facade." I showed her a photograph my mother had taken of me at the age of three, smiling mischievously, white chalk sticking out like a little cannon from my right fist, posed beside a blackboard on which she had printed LEILA BURTON IS A GOOD GIRL. "Omnipotent God parent, a compulsive super-ego promising protection on the condition of submission, all the same thing," she said.

I liked to do things that would merit the praise of "That's a good girl," but I was not the perfect child you seemed to be, Elsa Cloud. I lied, as one does to people on whom one feels dependent, or toward whom one feels angry. I stole things— symbolic, I've read and been told, of mother's milk and the power and strength all little girls associate with their father's genitals (though I never saw my father naked until I was an adolescent, and then only as a reflection in the glass door of the shower when he left the door of his dressing room open by mistake. You, darling Veronica, often saw your father naked and actually pulled your little brother around by his cocky-locky, as you called it, like a wagon). I often did what I knew I should not, even when I thought it was at the peril of my life. "But I tried to be good," as I once confided to Kate, "I really *wanted* to be good." Intending to be reassuring, doubtless, but patronizing all the same, she replied, "Of course you did, lambie," and then launched into her customary text-book script. "A child has an astonishing ability to perceive and respond intuitively, unconsciously, to her mother's narcissistic cathexis, to take the role unconsciously assigned by the mother which secures the mother's love and which provides the child with a degree of security, as well, to be needed." Children who fulfill their parents' conscious or unconscious wishes are "good." I took it for granted she was talking about me, but perhaps she was talking about adorable baby you.

Oh, darling Elsa Cloud, I vowed I'd never be the way with you my mother was with me, but just as my mother wanted to live vicariously through me—a realization that makes me sad because I wasn't able to say to her, "Look, Mummy, I know you'd like me to do so-and-so, but I would feel happier if I did such-and-such, and that doesn't mean I don't love you"—perhaps, as Robert's mother would have explained in that arglebargle of hers which I acquired as readily as any self-indulgent habit, "feelings rising from the depth of my unconscious may have sought gratification through you." I remember your saying once, "How can you say you love me, Mummy, when you don't do what I want you to do?"

Both you and I share a desire to please, a need to be liked, needed, approved of, and the need for someone to love and be loved by. I can't imagine anyone wanting to be dominating or possessive about love, or wanting to be dominated or possessed by love, because love loses its value if not freely given. And yet . . .

The summer you were twelve, you wanted to go to camp in Nova Scotia. Nova Scotia: New Scotland. I liked the name. The girls at camp chose you to be their Mermaid Princess in the Grand Procession which marked the end of the summer. I can see you enthroned on a white-and-blue crêpe paper–covered float, in a chair tricked out with cardboard painted to look like a giant clam shell. From your waist to your toes, you are encased in chicken wire that has been shaped into a long, finned tail, stapled all over with sequin-sprinkled green sateen. You are wearing a silver-sequined, elastic bustier and a silver-sequined crown. An inarguably tacky get-up, but just as inarguably effective.

Your skin is summer brown, which makes your eyes, by contrast, even brighter blue, like chips of faience. You have braided your hair the night before, so now, brushed out, it is as rippled as the hair of the Grecian goddesses in the illustrations of Bulfinch's mythology.

When your float rumbles down the street, the applause is tremendous.

A man behind me says, "Jesus, what a gorgeous piece of tail."

I turn to him amiably, saying, "Yes, isn't it? It took my daughter hours to make it with chicken wire, sequins, and Sobo glue." Then I realize what he is really saying, and what I am saying and I turn away, remembering the spring before that summer when a smart-aleck boy in Central Park told you he would like to play with your pussy, and you told him you were sorry he couldn't because you had left Minou at home.

"How did he know about Minou, Mummy?" you asked me later.

"He didn't," I said angrily. "He didn't want to play with Minou. He meant he wanted to play with your weewee—which is an idiotic enough name, God knows, but when I was your age

I had to grow up listening to your grandmother referring to it as your 'private parts,' or your 'shocking parts,' and pussy is just another name for it, but don't say it. It's not a nice word for young girls to use, and stay away from people who say they want to play with your pussy or want to see it. They just want to have sex with you, not love."

I feel I have failed you, but I swivel away from blame. "Oh, God, *New York!*" I say. And then, trying to better the situation, I add, "I'm not angry with you, darling. I'm just angry with that shitty little bastard. And don't say that, either, darling."

"Oh, no, Mummy. Of course not, Mummy. I know it's not nice to swear," you reply in that sweet little voice which makes me feel like an oaf.

Later, I'm all rationalizations and apologies, telling you that I just don't want to be with you the way your Granny was with me. "When I was fifteen," I say, "imagine, fifteen, four years older than you are, I came back from a teenage excursion with friends to Coney Island wearing a button that said, 'You can play with my doggy, but leave my pussy alone.' Your Granny frowned, looking horribly disapproving, and told me to take the button off and never, ever wear it again. 'Throw it in the garbage,' she said sharply. 'Throw it out at once.' I asked why, because I didn't understand, but she didn't explain. She never explained anything about anything, just handed down fiats. You know, fiats, commands, not the cars. I knew so little about sex when I first got married that I thought people did it in the navel." I really did think that, Elsa Cloud, truly. The only time my mother mentioned sex to me was on my first wedding day, when she said, "Don't worry, dear, sex will only last a year." All the brouhaha about having my hymen broken I thought had to

do with some ritual wedding rite. Hymen, like a hyphen, connecting pre-marriage and the wedding night, the wedding
knight who was to carry me away from my parents to another
world, another life where I would do what he wanted me to do
and be the wife of a young lieutenant in the officers' quarters of
an army camp in Louisiana, and where I would sleep with him,
as he had promised me, in twin army beds hooked together.

My mother never let me see her naked. Even when I was
grown-up, she made a dramatic show of covering her "shocking
parts" with a wash cloth when she was having a bath, and
crossed her arms over her bosom. She was either embarrassed
and uncomfortable about her body or expressed its value in the
modesty she accorded it and insisted that I accord mine. She
said, "Ladies don't have bottoms," so I dutifully wore the girdles
she bought for me, and backed out of the bedroom when I had
to go to the bathroom on my wedding night. By the time I
learned to be unashamed about my body, I needed reassurance
that its allure was still there. I would often stand in front of the
mirror, wearing only pantyhose or a petticoat, sucking in my
breath, and say to myself, "My breasts aren't very big, but look
how tiny my waist is, how flat my stomach."

Your sister, Allison, had once said blithely, "Mummy, you
look like a princess, an *old* princess." But your reaction was
different. Though you didn't openly condemn me for my im-
modesty, my vanity in being remarkably well-preserved, as I
put it, there were times when I felt you looking at me with a
superior and silent contempt. But why? I was no rival of your
soft curves and purring flesh. I seemed to take pleasure in them
more than you did. I never saw you preening before a mirror as
I did or as I had seen my mother, brushing her long hair before
she had it cut into a becoming, fluffy gray helmet.

The plane has touched down in Frankfurt. Men have come aboard with vacuum cleaners and trays of pastries with coffee. The flight seems interminable. I light another cigarette. Nervous tension. Oral pleasure. Boswell in the *Tour to the Hebrides* quotes Samuel Johnson as saying that smoking is a shocking thing—"blowing smoke out of our mouths into other people's mouths, eyes, and noses, and have the same thing done to us." Defensively, I remind myself that Samuel Johnson had to contend with corpulence, melancholia, and a scrofulous taint, that Boswell had remarked, as a corollary, that smoking preserves the mind from total vacuity. The summer before my grandmother died, the last summer I spent with her, she read me parts of Boswell's *Tour to the Hebrides*. Ashes fall from my cigarette onto my lap.

Thinking about the confluence of worlds in which I have lived, seeing clouds scudding past below, I feel my guilt vague as original sin. I remember my grandmother reading the familiar gospel according to Saint Matthew with all its comforting and loving references to children exempt from the evils of the human heart, able to see God, able to see and hear things hidden from even the wise and prudent. I explained everything to you about making love, and told you that you shouldn't make love until you were—I was about to say "married," but this was in the early sixties, and I realized that times had changed, and emended this to "When you're sixteen," which seemed far enough away for you to be a grown up and take charge of your own life, and for me not to be concerned anymore about the possibility of your having sexual misadventures. I felt I had explained everything. I had told you what to do and what not to do, and thought that was all there was to it. Now I wonder if explaining everything was better than explaining nothing. Was I too open, too direct, too indulgent, too casual about other things, too free in expressing feelings of pleasure, displeasure, approval, disapproval, love, laughter, anger, hate?

The thought is too painful for me to examine, and I push it away and return to the image of twelve-year-old you as the Mermaid Princess. Transcending your chicken-wire hobble— it took a week before the welts around your thighs faded ("The colors are just like a very long sunset," you observed)—you smiled and waved with an unexpected regal detachment, the remote countenance of a patrician acknowledging the plebes. It was a new look. Elsa Cloud. Elsa Nuage. Elsa New Age. It was a look heralding a new age.

Do you remember your "electric dress"?

I was an editor at the *Saturday Evening Post*, planning a story about a designer of battery-wired clothing whose wearers could glow and blink and flash like the discothèques in which they danced. You came to visit me in my office cubicle, saw the dress, read my outline and my suggestions for the pictures and the layout. In the softest, most compelling whisper I had ever heard, you begged me to let you model the dress live on location at a disco called the Electric Circus. "Of course," I said. You were the darling of all the editors and art editors and their assistants who were always looking for models with fresh faces. Why not? I wouldn't let you go alone, of course. I'd be with you.

We arrived at a place carpeted with Astroturf.

"Grass," you murmured, giggling.

I was overwhelmed by the pungent smell of marijuana, deafened by the aggressive, sexual rock music; confused by all the flashing strobe lights and the crowd of bedecked and bedizened revelers. Not you, Veronica. With a slight smile to show you were conscious of the admiration you exacted, and with the enjoyment of one who projects herself into the impression it must make on someone who has never seen anything like it before, you danced with the photographer.

"You dance so well," I shouted at you when you moved close to where I was standing.

"Oh, no, Mummy. I'm just warming up," you answered in a normal voice as the music stopped briefly. You whispered to the photographer and then, saying "Here I go," you turned on the batteries of your dress and whirled away to reappear on top of a small exhibition platform. In the spinning prismatic light with the red hearts on your shiny white dress flashing on and off so that they seemed synchronized with the beat of the music, you began to dance. How could I have ever called you Miss Priss? Your dancing was wildly erotic, controlled, but suggestive of passionate copulation. Your sexuality frightened me. You were absurdly young. How could you know how to dance as well as you did?

In another sequence in my mind's movie-house, on another sound track, I am in my grandmother's ballroom watching the bright patches of light cast by the crystal prisms of chandeliers shimmering over the yellow damask walls. *Whaaaap!* The per-forated roll of paper in the player piano signals the end of *Tristan and Isolde* like a too-rapidly-pulled window shade. Shall I replay *Carmen* or *Swan Lake* or *Coppélia*? All are glorious. Never having heard an opera or seen a ballet, I dance my own whirling, jump-ing, leaping dances, sing my own songs. Conscious of my own awkwardness, knowing I am not singing on key or in tune, but so thrilled with the music that I don't care, in my mind I am as light and free as a leaf in the wind and close my eyes to the mirrors which tell me I cannot will my body to move as I feel. Some further self within me resists release.

But you, Elsa Cloud, fast, supple, sensuous, you danced with the concentration of an incantation. Arching your back, twisting, swaying in perfect rhythm with the violent drums, your arms moving as sinuously as the elegant windings and contractions of snakes, you danced with your pale gold hair swinging and your dress's flashlit hearts pulsing on and off like the mating lights of giant fireflies. Other dancers stopped to watch, and gradually you became the only one dancing in the huge ballroom. I was appalled and proud and fascinated.

"Beautiful!" the photographer shouted. "Fantastic! Great! She's fabulous!" When you stopped, people clapped, shouted, whistled in applause, yelled for more. But like a child, you reached out your arms to me to be helped down from the platform. You fell asleep on my shoulder in the taxi going home.

Now in a dissolving flash, I see you sensual, even as a four-year-old, dancing in Africa, swimming in Jamaica. *A girl she don't like swimming and dancing none, she never be able to be making love.*

Three

Flying to India, not on a magic carpet with a roly-poly, turbaned genie by my side, but in a plane, with my Louis Vuitton tote bag propped against the arm of the empty seat beside me.

Would that I were in the compartment of an old-fashioned train, watching the scenery reel by, or in a boat under sail, or even enjoying the discomfort of riding on a camel or in a canoe. Any form of transport would be preferable to this particular plane that is propelling my body forward to Delhi, while my memory, my conscience, my mind are reluctantly led back.

By now, it is as if those years had happened to two other people, not to the Veronica embodied in her telephonic voice, not to that self my therapist claims, in that ever and probably over optimistic way of his, has "grown and developed" away from her past guilts, depressions, feelings of anxiety and inadequacy.

When Veronica was thirteen, in the mid-sixties, she began to spend more and more time on the weekends and after school in Central Park, in Sheep Meadow and around Bethesda Fountain where all the hippies danced and idled. In the morning she would set off in her private school regimentals of plaid skirt, white blouse, navy blue knee stockings, and navy blue blazer. She would return at night (sometimes in time for dinner, sometimes not, having telephoned to say that she was "with friends"), wearing blue jeans and a T-shirt through which her nubile nipples stared. She was an A student, for the most part, but there began to be trouble. She wrote compositions so complex that her English teacher accused her of plagiarizing them. Even though I told Veronica that this had also happened to me when I was her age, she felt affronted and was resentful. When I was accused of plagiarism, I fancied I evened the score by copying poems that weren't mine and handing them in as originals, shaking with soft, silent laughter when the teacher corrected Edward Guest or said Thomas Hardy was no good, and panicky when a poem by Eugene Field was printed as mine in the school magazine and I was sure I could be caught out because clearly it would be unfair if I wasn't, and yet what would I do or say if I were? Veronica's spirit was purer. She refused to change her style but she altered the content of her stories and wrote about flower children in the park, drugs, and other subjects her teacher felt unfit for a thirteen-year-old to know about.

"But a lot of girls at school are smoking grass," Veronica protested. "They go down to Stark's restaurant where a man comes around and sells them joints."

"Ridiculous," the teacher said, and telephoned to inform me that Veronica was making up wild stories and was being rude and insolent.

Supremely indifferent to criticism, Veronica assumed an impalpable air of detachment, speaking politely while looking at me with a flat, blank expression, the whites of her eyes tinged with pink, the pupils strangely large and dark. One moment she would seem lost in her thoughts, the next she would smile foolishly, giggle, talk in a loud voice. Accusing, pleading, arguing, lecturing, shouting, I battled with her about smoking pot and using drugs. I don't remember what she said in response. All I remember is that nothing I said seemed to have any effect, and running out of new things to say, I said the same old things a thousand times over. From her there would be a shrug, a blank or stubborn look, outrage passing across her eyes like wind over a lake, a mocking smile.

My friends' children used to rationalize their smoking pot by accusing their parents of drinking and saying that pot was no worse than alcohol. I didn't drink—my father had been an alcoholic—but ever since we had returned from Jamaica to New York, I had been taking dexedrine tablets, prescribed by doctors to counteract my low blood pressure, to increase my energy, decrease my appetite. Those miraculous little pills were actually "speed," Veronica knowingly said. "Nonsense," I replied. "The doctor says they're good for me." Veronica said they were making me "insane." When the powers that be declared dexedrine illegal and stopped my prescription, my doctor cautioned that I might have a reaction to a possible chemical imbalance, that I might feel "jittery, tired, nervous."

"Did he tell you you'd become a total bitch?" Veronica asked.

Around this time, the *Saturday Evening Post* folded; I was out of a job and worked on a book and articles at home. The telephone rang incessantly with calls for Veronica from a bewildering spectrum of male voices. In the evening, if she were home, it was not unusual for her to be talking on one line, with two other callers on hold.

"Who was that?" I would ask.

"Just a friend. You don't know him," she would reply.

"How do you know him? Where did you meet him?"

"With friends." "In the park." "Around."

We see what we want to see. We hear what we want to hear. Without Robert's anchoring presence, I indulged in magical thinking. I wanted everything to be wonderful, happy, safe, and therefore, that was the way it would be. For a while, I was exhilarated by the sixties' surface ambience of freedom, fun, and fantasy, enthusiastic about all the strange new food, intoxicated by kinetic art, psychedelic colors, and the songs of the Beatles. If Veronica smoked pot, experimented with drugs, that was all it was—*experimental*, an expression, unwise though it may have been, of her availability to experience, a quality of which I thoroughly approved. I had said my say on the subject of the dangers of drugs. If Veronica appeared unmoved, that was natural, wasn't it? Didn't all children go through a rebellious stage, particularly during adolescence? If I hadn't battled with my parents, it was not that I had not wanted to. It was simply that I had been brought up to believe that children were not allowed openly to do so. My daughter was—well, simply more *open* than I had been, that was all.

I gave Veronica the poems of Gerard Manley Hopkins, T. S. Eliot, A. E. Housman, Robert Graves, and Yeats, and borrowed her copy of Jack Kerouac's *On the Road*. Ghastly book. Everyone has to get his kicks speeding, taking drugs, stealing cars, bedding down promiscuously; crazy, wild, aimless people; people wanting to be hoboes; mad ones, mad to talk, mad to be saved, mad to live, mad to have their fixes and their orgasms naked in the front seat of cars; shared sexual ménages and the ridiculous jargon of "What you doin', man?" and "Do you dig me, man?" And *Dharma Bums*, page 136, was turned down. On the small, neat triangle Veronica had drawn a smiling face, and lightly penciled the last paragraph:

"Didya hear about the disciple who asked the Zen Master 'What is Buddha?' "

"No, what?"

" 'The Buddha is a dried piece of turd' was the answer. The disciple experienced sudden enlightenment."

" 'Simple shit,' I said."

Could Kerouac influence Veronica as Kim and the Holy One, Byron, Boswell, Shakespeare, Dick Tracy, and Nancy Drew had influenced me? Of course not. Unthinkable. Impossible. No way. The books might be piled in the stack of books by her bedside, but she used them for pressing flowers.

Darling, darling Elsa Cloud. I see her lying on her bed and myself sitting on the floor beside her with the ethereal strains of Pachelbel's Canon in D Major pooling around us and flowing through the apartment. She raises a glass of grenadine syrup and ice water to the light, swirling the ice cubes.

"Isn't it a lovely color?" she asks, and offers me the glass. "Have some," she says. I do, and together we examine the flowers she has pressed inside the covers of *Dharma Buns* and *On the Road*. Ivy leaves, violets, Queen Anne's lace, daisy, fleabane, yellow goat's beard, and amber, or St. John's Wort, as I had called it as a child when I stayed with my grandmother in Scotland. I tell her I remember picking it in great bunches, before sunrise, while it was still wet with dew, to be smoked in the St. John's

Eve bonfires and used to protect the animals and people against devils, demons, witchcraft, and all other evils. I tell her about the magic ceremonies of pre-Christian times when fires were used to protect the harvests, the people, and the farm animals, and how the festival was adopted by the Christians as St. John's Day because he was "a burning and shining light." And I tell her about the flower, *hypericum perforatum*, called St. John's Wort because of its yellow-like-the-sun flowers and its red juice, which would be likened to the blood of St. John when he was beheaded. "See the glandular dots in the leaves? In white magic they're called the 'signature' of wounds or perforations, which reinforced the signature of the red juice, so that it's a vulnerary as well as magical plant."

"Oh, Mummy, you know so many interesting things," she says, holding out her hand to me.

I reach out to clasp it, and lean closer to that invisible magnetic field of her unaffected grace to receive its imprint, like breath on a pane of glass, to be immersed in the scent of lavender soap, and her freshly washed, undried hair. There is a fusion between us, mother and daughter, daughter and mother and the child I was, showing my grandmother the bunches of dew-wet St. John's Wort I had picked.

One morning, an acquaintance of mine, a member of the international gay-is-chic group, called to ask if he could borrow Veronica to do a tape-recorded reading for a special church service.

"That sounds nice," I said. "Episcopalian, Presbyterian, or Catholic?"

"Ecumenical," he replied. "About love."

Dressed in her school uniform, Veronica went off to make the recording, and returned a few hours later.

"What did you read, sweetheart? Corinthians XIII?" I asked. Charity. *Caritas*. Love. Speaking as a child. The chapter came to my mind as a likely choice.

"No."

"Well, what then, darling?"

"Just a lot of words," Veronica said.

"Well, what words?" I asked, puzzled.

"All the words you see carved on park benches and written on walls. He said not to tell you, Mummy, but it was all for a Black Mass. What's a Black Mass?"

"What words?" I repeated, gripping my hands together so that my arms were pressed tightly against my ribs, trying to contain myself, trying to hold myself together.

"Oh, you know, Mummy," Veronica said in that clear, high, bell-like voice which admitted such purity and innocence that I began to understand the decadence in whose service it had been used. "Shit and fuck and motherfucker and cocksucker and asshole and words like that."

When I discovered birth-control pills in her top bureau drawer, she had a ready excuse which I was equally ready to believe. She was studying estrogen in her biology class. She used the pills for a poster design. Something like that. "You're such a worrier, Mummy," she said, and made a book of collages for me describing me as a loving, inspiring, and caring mother. She painted an out-of-season valentine for me, and glued a brass keyhole to an iron bolt and covered the opening with an inked inscription on tracing paper: I love you. She knew what would please me and reassure me, and there were weekly offerings of endearingly comic or exotic trifles she had found in her wanderings about New York. Sample bottles, the length and width of a paper clip, filled with oil of jasmine; wands of incense like miniature bulrushes; a sandalwood fan; a stone she had painted with a geometric design; a cut-out of a pensive Victorian cupid; fortune cookies; paper butterflies and silk flowers. Allison and Sam were mindful of my need for love and reassurance, but it was Veronica who knew best what I liked to hear and what would give me pleasure. When she played the guitar and sang in her clear, high voice, looking so pure, so innocent, so beautiful, I felt a pleasure of almost blinding incandescence.

She showed me a cardboard box, white on the outside, midnight blue inside, threaded with discs, each disc about an inch in diameter, pasted on one side with images of flowers, birds, trees, animals, faces, colors, designs, the sun, moon, and stars, and on each obverse was a message to complete the phrase, "Loving is . . ."

> Loving is being often very jealous
> Celestial and magic
> The key to much of my misery and all of my happiness
> Something terribly upsetting
> Being someplace faraway and quiet with you
> Mysterious and often elusive
> Very intense
> To be meditated upon
> *La fleur de ma vie*
> A reflection of one's own beauty
> Being healthy and naked with you
> Watching the sun set when it's Turneresque
> A feeling of great security

The fitting together of both of our natures
Watching you always when you are awake and asleep
Having a shoulder to lean on
Worrying about you and waiting for you to come home.

Who had she been thinking of when she wrote this? Had she been like me as a schoolgirl, imagining a lover? All she said was, "Here, I made it. Maybe you'd like to have it." Her face was like a bud, straining against its petal-like sheath to reveal the withheld beauty of its inwardness.

Then, one day, when I was tidying her cupboard, I came upon an unlabeled shoe box with what looked like three birds' nests inside. I remembered how, when I was a little girl more than half Veronica's age, I had collected shoe boxes filled with sheep's wool gathered from Scottish hedgerows and fences. Birds' nests. Catbirds' nests? Where had she found them? When I examined one, and then the others, I saw that they had been fashioned out of assorted pubic hair, the tufts of crinkly coarse, reddish, dark brown, yellow, and black hair carefully interwoven and secured with thread. Each "nest" was different in the color predominating, and one had grayish hair woven in with the other colors. On the inside of the shoe-box lids written in Veronica's minuscule handwriting was a list of names, Bill W., Kenny T., Guy M., Mr. Macintosh, Dr. Russell S., Danny R., on and on. When Veronica came home from school, I shouted and screamed and carried on, crying with pain and with anger. Why? Why? Why?

"I think I'm frigid," Veronica said. "I just wanted to find out." Even in her scruffy blue jeans and ratty T-shirt, she looked like an angel with eyes as China blue as harebells.

"But you're only thirteen. You're supposed to be innocent

and shy and virginal at thirteen. Sex without love is no good, anyway. If you don't know what love is, how can you be frigid? You're only *thirteen*!" I burst into tears with an excess of anger, grief, and despair that could find no other expression.

"Age doesn't make any difference," Veronica said calmly. "Your nose is running. There's Kleenex in the bathroom."

I hated Veronica for betraying my image of her, and I hated all the owners of the shorn pubic hair who had not told Veronica the difference between love and sex. I hated Robert for quitting the unassailable citadel of our marriage to seek an illusory fortune in the Philippines, for leaving Veronica without the security and protection of a father. I hated myself for having failed as a mother. I hated the sixties. I hated the world. And naturally, everything went from bad to worse. Everything always gets worse, I reminded myself, before it gets better.

One evening, Veronica came home hysterical and partially paralyzed. A friend had given her LSD, laced with strychnine. She could hardly move her arms or her legs. All the color had drained from her face.

"It's just a bad trip, Mummy, a bummer. I'll be all right. I promise I'll never drop acid or take any drugs ever again, except maybe a little grass." The pupils of her eyes were so dilated that her eyes looked almost black.

In the opinion of diagnosticians and specialists frantically consulted, there was the "possibility" of brain damage and the expectation that Veronica would "probably" not regain complete muscular control of her arms and legs.

As I added doctors to my hate list, I realized that in my own way, I was as much a rebel against establishment thinking as

Veronica was in hers. What does one do in a moment like this? I turned to God. Veronica had paid sufficient penance for her sins, hadn't she? Now she would get well.

Ask for a miracle, and sometimes you get one. Veronica recovered. She returned to school, and was commended by her history, biology, chemistry, and English teachers as being a delightful and brilliant student.

A state of grace was temporarily achieved until, after four years' absence, Robert returned. He had failed to make his hoped-for fortune and was angry and resentful. I was angry and resentful that he had abandoned us. Our marriage no longer seemed possible, and I flew to Tijuana for an uncontested divorce.

Unable to comprehend the problems of our marriage and the reasons which made divorce necessary, the children became critical of me, blaming. Disillusioned with Robert, angry with the children for not understanding, I took to ruling the household with the tyranny of a spoiled brat, demanding that everything be done the way I wanted it to be and only too ready to have a tantrum if it weren't. The therapist I was going to at the time assured me that ventilating problems was far better than repressing them. So I shouted at Veronica for not wearing a bra, and she shouted back. I slapped her face for being late for dinner. She slapped me back. "Fuck you, Mummy," she said. Once, when she had been gluing seashells to the plastic frames of stand-up mirrors, I became so angry about her having gone off on a weekend without telling me where she was going that I seized one of the mirrors and hit her over the head with it. She seized another and did the same to me. Although we were tearfully apologetic later for these psychic squalls, our inner images and the images we had of each other shattered into fragments like the cheap mirrors with which we had attacked each other.

We have landed at Teheran. We have taken off from Teheran. We have been flying, landing, taking off for some twenty-eight hours. I hold on to the handles of the Louis Vuitton tote bag to keep it from sliding off the seat next to me—L and V, Leila and Veronica, interlocked like Yin and Yang—as the plane tilts, descends.

Part Two

'Four

We have found each other quickly, Veronica and I, as if we were the only ones in the airport. We have embraced, kissed, hugged.

Now we sit on the lid of one of my fibreboard cases playing backgammon while we wait for the customs official to finish his examination of my luggage. Veronica is wearing a clean but shabby loose-sleeved, ankle-length white cotton dress and pink plastic Punjabi slippers with toes curled up like handles. A high, straight forehead, glinting cheekbones, straight nose and a grave, full mouth are a setting for her eyes which are dark-lashed and forget-me-not-blue. Her hair, parted in the center, falls smooth and honey-colored in a long fringed cape around her shoulders. Like an Arcimboldo portrait in which bodily components assume other forms of nature, her skin seems to have borrowed its colors from glossy fruit and brown eggs. Her fingernails, cut short as they had been when she was a child, have the shimmer of butterfly shells wet from the sea. She is calm, more serene than I remember her.

She takes charge at once, summoning porters to bring my

packing cases, coolies to undo the lock straps, smiling a slow, sweet smile when I assure the customs official that my possessions are all personal effects for my own use and for my daughter. Veronica looks at me with approval. "Now it's best not to make any more conversation while he goes through it all," she said. "He won't pinch anything. It'll just take hours, that's all."

So out has come the traveling backgammon board with its magnetized pieces. Veronica and I don't talk much. I touch her hand in acknowledgment of this silence, which I take to be a sign that she feels too much to say anything, just as I do.

Boswell, when he wrote about draughts, might as well have been writing about backgammon: "The game of draughts as we know is peculiarly calculated to fix the attention without straining it. There is a composure and gravity to draughts which insensibly tranquilizes the mind." And perfect, dear Bozzy, had you but known, for whiling away the time during enforced stays in airports. The last time Veronica and I had played backgammon had been at Reykjavik Airport, waiting for the announcement of the arrival of the hotel bus.

At the end of the sixties, Veronica and I were wedged together in a parenthesis between being and becoming. If only Robert had been there to tell her that fucked-up situations fuck us up, to remind her that it was her mother she was talking to, to ask her to tell him what the problem was. But Robert wasn't there.

"She's flaky," Sam said.

"She's spacey, Mummy," Allison said.

"It's just the age, dear," my mother said. "She's always charming and delightful when she visits me."

I suggested that Veronica have a few sessions with a therapist.

She muttered something derisive and snubbing, and wheeled her bicycle out of the apartment, dismissing the subject. Not long after that, she announced calmly that she wanted to go to another school.

"You do it," I snapped. "You enroll yourself in another school, fill out all the forms, make all the arrangements, and I'll pay for it. I can't cope with any more problems. I've reached the end of my tether."

I tried to be another person, one who wasn't angry, high-strung, forever apprehensive about money. I asked Veronica to come with me to Iceland and England on one of my travel-writing trips. Surprisingly, she said she would. Iceland's simplicity and cleanliness came as a relief, its law-abiding and orderly ways a tonic for us both. Breathing in the cold, clear sea air, traveling from the airport across a lunar landscape of volcanic tuff that stretched to the horizon, the Northern Lights flickering pink and amber in a misty November sky, I would begin to believe in the perfectibility of the world.

Veronica had never seen the Northern Lights before. Her face was taut with concentration as she looked out the bus window, the pink and amber lights fingering the cartilage of her ear tip, the waxy outline of her profile, the strip of eyebrow above the cave of her eyes. "Oh, Mum, isn't that *something?*" Her voice echoed her childhood's touch-the-heart tone.

Then, settled in our Reykjavik hotel, she and I indulged ourselves with steaming baths of sulfurous water. We swam for hours in the indoor swimming pool. We shopped for sweaters. We photographed puffins on the bird-breeding cliffs of the Westmann Islands, took the ferry to Akranes for picnics, foundered ourselves on smoked salmon and local cheeses, Vinarbraud hot from the oven, pancakes with whipped cream. We foraged in bookstores for copies of sagas which we read aloud to each other, along with the poetry of the *Eddas* and the names from the telephone book. That every Icelander is known as the son or daughter of his or her father was a fascination; Augusta, the daughter of Bjorn, or Augusta Bjornsdottir; Helgi, the son of Arna, or Helgi Arnason. And how commendable that every woman was allowed to keep her maiden name after marriage. Even more commendable that Iceland had no poverty, no pollution, no unemployment. Like lovers, Veronica and I created a cherished store of common knowledge and experience.

It was in Iceland, standing in the cool, clear, bright air by the harbor, that Veronica, her arm linked in mine, exclaimed, "Oh, Mummy, I'd like to be the sea, the jungle, or else a cloud." And Elsa Cloud she had become by the time we reached London, where a chance incident became a turning point in our lives.

Veronica left one of her Icelandic sweaters on a bench in Regent's Park, and I urged her to go back and look for it. "Well, it won't be there anymore," she said. But it was. This was London, not New York. "It wasn't ripped off," she reported with exuberant incredulity, and made up her mind, just like that, bingo, that she wanted to live in London. "If I go to a tutorial school, I can do my O and A levels and get into Oxford," she said persuasively.

Why not? The thought of Veronica at Oxford thrilled me. She would need a legal guardian, but there was bound to be some friend or kinsman who would be willing to take on that responsibility. She could live with friends while she was being tutored. I could pay for the school, send her a little money. "And maybe you can eke out the rest baby-sitting or something," I said, hopeful that jobs would fortuitously crop up for her as they had for me. Except for writing, I never knew what I could do to make money until someone offered me a job and asked if I wanted to do it. Secretarial chores, fund-raising, public relations, organizing parties and charity events, research, editorial work, journalism, office management—I fell into jobs as easily as a fly into a spring-garden syllabub. "The point about a job is that you should learn from it and like doing it," I told Veronica, and left it at that.

When she was eighteen, she wrote an encyclopedic account of the world's demons, and illustrated a book about charms and talismans. Both books were published simultaneously in Great Britain and America, and enjoyed a respectable sale. "The occult pays, Mummy," she said by way of explanation. I felt reproached (I was not making much money as a writer at the time) and relieved (she was not seriously involved with demons). Then she headed an avant-garde poetry society in London and edited a poetry magazine. She was a model for photographs in an adventure magazine. She worked as a salesgirl in a bookshop and for an antique dealer. She studied carpentry. But having been successfully tutored for and accepted by Oxford, she decided that she preferred "experience" to formal education. "Oxford is for bank clerks," she said. "I want to leave London and travel. I'm tired of seeing black pimps in white Cadillacs and listening to writers being pompous."

How could she? Education is imperishable, the only thing no one can take away from you. I gave up going to Radcliffe to marry Bryce before he went off to war. Veronica was giving up Oxford—for what? In one of our transatlantic telephone conversations, I screamed like a blue jay about her defection—and in the next, was overjoyed when she said she was coming back to New York for a month's visit.

She arrived accompanied by Jean Luc, a Luxembourgeois lover with whom she had shared a flat in Tooting Bec. ("Tooting Bec? Don't ever tell anyone she lived in *that* awful neighborhood," my mother said, her horrified disbelief turning into anxiety for all our reputations and then into a kind of frustration and exasperation for which there were no words.) Jean Luc wore his hair in a pony tail, and refused to carry the garbage down to the basement. "I'm a poet," he said. "Poets aren't garbage men."

She left New York and Jean Luc to travel in France. She traveled in Spain. She lived and worked in Zürich as a char for a rich Swiss industrialist who shouted at her when she cleaned his bathtub and left one of his hairs in it like a little black S, and never noticed the Alpine flowers she arranged. I couldn't imagine Veronica, with her scrupulous, delicate, unconventional rhythms, adjusting to the bourgeois beat of Zürich life in the guise of a chambermaid—it was something I could never have done. But Veronica's uncompromised strength hinted at undertows of insecurity, fear, and anger that had also often unsteadied me, and I was glad when she left Zürich after a few months and went to live in Rome. After Rome she spent almost a year on Paxos, an Ionian island pendant of Corfu. Then, with only a backpack, she boarded a schooner bound for Istanbul because, she thought, it would be a good place to buy Christmas presents. But Istanbul was the pits, and on she went by bus through Pakistan and Afghanistan, writing at last that she had settled for the moment in Dharamsala, a small Indian town in the outer Himalayas, the seat of the Tibetan government in exile. Describing it as a Tibetan tourist trap, she wrote, "The fleas that

tease in the High Pyrenees are nothing compared with the fleas
hosted by Tibetan refugees." By return airmail I sent her the
flea collars and medallions which she gave to the Dalai Lama for
his Lhasa Apso.

The next I heard, she had been given a cell-like room in the
Library of Tibetan Works and Archives so that she could attend
classes in Buddhism. She found the teachings so stunning that
she has lived in Dharamsala for the past three years, studying
the Buddha Dharma at the Library where she is a volunteer
helper in the compilation and translation of ancient Sanskrit
and Tibetan texts. Recently, she has taken time away from
Dharamsala to attend classes in Tibetan grammar at the Nyingmapa Lamas' College in Dehra Dun, to study at Abo Rinpoche's
Gompa, a monastery-university in Manali near the Rohtang
Pass at the end of the Kulu Valley. She speaks, reads, and writes
Tibetan with the same fluency as she does French, Italian, and
Spanish, but Sanskrit seems like an iron bar that she is trying to
stroke into a needle with a feather. Shortly after her arrival in
Dharamsala, she wrote that she had decided to become a Buddhist nun. "I think I would be good at that," she said. "I can't
stand the sound of another fly being unzipped. I'm sure Geshe-
la, my guru, will understand." Geshe-la, thank heavens, had
understood. It would be far better, said this wise man, for Veronica to continue her studies in Buddhism, not as a nun, but as
a scholar, an occupation for which she was ideally suited.

Veronica wants to be free. I have gladly paid for her freedom.
The most frugal of my four children, and the most extravagantly
generous about giving to others, she is currently living on the
proceeds from the sale of a Joseph Cornell collage of an owl
surmounting her constellation of Scorpio. She was going to sell

the collage to an art gallery, but I asked her to sell it to me instead so that we could keep it in the family.

"Thank you, Mummy. I like to be free to come and go as I please," she said. Later she wrote that welfare states, neon and Naugahyde, decadence weren't for her. Who needs another industrialized, air-conditioned country with a national neurosis for security? "I like the weeds and wilderness of this innocent, patient country," she wrote. "Why don't you come and visit me here?" So here I am, at Palam Airport, throwing dice on a backgammon board.

Part of me is giddy with happiness. My smile wheels around my face, my cheeks flush with pleasure and press up like little apples beneath my eyes. Quivering, yet, at the same time, numb, still, blank, I wait to be filled in, like an empty page in my notebook.

The Customs official finally exacts a duty of a few rupees and allows us to pack up and leave. From the dimming, dulling ambiance common to all large air terminals, we are propelled into the morning and hubbub outside. Coolies detach themselves from the crowd to rope one packing case on the roof, the other into the boot of a taxi that is a British Raj left-over— high, wide, and black, with a running board.

Veronica and I settle ourselves and my LV tote bag in the back seat. The driver and a Sikh who wants a lift to New Delhi climb in the front. With a scratchy roar from the engine the taxi shudders, but it does not move forward until at least a dozen men have flung themselves at its back and sides to push it to a jerking start. With shouts and waving arms they send us on our way.

"We should have given them *baksheesh*," I say.

"No need."

"Ask the driver."

Veronica obediently leans forward, resting her arms on the front seat, to confer with the driver, whose primrose pink turban is bobbing like a balloon on a stick as we jolt along.

After a brief conversation, Veronica sits back and says, "Quote-unquote. They are his countrymen. Countrymen are his friends. Friends are glad to help each other. Remember you're in India, Mummy, not in New York." The blue flowers in her eyes die as she puts on her granny glasses and looks out the window on her side of the taxi.

Oh, Elsa Cloud of the opaline expressions, how superior you can be. Feeling chided and culpable, I, too, turn away and look out the window.

All along the roadside, in the trees and in the sky, birds flash and jostle. Black-winged kites sail in the air on thermal highs and hover above the telegraph poles and the connecting wires, which are beaded with sparrows. White-backed vultures wheel in the sky and screech harshly at each other on the ground. Noisy parties of verdigris-green parrots with red beaks chatter in counterpoint with the curdled cries of rock pigeons, iridescent-necked, that cluster beneath trees by the road's edge. A pair of red-vented bulbuls with white rumps and crimson bibs fly into the sun-burnished canopy of a banyan tree and are gone. "Fine feathers make fine birds," my mother sometimes said when I was dressed in party clothes. In the seasonal rhythm of my childhood, winter was the only time when I could see as clear and close as I do now such a dazzling, dappling whirl of birds, when they winged in for the suet, the birdseed and the peanut butter I set out for them. I was an apprentice to St.

Francis then, and years later, when I read about Konrad Lorenz, it seemed to me that I, too, had had the magic power of whistling birds out of the sky, if not to perch on my shoulder, then at least to feed from my hand.

I see myself in my dark blue hooded ski jacket, wool pants and boots, the cardinals and blue jays luminous against the snow, and I feel the daily rhythm of mealtime, bedtime, time to do homework, go to the bathroom, listen to Little Orphan Annie press in on me again—great excitement when the shake-up mug (a cup with a removable domed top) for my Ovaltine arrived after I had sent in my quarter for it—time to try on new clothes, write thank-you letters, practice on my green upright piano in my room, or the grand piano in the living room. There was so little time in the spring, except on weekends, to follow birds beaking twigs and grass to nests I searched for, or to loll about the pigeon loft watching eggs turn into squabs, and the horrid squabs, their eyes bulging blue beneath a membrane of boil-pink skin, become transfigured into fledglings with back feathers elegantly fitted to them in pinecone patterns. I wished then that I could be a baby wren in the feather-lined cup set in a matrix of dried grass and twigs on the inner rough ledge of my playhouse, or an oriole in its hanging nest of woven grass, or a barn swallow in its chalice high up on the molding of the garage wall.

As the car scatters the gleaming, chestnut-winged, bronze-black crow pheasants that have been occupying themselves on the road in their clumsy fashion, one searching for a beetle, another in a little jerking run chasing after a lizard, our Sikh traveling companion says in the guttural sing-song manner with which almost all non-upper class Indians transform the English

language, "They are being called coucals by name. Hindi name
kuka."

"*Really.*" I dutifully record this information in my notebook.
"Would you like an apple?"

"From where is it coming?"

"From the plane. From America."

He takes the Golden Delicious apple I offer him and bashes
it smartly on the dashboard. I think he is expressing his dislike
of planes and the United States, but then I realize his action
simply has been to divide the apple into two pieces, one of
which he gives to the driver.

He bites into his half. Crunch. "Umrican apples are being
like Kashmiri apples," he pronounces. "Good. *Dahnayvat.* That
is how we are saying 'thank you' in Hindi. In Urdu, *shukria.* I am
coming from the Punjab myself. In Punjabi, we are also saying
shukria."

In front of the Oberoi Maiden's Hotel, sleek, dark brown
mynas make bouncing shadows on the lawn, and a pair of hoopoes, easily recognizable with their black-and-white barred
wings and rayed crests, are busily probing the driveway's cultivated edging of magenta bougainvillea.

"Mr. Sikh birds, we are calling them. Because they are having
turbans," says the driver, pointing at the hoopoes.

Nonsense, I contest to our friend. Hindus and Muslims also
wear turbans. Sikhs are renowned for their cleanliness. Hoopoes have notoriously dirty nests. Sikhs are required by their
religion to wear undershorts reaching to the knee; to wear an
iron wrist bangle; to pin up their hair, which must always be left
unshorn, with a special wooden comb; to carry a small two-
edged dagger or a large sword. Surely it was not for their crests

but for their long, curving, sword-like bills that hoopoes had been named Mr. Sikh birds.

I hear myself trying to echo and recall the rational, academic tone of Robert, to give Veronica the feeling that her father still lives in me, while riding on the desire that rises in me, when traveling, to fit in, to show that I am interested in and not entirely ignorant of local customs and information.

Our Sikh companion rewards me with a gust of flattery that I hope will impress her. "Mummy's little triumph," Veronica says softly, and her smile is reassuring in its complicity, and forget-me-nots and harebells have come alive again in her eyes.

We are welcomed by a commodious suite with high ceilings, *punkah* fans, a bedside table containing a Gideon bible and the Bhagavad-Gita, a bedroom festive with a basket of fruit, and vases of flowers which Veronica ordered ("I told the *mali* you liked tuberoses, white roses, delphiniums and pinks; otherwise, he would have given us marigolds and gladioli").

I begin to unpack, while Veronica goes at once to the bathroom to draw a bath so hot that it mists all the mirrors in the bedroom.

"Oh, Mummy, *quel luxe*! A *flush* john and *running* hot water! Did you bring any herbal shampoo? Indian shampoo is the pits, all coconut oil that doesn't rinse out and no lather."

I have brought eighteen bottles of her favorite kind. Pleased to be able to please, I trot one into the bathroom to her. "Shall we give room service a ring?" I ask. "I'm hungry or thirsty—I don't know which."

"You'll hate the food," Veronica replies knowingly, holding out her hand for the shampoo as she steps into the bathtub.

"But you'll like *lassi*. It's like a yoghurt milkshake, sort of. You can have it plain, or with sugar or salt, or both. I like it with sugar. How do you want it?

I know about *lassi*. "How do I say I'd like it plain in Hindi?"

"*Ek lassi sada.* Just be sure, though, say 'no sugar, no salt'; that's *cheeni nai* or *meeteye nai*, which are the same thing for the sugar, and *namak nai*, which is for the salt."

Sitting in the bathtub, Veronica closes her eyes, lathers her scalp with Herbal Essence. "Ah," she sighs luxuriously, "the old boustrophedon scrub."

Ox-eyed Juno? More like Renoir's *Grande Baigneuse*, charged with a glowing exaltation of the female body.

"Clerks and waiters don't really like it if you try to talk Hindi with them," she says while her fingers continue to plough back and forth, sculpting her hair into a soapy wig worthy of Madame de Pompadour. "They think you're being patronizing. Besides, they want to show off their English. Almost everyone in restaurants, shops, and hotels speaks English. Not always the way *you* speak it. You have to speak it the way *they* speak it. *I'll* do it, Mummy." Naked, unshy, full of grace, she steps out of the bathtub, an admirable genetic mix of straight back, long legs, narrow waist, dimpled bottom. Robert once told me my bottom and my nose were both uptilted to the same degree. Veronica has inherited Robert's long legs. No wonder men seek to know her through her body. She walks with the sexual confidence and pride men recognize at a glance.

"You look like a vision," I say to Veronica. "You *are* a vision." And so she is. She looks so pure, so beautiful, so childlike in her easy grace, so happy, so healthy, so relaxed, so everything I have longed to see her be, that I put my arms around her and kiss the tender hollow of the nape of her neck, the way I used to, when she weighed little more than her teddy bear.

She makes a crescendo-diminuendo purring sound in acknowledgment. She picks up the receiver. Slowly she says, "Room zerviss, bleez. Room zerviss? Our zveet number is being four-oh-tree, and we are wanting, bleez, two are-runge Jews. *Nai*, two, dough, *do*, hanh, two. And two *lassi*, one with sugar, yes, *hanh*, *meeteye*, and other blain, *sada*, *cheeni nai*, *namak nai*. And . . . and . . . and . . ." She orders a meal that sounds like the entire menu of an Indian restaurant. "And bring it guigly, bleez," she adds. "*Atcha. Guigly. Teek. Atcha.*"

I look at her with amazement. "Oh, sweetheart, please be serious. I can't bear you talking like that. You sound so awful, they must know you're making fun of them."

"But I'm *not*. They don't understand if you speak English the way *you* think it should be spoken."

"I don't believe it," I retort, and promptly tell myself not to be swayed.

Are you trying to be helpful, Elsa Cloud? Or are you being consciously or unconsciously condescending, patronizing, superior? Are you replaying the way I talked with you when you were a child? Or am I being overly sensitive?

Dripping soapsuds, Veronica returns to the bathroom. There is the sound of the shower turned on full blast, water gurgling down the drain. Silence. She reappears in a cotton wrapper, her hair turbaned in a towel in time to sign the chit and tip the waiter, who has set down a cloth-covered tray on the coffee table in the sitting room. He whisks away the cloth, lifts off

metal covers to release the fumes of turmeric, cumin, and coriander.

Unpacking, I have come across the collection of art postcards
and, as we sit down to eat, I thrust them at Veronica. I watch
her as she examines them, listening to what she has to say about
these images I have chosen because their energies are attuned
to my own in some mysterious way. If Veronica doesn't like
them . . . she *must* like them. Thank God, she *does* like them.

"Each picture is like a mantra," she says, smiling. "Each has
its own vision." About Picasso's *La Vie*, she remarks, "Picasso is
never ashamed or withholding. He shares all the visions of the
world that arise in his mind." Her breasts lift beneath her wrapper as she inhales. She glances up at me. "I miss Western art in
India," she says. "Indians don't go in for paintings all that much.
Why do you suppose that is? Is it because their life is their art?"

Is this a test? I had asked Mulk the same question. Because in
India there's a union of art, sex as the mystical force of creation,
and religion, he had replied. As in the mind, in dreams and in
the unconscious, the mysterious, creative, regenerative power
of art flows together with sex and religion in a primal trinity.

No test. Veronica does not give me time to answer. Resuming
her preoccupation with the postcard prints, she murmurs in a
soft, loving moan, "Turner, Cranach, Monet, Pissarro, Seurat,
Cornell . . . darling Joseph."

She had been the inspiration for one of Cornell's simple and
playful boxes in which he had stacked children's building blocks
in a tipsy column with a rubber ball alongside that could be
guided into a knot-hole. There were eight picture-letter blocks
in all, eight the number of regeneration and the symbol of the

infinite, but all I can remember are the ones with a letter O representing the feminine principle that ensures birth and re-generation, eternity, the monogram of God; and two deer, one placed right-side up, and the other beneath it, upside down, an inversion for emphasis. When Joseph gave the box to Veronica and me, he told me there had been a pair of statuary deer at the gateway of his mother's house. His mother's deer, his dear mother, mothers at the gateway of life, guardian mothers.

In a booklet of collages in which she extolled my virtues as a mother, twelve-year-old Veronica had depicted me as a hen, a Rhode Island Red, shielding her chicks beneath her wing. Was she overdoing the imagery to the point of derision? Or had the image been chosen because Robert used to sing a song about a little red rooster to her ("I love my rooster, my rooster loves me, my little red rooster 'neath a cottonwood tree . . ."). I felt happier twelve years later when she sent a painting from Dha-ramsala, showing me as a white cat, looking severe, with a white kitten in the foreground, an orange-and-black patch on top of its head, its expression an unmistakable I-want-to-please one. Three other kittens, marmalade and black-and-white, were vis-ible, half-hidden behind the foliage of dried Himalayan flowers Veronica had meticulously set in place.

Mother Hen. Mother Cat. Mother Deer. Mother Dear. My eyes fill with sudden tears. Veronica expected as much of me as I did of my mother. I'm only human, I want to tell her. I did the best I could. And so did your mother, a voice inside tells me. But I am not ready to listen.

When we have finished our meal, Veronica makes another call to room service. I smile indulgently, wanting to believe that the macaronics she has affected have become less pronounced as I listen to her telephoning. "We are wanting a *malish-wallah*. Guigly, *hanh, jaldi*."

Male or female, masseur or masseuse, *malish-wallahs* are one of the most comforting of Indian conventions. Resident at all the good hotels, quick to present themselves at most tea shops and bus stops throughout India to rub your head, your body, your feet for as long as you wish or until you fall asleep, *malish-wallahs* offer their services for prices adjusted to what they feel their clients will pay and then, unlike the rest of bargaining India, give you the easy satisfaction of offering a discount with no prolonged haggling.

I reach for my notebook. Writing is a way of life as natural as breathing to me, in-taking and then releasing. Besides, I've got travel articles to write. "Why don't you start writing again?" I ask Veronica.

"Writing is a form of self-aggrandizement," Veronica replies, as though she were stating a fact so obvious that nothing more need be said.

Disagreement with and resentment of this put-down make the inside of my head tingle with the pins-and-needles feeling of a cessation of circulation of blood. I cup my hands above my eyes and press hard against the ridge of my eyebrows to relieve the tension and push back the anger, but it is the *malish-wallah* who calms me. She glides into the room, a middle-aged woman with skin the color of cinnamon. She is wearing a neon-pink sari and gilt sandals, and her diaphragm, bare beneath her short, tight-fitting blouse, is ringed with quoits of fat. I fall asleep having my toes rubbed with coconut oil, listening to a murder of gray-headed crows and a dule of mourning doves in the courtyard below.

Six hours later I wake to see Veronica sitting on the floor in the cross-legged lotus position, her eyes closed, her lips moving silently. Buddhists believe that saying mantras, humming a syllable silently, repeating phrases over and over again, is an assistance to higher consciousness, calming and steadying to the mind, but I have a distrust of incantations. After watching Veronica for a few minutes, I say, *"That's* a sight guaranteed to warm the cockles of your Presbyterian mother's heart." Then I dislike myself for being intolerant, obtuse, and horrid.

Veronica opens her long eyes. "I'm meditating, Mummy." She smiles sweetly, and stands up the way a ballerina does, as if gently lifted by a current of air. "Would you like some tea? I'll order some. Here's your dressing gown. Do you want to look at the papers? I'll fetch them from the sitting room. Read the matrimonial ads. They're the best part."

In no time, the tea is ordered, and the newspapers are folded and stacked neatly on the table by the bed. Like her father, Veronica is serious in matters of esthetics: clean, orderly, precise; as a child, she licked her ice cream cones into smooth pyramids that never dribbled.

Robert's mother used to tell me that compulsive neatness is often a sign of interior chaos, a reaction formation, a defense to ward off the feeling that one is going to pieces. The mute rejoinder would spring to my mind that neatness and order simplify life. A place for everything and everything in its place, as my mother would say; everything easy and quick to come to one's hand, I would say as a corollary. Since childhood, when I had heard in church that Christ would come to judge the quick and the dead, I had urged my mind to be nimble. My quickness, even in its guise of the "speedy Western aggressiveness" Veronica faults me with, remains desirable to me, the opposite of being dead.

Still smiling gently as Lord Buddha, Veronica resumes the lotus position, seating herself as though she were a puppet being lowered slowly to the floor, crossing her legs deftly, cradling her right hand in her left with both palms up, closing her eyes.

You have tender eyelids, Elsa Cloud, tender eyelids with thick, dark eyelashes, innocent of mascara, and you're angry with me because I'm not being understanding or sympathetic or wholehearted in my acceptance of whatever it is you believe in. And there you sit, not defensive or cross—*that* I could manage—but feigning loving-kindness and compassion. Well, I *think* you're feigning, playing a part you think you should play, very saintly, like a Buddhist Elsie Dinsmore.

Picking up the papers, I retreat to the sitting room and begin to skim through them. International news, local politics, a search for a tiger that has killed everyone in a village in West Bengal, robberies, accidents, murders. Veronica is right: the advertisements for partners sought in matrimony are the best part.

> Wanted: Settled groom for Brahmin girl, 25 yrs., M. Sc., 158 cms, wheatish complexion. Father Gazetted Officer.

> Matrimonial correspondence invited from well qualified and settled Bengalese for beautiful, attractive, fair complexioned and high accomplished (M. Sc.) Bengal girl, 166 cms., 26 yrs., working abroad in responsible position. Girl's father holds top-ranking job abroad.

> Wanted: Suitable match for Arora virgin girl, 30, M.A. (Music), 155 cms. Early marriage, respectable family.

Wanted: Extremely beautiful, white complexioned, twenty
years Brahmin bride preferably. Convent-educated for
Architect, Civil Engineer, four figures salary, reputed family.

Wanted: Match for Sikh boy, 27 yrs. Post-graduate, medical
Res., earning 1600 Rs. p.m. Caste no bar. Early marriage.

Wanted: Really pretty, fair maiden match for handsome
teetotaller Punjabi bachelor, 34–35, younger appearance,
160 cms. Diploma Engineer, locally employed, income
1900 Rs. p.m., local preferred.

Wanted: Beautiful match for a cultured, smart, fair complexioned and very handsome Deputy Superintendent of Police,
24 yrs., 167 cms., from a sophisticated and very well placed
Vaish family. Girl's merit and family the only consideration.

Physical appearance, especially complexion and height
(weight was never mentioned), along with age, money, position,
education seem to be of prime importance. I read dozens of
these advertisements, seductively foreign in their vocabulary,
grammar, and substance, and find little mention of personal
characteristics or interests. Is humor of no importance? Is no
one interested in someone serious, playful, fun-loving? Are
there no ardent gardeners, amateur archaeologists, stamp col-
lectors? No book, dance, theater, or music lovers? No fishermen, mountain climbers, good cooks, weekend painters? Bemused, I read until the strong Darjeeling tea is brought, then
put the newspapers aside.

Veronica emerges from the bedroom to ask if I've signed the
chit. She has changed into the new sandals and one of the
dresses I have brought for her, and I feel self-congratulatory, for
the dress is a style similar to what she had been wearing at the

airport, but an improvement in cut, and becoming in its color, deep blue.

"It fits!" I exclaim happily.

"I'm the best-dressed recluse in India," she replies, striking a model's pose, her expression of satisfaction a reflection of my own. Then, in a more serious tone, she adds, "Of course, Mummy, you realize that I'm enchanted with everything you've brought without really being attached to all these wonderful goodies. I mean, that's one of the reasons for meditation, non-attachment."

She smiles provocatively, her eyes full of cool secrets, and pours me a cup of tea. "Meditation has to do with intuiting the true nature of existence, letting you experience calm, peace, and tranquility while it enables your mind to turn itself inward upon its own awareness," she says, sounding like a textbook. "*Nowness*, learning to let things be as they are, achieving single-pointedness of mind, letting images come and go with no attachment. Meditation stills the mind, scours it of intellect, emotions, senses, the way people in television commercials wipe the stains out of the kitchen sink." She looks at me to see if I comprehend this amusingly simplistic analogy. How Veronica and I do enjoy imparting information to each other. Yet how difficult it is for me to appear to be interested in what is only of interest to me because it is of interest to her. I feel stupid, ignorant, irritated. Are we on different levels of consciousness, different planes of spiritual development? Is that the problem?

I try to look intelligent. I know from Veronica's letters, written in the neat, orderly, minuscule, measured writing that is startlingly like her father's, that meditation has nothing to do with thinking, contemplating, or praying for guidance; that it is a difficult discipline, hard to acquire, and a help in ridding the mind of attachment. I also know from the tissue-thin pages of those lovely letters of hers, which fill an entire drawer of my filing cabinet, that she takes a firm stand against attachment. Attachment comes from clinging and desire, she tells me. All suffering will cease if you can eliminate desire, if you can be without clinging or craving, freed from worldly attachments to people and things, freed from memories and past associations, killing off your ego, obliterating the need for a separate identity . . . I remember when she used to spend hours placing Peter Pan patches over the holes in the pages of her ring-bound school notebooks so that none of the pages would fall out.

She stops talking and carefully tears open a small package of Mangalore Ganesh beedies, native leaf-wrapped cigarettes about two-and-one-half inches long and about half the width of a pencil, tied with a minute magenta thread to keep them from unfurling. She lights one with a wooden match. "It smells like pot, but it isn't," she says. We both concentrate on observing the match as it flares at the tip of the beedie. The beedie tip burns bright as she inhales, then exhales, releasing a blue plume of smoke.

Five

From the open corridor outside our sitting room I watch the *mali* in the garden below slowly hunkering about, walking in a squatting position, sweeping the lawn with a twig whiskbroom. With supernatural patience, he brushes off the garden furniture, tilting the legs of chairs and tables to sweep under them and to straighten the nap of the grass, brushing up a fallen rose petal, a feather, a twig.

At the edge of the garden, a tall silk-cotton tree is in bloom. Glossy scarlet flowers with cup-shaped calyxes and five curling petals bunch at the tips of its leafless branches, and the promise of these fistfuls of nectar has attracted a swarm of chattering and singing birds clustering like chromosomes. There is a joyful sprinkling of musical calls, and the *mali* stops smoothing the lawn to look and listen to a bulbul with cheeks as brightly red as the silk cotton flowers.

Made much of in Persian poetry, and associated with the idyllic romance of Krishna and Radha, the bulbul sounds poignantly sweet. Also, it sounds extraordinarily familiar. Its song is like the prototype birdsong of the singing-bird automata of the nineteenth century, one of which I have in my bedroom in New York. Perhaps in trying to reproduce the elusive liquid siftings of the brown-bright nightingale, the European music-box masters had, by accident or intent, managed to duplicate the sound of its Oriental cousin.

As I listen, conditioned by association, I anticipate hearing the bulbul's song run down and fall off in quality, indicating the bird's need to be rewound. Would Veronica, I wonder, having emptied her mind of association through meditation, have any such odd expectancies? Would she be able to share with me the sudden consciousness of my pleasure in being in India, where bulbuls don't have to be rewound, and where, for the moment, I can enjoy a delicious confusion of live bulbuls with their artificial counterparts?

She has gone off to round up a car and a driver. Now she comes twinkling down the corridor with a sizable Sikh in tow. Tall, thick-bodied, wearing a purple turban, sandals, starched white trousers and a starched white coat that is buttoned up the front, with his stand-up collar partly hidden by the full gray beard which is tucked under and braided with his sideburns, he is the apotheosis of Little Orphan Annie's faithful and omniscient Punjab.

"This is Gurdipji, Mum," Veronica says, politely using the honorific. "Gurdip Singh Randhawa."

All Sikhs take the affix of Singh, which means lion, and appreciate being addressed, when their first name is unknown, as *Sirdarji*, Honored Chief.

"I was listening to the bulbul," I hear myself saying as if in a dream and then, "*Sirdarji*. Gurdipji. Good morning, good morning."

"Good morning, Madam," Gurdip replies. "*Sat Sri Akal.*"

A lovely greeting. Hindus steeple their hands, bring their palms together before their faces to say "*Namaste*," a Sanskrit phrase meaning "I salute the divinity within you." Sikhs say simply without gestures, "*Sat Sri Akal*. May the truth be exalted, truth is imperial."

We are going shopping.

The prospect of an alien, hot country where I can bargain for hours for the fine work of artisans and craftsmen always sings a siren song for me, and nowhere more impassioned than in India.

I want to shop while I still have my New York eyes, before the obscuring glaze of familiarity makes the Indian largesse of lapidary intricacies a commonplace. I want to see belled toe-rings and wide ankle bracelets weighed in a pan scale for their value by their *tola* weight. I want to watch merchants fling lengths of billowing golden silk cloth around me for the pleasure of my selection. I want to look for treasures and curiosities and objects of everyday life whose purpose I will not know until told. I want to steep myself like a teabag in fantasy and reality, a brew of romance and the genial trickeries of bargaining.

With the exception of my mother's older sister, my casually generous and open-handed Aunt Vera, I had grown up among people to whom demanding discounts and bargaining for the best deal possible were subtle indications of social position and solid financial worth; these practices showed that you were careful about money and respected its value. I dislike that sort of bargaining. As a child, I shriveled when my mother would boast that she got Schiaparelli to give her ten percent off because she was such a good customer.

Oriental bargaining, on the other hand, is a way of life and a ubiquitous custom, so shopping and bargaining become a rite of passage, an initiation into the local society and aesthetic idiom. Instead of feeling self-indulgent and extravagant, I feel virtuous; it's like doing research, an exercise in selective acquisition, a way to become instantly connected and accepted.

Chandni Chowk is the main thoroughfare of Old Delhi, where the Middle Ages joins the twentieth century in a wild and clamorous confusion of ox-drawn carts, motorcycles, cars, bicycles, horse-drawn carriages, buses, trucks, and a human rookery flapping and flying underfoot, overhead, every which way, indiscriminately displaying beauty, infirmities, diseases, garbage, grime, a multitude of patterns, and a brilliance of colors that attain the dazzling intensity of stained glass.

"Don't panic, Mummy," Veronica cautions as Gurdip drives away. We stand on the arcaded sidewalk with the traffic-jammed street on one side, and a rush and pour of people and merchandise and food all around us. I am a wren in the tumult of a tropical aviary.

Motorcycles roar past, a preposterous cavalcade of turbanned gentlemen with their ladies riding postilion. Some ride sidesaddle, their heads mantled like madonnas with the ornate borders of their saris. Others, in the Punjabi dress of princess-style tunics worn over full pajama pants tightly cuffed at the ankle, ride astride. Mogul miniatures come to life, they zip by on Hondas, their scarves streaming behind them, their thick, be-ribboned plaits of black hair bouncing on their backs, children clinging to them like baby possums.

Vans and open-windowed buses rumble by, decorated with symbolic good omens—flowers, peacocks, elephants, tigers, cobras—that look like the art of talented children. With similar style and an eye for pure color, fruit and vegetable vendors heap limes, lemons, and eggplants in elegant formations; an old woman, attenuated as a praying mantis, has wrapped herself in a length of peacock blue.

Wooden-wheeled carts lumber past, drawn by hump-backed, cream-colored Brahma bulls whose horns are painted red and blue and tasselled with brass bells. Three-wheeled scooter-taxis skitter like water beetles among wheel-squealing horse-drawn wagons and cars with signs saying "Horn Please" posted above their license plates. Bicycle rickshaws. Men trundling handcarts heaped with sacks of coal and grain and teetering wooden cages filled with roosters and hens. Four tiny children skip through the onrush of traffic, one of them a Sikh boy-child, his hair secured on top of his head so it looks like a handkerchief-covered apple with an elastic band around the base. All male Sikhs wear their hair in this fashion until late adolescence, when they learn to wrap a turban. "I used to think that a branch of the Sons of William Tell Society was active in northern India," I say to Veronica, smiling as she smiles.

With all the coolies loping along shouldering tin trunks and jogging with yokes slung with swaying, bulging bags, I am astonished that my personal envelope of space remains intact. No one bumps into me, no one brushes against me as Veronica and I make our way to the entrance of a side street called Dariba.

We pause at the corner for a jellaby. Jellabies are hot, honeyed confections deep-fried in clarified butter, or *ghee*, as everyone calls it in India. When I was a child, I tell Veronica, I thought of *ghee* only as the delicious syrup of melted tigers Little Black Sambo poured on his pancakes.

"I did, too," Veronica says. "You and Daddoo used to read me that book, don't you remember?"

"I remember," I say. Now *ghee*, the delight of childhood fantasy as golden tiger-melt, glistens again before us on jellabies piled high in orangey-yellow pyramids on dark, leathery, lobed leaves that are almost a foot long and only a little less in width. The leaves curl at their edges to show pale gray undersides. Karnikar leaves, good for keeping away insects. The vendor twirls two leaves into cornucopias for the jellabies he ladles from the brass wok in which they are spinning and sizzling. Veronica nibbles hers while I munch on mine, a debauchery that makes my teeth cringe and produces a soggy feeling in my stomach.

Both sides of Dariba Street, which is not much wider than the span of an ox-cart, are lined with shops, small stalls raised above the street that purvey silver and gold jewelry and objects, an array of extraordinary magnitude. "They've even got silver foot-scrubbers," Veronica remarks. "They're usually made of brass." She points out several animal and bird figurines mounted on squares and lozenges that are runneled and scored on the undersides of their bases. "See? You just use the swans or the dog as a handle and scrub the soles of your feet with it. It's just like a pumice stone that never wears out."

Hadn't I wanted to look for objects of everyday life whose purpose I would not know until told? Like hearing a new word and then seeing it and hearing it with surprising frequence, from now on I will see foot-scrubbers shaped like small playful animals everywhere.

Up and down the street we go, peering at all the little cubicles. Some have white sheets thrown over the floor for the sake of cleanliness. Most of them smell of incense from miniature bulrush-like wands set to smoke before an image or gaudy print of Lakshmi, goddess of prosperity.

"Yes, yes, good morning, good morning," Veronica patters. "Yes, we are coming from Umrica, but I am living in Dharamsala and Manali, and *Mataji* has traveled all over India, so we are knowing the quality of your merchandise. *Nahin, nahin,* we are not interested in tourist stuff. What are those Rajasthani belts costing? And these rings? And these earrings? Fifteen rupees a *tola*? Surely not. No, no, Mummy, we mustn't buy here, the prices are too high. Come. Let's go next door."

"No, no, ladies. I am making you a special price. These earrings are old, very good price I am making you."

"Surely you are mistaken. These earrings old? *Nahin, nahin.* You are teasing us!"

Face-saving laughter all around, and more fervent assurances from the shopkeeper that the earrings are old, very old.

"He just means second-hand, Mummy. And eight hundred rupees for these necklaces? I've seen them for three hundred roops in Madhya Pradesh where they are coming from."

"But not the same quality. Seven hundred and fifty rupees."

"Four hundred is all we can pay."

"But look what they are weighing. Look at the scale."

"Well, four hundred and fifty rupees."

Would you be caring for tea, ladies? Jews of fresh mangoes? Fruit drink?"

A tray of courtesy tea in thick-rimmed cups and chemical-colored bottled soft drinks to be decanted into clouded glasses is set before us, a customary offering to confer both a sense of obligation and the false sense that you are getting something for nothing. Intermission time in the bargaining process. I pour my tea from the cup into a dark blue plastic-fantastic mug I have brought with me from New York. Veronica silently, with expressive eyes and lips parted in dismay, apologizes to the shopkeeper for my behavior. A look of pathos, of martyrdom, a plea for understanding, Veronica's I've-got-a-weird-Mummy look.

It's the in-dwelling ghost of my mother, of course, who has insisted I bring this nice, new, clean, unbreakable, unchippable mug with me. *My* mug, untouched by anyone's lips but mine, mine, mine. My mother had a horror of eating with silver or drinking from glasses or cups used by anyone she didn't know. She refused even to sit on a chair that was "warm from a stranger's sit-upon" and I remember well the autoclave she insisted on bringing with us whenever we traveled abroad so that cups, plates, and eating utensils could be sterilized before my nanny and I were allowed to touch the food carted up by room service. Veronica views my mug as a portable insult. I regard it as a harmless hangover of childhood, and a definite esthetic improvement over vein-cracked cups. Heaven knows, I am far less plagued than my mother was about bacteriological bugaboos, thanks to the cheerful promises of those Zulu and Xhosa nannies who helped me look after Victoria. Their "Dirt that don't make dead, fattens" is a reassuring comfort. Veronica has scant regard for germs, but her concern about wounding the feelings of the shopkeeper seems to me self-defensive. She doesn't want him to associate her with my behavior. But what about me? Why isn't she more concerned about my feelings than the feelings of a sly merchant? Or is her attitude a latter-day version of my mother's admonition, "Not in front of the servants, dear"? One thing that is sure is that rarely, even as a grown-up, would

I have dared let my mother know, even by a gesture, that anything she did embarrassed me.

Protective though Veronica is of the shopkeeper's feelings, she also is aware of his beguiling slyness. A persuasive bargainer, she gets the price down to five hundred rupees. I hug her with delight. She looks flustered at this display of affection, but the merchant smiles so widely you can see his gold-capped teeth. "The mother is loving the daughter. The daughter is loving *Mataji*. It is being a sign of long life and happiness."

The variety and profusion of the shopkeeper's jewelry enthralls me. "Jewelry," Mulk said once, "has been a lovely and splendid part of Indian culture for millennia. Though sparingly worn, it is as significant to Indian men as it is to Indian women."

There are ornaments for the head, the hair, the ears, the nose, the neck, the arms, the wrists, the hands, the fingers, the waist, the ankles, the toes. Everything made from silver and gold. Repoussé, chased, filigreed, enameled, twisted, and knitted and carved and tasseled with beads and bells and decorative pendants. Boswell quotes Dr. Johnson as saying it is by studying little things that we attain the great knowledge of having as little misery and as much happiness as possible.

"It's all so beautiful. How can I choose?"

"Anything beautiful has to have quality of intention as well as quality of skill," Veronica comments. An excellent criterion, but my eyes have to learn to see and to judge the unfamiliar. I think of the baby jewelry I had—fine coral and crystal beads, pearls, a bracelet of pale blue enamel piglets, little white enamel pins in lozenge shapes with bands of inset seed pearls. Only a pearl necklace had been kept to be worn by Veronica at her christening along with the christening dress of Indian mull and lace that

I and my mother had also worn. The dress is gone, but the pearls rest safely in one of my grandmother's purple leather jewel boxes from Tiffany's, when Tiffany's was still in Union Square.

Veronica looks blank when I tell her this, and informs me that a rat almost pinched the opal ring I had made for her from one of her father's cuff links.

"I suppose he thought it was something to eat," she says, "and when he found it wasn't, he dropped it. How much is it worth, Mummy?"

"Don't sell it. You don't want to sell it, do you?"

"Well, I don't wear it much."

I make a note to myself to give Veronica enough money so that she won't be tempted to sell the ring. I tell her not to be non-attached about the ring made from her father's opal cuff link.

She tells me not to worry.

Oh, Elsa Cloud, I know you don't care about the ring in the way I do, but thank you for pleasing me by saying you'll keep it—which I know you will, because you are honest and truthful.

I hold up a bangle, self-congratulatory that I know what it's made of. "Lac," I crow. "Lac from the exudation of a female insect, as opposed to lacquer from tree sap." There is no response from Veronica. Why should I think that bits of information, which attach themselves to my mind the way fragments of shells do to the spines of sea urchins, should be of interest to Veronica? Facts are reassuring to me, but maybe I'm making a mistake by telling Veronica about facts. Facts are too confining, too specific, and perhaps, like so many other things I say to her, my factual recitatifs are unsuccessful attempts to say something else.

I try again. "I like something you wrote in one of your letters to me, something very profound. You wrote that a man never discovers anything new, that life only stands more revealed. I liked that enormously."

"I'm glad." She tries on a lapis lazuli ring carved with champak buds. "Flowers are good omens," she murmurs. The essence of flowers, their color, their shape. I think about my voice. If my voice were a color, it would range from maroon to navy blue to Tyrian purple. I visualize Veronica's voice as sky blue delphiniums, violets, and lilies of the valley.

I buy her the ring. I buy presents for her to take to her friends in Manali and Dharamsala. I buy two heavy silver belts from Rajasthan with clasps secured by screwing in a bolt that turns counter-clockwise, the opposite direction of Western-style closure and, therefore, both awkward and endearing. I buy *bana lingams*, heavy silver boxes shaped like eggs, and some like rectangles with stylized horns, to be worn as lockets on thin silver chains. Indians use them for carrying good-luck talismans with religious significance. International hippies passing through India find them useful as "hash caches."

"They're really for men. They've got phallic connotations," Veronica points out. Their feel, their weight, their look pleases me. "I like phallic connotations," I say defensively.

Foreign money is play money, tipsy money, gypsy money. I part with it easily and without regret. Guilts and anxieties about spending money in New York are dissipated in the reckless joy of spending in India. I've always alternated being broke and frugal with wild sprees when I was solvent. "Luxuries are my only necessities," I once said to Robert. "You mean the moon for thimblerig?" he countered with an affectionate smile. "I don't know," I replied, happy to be considered frivolous because playfulness, to my way of thinking, is not a sin, but one of life's greatest pleasures.

Money. When I married Robert, I put everything I owned into a joint account that I left for him to check and balance at the end of each month, and having been brought up to believe that money was a serious matter, a man's province, I was content that this should be so. Whoever would have guessed that serious, competent Robert would become enamored of get-rich-quick schemes and foolishly invest my inheritance? Who would imagine that the children of our marriage, Veronica in particular, would all have an almost unerring sense of how best to make whatever money they had go the furthest in their varying ways of life?

I buy glass-faced circular lockets containing miniatures of Krishna and Ganesha, the elephant-headed sovereign over demons, often invoked by Indian mothers to protect their children.

I buy bell-shaped ear drops, silver hairpins capped with jingling bells, toe rings, hair pendants, and a crescent of garnets and turquoise to wear like the moon around my neck. My analyst would say I am paying undue attention to the inanimate in order to avoid intimacy with Veronica, or that I am feeding myself, rewarding myself with the love and attention my mother didn't give me when I was a child. But I don't want to think about that, and instead, I reach for the heavy solid silver and gold ornaments worn in the rural areas that are bold, beautiful, and dramatic—as well as being investments against emergencies. I prefer their heaviness to the delicate and sophisticated pieces worn by urban women. My mother always deplored my "peasant" hands and feet, but in India, I feel they have come into their own to be cherished and adorned. And why not treat myself to one of those whimsical foot-scrubbers? I buy one, and then several more, a swan, a peacock, a sturdy bull, the vehicle of Shiva, bath-toys for my feet.

The silver belts I have bought are too large, a ring that covers my entire finger fits too tightly. With a lovely old man's grin, the shopkeeper nips and solders, and there, *"Meherbani"* (Please, thank you), adjustment to perfection.

I can't stand things that don't fit. I can't stand anything chipped, broken, in need of repair. My father used to call my mother Mrs. Fixit, and I suppose I am the same way, not as my mother was, meticulously gluing handles back on cups, but if I see a bent fork tine I can hardly wait to rush it out of the house to the repair shop, and quick, buttons must be sewn on again, nicks in the furniture polished over, cracks filled in.

"When you were a tiny little girl in Johannesburg," I say to Veronica, "you were out on the lawn with your nanny and you saw a crippled old man walking past. You called him the 'crooked man,' and you couldn't stop talking about him for weeks. Do you remember that?"

"Yes."

Silence. I feel she is seeing him.

"And you didn't get over it until Robert sang you that funny song about 'this old man, he played two, he played knick-knack on my shoe.'"

"With a knick-knack paddy-whack, give the dog a bone, this old man came rolling home," Veronica murmurs. "Yes." She pauses. "Gosh, Mummy, you do think of the weirdest things."

When she was a teenager, she used to bring home boys she

had met in Central Park who were on quaaludes or cocaine. One of them told me he had needed a fix but Veronica had told him that if he talked with me, I would fix him so he wouldn't need a fix. So what had I done wrong? Why had Veronica taken to using drugs? Doctors had recommended dexedrine to me, prescribed it to give me energy, keep me thin. Regrettable the compound of their mistake, my vanity, my need to be quick, unfortunate the results. But what had Veronica needed drugs for? Escape?

Escape from what? A nepenthe? An anodyne? Or was it just that everyone was taking drugs in the sixties, that it was the thing to do? I put on one of the silver belts and take some sort of perverse pleasure—vain, masochistic, who knows, who cares, I think angrily—in cinching it so that it feels stingingly tight around my waist.

Once more we are caught up in the swirl of the street. We have arrived in one of those sections in the bazaar where the first-class shops are glass-fronted repositories of curios and antiques. In front of them, on makeshift wooden stands with shabby canvas awnings, fireworks and Western-style Japanese kewpie dolls are enjoying a brisk sale. Between the marvelously costumed crowd and the street, at the sidewalk's edge, are vegetable sellers, sweetmeat sellers, *paan* sellers, and a drift of hawkers whose wares are spread out on newspapers and cardboard: ballpoint pens, plastic combs, pencils, safety pins, pocket mirrors, and whatever else the vendors find easy to bundle away at night and take home. Veronica moves forward in an unhurried way. I follow her for several long blocks until "Here, Mum, this looks like a decent place," she says, leading me around the corner into an eclectic treasure trove.

We steeple our hands in greeting. I no longer feel self-conscious doing so. What had seemed an affectation in the early morning has become the simplest of courtesies. All day I have been conscious of the grace of hands coming together like butterfly wings, a salutation and a blessing.

Fascinating, how the Sumerian gesture of copulation, invoking fertility, the right thumb encircled by the thumb and index finger of the left hand, should have been the prototype for the steepled-hand gesture of Oriental greeting as well as the symbolic gesture of Christian prayer, that this gesture should have evolved to its stylized, simplified form because it was so difficult to sculpt in its original version. Copulation as a symbol of creativity and fertility, a mystical union with spiritual force and energy, displayed with a balletic show of hands, is a veritable dance of life, no mere abstraction or translation of life, but life itself. Some of the most beautiful parts of the present are renewed visions of the past. The starfish hand of an infant appears from the sea of memory, a hieroglyphic hand as a sign of manifestation and giving: the Roman *manus* of protection and strength; the magically potent amulet of the hand in Islamic culture. Love, health, humanity by reason of the symbolism of the number five.

Stars, I used to think when I was very young, were the handprints of angels, and the loving hands and eyes of the dead in heaven. The Right Hand of God. "He leadeth me, O blessed thought! O words with heavenly comfort fraught! Whate'er I do, where'er I be, Still 'tis God's hand that leadeth me." My therapist used to tell me that it was the intake of breath and oxygen that made hymns and carols seem so inspiriting, that birds and angels were phallic symbols, that religion really had its roots in pagan rituals revolving around the agrarian cycle, which in turn had its origins and homeomorphic representations in the act of sex. I suppose if I told him that I had been conscious all day of the balletic grace of hands steepling like butterfly wings, he would tell me that the butterfly is an emblem of the soul, of unconscious attraction toward the light. More interestingly, he might tell me that the purification of the soul by fire, represented in Romanesque art by the burning emberplaced by the angel in the prophet's mouth, is illustrated by an image of love holding a butterfly close to a flame. Jungian psychoanalysts regard the butterfly as a symbol of rebirth, fetus-like larva encased in womb-like cocoon, metamorphosed, transcendent, winged.

I am astonished when Gurdip enters the shop a few minutes after we have. He has tracked us, he says, "by making the proper inquiries."

"Can you imagine thinking you could find someone who had just gone shopping in Bloomingdale's, Lord & Taylor, The Woman's Exchange,* Tiffany's? Isn't it amazing that Gurdip found us?"

Wanting Veronica to affirm this minor miracle in order to establish the solidarity of our shared experience, I know before the words are out that I must sound silly and alien to her. I sound so even to myself, for I have cited my mother's favorite shopping places as though they were my own. Would Punjab ever lose track of Little Orphan Annie? Hadn't Kim always managed to find the Holy Man?

---

* Properly, The New York Exchange for Women's Work, referred to by my mother, and now I realize by me, as The Woman's Exchange.

"Yes, amazing," Veronica replies, gazing at the ceiling, then looking away. Straw stools shaped like the torsos of wasp-waisted women in the frescoes at Knossos are fetched and dusted off for us to sit on. Tea is brought. The shopkeeper flourishes his card. I present him with one of mine as proof to him, and reassurance to myself, that I also am prepared to exchange formal evidence of credibility and reliability.

I study the contents of the shop with the same intensity with which I squinted years ago through an Easter egg I had given Veronica, the sort of egg that looks like fresh snow packed into an oval, with a glass-covered hole at one end, and a miniature world of its own inside, where everything is like a dream world, the strange and the familiar compressed. Useful objects that are decorative, functional objects that are beautiful, everything made by hand in India. Work is worship. Every aspect of Indian life is governed by religious law. Every tool is daubed with a sacred mark of saffron. Mulk had told me that. The plough is sanctified as is the bullock's forehead. The handle of a hammer has a sacred tassel tied to it. There is a ceremony for the sanctification of the pen and inkpot. Hands are joined to salute the image of Ganesha set over the doorway of a shop before buying and selling can begin. Musical instruments are blessed before they can be played. The dancer touches the guru's feet before beginning to dance.

"In many instances, religious motif may become ritualistic habit or secular impulse, dimly informed by the awareness of the original inspiration given by the gods," Mulk had rattled away in his academic English, so strangely accented and so pulsing with emotion that his enthusiasm was in an odd alliance with his words. It is the daring craftsman who, presuming that he has inherited the known forms prescribed by iconography, creates new shapes by adding the twist and turn which his own artistry inspires, or whose fantasy gives a bird-shape to a vegetable cutter or a fish form with wheels to a betel box. All creations tend to become decorations, and all decoration involves the assimilation of the forces of nature. The tree becomes the symbol of life, flowers and shrubs turn into lyrical patterns. Animals express an essential significance; the lion represents a monarch's power; the fish is an image of fertility; the elephant is wisdom personified; the horse is symbolic of speed; the peacock is the acme of joy; the snake is an aspect of the curvacious flow of the soul. Everything is symbolic and sanctified to give depth to the creative life.

Universally symbolic objects, yet each is unique, each quivers with a life of its own. The artist's spirit is as much a presence in the object the artist created as everyone who is important in my life is present in me. My grandmother's voice, reading Tennyson's *Ulysses*, sounds softly in my mind: "I am a part of all that I have met, yet all experience is an arch wherethrough gleams that untravelled world, whose margin fades for ever and for ever when I move—life piled on life were all too little, and of one to me little remains." Tennyson's *Ulysses* had been superseded by my own discovery of Stephen Dedalus in Joyce's *Ulysses*, who asked his mother to tell him the word known to all men, the word she will not tell him, but what else would it be if not forgiveness or, better yet, love? Stephen Dedalus, another image of a bird, wings through his own rite of passage. Daedalus, the cunning worker in Greek legend, a personification of skill in the mechanical arts; the patron of artists' and craftsmen's guilds. That does not seem too unlikely an association to have, I think, as I begin my own symbolic search among the objects in the shop along with Veronica, my flower in Bloom, as it were. I smile to myself at my own wordplay, and hear myself humming, "Within the maddening maze of things, to one fixed trust my spirit clings, I know that God is good."

I accumulate treasures that I can bargain for later in great heaps on the counter. There are brass spice boxes with a central peacock that turns to release the sliding lids of eight scarab-backed containers. There are Brahmin slippers of silver plate on wood, with toe knobs, for general wear in a society in which articles made of leather are prohibited by religion. There are hair-drying pins of brass, cunningly fashioned like gazelles.

A nutcracker with curving handles is decorated with a goddess riding on a peacock. Another is in the shape of a mother holding a child, the figure splitting in half for nut-cracking. And here is one in the form of an amorous couple. Many have tiny bells attached to them to cater to the penchant all India seems to have for the jingling of bells set in motion by bodily movement or by the wind. The sound of bells is a symbol of creative power, bells related by their shape with vaults and, consequently, with the abode of the gods in the heavens. Religious images, a mass of art metalware that has silver designs engraved and inlaid on dark backgrounds that appears as a synecdoche of glittering stenciled patterns.

There are filigreed silver trays, brass inkwells and pen cases, and lamps for burning *ghee* or oil decorated with elaborate sculptures of human and animal figures that Hindu craftsmen, associating the forces of nature in their work, have carved and hammered with holy zeal. Here they all are, snakes, elephants, tortoises and camels, people and pagodas set about a lamp of lyrical harmony and line. The lacquered brightness of boxes, circular and rectangular, meticulously painted with trees, people, animals, butterflies, and flowers, tells of the closeness of artisans from Kashmir to a magical world of myth, legend, and nature.

From nearby Agra comes *pietra dura* work. Chess tables and trays of white marble glow with semi-precious stones set in geometric and floral patterns.

There are shelves of *dhokra* objects from Madhya Pradesh. Ingenious molds of horsemen, lamps, pots, and figures that are first made of clay, then wrapped with bell-metal wire that has a coppery-silver sheen. When the clay is knocked away, the wire creations remain. No clay feet, how wonderful, like Nebuchadnezzar's dream. I bet Nebuchadnezzer never dreamed of images like these.

There are receptacles for burning oil and storing water which seem, from certain angles, to have a fantasy life of their own, an other-worldly metallic ballet sparkling in the light of the late afternoon sun.

There is a brass gong suspended from a pair of elephant tusks, and a sarcophagus-sized brass chest mounted on wheels. Made in Gujarat and called a *pathera*, it is used for storing clothes and household materials. I wish I could buy it, but it is expensive, and the cost of shipping . . . No.

Next to a forest of attenuated gold art figures from Bastur, fashioned by tribal Giacomettis, are Buddhas of bronze and gilt, conch shell trumpets tipped with silver, prayer wheels that look like bronze cans on sticks, wooden daggers that look like tent pegs ("ceremonial ego stabbers," Veronica tells me), and trumpets made from human thigh bones coated with copper that are absurdly phallic. "Don't buy any of this Tibetan stuff here," Veronica says. "Wait until we get to Dharamsala."

Farthest back in the shop are painted wooden dowry chests from Rajasthan, some like cabinets with drawers, some like gaily painted dolls' trunks. The hinge of one I like is broken. Mr. Singh beckons an assistant, a grubby boy with hands black from polishing brass and silver, who whisks away the damaged chest to be repaired.

The objects that have attracted me seem to be in some way metaphorical images of my own interior life. I feel as unhinged as the trunk.

"Psychological hang-ups," I say to Veronica, pointing to ceiling lamps suspended on chains. Robert's mother would have laughed, but Veronica, like her father, finds psychology and analysis boring and irrelevant. A ridge and two vertical lines form between her eyebrows. "Why do you have to bring psychology into everything?" she asks.

"I don't know. The life not examined isn't worth living." I move on to look at cauldrons, lidded milk containers, and water pots of bell metal, a mixture of copper and tin with the tint of old gold; a huge brass tray with a raised rim worked in a piecrust pattern; an oval, high-necked copper water pitcher from the Himalayan foothills; a bronze Nataraja from Tamilnadu, dancing his dance of life; a ceremonial silver pot, shaped like three pots on top of each other; an image of Parvathi, the supreme goddess, the wife of Shiva, the mother of Ganesha, a power both destructive and creative. Her eyes are fish-shaped, elongated, amygdaline.

"Just like yours," I say to Veronica. She smiles, stretching her lips into a soft curving form, concealing her teeth. She is masking anger.

I have seen a similar expression of abstraction on my mother's classically beautiful face, a tuned-out, absent, empty nest look.

"You used to be such a sweet, happy agreeable little girl," my mother said to me once. "I don't know why you've changed so."

Quick, I call out to Mulk, the intellectual mentor I wish my father had been, a father surrogate who can calm, soothe, relax me. Talk to me in words of the classroom, expand my mind, let it learn, grow, acquire knowledge, wonder, think, imagine, play. Tell me once more, Mulk, about the national Indian obsession with ritual, pattern and order imposed on chaos, about there being a time and a place and a name and a way of doing and making everything. Tell me about the harmonic structure and molded melodies of *ragas*, music intended to create certain moods and emotions in the mind of the listener, and about how everything relates to the six seasons and to the different parts of the day. I feel in accord with this. It's like my childhood all over again. There was a time for corn-on-the-cob, asparagus, strawberries, hot oatmeal, peach ice cream, and other ritual, seasonal foods. There was a time to do everything, a rhythm to everything. Weekday mornings at half-past eight, the chauffeur drove me to school, and picked me up at half-past four. Monday was the day the laundry was done; Tuesday was when the clockman came to wind the clocks and adjust their chimes; on Wednesday, like Sunday, there were pancakes and maple syrup for breakfast, and the *Tatler*, *The Queen*, and *Illustrated Country Life* arrived for Mummy to check out the people she knew and the prices of antiques. Thursday was the cook's day off, meaning hard-boiled eggs and cream sauce for supper; Friday was Fish Day; Saturday was for riding, shopping, errands, haircuts, and appointments with the dentist or the doctor. Church was on Sunday, with Sunday lunch comprised of roast beef and Yorkshire pudding, ice cream, silver gravyboats filled with hot sauce—chocolate, butterscotch or fruit—and a splendid cake served with the ivory-handled silver trowel my father used at the age of five to lay the cornerstone of Woodbine, his family's place in New-burgh on the Hudson. Every other month or so, the dressmaker came for a week, sometimes two, or a "fortnight," as my mother said. Mr. Sherman, my piano teacher, came once a week, and when he died, Mr. Hollett came. The piano tuner came and went. So did a man who sold linens and a man who attended to whatever was chipped, cracked or broken by the dogs, who were forgiven, or by the maids, who were not.

"To everything there is a season . . ." It is my grandmother reading aloud again, a reassuring presence in purple panne vel-vet, pearls massed around her neck arranged to fall in loops of ascending magnitude. "A time to weep, and a time to laugh; A time to mourn, and a time to dance; . . . A time to keep, and a time to cast away; . . . A time to be born, and a time to die; . . . A time to plant, and a time to pluck up that which is planted." Trees, flowers, birds, seasonal changes, recurrent holidays have melted and fused within me, ready to be recalled, re-formed as images, all those Easter eggs, Christmas tree-top angels and ornaments, birthday candles, and Fourth of July sparklers and fireworks.

Is there no Oriental bezoar to be found in the Oriental ba-zaar? Some antidote to all this anecdotage? Some alimentary, elementary food for thought? A rush from that fountain of Mulk's human kindness?

Tell me more, Mulk, about the craftsmen of India. I want life to be like a wedding *shamiani* in which everything flows together and becomes a part of everything else. Contrarily, I also fancy life like a tray for printing type, with scores of little open boxes separated one from the other so that all the material is there for writing and thinking, all orderly and sorted out, systematized, as tidily arranged as Robert's desk drawers and my father's. I remember Mulk telling me that before making images of deities to be worshiped, craftsmen not only must learn the physical measurements to ensure the proper proportions of the images, but also they must familiarize themselves with the verses in the Vedas, the primary scriptures of Hinduism, which describe the characteristics, the symbolism, and the esthetics of each deity.

The rules in icon-making, the idea of a right way of doing things, is in accord with the way I was brought up, and delights me. In particular, I am most entertained by the rule in which each part of the body is likened to some object from nature.

"Mr. Singh, Mr. Singh, please tell me how it goes," I cajole the shopkeeper. "The thigh is like the trunk of a banana tree; the kneecap is like a chin, the eyebrow is to be shaped like a fish or a neem leaf . . ."

"The nose is being like the sesame flower; the upper lip is being like the archer's bow . . ." he adds.

"The chin is like a mango stone," I chime in with the elation of a child excelling in a classroom recital, which is probably what I am doing, I think, making up for all those years I stuttered so badly that teachers felt it kinder not to call on me. Time has muted the silences, sibilances and percussions of my stuttering. Now, I often think I have moments of talking too much.

"The neck is being like a conch shell . . ."

"And here's Krishna with his hand in *tripitaka mudra*," I say, pointing to a small statue in which the deity's thumb and the third finger bend to touch each other. "And that *mudra* symbolizes destruction, doesn't it, Mr. Singh?" I go on shamelessly, indicating a bronze Nataraja of Shiva stepping on a demon with his right foot; his upper left hand with open palm and extended fingers pointing downwards obliquely across his body.

I know I am being awful in Veronica's eyes, but once started I cannot stop.

"Correct. And you are knowing what meaning is the hand like so?" Mr. Singh holds his palms open toward me with his fingers extended.

I make the nasal noise of assent. "Divine assurance and protection," I reply. "And the hand pointing to the foot that's raised signifies deliverance. And the drum is symbolic of the rhythm of the primary creative force. And all the flames behind Shiva symbolize the cosmic function of creation and destruction, the eternal circle." There is more, of course, but this is all I can remember from Mulk's basic training in the art of Nataraja appreciation.

"Any five-year-old Indian child would know, wouldn't they, Mr. Singh?" Veronica says. Affirmation of this fact is so obvious that instead of waiting for Mr. Singh's response, I turn away.

With sudden peripheral vision, I glimpse motion and a change of light. Turning my head, I see that a *saddhu* with a begging bowl has come to the doorway, and that Gurdip is walking toward him. Gurdip? In an eye-blink, it is not Gurdip, but my mother, interposing herself between me and any other child or grown-up, fearfully, as though they might have a contagious disease or do me harm. Gurdip is protective. But surely, he doesn't believe the *saddhu* is a dacoit in disguise? No. Gurdip is smiling and funneling small coins into the holy man's begging bowl.

The *saddhu* is wearing the standard white *dhoti* and long-sleeved white collarless shirt of thin muslin that is the most common of local male costumes, and a necklace of holy and talismanic rudraksha seeds, dark reddish-brown and somewhat smaller than nutmegs, that reaches to his waist. His shoulder-length flowing white hair, his ash-smeared forehead, the biblical radiance of his beautiful old man's face have already become for me a visual cliché. Leaning on his shoulder-high staff, he looks serene, patient, tired.

Veronica, easily moved by tears and frailty, quick to defend the old and weak, reaches into her purse for a fifty *paisa* coin, worth about six cents. "This is enough for both of us to give him, Mummy. Don't you dare give him that five rupee note."

"Ten paisa is being plenty," Mr. Singh says, showing me the coin he has in his hand, and extending it to Veronica to add to her donation.

"But he'll think I'm a greedy, stingy monster, sitting here with all this loot and giving him three cents," I protest, feeling culpable.

Veronica is exasperated. "I've told you before, Mummy, that it's just a matter of *karma*, good *karma* if you are rich, bad *karma* if you are poor. No one is jealous or envious in India the way they are in New York. You don't have to feel guilty, Mummy. Just be happy you have good *karma*."

I need more than *karma* to feel calmer. Looking in my bag, I find I have two pears and two pieces of plastic-wrapped raisin cake to eat with our tea. Scooping them up, feeling ridiculous,

I hare out of the shop after the holy man. Kim would have approved.

The *saddhu* receives my offerings with dignity, smiles at me with approval. With the thumb and forefinger of his right hand, he pinches off a fragment of the ash caked on his forehead and, triturating it with his fingers, sprinkles it on my hair, all the while speaking to me and fixing his dark eyes on mine.

When I return to the shop, Gurdip says, "That was a nice thing, Madam, that the holy man blessed you. *Shabash!* (Well done!) You will have good luck."

"Yes, Mummy, now you have sacred cow dung in your hair," Veronica's low murmur changes into bubbling, back-of-the-throat sounds of suppressed laughter.

We regroup to begin bargaining. As a seductive tactic, Mr. Singh brings forth the paraphernalia of *paan*-chewing: a large, round, brass box which opens to disclose a tray, cutting and paring utensils, open and lidded containers for all the accoutrements; a betel nut case of silver, the size of a matchbox, nicely etched with a romantic scene of Shiva and Parvathi who, during moments of sublime conversation with her lord and lover, is often depicted handing a *paan* to him. As a symbol of fecundity, Shiva incarnates perfect pleasure, and the etching shows him with his principal left arm around Parvathi, while his principal right hand, held before his chest, silently instructs her. Next to him is a couchant figure of his bull *nandi*, gazing at his lord with adoration. Veronica says that *paan* is a Sanskrit word that means both drinking and kissing, and points to one of Shiva's ancillary hands, which holds a cup. There are four kinds of *paan*, she says: the poor man's Poona variety; the middle-class Benarsi kind that comes from Benares; the large, dark green Calcutta leaf with its strong scent; and the subtle and expensive *maghai*, considered a regal pleasure, and the variety which Mr. Singh has produced for us.

Maghai. That was what Mulk had chewed. I had tried it, and it had tasted to me like a sour leaf with a crunchy, spicy wad of bicarbonate of soda enclosed in it. What I enjoy about *paan* is watching its ritual orchestration, the putting together of all its ingredients. Street vendors do it best, spreading the necessary items in an array of captivating detail on slips of bright magenta paper on a shining brass tray, the betel leaves fresh and glossy, the cloves and cardamom in tiny pyramids; the betel nut, like slivered almonds, composed in fan-like arrangements; a white pile of powdered lime; sometimes, as an additional luxury, silver beaten into translucent tissue wafers for a coating. Mr. Singh has an enameled box of these silver squares of *vark*. "In honor of your presence in my shop," he says, furling one around his *paan* before he pops it into his mouth.

After the prelude of *paan*, we are ready for the counterpoint of bargaining. "You are having a wonderful eye," Mr. Singh says, as we examine a domed carriage pulled by bullocks, artfully sculpted in brass. "That is being one of my best pieces. Not everyone would I show it to. But just looking at you, I am seeing that you are the type to be appreciating it."

I smirk at this unctuous flattery. "How much is it?" I ask.

Some astronomical figure is proposed and Veronica quickly says, "*Mataji* cannot possibly afford that. And it's so heavy. How could she be taking it back with her to Umrica? It will cost too much to ship and then she won't be able to be buying anything else, Mr. Singh."

"*Ohé*, your *Mataji* could be buying my whole shop. It is only that I am wanting her to have it that I am quoting a lower price than I should," Mr. Singh challenges her.

"How much are the Brahmin slippers?" I interpose a diversion.

"Yes, yes, the Brahmin slippers." Veronica smiles winningly. "I am wanting to give them to *Mataji* as a present. Eighty rupees?"

I would gladly pay twice that. With a kingfisher flash of her eye, Veronica wings a knowing look at me. Leave this to me. I am the expert.

More prices are quoted for other objects. "I would not care to be parting with that except I am knowing you would be taking good care of it, that you would be looking after it with the attention it is deserving. You must be having what you are choosing because you are being so special and appreciating the quality of the work." Dispensing smarminess, Mr. Singh picks up a pocket calculator and begins tapping numbers with his long, slender index finger. Twenty-five years before, he would have been pushing balls back and forth on an abacus. Twenty-five years is the span of Veronica's lifetime. Behind the shopkeeper's back, she is waving the Brahmin slippers triumphantly.

Oh, Elsa Cloud, darling Elsa Cloud, your expression is the same as it was when you were less than three feet tall, wearing a woolly blue dressing gown with a tasseled sash, hugging your "bunny labby" and your "wow-wow," and waggling their paws to say goodnight in our living room in Johannesburg. Your Daddoo teases you, imitating the way you talk, asking you if you would like him to play his "honnymonica."

"Come along, Mum," Veronica is saying. Gurdip, the faithful courier, all devotion and ready to offer any personal service to make our lives simpler and easier, strides beside us, ever on the lookout for the most comfortable way, the safest path where neither *goonda* nor *thuggee* would dare harm us. There is no one or nothing Gurdip is unprepared to take on in our defense. "I am always carrying a snake-bite kit and a sewing kit," he says, slapping his pockets, "and I have a *kukri* in the car beneath the front seat."

We walk along a street devoted to the sale of items for marriage celebrations. Ceiling canopies and *shamianis* of brightly colored appliqué are worked in motifs of people, animals, birds, and flowers that are unified through a natural flow of connecting lines, a phenomenon of Indian life and culure, and a metaphor of life itself.

The fringe of tassels on the embroidered mantle for the bridegroom's horse suggests that in being tied together, separate entities become interwoven and joined, just as the broken bits of mirror embroidered into the *shamianis* catch the rays of the sun and send reflections spinning on the clothes of passersby, just as the crystal chandeliers in the ballroom in my grandmother's house used to send rainbow baubles of light to dance with me. On one cubbyhole's white-sheeted floor, ready-made wedding turbans in circus pinks, blues, and mauves, flecked with gold, are set about and covered with plastic wrappings. For those who can afford no better, there are bridal diadems of flexible cardboard, sewn with spangles and sequins and fringed with looped strands of fake pearls, as well as creations of gold and silver thread worked into the scarlet colors suggestive of a wedding's promise of fertility.

I am disheartened to find that custom-made, hand-crafted

objects are being replaced at every turn by mass-produced items, but the quest for the past is often a quest for the unattainable that ends abruptly in reality. Veronica shares my nostalgia for past landscapes and hand-made objects that shake you with their beauty. She argues, however, that the plastic Punjabi slippers, replicated with embossed designs in a nasty blistered boil-pink, keep one's feet drier during the monsoon season than their cloth and leather originals.

"Cloth and leather get moldy and rot," she says. "Rubber and plastic are the only things that hold up in the monsoon."

When Veronica and I return to the hotel room, we kick off our sandals and turn on the air conditioning. We wash our hands, faces, and feet, comb cologne coolingly through our hair, then fling ourselves on our beds, each of us making little noises of pleasure as though caressed by a paramour.

"I love you," I say to Veronica.

"Thanks, Mum. I can't talk now. I've got to meditate."

"So have I." My meditating is not the same as her meditating. She lets her images come and go. I cling to memories, want to decode them, give them a framework, set them in order, know what's what, get to the root of things. Not just recollecting, but *re-membering*, an active, purposeful task of reconstructing, different from the fragmentary, flickering images and feelings that drift along like flotsam and flottage in the flow of consciousness. Am I rationalizing, trying to encourage and comfort myself? In Hindi, *kal*, time, is a word used both for yesterday and tomorrow. Mnemosyne, goddess of memory, the mother of the muses, also works both ways, carrying one back into the past and projecting one into the future, just as my therapist said Veronica does to me. I try to find a cool place on the pillow and flick Veronica a sideways glance. She has steepled her hands, her wrists resting on the sash of her dress. She is lying perfectly still. If she were a baby, I'd be worried that she wasn't breathing.

Six

It is another morning. The day feels open on all sides, begging exploration in the sunslant. Walking with Veronica through the labyrinth of Old Delhi's lanes and alleys, this maze of byways seems no simpler to codify than a rain-forest crisscrossed with animal paths that lead to water, caves, burrows, hollows, and sleeping trees. And yet for me, there is a sense of the familiar, of something known through some other time, some other place.

The high double doors, embossed with hand-wrought iron and brass, ancient, mysterious, remind me of entranceways in Middle Eastern and North African cities, of old cathedral and university towns in Spain. But instead of greenery, flowers, fountains, the doors open onto tunneling corridors or courtyards with patches of sky as blue as morning glories, mud-brown puddles, and a surface skim of litter.

There is a long stretch where the upper stories of houses jut outward so that the alley between the dwellings is lit on either side, with a wavering ribbon of white light winding, twisting, hot as lava, shimmering with the intensity of a mountain's torrent of white water along the cobblestones.

"To explore is to penetrate; the world is the interior of the mother. . . . From mythology and poetry, towns, citadels, castles, and fortresses may be taken as symbols for women. . . . Symbolic equivalents for the inside of the mother's body are discovered in external objects, the toys. . . . Growing up consists in finding new toys, new symbolic equivalents, so that in all our explorations we are still exploring the inside of our mother's body." These scattered sentences from Norman Brown's *Love's Body*, a book I read a year or so after Robert abandoned us, return to me. Before me, the light shines like a magnification of Ariadne's clew, a shining corridor through a cave.

"It looks like a diagram of a ritual, ceremonial dance," I say to Veronica, the sound of my own voice droning in my ears. "You know, like the Cretan labyrinth where Ariadne and Theseus danced." In primitive societies, the labyrinthine paths followed in ritual initiation dances represent the archetypal endeavors of the divine ancestor, the prototypical man, to emerge into this world, to be born.

"I don't know about myths much," Veronica says.

"But didn't you research them when you were doing that book on demons?"

"No."

Down comes the portcullis on the castle of thought and communication. Chop goes the guillotine. Off comes my head to fall in a basket as neatly as a peony clipped by my mother's gardening shears. My daughter, the executioner, walks ahead, then glances back. Her dispassionate expression is again my mother's. A nanny had also looked at me the same way. A shiver creeps up and down my skin, pausing to tremble in my groin. My perspiration evaporates with a frightening chill.

I sustain the sensation that I am myself as a child, myself as I am now, that Veronica is both a second self and my mother. In this narrow street, in this setting of overhanging houses, the feeling swells within me.

I see myself in a sepia photograph as a plump toddler, wearing a bathing suit with a sleeveless, round-necked top of cross-hatched net attached to a pair of woolen trunks. They were orange-colored, I remember. Facing the sun, I scowl at the photographer.

My stance is wide-legged, defiant. My arms are limp and end in little mittened fists. I have survived the panic of the disappearance of my first nanny, presumably dismissed by my mother for reasons of possessiveness, jealousy, and her vulnerability to the fear that I could be happy and contented in the care of someone else. It was the beginning of a pattern. Whenever I felt affection for a nurse or a governess, that nurse or governess would be dismissed and arrangements made for her to leave when I was asleep or at school. Whether my mother told them it was preferable that I not be alerted in advance of their departure, or made some pretext to fire them on the spot, no nurse or governess ever said goodbye to me. Where they had gone, I never knew. I never saw them again. I behaved, I was told, as though nothing had happened. To this day, however, all partings and departures are freighted with the fear that I may never see the person or persons I care about again, a fear so intense at times, so emotionally disturbing, that there were years in which I could not bring myself to say goodbye or even hear goodbye said by anyone close to me—the word itself was so fraught with anguish. My sadness was so out of proportion to appropriate feeling, my terror of such magnitude, that it took fifteen years of self-analysis and dozens of visits to the offices of psychiatrists before the "traumatic affect had been attenuated" to proportions with which I could cope.

I remember. My mother who never enjoyed the beach, who had a cat's dislike for cold water, has photographed me and gone away, probably to the beach club for lunch. I run from the nanny to splash at the sea's edge, fall down, and get myself trapped beneath the thick safety-line. As the waves draw back and roll over my head, I shriek for help and swallow salt water. The new nanny, sitting upright on the clean, white, soft-sugar sand above the wrack line, knitting bag beside her on the striped beach towel, obviously thinks I am screaming with delight, waving simply to show off and attract attention. Wailing with panic, my eyes stinging with salt water, my mouth and nose filling with water every time I try to catch my breath, I can see the new nanny, sitting there insensible, uncomprehending. With the sense of self-preservation inborn in me or newly-born at that moment, I struggle out from under the weight of the rope that crushes me down with the force of the undertow and, arms flailing to keep my balance, scramble beyond the waves' reach, belly-flop in the sand, gasp for breath, heave, choke, vomit. The spasms subside. My bathing suit feels icy in the sun. Through tear-blurred eyes, I see the white-stockinged legs of the new nanny, her white shoes half-buried in the sand. I yearn for comfort and sympathy, but am unable to form words or sounds to explain what has happened. The new nanny scolds me for getting sand and seaweed in my hair.

Suddenly, I am caught up, lifted, hugged, and held close to the warm chest of a lifeguard who has seen what happened and has raced across the beach too late to rescue me, but not too late to comfort me and to berate the new nanny for her carelessness. He carries me to the clubhouse where I am reunited with my mother and father. I am loved. I am understood. No longer drowning, no longer exiled without communication, my needs have been made known and have been adequately responded to. I am happy, content. From that time forward, words and communication take on an immense significance to me. There are times when I am beset with the fear that I will be cut off, unable to communicate, annihilated. "Speech is silver, silence is golden," my mother used to say. "Of our unspoken words we are masters, but our spoken words are masters of us."

I remember. My mother had my room redecorated as a reward when I won a prize at St. Timothy's for neatness. But when I won the history prize and the poetry prize, she paid no attention. It was a day that sought to take all that was precious from me, the day I won the poetry prize, and received a National Certificate of Honor, a scroll "suitable for framing," both of which arrived in the morning mail. "That's nice, dear," my mother said. Unabashed, I went jigging away to flourish the rectangle of parchment with my name on it at the cook, the maids, even to waggle it at the poodles. Daddy was out golfing, but his sister telephoned.

"Tell her, tell her," I shamelessly prompted my mother in an insistent whisper, waving the certificate before her eyes, my fingers clamped on its corners like clothespins. "Tell her, tell her," I mouthed, already elated by the prospect of the instant gratification of our three-way shared delight. But my mother was deaf to my whispering and impassioned miming. A wave of anxiety swelled within me as she closed her eyes and went on talking.

"You didn't tell her," I protested, near to tears, when she hung up the receiver.

"She wouldn't have been interested, dear," my mother replied. I felt a thud inside, like the sound of an apple falling, and the sensation of part of myself suddenly closed off as though a magician had slid shut the horizontal panel of a trick box, enclosing its hidden secret.

I remember. "Buttons!" my mother exclaims with the same high-pitched tone of enthusiasm she uses when she says "Walkies!" and "Dindins!" to the dogs. "See all the pretty silver buttons." She spreads a Tyrolean cardigan on the bed before me to impress on me, as usual, the unique quality of what she has given me. Mute as a cobra, I look at the heavy white woolen cardigan with its cheerfully mocking Alpine flowers. To please her, I count the flower-carved silver buttons. Five down the front, three on each sleeve. I had asked her to get me, *please, pretty please*, a plain navy blue cashmere turtleneck pullover. How sharper than a serpent's tooth and all that, but oh, the co-existing irritation and exasperation when Mummy paid so little attention to my wishes and desires. Yet she would ask me what color rubber band I wanted, how large, how wide or thin, and what sort of scissors I needed, for what purpose, for cutting fingernails or toenails, thread, paper, cloth, wool, "Or would you like pinking shears, dear?" I was terrified that I would be caught using paper scissors to cut up felt for the Christmas tree ornaments that were hung at the back of the tree, invisible behind the array of satin balls stuck all over with pearl-topped pins that she bought in quantity at the Woman's Exchange.

My mother had an Edwardian reserve, was unable to discuss her feelings except those of anger, irritation, and indignation at the behavior of others; she preferred a cool proximity of being.

To be personal was "not done." Almost all the cooing, baby talk, and demonstrative loving at Northlea was lavished on Robin, Jackie, and Brother—the poodles I was convinced she loved more than she did me. She preferred dogs to people, she often said, because they were always glad to see her and never said anything irritating. In her rigid code of conduct that was paradoxically so unpredictable, it was vulgar to show one's feelings about people, yet permissible to lavish emotion on animals. When my grandmother died, when my father died, when Aunt Vera and my uncle died, Mummy appeared unmoved. Yet when Brother, her favorite miniature poodle, was run over by a truck, she was hysterical with grief.

Was it her need to be irritating or the awful lying rectitude of the truly devious that imparted to me bewilderment and confusion about almost everything she said? Her "I'll be thrilled to see you," to an acquaintance on the telephone would be transformed to "I thought she would never leave," after the visitor departed. Her "I'll do that . . . I'll ask . . . find out . . . come . . . be there . . . pay for it . . . get it . . ." promised with assurance, for one reason or another, would rarely come to pass. "Thank you, dear, how nice," she would say whenever I gave her anything I wrote. "Did you read it? Did you like it? What did you think of it?" I would ask a week later. "Oh, I haven't had time," she would reply. "There's been so much to do."

Nannies, governesses, or maids might have comforting things to say, pleasant questions to ask, but it was to my mother that I wanted to address myself, my mother with whom I wanted to share my joys, triumphs, sorrows and to share hers in turn, if she would let me. But no matter what I would report, she would respond vaguely, nod her head, say "That's nice, dear," and resume her scan of the evening paper, sipping her tea, or concentrate on the faint hiss of silk being drawn tight on the circular frame of her crewel work, that crewel, cruel barrier between us, her attention focused not on me or on what I was saying, but on images of flowers and birds and trees.

From the time I was in kindergarten until my first marriage, when I could only whisper "I do," I was often not able to talk without stuttering terribly—that is, if I could get the words out at all. The green-painted upright piano and books were my salvation. The piano was in a corner of my bedroom. Long before Mr. Sherman arrived to give me lessons on it, I discovered that I could make the piano talk—express my feelings— and that I could sing without stuttering as I picked out tunes by ear I played in tandem with two-and-three-note lower-pitched chords. Books were even more satisfactory—pop-up books, Big Little books, comic books, any books I was given, any books I found to read in the house—because when I read, my body disappeared from consciousness and events took place behind my eyes. Books were portable. I could carry them outside to my tree house. I could toy with their words, croon myself to sleep with their poems, and once I had read them, they were mine to keep or throw away. Like the green upright piano, books could express what I had no words for.

By the time I married Robert, the worst of my stuttering was over. "You don't deserve a man as nice as Robert," my mother said. "You used to be such a sweet little girl, I don't know why you've changed so." I simmered with silent anger, then heard my voice roiling forth past a barricade of clenched teeth and lips that moved hardly more than a ventriloquist's. "You never loved me." I was astonished that I had voiced what for so many years I had felt but left unsaid.

Damn. I wanted to be what Granny called my "sun-dial self" today, recording only the happy, sunny hours. Determined to be that sunny self, I stop next to a brightly painted image of the elephant-headed god, Ganesha, brilliant as the plumage of a toucan's bib—and I know how brilliant a toucan's bib can be, for before Veronica was born and until we left California to go to South Africa, Robert and I had had a pet toucan (named Livecheaper) who perched amiably on the carriage of my type-writer or on a verbena branch wedged above the kitchen stove, waking us each morning with hoarse and retching cries—I *gladly* let the elephant-headed god sing to me with the jubilance of a hymn. My thoughts arabesque to a plush elephant Robert won in a shooting gallery at a country fair, to a rogue bull elephant that thundered after our Landrover in Botswana, to the herd of elephants we watched together at the water-hole near the Angola border. We had so much to talk about, Robert and I, so much to tell each other, so much to share. I run a finger along Ganesha's trunk. "Do you remember the orange canvas cushions, just this color, that we had on our white wicker fur-niture on the porch in Jamaica?" I ask Veronica. "Do you re-member how beautiful the garden was, the great orange cups on the tulip tree flown through with hummingbirds all day long? Do you remember the night when a hummingbird, attracted by the light, flew through the open jalousies and came to rest in my hair? Your Daddoo claimed it had collapsed out of metabolic exhaustion and managed to disentangle it and we laid it peace-fully to rest on the windowsill, and then, in the morning, it flew away in a whir of almost invisible wings. Do you remember that?"

"Sort of."

Jamaica was a paradise for me, our Garden of Eden, even though, Elsa Cloud, you once terrified me by calling out that you had found your birth-sign beneath a stone, and I raced to topple you out of the way and to kill what you rightly had identified as a scorpion. But oh, that garden and the view of the mountains at dusk, all greenish-mauve and pink in that light. And the pineapple patch with pink-purple buds. Bougainvillea. Ferns with their growing tips coiled like sun-dial shells and the tails of chameleons. Hibiscus. Clear, lemon-colored blossoms on the dogwood tree and, at night, the twittering purr of the guinea fowl in the lignum vitae. White star jasmine. White tuberoses. White bell-shaped flowers of datura. A pair of white owls perching on the railing of the balcony outside your bathroom. You saw them while you were having your evening bath, and rushed wet and naked into my room to tell me to come and see. Breadfruit. Star apples. Bananas growing upward, enormous hands of bananas bannered with fringed leaves whose stems, when cut, left ineradicable brown stains on clothes. Red ackees with their shiny black almond-shaped seeds, "like a daisy," you said, in their center.

We stop at a fruit vendor's barrow mounded with chikus, dusty fur balls, and rambutans, a bright red fruit quilled like a hedgehog; clusters of hard yellow gooseberries, mangoes, limes, oranges, and finger bananas, the obvious easy choice to buy and eat while we stand in the shade of the vendor's black umbrella. As we drop the banana skins into a basket of refuse covered with Ganesha-bright spirals of orange peels, I have to catch myself before I actually tug at Veronica's sleeve, wanting her attention, yearning to share with her—what? I try again. "At school, a girl once made fun of my name and called me

Leila-Leila orange peela, all in fun, but I thought she meant I was a cast-off, a reject, garbage, and burst into tears. But then, *mirabile dictu*, a wonderful English teacher said, 'there, there, never mind,' and told me that in Christian symbolism the orange tree is symbolic of purity, chastity, generosity, that in representations of paradise, it alludes to the fall of man and his redemption. And she told me about a poet she knew called Rainer Maria Rilke who had written a poem about dancing the orange, dancing the taste of the fruit and becoming a pure resistant rind as well as the juice that fills the happy fruit, something like that. I like the idea of synaesthesia. Or are you going to tell me to go and synaesthesia no more?"

I hear myself sounding artificial, contrived, abstract, a phony-baloney dinner partner trying to make conversation, not a mother sharing thoughts and feelings with her daughter, certainly not me, but one of my protective, acquired selves, wanting reassurance. Still, I go on. "If you were a mapmaker and were mapping this area, would it look like a tree in winter with the twigs growing like birds' feet from the branches, and the branches swirling up and out from the trunk? Or like an anatomical illustration of capillaries, veins, arteries? Or like a diagram of all the constellations in the spring sky?"

"I like real places better than maps. I just like the Fellini flux of Old Delhi." Veronica's clear, high, lilting voice chimes with impatience.

"Okay. So be it. Right you are. I'll shut up." Better the Fellini flux externalized as Veronica is experiencing it than to be caught up as I am in an interior whirligig of words and thoughts that will not stay still, will not stay in place. And in what context have I heard that phrase? "Words move, music moves only in time; but that which is only living can only die. Words, after speech, reach into the silence. Only by the form, the pattern, can words or music reach the stillness, as a Chinese jar still moves perpetually in its stillness."

"Words strain, crack, and sometimes break under the burden, under the tension, slip, slide, perish, decay with imprecision, will not stay in place, will not stay still." Ah, Mr. Eliot. Thomas Stearns, T. S., teasing ever teasing and somewhat tormenting, Mr. Eliot, my adolescent schoolgirl pash, Mr. Eliot!

"Are you absolutely positive, Granny, that T. S. Eliot isn't a cousin?" I had written.

"Definitely not," my grandmother had replied to me in her looped, rounded penmanship formations. "He came from a different family altogether. *We* descended from the Saxon Elwolds; his was a Norman family who descended from the Alyots. Double L and single T, the Elliots of Minto and Wolfelee," she reminded me, were *our* cousins. "Double T and single L, the Eliotts that in Stobs do dwell," were ours, too.

My grandmother was the Dowager Lady Eliott of Stobs, a name that means "the wood," and styled herself simply on envelopes to acquaintances as L. Eliott, with her address. On letters to my mother and me, she never bothered with either name or return address. She had implicit faith that what she wrote to us would never go astray, and her faith, as far as I know, was not disavowed.

"Single L and single T, the Eliots of St. Germains be." That was the crusher. No relation at all. What my grandmother said was always the truth. My grandmother, natural, straight and true, could never, by any possible freak of fate, become anything else. How I cherished that thought, growing up, when my own mother seemed so unpredictable. Veronica has written me many times that existence is in perpetual flux, that nothing is permanent, that the Self, our Selves, are constantly changing. I suppose this is true, but I like certainties. I like character traits you can count upon.

The overhanging facades have become arched tunnels now, a proliferation of pentagonally shaped bay windows with diagonally latticed wooden shutters, the *moucharabiehs* from behind which women of the *harim* could watch the passing parade without being seen. Below, in a courtyard, the string webbing of a *charpoy* that stands on end casts sharp, diamond-patterned shadows against a gray-mauve-ocher wall, lovely in its impressionist coloring; a simple and satisfying inversion of pattern.

I stop to photograph the up-ended *charpoy*. The taut rectangular hammocks stretched across sturdy wooden frames, on which old men sleep with open mouths and children curl like commas, are a pleasing extension of my solitary child's pastime of the string game cratchcradle.

"Not cat's cradle, my precious," Granny had corrected me on several occasions. "Cratchcradle, in remembrance of our dear Savior's crèche. The lower classes just mispronounced the word, as they frequently do, vulgarized it through lack of proper education, thus obscuring the true significance of the charming diamond patterns." She tilts my chin so she can look into my eyes the way she looks into the hearts of the rose geraniums growing in the windowboxes of her London house—destroyed by a direct hit during the bombing blitz of World War II, luckily when she and Holloway, her ladies' maid, were in Scotland—"Remember, my darling, even when occupying your dear little hands making charming diamond patterns with kitchen twine—you did ask Cook if you could have some, didn't you? That's a good girl—remember to bear in mind the original reverence of this pastime, and to know that whatever you do is an offering to our Lord, because God is your help, your strength, your understanding. God is all love, His presence will never leave or forsake you and is with you now. That little diamond is a bit crooked, my treasure, just stretch your fingers a bit wider. That's it."

I blurt out this reminiscence to Veronica.

"Your grandmother sounds like an awful snoot," she says.

"Well, she wasn't," I say.

As though she doesn't hear me, Veronica says that the word *diamond* comes from the Sanskrit *dyu*, meaning luminous being, "an emblem that often indicates a radiant, mystic center. Like the Orphic Egg."

I wonder if Veronica remembers the day Robert showed her how difficult it was to break an egg held upended between the palms of one's hands. The Orphic Egg, that vast egg-shaped world, its golden yolk suspended in its elastic hammock, contains all the secrets of life. For out of the egg's snug, perfect entity, a creature emerges—human, bird, fish, reptile, animal—to complete the cosmic symbol of immortality, the equivalent of the Pythagorean circle with its central point like a navel, the umbilicus of the world. "That's why when children draw pictures of themselves with buttons marching down their fronts, it means that they are dependent on their mothers," I say to Veronica. "Buttons, with the little dot in the center where they're sewn on, are like Pythagorean circles, belly buttons!" Veronica confers on me a rather patronizing V of a smile, and on we walk, me behind her, for there is no room to walk by her side.

So much for my cheerful sun-dial self. I experience the houses I walk past now with an almost imperceptible visceral trembling, seeing in their place the house where I grew up, the perfection of its white clapboard exterior sheltering all those rooms with their proper settings and places for family, servants, and guests sandwiched between the terrors—yes, *terrors* is the word that springs to mind—of the cellar and the attic.

Outwardly, Northlea was of pure, simple proportions and a pleasing aspect. White, clapboard, gabled, fanlight above the front door, white-painted brick chimneys, white colonnaded brick side porch, back porch, and porch above the kitchen, black-green shutters and doors, the doors set with side-windows and centered near the top with polished brass door knockers. The interior of the house was labyrinthine. Some of its many rooms, including my own, were spacious and airy, gleaming with gilt-framed mirrors and the polished brass of fireplace fenders, shovels, tongs, and poker-handles. Other rooms, as well as the hallways and corridors, were too narrow for the massive American Empire furnishings with their marble tops and ormolu festoons that had come from Woodbine, my father's family's house in Newburgh, on the banks of the Hudson River, and the English antiques my mother preferred. Throughout Northlea there was the feel and shine of cleanliness, the scent of lavender and flowers, the fragrance of furniture polish that looked like butterscotch-colored saddle-soap in its tin. Delicious kitchen aromas were orchestrated to a tick-tocking wall clock loud as a metronome. The pantry was redolent with silver polish and the wooden drain board emitted a smell like stale beer. The laundry odor of the gaslit drying cupboard mingled with the perfume of lavender sachets topping wicker baskets of freshly ironed starched napkins, bed linens, and guest-towels that all had initials and the date they were bought cross-stitched in red on inner corners.

The dolls' house my mother gave me was a simplified version of Northlea and smelled only of oak shavings. It had been set on a rectangular platform in front of one of my bedroom windows, blocking my view of the blossoming Japanese peach tree, its flowers now visible only by opening the other window, putting my head on the sill, and pressing my left cheek against the mesh of its screen to have a pre-planned look. Gone the delight of waking up to that wild, gorgeous color, faced instead with the don't-touch-me stare of the dolls' house.

The dolls' house had eight rooms which were connected with a bannistered staircase, carpeted with a gray-blue-green runner, the color of my mother's eyes. Each room was wall-papered, electrically lit with an upside-down flame-shaped light in the center of its ceiling; a water tank made it possible to fill the bathtubs in two bathrooms and the sink in the kitchen. The rooms were furnished with English antique and Colonial American reproductions, and *real* antiques: a silver coal scuttle; a gold spectacle case with rose-colored glasses inside; a silver tea tray set with blue and white cups and plates and a silver hot-water jug, teapot, sugar bowl, and cream jug; tiny brass animals; a tiny mother-of-pearl telescope; and *this*, and *that*, and *these*. I remember Mummy holding a little leather bellows and other minikins tenderly in the cup of her hand. From tiny books with minuscule printing to even tinier real silver butter knives, noth-ing was missing. Lamps, children's toys, embroidered white crêpe-de-chine blanket covers and a silk one inset with lace for the master bedroom, fireplace utensils and fenders, Staffordshire poodles to flank the mantelpiece in the living room, a tapestry hanging for the front hall. My mother had searched antique shops in New York, London, and Paris for an inventory that was extraordinary in its detail and completeness. But once all this had been examined, what was I expected to do with the family of porcelain-headed dolls—mother, father, boy, girl, baby, nurse, cook, waitress-chambermaid—whose faces all had an expression of smiling vapidity? Like the collection of porcelain, rose quartz, crystal, jade, glass, and painted wooden animals—the cats' tea party and the monkeys' orchestra—that my friends admired and the maids fussed about the mantelpiece dusting, the dolls' house was one of my mother's enthusiasms, *her* plaything. I broke a fragile, tilt-top firescreen on the first day I dared to move the furniture around. A nurse carried the pieces to my mother, and Mummy carried the pieces back to me, raging, "How *could* you, how could you break this? After all the trouble I went to to find it . . ."

I came back from school one day to see in the place where the green-painted piano and bench had been, a ceiling-high 18th-century mahogany desk-secretary-cabinet. "Look at your new rich toy," my mother said, her voice pitched with hysterical pleasure. "And look," she exclaimed, "look at this matching miniature I got for the living room of your dolls' house!" As always, I did my best to be a mirror in which my mother could see herself reflected as the generous, loving, admirable, appreciated mother her psychic equilibrium depended upon and required, and me as her lucky and privileged child. Obediently, I inspected the midget clone, touching it with only my thumbnail.

LEILA BURTON IS A GOOD GIRL. My mother chalks this message

on a blackboard and poses me beside it, plump as a muffin with arms and legs like sausages encased in a rose-colored English woolen coat with a fur collar and cuffs and matching leggings. Beneath a pudding basin of a hat, also trimmed in dark brown fur, I am peeping out at the world, round-faced as a pocket watch, mischievous eyes sparkling, my smile a trusting but rather tentative crescent baring the little white corn kernels of my baby teeth.

The photograph is in black-and-white. Color film had not been invented then, but the intensity of that moment and that image captured by my mother's camera and reflected from her presence to my own has been preserved for my lifetime like the flowers of St. John's Wort in Veronica's copies of Kerouac's *Dharma Bums* and *On the Road*.

LEILA BURTON IS A GOOD GIRL. To ask to have the dolls' house moved away from the showcase window of the peach tree once the dolls' house had been installed would have been futile. The dolls' house would stay where my mother had instructed it to be put. To question her authority would only invoke her anger. "Take care not to come between the dragon and his wrath," she would caution me as I skipped downstairs to sit with my father in his study where he listened to the radio. But my father was seldom cross with me. It was the dragon wrath of my mother I feared.

Hence, the terror of the cellar and the terror of the attic. My mother had forbidden me to go to either of them. In the damp chill of the cellar, strange and unexpected things packed in elevated white-washed stone crawl-spaces—storm windows, wooden folding chairs waiting to be used for the Fourth of July fireworks display and my birthday parties, sleds and toboggans, broken towel-racks and cast-offs from the kitchen, mole traps stored here for convenience to save their being carted up in a wheelbarrow from the other end of the prop-erty—cast bogey-man shadows when the naked light-bulbs, hanging from twisted cords, were turned on, either from the kitchen switch or by pulling a string attached to their beaded brass chains.

Mushrooms were grown in tiered trays in the cellar; apples were stored in barrels. The kitchen tomcats sprayed there and the females had their kindles, of which all but one kitten would be taken off in a burlap sack by Karl or another gardener to be drowned, leaving a solitary mite pitifully mewing as the mother cat searched for the ones that were lost. There were rat traps everywhere, baited with raw bacon, and the reek of a rat that had escaped to die. A milk snake, long and thick, had been sighted several times in the cellar, and had never been caught. From outside or from the kitchen, the descent to the cellar was a test of bravery that fulfilled whatever need other children might satisfy in seeing the scary movies I was not allowed to see. "We don't want you having nightmares, dear," my mother said. But what nightmares were worse than these I could devise at will with a trip to the cellar?

The attic, while not quite as terrifying as the cellar, incorpo-rated the terror of being caught out and the attraction of the forbidden, and concertina-ed as well the inspiriting satisfaction of my need for exploration, discovery, and surprise, the feeling that some hidden thing was waiting just for me to find. Up the back stairs, past the walk-in cupboard, the storerooms, the roll of brown paper on the parcel-wrapping table, there was the enormous attic. In it, I found my father's high-chair, which had also been mine; boxes of black-bordered letters of condolence mourning the dead; my mother's porcelain-headed, kidskin-limbed dolls which I misprized; and elsewhere, an unending treasure trove in which to hunt out something I could use, give away as a present, or add to a matchbox surprise offering. The attic was a marvelous jumble of the accessible and that which was temporarily out of reach on high shelves, beneath or behind other boxes and packages, blocked by a platoon of trunks, or guarded by a dressmaker's dummy that had to be silently and carefully moved, my fingerprints appearing light or dark through its lovely pelt of soft gray mouse-fur dust.

"It's not like an attic, more like a cellar, my mind, that is." This was the first line of a poem I wrote when I was fourteen. "An attic has windows," I went on:

Sometimes you can fling them wide
And watch the alchemy of the sun transmuting dust to gold.
A cellar's not like that,
Although there is that same accumulation of
Discarded things, so hard to part with, so easy to keep.
You once looked at my thoughts,
A row of dusty jam-jars on a time-warped shelf.
One by one, you took them down, re-labeled them,
And set them in a row again.
I remember torn-off labels on the floor,
They looked like moths, dead moths, with moldy wings.
Yes, I know the cellar well.
I know the ghosts of things and people
Which just a word can so easily recall.
But when the frightening conclave begins
Of all the things I might have done,
Of all the things I might have been,
I run upstairs, and close the door,

Washing the dust smudge from my face
So that there will be no trace
Of what I have been doing.

I wonder who I thought I was, writing a poem like that.

I stored my secret thoughts, feelings, and dreams in an attic, and felt pitched to the greater excitation when I sallied forth on my sneaky little trips there than I did about my excursions to the cellar, where at least I was officially allowed to go once a year, on Hallowe'en, when Aunt Vera converted it into a Chamber of Horrors. Perhaps it was because greater secrecy was necessary in the attic, the barefoot tiptoeing so that I would not be heard and the fear that I would not be mistaken yet another time for a maid in the end room or a squirrel on the roof, the final feeling of elation as I closed the door triumphant at having not been caught, the secrecy with which I scrubbed the soot-black dust from the soles of my feet, the swell of fear as I hid my loot up my bedroom chimney in the fireplace damper or in the bottom of a clothes bag in the cupboard until I could make use of it or give it away—would anyone find my stolen treasure before I had?—and the fear subsiding when time passed and no one did.

To venture to the attic or to the cellar was not to risk being slapped or spanked, which I never was, or having my allowance stopped. My allowance, graduating from the quarters my mother washed in ammonia to "sterilize" them so I wouldn't be contaminated by other people's germs to mint-fresh dollar bills, presumably handled only by the familiar teller at the village bank, was never stopped. No, being disobedient was to defy the consequences of abandonment and annihilation, for that was what the withdrawal of my mother's love and approval meant to me. She might abandon me as my first nanny had, and I might almost drown again, or she might cut off my head with the same ease as she sheared off the heads of withered peonies, snip! snap! snip!, like the scissor-man in *Struwwelpeter*, a book my mother was fond of because she had read it as a child, who cut the thumbs off little boys who sucked them.

Sooner or later, my mother would do something far worse to me than I had ever done to her. She was bound to. She always did. Someone beloved, something cherished, missing, gone, vanished—that was always the form of retribution.

When, at the age of twenty-five, I set off around the world, I left my New York apartment rented, and asked my mother to find new tenants for me if I didn't return within the year. Eighteen months later, I got back to New York to find the apartment gone and most of my possessions disposed of, including a piano I acquired to replace the green upright piano of my childhood. "It was only an ordinary piano," my mother said. "You can stay with Dadzo and me until you find another apartment."

Instead, I flew to California to visit Robert, married him a week after I arrived, and installed in our little rented house an antique harmonium I had found serendipitously in a Los Angeles second-hand store, that totem foot-pedal organ I have clung to ever since. Six weeks later I was pregnant. When I telephoned to tell Mummy and Daddy the news, I said to my father, "I'm longing for you to meet Robert. I'm going to have a baby. Would you like to have a granddaughter? Robert says he wants me to have a little baby girl, just like me, except he says she will be like a fairy-tale princess, beautiful, wise, good."

Five days after that, there was a telegram from my mother. "Daddy died. Funeral service to be held in New York, March

28. Ever your devoted Mumsie." She said he had died of pneumonia, unable to breathe. I felt I had caused his death with my news, that he had loved me so much he had died of a broken heart.

I was incestuous about my father, let's make no bones about that—not physically, of course, but in my heart and mind, where bonds are stronger. I climbed into bed with him one afternoon during my nap time, when he was having his nap across the hall in his dressing-room. It was the nurse's day off. The maids were resting in their rooms. My mother had taken the dogs for a walk. I must have known all this, for how else, at the age of eight, would I have dared to rush from my bed and slip into his, put my arms around his neck, look into his eyes, look away, press my cheek against his tree-bark cheek and say what I knew everyone else would think was wrong to say, but what was right for me to say only to him. "Oh, Daddy, I wish it was always like this, just you and me alone here. I wish everyone else would go away and never come back. Couldn't you get Mummy to go away forever? I could make you much happier. I'd be so happy if it was just us together. Wouldn't you like that?"

"You bet, old sport," my father had said. "You're Daddy's good girl. I love you, old top."

I hugged him, pressed my cheek harder against his as he flung his arms around me to hug me reassuringly and hold me for a moment before he lifted the weight of his arms. "You're the best girl in all the world, old sport," he said, raising his arm and pressing it around me again. "You're Daddy's own girl. We understand each other, don't we, sweetheart?"

"You bet your sweet life we do." I heard the dogs barking,

the front door open, and all in one motion I hugged him, slid off the bed, and was back in my own bed, my heart pounding, before the first dog came kiyoodling up the stairs.

"You must miss Daddy terribly," I said to my mother the day of the funeral, as we were about to leave the New York apartment my father and she had begun to spend more time in.

"Oh, no, dear, there'll be so much more room," she replied in that faraway voice of hers as she stood gazing at herself in the vestibule mirror. She lifted the veil of her black velvet hat over her ears, carefully, so that it wouldn't catch on her pearl and diamond earrings. "How do I look in my widow's weeds?" she asked.

Within an hour, I was looking at my father, dressed in his vestryman's attire, resting in his coffin lined with quilted white velvet. I thought of him lying in the snow at Northlea, showing me how to make the imprint of an angel, moving his arms slowly up and down to form the outspread wings.

Within weeks, Northlea, too, was gone. My mother sold it, disposed of all its contents. Everything was gone. The grand-father clock with the sun and the moon on its face, the rich toy I had come to like with its ivory keyholes and secret compart-ments, my country clothes, and everything I had hoped to keep forever in the attic: diaries, notebooks, all the books of mine I had read before I went to St. Timothy's, my favorite childhood dresses; the Schoenhut circus with its tented top, its animals, performers, high-wire platforms and trapezes; the wooden jig-saw puzzles and the sandstone building blocks with their pillars, arches, and turrets for the construction of elaborate buildings; the red kaleidoscope; the bird-houses in the trees, the gray lead cherubs poised by the bird-baths, and the bird-baths them-selves that I had watched being dug and made. The house, the stables, the garage with the pigeon loft above it, the barns in the horse pastures, the playhouse—all would soon be razed to make way for a housing development.

Oh, Elsa Cloud, we seem to live, you and I, only by the standards we have set for ourselves. Self-styled perfectionists, although our styles differ in many ways and the extremes of our self-indulgence vary, we tend to exercise the form of vanity in which we are more ready to excuse the faults of others than we are to excuse our own. Of course, this doesn't apply to my mother. Is this because I'd rather hate her than myself? Is it because I see her in myself? If I could only understand why she was the way she was, I might in some way understand myself better, so that I won't do to you what she did to me, or be with you the way she was with me. And if I have already done this, maybe I can change the way I am, or the way you feel about me.

"Let's go shopping." The words bound from me as if loosed from a cage. I want to flee to the safety of objects I can cope with and escape the thoughts and emotions that threaten to overwhelm me, to take over, to fill my mind, to throw out all else like a cuckoo in the nest.

"Let's shop," I say again, pleadingly, knowing that in the timepiece of my mind while years can be distilled to seconds, minutes can also stretch into hours, and somewhat concerned that Veronica may not want to shop, may get cross with me for wanting to shop, and may not understand why I want to shop, need to shop—a therapeutic diversion as well as a pleasurable one.

"*Teek*," Veronica says calmly, soothingly, the way a Zulu houseboy would say, "*O.K., Baas*."

"Wonderful! Thank you, darling!"

Veronica is glancing back at me, stretching out her hand for me to catch on to, her peach-brown cheek glinting along the bone. She is cautioning me to watch out where I walk because we are coming to a slippery patch. As a child, I used to fall asleep pressing one hand into the other, making believe I was holding the hand of a beloved companion.

"You have to expect that in grungy, tenement areas like this," Veronica says, as a woman in an iridescent saffron and purple sari edges by, and then another in a marvelously risky color combination of magenta, electric blue, and orange, balancing a burlap sack on her head with graceful ease, a woman from some outlying country district, the light scintillating on her silver ankle bracelets, her wine-jar hips swaying as she walks. Then a man in a lime-green turban, another woman in fire-bright orange-red, a man in a turban the color of a robin's egg.

Tenement area? Elsewhere in the world, poverty is gray and brown and seems far more dangerous, unrelieved by dashing color, flash, and sparkle.

That clothes washed in the nearest river, pounded with stones by a *dhobi*, dried in the sun, and pressed with irons filled with embers should appear flower bright and spotless as Veronica's baby clothes had been is a comforting aspect of India's indestructibility, a small enchantment offering the larger hope of another chance in life to emerge cleansed of imperfection.

Seven

It is early March. Veronica and I linger in Delhi. The festival of Holi will take place when the moon is full, and Mulk has promised that he will join us then. Usually, I hate waiting. I operate on infant time, craving instant gratification for all my needs and desires. But as we go about Old Delhi and New Delhi, sitting in the back seat of Gurdip's taxi with the windows open to let in the silky spring air and the scent of cumin and coriander, as we wait for Holi to happen, it seems to me that I am finally "seeing things as they truly exist in all their richness and flux, accepting each moment as it is, feeling calm in action, intense when calm, living in a slowed-down way," as Veronica says, explaining what meditation does for her. Still I find it impossible to respond to things spontaneously, to see, hear, think, feel, touch, taste, "with no ego-self to separate you from the ocean, or the sky, or a mountain or a bird or a tree or anything." Nor do I think I would like to be this way, just letting images come and go with no attachment, leaving behind all residues of anger, pain, pleasure, association, so that every experience is just that: pure experience, uninterpreted. No, everything I see brings back memories, associations, and connections. Where I expect to see windows with *khus-khus* tatties, those thick mats of woven roots kept drenched with water so that the wind passing through them is cool and refreshing, I see boxes and grilles of air conditioners. And where are the goldbeaters flicking the pages of their books of tissue-paper, placing between every two pages a sheet of gold so fine you could rub it on an icon or dissolve it in your mouth? Vanished, gone like the use of abacuses. In the gaudy bazaars, you still can buy squares of *vark* for the decoration of food as well as for *paan*, but I see no one making it. The old, handmade, odd *vark*, I joke, a rare beast. Gurdip says that *vark* is now made in factories by machines.

Watching a brass-smith at work in an alleyway cubicle is like watching a gymnast or a juggler: how can the human mind direct such intricate operations? A tattoo with a hammer, and a perfect fish-scale design appears. A few seconds pinging with a spike, and there's a peacock with a tail like a fountain. "An apprentice, Madam," Gurdip says. "The real craftsmen are performing much better work." Gurdip's turban waggles with contentment when he imparts such information. His turban, or *puggree*, as he refers to it, is forty feet long and takes him five minutes each morning to fold, pleat, and wind around his head. Sometimes, when he is waiting for us, he washes his waist-length gray hair, treats it with asafoetida, curls it into a wet ball, and pins it to dry on top of his head.

Being a Sikh is the center of Gurdip's life, the spindle that keeps his mind's records of piety and courage, of swinging scimitars and happy warrior marches, aligned with the turntable of his hard-working daily life. One day, he takes us to see his temple, a new concrete building where an old one used to be, containing a series of high-ceilinged concrete-walled, concrete-floored rooms—"all clean and moderen" Gurdip says proudly —for sleeping, eating, religions observances, and meetings. Anyone of any race or religion is welcome to free food and a *charpoy* for three successive days. "Even hippies," Gurdip says.

"If they're in trouble, all they have to do is hide and go Sikh," I can't help saying as I examine paintings of Mussulmen beheading Sikhs. Fountains of blood spurtle from the victims' necks and cascade from lopped heads that are either suspended some distance above blood-dripping scimitars or hand-held in football-passing style by grinning oppressors.

Gurdip points out the dining hall, where free food is being dispensed to a crowd that includes several Westerners and a clutch of old crones in saris seated on raised benches with platters and cups placed on low stools before them.

"What are they eating? Curried favors?" I tease.

"No, Madam," Gurdip replies solemnly. "Curried *subji* (vegetables) and rice. It is costing the Sikh community much money, Madam. The beliefs of Sikhs are piety, obedience, purity of mind, self-restraint, and industriousness." He leads us to a railed-off enclosure where Sikhs can pray and place offerings. The floor is coated with copper annas and silver rupees. "Naughty boys sometimes spread flour paste on their palms. When they prostrate themselves, they pick up some of the coins," Gurdip comments. Then he adds quickly, "Not *educated* boys, just poor ones."

Another day, we explore a residential section where an occasional ox can be seen pulling a mower in silvery circles on a lush green lawn. The lawn is dovetailed with dark *ashoka* trees clipped in umbrella shapes, and a few gnarled mountainous banyan trees, linking the underworld, earth, and heaven with their roots, trunks, foliage. Veronica counters my murmurings about the tree of life and the tree of knowledge by saying that in India people believe in upside-down trees, a classic symbol of the reality that underlies or is hidden by life in the world, with its false goals and misleading perceptions. She says you can read in the Upanishads about the roots of mythical trees that generate in heaven, with branches below that are ether, air, fire, water, and earth. I tell her I like upside-down things, inversions, that I used to croon myself to sleep with a poem that up-ended itself called *This is the Key of the Kingdom.*

> This is the Key of the Kingdom
> In that Kingdom is a city;
> In that city is a town
> . . . a street . . . a lane . . . a yard . . . a house. . . .
> In that house there waits a room;
> In that room an empty bed,
> And on that bed a basket of sweet flowers
> . . . flowers in a basket . . . on the bed
> . . . in the chamber . . . in the house . . . in the yard . . . lane
> . . . street . . . town . . . city . . . kingdom . . .
> Of the Kingdom this is the Key.

"Sort of a mantra," I add, and wait for Veronica to correct me, but she doesn't.

The sight and scent of frangipani through the open car windows, their large, creamy blooms inlaid like random ivory on the boughs, flowers which symbolize immortality to both Muslims and Buddhists, make me think of Robert. I see him looking upward, gulping in the fragrance of frangipani the way we once saw a boy in the Riffi hills in Morocco gulping water from a spigoted jug held as high as he could reach above his head. I see Robert in a Landrover in Botswana, and myself sitting beside him, watching the flamingoes lift like a pink carpet off a lake in the Kalahari desert. We are jouncing along toward the oasis of Maun, where we shoot crocodiles at night from a flat-bottomed boat poled through a swamp of lotus and papyrus with the trees lit here and there with little green eyes that Robert says are baboons or maybe lemurs. The crocodiles' eyes are red when the oarsman shines a flashlight at them.

Robert always knew the names of trees wherever we want. It's a belief as old as the hills, he used to say, that to know the name of someone or something is to give oneself mastery over the object. Not only to know the name, but to be able to say the word. To know that even if I still stuttered on some sounds and not on others that I was almost free of the censorship of stuttering, yet still to keep lists of synonyms in my mind just in case a troublesome word cropped up increased my interest in all the taxonomical terms Robert compiled. I smile as I find myself asking Gurdip and Veronica to tell me the names of the trees we pass by.

"The outside—how you are saying it, bark, isn't it?"—of the casuarina, or the *jungli jhao* in Hindi, "is very good for complaints of the belly," Gurdip says. "And the twigs of the neem trees many people are using for teethbrushes."

"The leaves of the Bauhinia are used for beedie-wrappings." This from Veronica, who points a long, tapering index finger at a tree with kidney-shaped leaves and lavender flowers.

"My mother used to tell me never to point at anything except pastries," I say, and point at once with my child's stub of an index finger at a Tickell's flowerpecker making sharp chick-

chick-chick catbird-like sounds in a *gul mohr* tree that sparkles with splashes of flaming orange and crimson.

"A Tickell's flowerpecker?" Veronica finds this hilarious. She says she'd rather *see* than *be* one.

Two white hump-backed Brahma bulls suddenly block our path. Gurdip brakes and impatiently revs the motor. Blinking at us, the bulls stand motionless, switching their tails. Notwithstanding the precept of *ahimsa*, of non-injury to living beings, of not taking life, a precept Hindus and Buddhists observe as Christians do the Ten Commandments, I wonder why cows should be more respected than other animals, venerated so that one thinks of them as "sacred," as "holy." Because . . . *pecus*, cow, the voice of Mr. Green, my Latin teacher returns to me. *Pecus*, because. Because to be without cows, without cattle, is to be *impecunious*. Impecunious, without cows, without milk, meat, hides, without money. "To ask how many cows a man owns is as rude as asking him how much money he has in the bank," a Zulu chieftain had told me in Africa. Now, here in India, I hear his voice above the revving of the motor.

Gurdip informs us that cow protection is coming to an end, with some states upholding the cow slaughter ban and others, like Kerala in the south, fighting it by setting up cow slaughter houses and meat-packing subsidiaries. "The cows are numbering twenty *crores* (200 million), Madam. Turned loose, Madam, they wander at large, Madam, eating crops, *scavenging*, Madam. In Bengal, the west side, near where I am living with my family on a farm, there are many, many eating up maize and wheat. But in Bengal, they have organized a meat-packing industry, and a very good thing it is, too, Madam. Many Hindus are now eating beef, Madam. Not the old and the true orthodox Hindu believers, but the young. Beef is cheaper than chicken, Madam. The *Tibby*tuns, are they not also eating beef, Miss Veronica?"

"Oh, yes, Gurdip, they are."

Tibetan monks and lay Buddhists eat beef? "How come they eat beef if it's against their religion to kill anything?" I ask.

Veronica's response is cool, patient. "Buddhists don't kill the fish or meat they eat, Mummy. Someone else who is not a Buddhist does that. Buddhists just *buy* fish and meat to eat."

"And sometimes they just rescue poor helpless fish from drowning, isn't that so?" Gurdip says, all teasey and jolly, swiveling his head around to wink at Veronica.

"Oh, shame, Gurdipji. You're so naughty."

Veronica and Gurdip can talk in an easy, cosy way about religion. He is always telling me I have a very religious daughter, and somehow I am made to feel like a heathen, an infidel, Mummy the *giaour*, the ja-ooooor.

We drive about. We walk about. From the dark, house-filled grotto of a lane, Veronica and I emerge into the scalding, momentarily blinding light of a main thoroughfare, with the Jama Masjid unexpectedly springing into view, its three white marble onion domes shimmering against the primal blue of the sky.

"Here, Mum, let me take your pack and camera." Veronica holds out her hands. How does she know I want to feel completely free to hug the Jama Masjid, to embrace the sight of it as you would embrace a dear friend you had not seen for a long time?

By physically unburdening me, Veronica sets me free emotionally. Standing there unencumbered, my hands raised and pressed against the sides of my head, I can race back in time and ascend the graduated stone steps to the plinth of the granite courtyard, where pigeons with undulating breasts cluster and flap about. The surrounding pillared cloister, its crenellated roof set off with four *chattris*—the cylinder forms pierced with arches and topped with the domes and golden finial spires so dear to the hearts of Mogul architects—is where I imagine myself. I would stand in the shade facing the courtyard's cusped entrance with its calligraphic inlays, and the great mosque's minarets. Three centuries past, the royal procession of Shah Jehan, the passionate builder, who fashioned his dream in marble on the banks of the Jamuna, a courier's ride away, had traveled here every Friday from the Red Fort with his retinue. I could see the royal slaves dressing him for this occasion, handing him his jeweled necklaces and bracelets in the same grandiose fashion that Louis XIV had his courtiers appointed to deliver particular articles of clothing. I see Shah Jehan in my mind's cinema. I see the Sun King. I see them both sharing the endearingly grand gesture of a child extending a foot to be shod. I see myself. I see Veronica. I see my grandmother, her lady's maid kneeling at her feet to fasten the buckles on her satin evening slippers. My mother always dressed in private. No one was admitted to her room while she dressed. Was my mother ever endearing in a childlike way as an adult? No, I say fiercely to myself. No, no, but there is more to it than that, and I shall get to it all soon enough.

Here I am, back in the street again, my hands still pressed on either side of my head, staring at the white onion domes which appear to be as pierced with cloves as the pomander balls I used to fashion from oranges as an offering to my mother to scent her clothes cupboards. I remember my heart bursting with excitement at the prospect of giving and the gratitude I would receive as I pressed the smooth-headed cloves and the four-spiked, pronged, decapitated ones in serried ranks through the rind.

"Pigeons, Mummy," Veronica says, answering the question I have not asked.

I watch the cloves turn into pigeons that lift and rise into the sky, transfigured by a trick of light into a swirl of white confetti, then settle, drifting like the flurries of snowflakes in a snow globe, to become again the cloves they were, stuck like preservatives in the nurturing breasts of the white, gold-nippled domes.

On another excursion, at the Kutub Minar, we encounter what appear to be players from a lost circus, two clowning giantesses. They are *hijras*, transvestites, eunuchs, who deliberately make a nuisance of themselves so they will be paid to leave. The *hijras* are new-style noisy and grotesque, but better by far than the deformed and mutilated Picasso-faced beggars one sees outside other national monuments.

The ancient minaret charms Veronica and me. It looks like a colossal tilted telescope with its eyepiece pointed into the sky. Each story is fluted and knife-pleated, each platform is differently patterned. Ruched with a corbeled balcony, banded with Islamic calligraphy, it is music for the eyes. We tilt our heads back to our shoulders to look up at it. We walk around it several times.

"Like monks," Veronica says. "Like monks circumambulating a temple. Except that monks never look up, and they circumambulate in a clockwise direction, and we're walking around the other way."

She doesn't circumambulate temples, does she? Oh yes, she

does. All Buddhists do. In a clockwise direction. "We drop pebbles on the window ledges, sometimes, to keep track of how many times we have circumambulated. It makes me feel like Hansel and Gretel dropping crumbs in the forest."

I hurl out Christian indignation, a lightning bolt that is metamorphosed in mid-air to a critical, querulous dart tossed at the Kutub Minar. "The first three storeys are the beauties. The top two storeys added on later are all wrong. Horrid."

Having articulated my critique, I stop, feeling like the wicked witch, but Veronica twigs on right away. "Don't grump, Mum," she says with a look of pity and condescension. "I'm so glad we came."

I put my arm around Veronica's shoulder and tell her that I am glad she is with me. I tell myself that life reveals itself. Be patient. Be compassionate.

In a cloistered courtyard we run our hands along the smooth and sun-warmed shaft of the famous iron pillar of the Gupta age, sacred to Vishnu. It remains uncorroded by rust. Magic powers? The purity of the metal? The metallurgical skill of ancient India? Who knows? Veronica tries to read the Sanskrit inscription on the column. "Can't do it." She sighs. "All I can do is make out Vishnu's name." She trails her finger along some pennant-like marks like the leaves of ferns in our garden in Jamaica.

Near the exit, a snake charmer presses close to me with the evident intention of looping a fat, wriggling python around my neck.

"There's your chance, Mummy, to wear a real python instead of a feather boa."

Veronica laughingly fends off the snake charmer, who then

gestures toward half-a-dozen drugged scorpions spread out on a woven palm frond mat beside him. His face is as dimpled with smallpox pits as a golf ball. Beside him is a brass water-pipe with a clay *chillim* on top to hold a few shreds of blackened tobacco. The ivory mouthpiece at the end of the magenta flex that leads from the hookah has been neatly placed on a large leaf next to his basket of snakes. I hate myself for liking these tourist sights, and like myself for hating them and hate myself for gawking as he tries to prod the scorpions into action with a twig.

"Your birth sign, sweetheart," I note.

"Did you know that Indians think scorpions are symbolic of frenzied sexual passions?" she asks.

I immediately wish that Veronica had been born in October or December. "Is that because the scorpions mate wildly or because of some love-death equation?" I ask.

"No idea, Mum. Just a curiosity for your notebook." Veronica doesn't trust me to know what to tip the snake charmer. She selects the appropriate amount from a chamois change-purse I remember her buying in London.

We are fair game now for the fortune-tellers. One waves a testimonial from an American girl in Ohio: "You remember me, don't you? I was the blonde girl traveling with a black and a homosexual . . . And you were absolutely right about the boy who said he wanted to marry me. It never would have worked . . ."

"Pick a number from one to five," he instructs us. "Think of a flower . . ." I do, and there on a slip of paper drawn from the fortune-teller's pocket is scrawled "Three" and "A Rose." "Good luck, good luck. *Ram! Ram!* You'll be living to be eighty-five. You have money, but don't save it." The fortune-teller holds out his hand for baksheesh.

Veronica is impatient. "Three and a rose are the most obvious choices," she whispers. "He had the answer already written before he even asked his silly questions." The fortune-teller smiles, slips his hand once again into his pocket, and draws out two wadded pieces of paper that he gives to us unfolded. Mine says Leila. On the piece of paper Veronica has unfolded I can see untidy letters spelling out her name.

I tip the fortune-teller. How had he guessed our names? Had he and Gurdip made a game-plan beforehand? Or are some people really able to tell what's on your mind and what happened in your past, and to make educated guesses about your future?

"Your father, you know, was not only an excellent geologist, but an excellent scientific generalist," I say to Veronica. "He always said that it is possible to tune in on the brain processes of other people, that just as an encephalogram can record the electrical activity of brain waves and pick up signals that accompany neurological activity, so someone who is sympathetic to your brain waves can resonate like a tuning fork and tune in on what you are thinking about."

"I suppose," Veronica says in the agreeable tone of one who is not really convinced, but who hasn't the energy to marshal a strong argument to the contrary. "I suppose," she says again, and her lips began to move, forming the soundless words of a mantra.

Later, back in our hotel room, she brings up the subject of non-attachment once again. Speaking of a single-pointedness of mind, where every experience is pure experience, uninterpreted, "in which your mind, body, nature, and everything around you all come together, are one, so that you pulse with the same rhythm of the world, the universe," she sounds inspirational. But what state of mind is she describing? Mystical communion with God? The passionate act of love? Rebirth, renewal, escape from the past? Alive, alive-oh? From the sublime to the possibly absurd, what Robert had said and what Veronica is saying might also lend credence to mind-reading and fortune-telling. Yes, Veronica?

No, Mummy. She says I've got it all wrong, that I don't understand. "You don't really believe in all that, do you? Fortune-telling? Why, that's like tea-leaves!" she teases me, expressing indulgent incredulity. "Astrology, yes, of course, but not fortune-telling. *Really*, Mummy."

"Well, maybe it's just that heightened perception and mind control are more of a commonplace in India than anywhere else in the world," I say, hearing myself sound feeble and ridiculous.

At least three or four times a week, Veronica and I visit people to whom I have letters of introduction. We go to parties, often grumbling as we get dressed, and then usually have a good time when we get there.

Tonight we are invited to dinner at the home of Patwant Singh. Patwant is the editor of an architectural magazine and has invested most of his considerable personal fortune in building a private research hospital on the outskirts of Delhi where the rich and those who have no money to pay for treatment can share equally in the benefits of modern medicine. "*Merci beaucoup*, as we say in the Punjab," Patwant says with a jocular air in response to the book I have brought him. "It looks like a turban raiser." Fiftyish, sartorially splendid in his black silk Sikh's turban and Saville Row bespoke gabardine suit, he is an attentive and generous host.

In an air conditioned dining room, houseboys have set out the dinner buffet. There are candles in pierced brass globes, silky pink puffs of rain tree flowers mixed with white roses, and before them, a steaming *Shahjehani biriyani* of rice roasted with spices and meat, to which saffron, dried fruit, nuts, and hard-cooked eggs have been added, a Mogul recipe hardly changed from the seventeenth century. There is *pulao* of rice with prawns, cashews, raisins, mushrooms, carrots. There are fresh chick peas, *pakoras* (vegetables fried in batter), and a platter of *dal*, lentils prepared with cumin, ginger, onions, garlic, coriander, turmeric, cardamom, chilies, and peppercorns, with green peppers or *capsicum* as a garnish. ("Don't eat too much of it, Mummy. It will give you the trots," Veronica whispers.) There is a silver platter of *kofta* (meat balls) garnished with fresh mint. There is *paneer* (cottage cheese). There is *murga masalam*, a spicy, peppery chicken curry. There are salads of fresh fruit and salads of fresh vegetables. I watch with fascination as the Indian guests heap their plates and then proceed to eat everything using only a *chapatti* held in their right hands, a circle of wheat dough fried to the consistency of a stiff pancake, to pinch the food and carry it to their mouths with deft, neat motions. Silver forks and knives are provided for foreign guests, and we are all provided with silver spoons for the dessert, mango soufflé with whipped cream and sauce, and crisp, rich, sugary cakes.

As I am savoring the soufflé, a stern-faced man, tweaking up the legs of his trousers and stretching out his sockless feet, his toes visible beyond the leather criss-cross of his *chaplis*, asks if I believe in auto-urine therapy.

"I'm a one-man piss-mission," he confides. "A naturopath."
He tells me that he ascribes his good health to a regimen of
drinking his own urine two or three times a day.

"Urine is the nectar of life," he says. Drinking one's own
urine is a therapy first imparted by Lord Shiva to Parvathi and
has thus come to be called *Shivambu*. He assures me that *Shivambu* is a cure for poor eyesight and diseases of the urinary
tract, and a general benefit to one's system. The nails on his
straight, unblemished toes are as perfect as Veronica's fingernails, as perfect as the sandaled feet on classical Greek sculptures. Do I, as a Westerner, find the practice of *Shivambu* repul-
sive or acceptable? he inquires.

I think of advertisements I doubt will sweep America: Urine
for a surprise. Urine for a treat. "I don't think it will replace
Coca Cola," I say, smiling.

"*Atcha*. But if the West does take to it, more Indians will
follow the practice. We in India like to borrow our own gifts."

The following evening we attend a black-tie dinner called for
nine o'clock, given by Goodie and Biki Oberoi, who have a
genius for the calculated risks of the hotel business. Thirty-six
guests finally sit down at half-past ten. Round tables covered
with black linen cloths are set with silver service plates, crystal
wine glasses and water goblets, and silver centerpiece bowls
filled with passion flowers, roses, and cineraria. At each table, a menu set on a silver pedestal announces that dinner will
be Vichyssoise, lobster-stuffed avocado, creamed chicken, broccoli hollandaise, chocolate mousse cake. After dinner, coffee is
served in the drawing room and bowls of shredded anise and
cardamom kernels to crack between the teeth are passed
around as an aid to digestion. An Australian senior citizen, her
hair like boiling milk, says to her companion, "I *love* Indian

women. They look so cute going about wearing evening dresses all day long."

Conde Leopoldo de Santovenia, the Spanish ambassador, gives parties in his garden through which Indian women in their drifting saris glide like apparitions, and servants in their white uniforms float like lilies in the shadowy expanse of the Embassy's lantern-lit lawn. Laughter booms and ripples in coloratura ecstasy. Voices tinkle like ice cubes, crackle like fire. To a guest who is nattering about the "poor things" sick and sleeping in the streets, the Count says that he envies them. "I'd rather have them as companions in my old age than die alone in one of those nursing homes in Madrid where the well-to-do are put away so as not to inconvenience their families." Turning to me he adds, "I just swim with the tide, my dear. It is too hot, and nobody has the energy to do otherwise." I see him later, courtly and charming, fetching champagne for Veronica.

The food differs at the parties we go to, the settings vary, but the voices and faces become increasingly familiar. Veronica faults me for wanting to show her off to people. "Why do you have to tell everyone I'm translating Tibetan and Sanskrit and studying Buddhism? They'll think I'm some sort of religious freak," she says. And "Do remember to use your right hand in passing things and giving things to people. It's not done to use the left hand." And "Don't cross your legs, Mummy, and don't show the soles of your shoes or feet to anyone, particularly holy men. It's not polite." And "Don't talk about the Tibetans. They are refugees, and even the Dalai Lama is a touchy subject with the Indians because of the political relationship with the Chinese. The Indian government wants to be polite to the Chinese by not demanding that they give Tibet back to the Tibetans, and they also want to be polite to the Tibetans so that they won't start a war between the Tibetans and the Chinese on Indian territory."

I feel myself a child again. "What a busy little bee you are," a nurse said to me when I was five and sitting in bed with a bed tray fashioning valentines from red paper, paper doilies, and pasteboard sheets embossed with tab-joined pictures of birds and flowers and old-fashioned children. Down the little red lane. Little pitchers have big ears. Children should be seen and not heard. You look as pretty as a speckled pup (this from my father). Did you wipe yourself? Eat your carrots, they'll make your hair curl. Eat your spinnidge, it's good for you. We'll kiss it and make it all well (always from nurses—my mother would rush for the bottles of peroxide and mercurochrome). Don't bolt your food like that. Don't smile too much, people will think you are too friendly (always from my mother. Away from her gaze, I smiled at anyone whose face attracted me because it made me happy to have them smile back.).

Are you sure you have clean gloves and a nice clean handkerchief and clean underwear? What would people think if you were run over? (from all the nurses and governesses, except the French ones). Good riddance to bad rubbish. Brush your teeth and say your prayers. Pick everything up. Mind your manners and your language. Don't ask so many questions. Get your derrière up off the saddle when you jump, for Christ's sake (this from my father). But me not butts, only goats butt. Good shot, old top; good work, old sport (praise from my father on almost any occasion). What's worth doing is worth doing well. A place for everything and everything in its place. Fidgety Phil wouldn't sit still. Don't make faces like that; if the wind changes, it will stay that way. Leave something on your plate for Mr. Manners. Cover yourself up, treasure, it's not nice to be naked (my grandmother). Just look at your hands and knees, what will people think? Cleanliness is next to Godliness. Sit up straight. No elbows on the table. Write thank-you letters the day you receive a present. Put your gloves on. Don't talk so loudly, dear. It's not nice to make personal remarks, dear. You must suffer in order to be beautiful (said while my hair was being put up in rag curlers, or being braided). See a pin and pick it up and all the day you'll have good luck. Good, better, best, never let it rest, 'til your good is better and your better best. Your hair is like heaven, there's no parting. If you don't eat, you'll never grow tall. You can always tell a lady by her luggage, shoes, and handbag; they must all be good leather and well-polished. Save your good writing paper for people who matter (from my mother). Skin a rabbit! (said when I was being undressed). The Devil finds work for idle hands. Haste makes waste. You're coming? So is Christmas. Don't bite off your nose to spite your face. Fine feathers make fine birds. Two wrongs don't make a right. Have you been? Do you have a dollar for the collection plate?

Telling Veronica that I am proud of her, that I'll always remember about using my right hand and about not pointing my feet at anyone, and that she must know by this time that I never get involved in political discussions, seems to reassure her for a while. But with the expression of a grumpy cat that has to be stroked before it will purr, she repeats parts of her advice, if not all of it, each time we set forth.

At tonight's party, I move from a man with enamel and gold buttons on his achkan who is asking if James Joyce's "quark for

Master Mark" has any connection with the theoretical particles that are a fundamental ingredient of matter, to plump myself down beside Tara Ali Baig, whose *Moon in Rahu* I've read and liked. She is the president of the International Union for Child Welfare, the daughter of a Bostonian mother and a Bengali father. I ask her why the dot of vermilion sandalwood paste called either a *tika*, a *bindu* mark, or a *kumkum* dot worn by married women on the center of the forehead never smears or smudges the way lipstick does. She tells me that if they are ready-made paper circles, or applied with spices and powder, they can blow off or streak with perspiration, particularly if you're playing tennis.

"They adhere better if you use a dab of coconut oil and apply a *tika* of spices and powder with a nailhead," Tara says. Traditional red *tikas*, she tells me, are now being replaced with metallic colors and pastels to match saris.

Meenakshi Devi, a poet and antiquarian, tells me that dyes and spices for *tikas* may be bought at the Mohan Singh market. As she tells me what she thinks Veronica and I would enjoy seeing, India becomes Meenakshi's own poetic haven. "Darling," I call out to Veronica, who is not far away, "*darling*," conveying that I want her to come and meet Meenakshi and hear what she is saying. Veronica joins us as Meenakshi is describing fossil-collecting in the Himalayas. Trilobites are her favorites. She tells us about doves made of pewter perching on chattris of black marble in a garden called Sehelion ki Bara in Udaipur; about white tree peonies, temples, mountains covered with wild eglantine, fields of poppies, wisteria in great purple sheets hanging on poplars winged around by blue kingfishers and dragonflies in Kashmir. When she speaks of Kashmir, her face is like a candle at first lighting. And Ooty, Ootacamund, if we aren't planning to go to Kashmir, we must go to Ooty.

"Oh, yes," Veronica says. She has seen a television film in London about Ooty. She'd love to go to Ooty. She and I delightedly accept Meenakshi's invitation to dine with her the next evening.

Meenakshi's flat is all sea-greens and blues, with a profusion of books, paintings, photographs, painterly arrangements of coins, seashells, boxes, sculpture, flowers. An owl is nesting on the ledge of her bedroom window, and there are ovals of Floris soap in the soap dishes. Meenakshi has the grace of tradition, an elitist's style, and the probity of a convent education under the tutelage of Catholic nuns whom she still visits. She speaks of them with affection, showing me the lace-edged linen sheets and napkins they have made, and the hand-towels embroidered with roses, two of which she gives me. She hasn't forsaken Hinduism for Catholicism, and she speaks knowledgeably with Veronica about Buddhism.

Meenakshi does all her own cooking, which she insists on serving to us, unaided, unassisted. We sit by a window through which we can see the moon like a melon slice in the sky, and listen to recordings of Ravi Shankar, followed by the Peer Gynt Suite. "When you were first learning to read, you used to call that 'Peer's Giant Suit,'" I say to Veronica. Meenakshi tells Veronica about doctors and dentists who are "good," and says that Veronica is always welcome to call on her for advice and help and to stay with her whenever she is in Delhi. She tells Veronica how to cook rice so that each grain will be separate from the other, and about the sweet rice eaten in Kashmir with thick cream and curds, flavored with saffron, cooked with raisins, orange segments, pistachios and almonds, which she has made for dessert. Over this confection, she pours fresh heavy cream from a pitcher painted with lilies-of-the-valley, and then glides away to turn on another splendid recording. Brahms's First, which I mistake for Beethoven's Ninth. "Even Brahms said they sounded the same," Meenakshi assures me. Formerly the wife of an Indian ambassador, she has a great flair for diplomacy, as she does for domestic sensuality, order, and hospitality. She tells me that what I refer to as *cashmere* is known in India as *pashmina*, the woven fleece of mountain goats, the only kind that can be woven into *shahtooshes*, "ring shawls," shawls so soft and fine that when pleated they can be drawn through a thumb ring. My grandmother had a light blue one on her chaise longue and now, for the first time, I know why she called it a ring shawl.

"How beautiful you are," Meenakshi says, looking at Veronica and then at me. "And Leila, how nice that you have an Indian name."

With her meditative, appraising eyes, Meenakshi seems able to scan the cellar and attic of my mind and all the rooms between, and to see them as I would like to have them seen, "bringing out my best," as my mother would say. To me, Meenakshi's mind and thoughts are elusive, no more easily grasped than a tempting pearl of quicksilver that rests in the palms, only to slip away when your fingers try to curl round it. Yet, like a coordinate, like the tangential notes of a bulbul's song that loop back and find the first note new again, she forms a link between Veronica and me, and the three of us talk until after midnight.

Veronica and I call on the American ambassador's wife at Roosevelt House for morning tea. Our accreditation has to be

presented at a sentry box staffed with Marine guards, extravagantly healthy in appearance and smartly turned-out in brass-
buttoned uniforms. The American flag rides high on a flagpole
above Roosevelt House. I feel a surge of patriotic pride. Inside,
all is cool, airy, light, an enclave of affluent and tasteful comfort.
I wait for Veronica to be moved to say, "Oh, Mummy, I miss
America so much. I want to come home." This is the way I know
I would feel if I had been living in India for several years. But I
am not Veronica, and she is not me.

We have our tea in the drawing room, and talk about art and
books and mutual acquaintances in India. Our sentences hang
in the rose-perfumed air. After an hour or so, the ambassador's
wife tinkles a temple bell to summon a bearer to clear away the
tea tray and the remains of the scallop-edged butter cookies and
cucumber sandwiches cut in crustless triangles. Veronica and I
take our leave. We stop at the Consulate library to buy magazines. Veronica tells me that she once sneaked into the commis-
sary in the American Embassy compound. "Marshmallows! Lic-
orice sticks! Of course, when I took my goodies to the counter,
the clerk said, 'What's your number?' I looked demurely hang-
dog, hoping he'd let me pass, but it didn't work."

Oh, God, she could have been arrested. "So then what?"

"So then I asked a pudgy henpecked man from West Virginia
if he'd be so kind, etcetera, etcetera. He was sort of gentle and
slow-talking. I felt embarrassed to ask for sweets, so I asked for
some Breck and Prell shampoo; and if it wasn't any trouble, for
a bottle of *vin rosé*."

Bryce, who could tell Chateau Latour from Chateau Lafitte,
used to banter that red was for meat, white for fish, and rosé for
cowards. Rosé. I see Veronica with a glass of it, the color of
melted rubies and grenadine. "And he got it all for you?" I ask.

"Oh, yes. He was very nice." Veronica looks culpable, but pleased by the remembrance. I make a mental note to send lots more shampoo and sweets to her when I return to America.

But there is more to Veronica's story. She tells me she also sneaked into the lounge where there is "a bowling alley that smells of Arrid deodorant, a bar with a billiard table, a restaurant serving roast turkey and all the goodies for Thanksgiving, and a coffee shop. I went to them all, feeling like a stranger in a strange land."

"Oh, my poor, *darling* Elsa Cloud."

Veronica smiles away my sympathy. "Oh, no," she says. "Everything was all right." And suddenly I am reminded of Robert. Like Kerouac, Robert celebrated the freedom of the road as an escape, I think, from all the things he disliked: routine, regular jobs, responsibilities, obligations, making decisions. He shied away from intimacy and emotions, was evasive and guarded about personal remembrances. He liked to think of himself as a nomad, a stranger. Freedom was a psychological necessity to him, freedom and a sense of space fanning out all around him. Perhaps Veronica likes being a stranger. Perhaps there is more of Robert in her than I had realized.

"Anyway, I had a tunafish sandwich and a banana cream pie and got indigestion. The place was full of wonderful short-shorted boys and girls, rosy-skinned and healthy looking. They had awful raucous voices. And there were Uhmurricans with short sleeves and fat arms talking about their lawns, getting weedkillers and seeding them and that sort of thing. I felt kind of ashamed to be out of the ordinary." She pauses. "Yet what could be more ordinary than getting up and doing my housework, washing my laundry in the stream?"

What could be more ordinary than discovering that happiness doesn't lie in owning things, although, of course, one may own a lot of beautiful things? Or discovering that happiness doesn't lie in achievement, but using one's intentions, skill, and wisdom to achieve a good cup of tea—*that* can be a source of happiness? "I guess that until one gets tired, one keeps on looking for something, or tries to maintain a standard," she continues. "I forget sometimes that what I'm doing is not some sort of exotic trip. I'm just doing what tired people do."

Veronica tired of life at twenty-five? I suppose I had expected her to unfold from childhood to adolescence to her twenties the way a novelty paper flower does in a glass of water—quickly, completely, problem-free. Just magically to grow up and be loving, harmonious, and in perfect communication with me. It occurs to me as an epiphany that both my mother and I, in different ways, shared a self-centeredness that made it hard for us to conceive of daughters who were not extensions of ourselves. Veronica is more like me than I am like my mother, yet conscience assails me, that awful agenbite of inwit I try to skip past by dwelling on all the things my mother did and said that were not consonant with my way of being, and the same with Veronica, the same patterns of behavior laid down over the ancient mother-daughter grid. Daughters expecting their mothers to be idealized extensions of themselves, mothers expecting the same of their daughters.

The Mohan Singh market, a great, dingy go-down spilling spoiled fruit and vegetables out onto the street, boasts a brightly lit, high-ceilinged, galleried interior teeming with people and produce. Away from the lurid skewers of meat and the counters of golden-eyed fish with silvery scales and fins, past counters of bright, sticky sweetmeats made of boiled milk and sugar, hippies are eddying with their canvas backpacks, their shoulder bags of woven cotton and wool, their shopping bags of netted hemp.

Veronica and I stop first at the candy counter to buy two crisp balls of the walnut-sized confections called *rasgulla* that have been layered on large and pointed leaves from a *Dhudi* tree, whose sap is known to keep milk fresh without changing its taste. Under the counter there are packets of *Dhudi* bark, used as a cure for dysentery, and *Dhudi* seeds, a multi-purpose remedy for dysentery, fevers, piles, and worms. "*Dhudi* is being the Hindi name. In Ingliss, Easter tree. In Latin dis dree is being called *Holarrhena antidysenterica*," I sing-song to entertain myself and to tease Veronica. "*Dhudi* is meaning milk-like."

Veronica gives me a rewarding smile, then leads me through the market's vibratory maze past a public lavatory reeking so strongly of disinfectant, excrement, and urine that I run, gagging, to distance myself from it. Solicitous, laughing, she quickly catches up with me, her words of concern capering as she holds my tote bag while I rummage for a handkerchief. I douse it with cologne and hold it with both hands over my nose like an anesthesia cone. As I stand, breathing deeply, calming the queasiness in the pit of my stomach and the base of my throat, disconcerted by my vulnerability to bad odors, I see a woman vendor staring at me. She has the look of many Indian women, an expression common to nuns, of women deprived of sexual pride. The sensuality of stone-carved faces in Indian temples and museums is rarely visible in the flesh. I see myself as I must present myself to the vendor: a foreigner, hands steepled in the ritual *Namaste* greeting, but inexplicably, over my nose rather than before it.

Laughter is in her kohl-ringed eyes. Impeccably polite, with crossed hands that are long-fingered and with skin as satiny and smooth as the finest glove leather, she has covered her smile, exposing only its parenthetical creases.

In India more than anywhere in the world, I am aware of hands graceful in motion, gracefully poised with beautifully shaped nails and delicately spoked tendons. Here in the market, hands silent as paintings, hands stretching, reaching, holding, hands pinching vegetables and fruit for the feel of freshness, these hands possess the sensuality that the faces lack. Everywhere gestures are visible harmonics, vanishing as they happen, as ephemeral as music.

I put my handkerchief back in my bag and give my short-fingered, wide, deplorably un-Indian hand to Veronica, who leads me up iron stairs stippled with patterns to the gallery floor. Coolies, their fingers splayed to balance the baskets on their heads, surge past us, as we hold fast to the railings and clang our way upward.

Bananas, mangoes, oranges, limes. The everyday fruit of India is arrayed above us and around us, suspended from the ceiling, stowed in open jute bags, heaped in baskets, mounded on brass trays, everything arranged with an eye for color and design. Cashew nuts are sent north from Madras in barrels opened now, and heaped with the curiosity of bunches of these nuts which grow outside their fruit, and look like pendants attached to the bottom of dried apples. There are coconuts, large, smooth, green ones for milk, and the small, dry, brown ones, whose hairy outer husks are processed into coir mats, and whose succulent meat is used for chutneys, sweets, and countless recipes. At the entrance of the first several recesses, where the specialties are dried fruit and nuts, pebbles of resinous incense, reminiscent of the amber-colored rock sugar for coffee my grandmother had always served after dinner, smolder in a brass bowl and mingle their cathedral perfume with the scent of sandalwood wands burning before a tin-framed portrait of Lakshmi.

There was a time when the whole of the known world was the marketplace for India, when silks, perfumes, precious and semi-precious stones, gossamer muslins, spices, and steel for sword blades were carried by mule and camel over the Khyber Pass to be bartered for the prizes of Afghanistan's harvest of apricots, figs, dates, almonds, raisins, and plums. The sun-dried fruits, fragrantly evocative of that historical past, look wildly romantic to me, even though most are stored in bins of galvanized steel and dispensed into assorted sizes of plastic kilo bags printed with the proprietor's name in romanized lettering as well as in Hindi.

Veronica smiles indulgently. "Miniver Leelee," she says. Leelee, my father's and her father's pet name for me; its referent coupling with a poem she knows is dear to my heart, Robinson's "Miniver Cheevy," is her own idea. She sees nothing romantic at all about dried fruit from Afghanistan. In unfaltering Hindi, she briskly orders five kilo bags of it to be mixed with cashews, almonds, and flakes of dried coconut. "Sometimes they run out of something," she explains. "I might as well get stuff now to give to Geshe-la and friends when we go to Dharamsala."

I'm sorry Veronica doesn't warm to the romance of history, pleased that she is generous, delighted that she is so organized, planning ahead. I buy several bags of plain dried fruit and several bags of Veronica's special mix for us to eat now and on our travels.

With the flourish of a magician producing a rabbit out of a hat, Veronica pulls from her drawstring bag a sack that looks as though it had been snipped from a tennis net and, insisting on lugging both her purchases and mine, leads me to a section where ice cream, *lassi*, and mango milkshakes are for sale. The recess is so jam-packed with hippies that I can barely see the counters.

In the context of an Indian food market, the cultivated shabbiness of the hippies' gear flaunting rents, patches, wrinkles, and the unlaundered look of poverty that the authentic poor conceal is riveting, and I gape unabashedly. Their multilingual, polyphonic words are tossed into the air like caps, their voices intersecting, progressing, sounding a contrapuntal motet to the uproar of the market. They classify themselves into two distinctive groups: hippies, the pot-smokers and only occasional users of hashish and other drugs; and funky-punkies, the junkies, addicts of heroin, morphine, and cocaine.

How can I tell who's who? I just can. As a result of some atavistic intuition acquired, perhaps, in my childhood, when I stuttered most atrociously only with people whose qualities were unlike or not complementary with my own, my first impressions are usually reliable.

I have never seen as many junkies anywhere, nor any who look as gaunt and sick as these. Many have band-aids and bandages on their arms. Why is that? I ask.

"They sell their blood to get money to live and buy drugs,"

Veronica murmurs close to my ear. "You don't have to talk so loudly, Mummy."

I haven't been conscious of talking loudly. I'm glad Veronica is considerate of other people's feelings, but I am appalled.

"Even the beggars in the streets look *cleaner*," I say.

"They probably have more money and can afford to pay for *dhobis*, Mummy." Veronica is all sweet reason and charity. "The incidence of hepatitis is very high among hippies and junkies. Most of them get amoebic dysentery, as well, because they aren't careful about what they eat, and because there's no place for them to get hot water and soap. They don't have any money, Mummy."

"Well, then, how can they afford milkshakes if they can't afford soap?"

"Most of them aren't *buying* food. A lot just beg or shoplift. Then they gather up here to socialize or bum money off each other if anyone has any."

"You mean they just pay their airfare to come here and then don't have any money left?"

"Oh, Mummy," Veronica protests. "They didn't *fly* here. They took the Magic Bus." Her voice is low, tickling my ear with that tone of forbearing condescension one enjoys with the innocent and the ignorant.

The Magic Bus, she says, offers a three-week, fifty-dollar ride from London to Paris to Munich to Budapest to Belgrade to Sofia to Istanbul. "Istanbul, that's where I got on. And then we went to Erserum and Teheran. And then by minibus to Herat. And then by public bus to Kandhar and Kabul. And then to Jalallabad and through the Khyber Pass, where you have to worry about bandits. When we got to Peshawar, we took the train to Lahore, and the bus again from Lahore to the Attari road, which is the border between Pakistan and India. And then another minibus to Amritsar, and then the train or bus to Delhi."

Elsa Cloud, Elsa Cloud. What fortitude. But how *could* you travel with people like these? Thank God for the teaching you found so stunning that you stayed in Dharamsala.

"So you see, Mummy, they're all right. They're just sort of lost and flaky and broke, that's all. *I* only had about fifty bucks on me when I arrived." She speaks with the pride of a survivor.

"But how did you manage? What did you *do*?"

Veronica shrugs. "I just managed, Mum. Anyway, we had those little *vade mecum* booklets for Asia that you can pick up for a few bob in London."

"And what might they be?"

"They list places where you can crash, hang out, buy cheap food. They tell you what you have to pay for bicycle rickshaws, pot, drugs, soap, bedrolls, tin trunks, hampers, the *kurtas* and pajamas and embroidered vests you see around. As long as we were on the bus trip, we just slept on the bus. Bought food and ate it on the bus."

"But what did you do about clothes? How did you pack and unpack and change clothes and get all your laundry done?"

"We didn't. There wasn't the time. I just changed my T-shirt when it got too gross to wear. You know, like that, Mum." Veronica lapses into hippie shibboleths as easily as she does Hindi and Urdu.

The hippies and funky-punkies hear her and recognize her as someone who speaks their jargon. Now we are claimed, surrounded by people in their twenties and thirties who identify themselves by their first names. They have come from France, Italy, Germany, Hungary, England, Australia, America. They roam as a vocation, a way of life, traveling "to find themselves" as if they were missing cuff links or coins that had rolled out of sight.

"*Je m'en foute*," a French girl says. She wants to get the hell out and go to Nepal. With all the enthusiasm leached from his words, a Hungarian declares the trip on "the Magic Booze" to have been "great" and "beauty fool." A funky-punky from Bremen allows as how the hash in Kabul is the greatest, and everyone nods and agrees that it is. They also agree that Teheran is heavy and that Nepal is great. When they hear that Veronica has been staying in Manali, an Italian hippie says, "Oh, man, Manali, the *bhang* and *charras* haven of the subcontinent." He can't wait to get there, and when he does, *maraviglioso*, he'll come and see Veronica. Veronica, mercifully vague about where she is living, tells me that *bhang* is pot and *charras* is hash.

"Yeah, man," says someone with a French accent.

We are joined by an English girl wearing an ankle-length purple Afghani skirt. Her arm is hooked in the arm of an American boy in blue jeans, white Indian *kurta*, and pepper-and-salt tweed vest. A heavy silver *bana lingam* in the shape of an egg hangs on a silver chain around his thin neck.

"We're going to an ashram," the girl says. "They meditate and levitate there. They're in a state of higher consciousness and can fly, really fly. They're disciples of Maharishi."

"They practice soul travel," the boy adds. "They can even travel out of this universe. With Krishna consciousness, you can transcend *karma*."

A nut, I think. A real nut.

Veronica believes in levitation. She has never seen it done, but she knows lots of people who have seen performances. Yes, indeed, levitation is possible.

She's cuckoo, too, I think. They're all cuckoo.

"I got a rip in my boot. I gotta find a *chamar*. The sole's coming off." A funky-punky sounds refreshingly sensible and realistic. He has an adolescent's deadpan delivery, sharp-eyed and self-defensive, and a tic that throbs and twitches on his upper right cheek, just beneath the cheekbone. He is wearing a filthy pair of pajamas and a sleeveless Anti-Nuke T-shirt. There is a pale yellow rash on his neck and a constellation of needle marks on both arms. All visible areas of his skin and his shaved head are lumped and scabbed with flea, fly, mosquito, louse, or bedbug bites.

The *chamars* are near the bottom of the Indian social ladder because they handle the skin of dead cows, but I know where they work. I hold out a map of New Delhi. My mother would have conniption fits if she could see me now. Defiantly, I move closer to point out the place on the map.

"Thanks, ma'am," he says with the nasal accent of a Chicagoan. "Thanks, ma'am. I gotta get the fuckers fixed fast."

A girl with a year-old baby strapped to her chest by a denim papoose rig shows Veronica and me a shopping basket filled with tamarind, cardamom, squash, chick peas, various kinds of lentils, carrots, and coriander leaves. "We're vegetarians," she tells me. "Eating red meat is like eating something half alive. It's gross. He's very healthy." She kisses the top of the baby's head which is blotched with scabs. I look away from the green-yellow slime clogging his nostrils, bubbling as he breathes.

On our way out of the market, Veronica and I see two Hare Krishna converts who are trying to collect money from passersby for copies of the Bhagavad Gita printed in English. "You ought to know better," I tell them in my fiercest voice. "You ought to be ashamed of yourselves for trying to take money away from the Indians for your phony-baloney cult."

Veronica approves. "Don't worry, Mum," she says. "They won't achieve Nirvana."

Love suddenly arrows through me, stirring up feelings of tenderness.

"Oh, darling Veronica, I love you so much," I say.

She is silent, but she looks pleased.

Whenever she has a craving for American food or Americans, Veronica says the only place to go, besides the Consulate, is the Ashoka hotel. "You'll hate it, Mummy," she predicts cheerfully. "It's a mix of *luxe* and lox in the snack bar, with hamburgers, ice cream, fried chicken. The hotel is the typical tourist's idea of India, but there's a swimming pool outdoors where a lot of Westerners living here love to come, and boutiques where there's good stuff mixed among all the dreck."

We enter the Ashoka's icily air-conditioned white marble lobby, ascend a white marble staircase of palatial grandeur, and come upon a snack bar with tented ceiling, and waiters in Hollywood-style Indian costumes of the sort featured in nineteen-thirties movies. Veronica and I try to behave ourselves, but we laugh with the conscious craziness of children. The balcony opening off the snack bar is crowded with Indians staring at the mixed nakedness of Westerners sunbathing around the swimming pool below. Veronica and I and the Indians speak quietly, but in the manner of people talking with a certainty of being overheard, sharing an experience as convivial strangers. Hunched like question marks, arms resting on the railing, we stare at the show below, play to each other's audience.

"Ouch! What a dive!"

"The man in the egg-yolk color is being like Humpitty Dumpitty with hairs, isn't it?"

"After all the cover-upitness, the contrast is extraordinary, isn't it, Mum?" Veronica turns the water-drop clarity of her eyes to mine. "Come on, Mum. Let's eat. I'm famished."

We take a table, and a waiter comes to hover over us, the liquid brilliance of his molasses-colored eyes pouring over Veronica as he utters conversational pleasantries. "It's Umrica you're coming from, isn't it?" He bends toward Veronica to confide the luncheon specials as if each were some luscious aphrodisiac, then darts off to bring back a red rose from the flowers arranged fan-like on a buffet table. He places the rose in my water goblet which he picks up and sets in front of Veronica. She receives the rose with a show of grace and pleasure. The waiter retreats to a far corner where he continues to gaze at her.

"Veronica's little triumph," I say. We joke. We laugh. I try to scribble an account of this incident in my notebook, but writing about shared laughter is like trying to paste a label on a soap bubble.

All at once, there is a stir. A procession of twenty or so persons enters the room. The procession is led by a shaved-headed monk, a tall, robust man wearing a maroon robe with an orange-yellow underblouse.

"Who's that?"

Veronica swivels in her chair. "Why, that's Trijung Rinpoche, the junior tutor of His Holiness." Her cheeks push up, squinting her eyes into a look of almost unbearable pleasure. "How extraordinary," she says again and again. She wonders what on earth he can be doing here. She says she knows some of the *shebjis* with him. *Shebjis?*

"Tibetan go-fers." She explains that they are followers who run errands for him, look after him, make his buttered tea. "Oh, Mummy, isn't it *wonderful*, a *miracle* that you can actually see Trijung Rinpoche?"

I try to look wildly pleased, as he and his entourage of *shebjis*—men, women, and adolescent boys, all in Western clothes (who, if Veronica hadn't told me, I would have guessed might be a gathering of Mongolians, Plains Indians, Eskimos, Burmese, Eurasians)—move outside to lean against the railing and look down at the sunbathers.

Shebji. The term, in sound and meaning, is so like the Egyptian shabti—a magical figurine, servant of the deceased, which will carry out on behalf of its dead master all the work required of him in his Other Life—that it's easily memorable.

Unlike the Indians, whose faces are mobile, expressive of astonishment, curiosity, amusement, and indecision, the faces of the holy scholar and his entourage remain unchangingly kindly. A *deep* look of kindness, I scribble in my notebook, as if that were the only trait they were capable of expressing.

Trijung Rinpoche is a *tulku*. As a child, he had been recognized as the reincarnation of a high-ranking religious personage, his qualification confirmed by his ability to select from objects presented to him those which had been the possessions of his predecessor and which therefore had been his own prop-

erty in a former life. All *tulkus* who are reincarnated for a purpose are called *Rinpoches*, which means precious ones. Rebirth
is for everyone, but people who choose to be reborn to benefit
others are reincarnated as learned scholars and spiritual men.
Trijung is a *Rinpoche*. He is seventy-five years old. His robe, the
color of port wine, reminds me of the robes of ancient Greek
philosophers. He is wearing an underdress of maroon that
leaves one pale shoulder bare. Over his underdress is an orange-
yellow surplice, and on top of the surplice is a one-shouldered
shawl-like garment that is draped from his left shoulder.

Veronica says that he is wearing a concealed sash, and that
the top of his underskirt goes over the sash like a lotus to signify
that in a deluded world you can still lift yourself above, the way
a lotus rises from the mud. She tells me that the folds of his
underskirt, which are hidden by the shawl-like garment, represent conventional truth, ultimate truth, the noble truths of
suffering and the cause of suffering to be accepted, the cessation
of self, and the path to enlightenment.

Trijung is also wearing steel-rimmed spectacles. He has high
cheek bones, the malar bones clearly visible, eyes dark and shining, and a beatific expression. I expect him to be wearing sandals, but instead he is wearing black wing-tip oxfords and socks
as red as a poinciana's blossoms. Surely the combination of red
socks and black shoes, well polished though they are, could be
improved upon, I comment.

Veronica's face goes still and obstinate. "Red is a sacred color,
Mummy."

We drink our *lassis*, eat our cheeseburgers, and continue to
watch Trijung Rinpoche and the *shebjis* who stand close to him,

a cluster of attentive kindliness in somber shades of brown, blue, and gray.

When Trijung Rinpoche and his entourage move from the balcony to the dining room, Veronica goes to greet him. They smile. They talk. After a while, she beckons me to join her. Unsure whether it is best to steeple my hands in the Indian salutation of *Namaste*, or to shake hands, I do both.

Trijung Rinpoche projects goodness and serenity the way an electric fan creates coolness, the way a wood-burning stove gives off heat. Whether it is the warm, sweet smile on his face or the clasp of his hand, I feel enveloped in an aura of peaceful contentment. How could I ever have quibbled about his red socks and black shoes?

"How extraordinary," I say later to Veronica, as we are walking down the marble stairs to the lobby. "Do you suppose he hypnotized me? I didn't expect to be, didn't really want to be, but I was awesomely bowled over by his presence. I just felt all peaceful, happy, good."

"Of course, he didn't hypnotize you." Veronica sounds scornful, then earnest. "Tibetan holy men really do project goodness and a sense of peace that is quite remarkable, because their own inner peace and goodness *is* remarkable."

"I know you told me about *darshan*, and that's really what I felt, a state of grace and blessing. *Extraordinary.*"

"I'm glad you liked him, Mummy, but lots of lamas and monks will make you feel the same way."

Oh, Elsa Cloud, you and your Buddhism. Is it you, or is it India and thoughts of Tibet? What is it that leaves me with these cryptic feelings and mystical intimations?

Eight

The moon hangs like a medallion in the depth of the sky. When it is full, we will celebrate Holi. Krishna's Annual Day of Judgment. The Festival of Colors.

"What do you suppose we're in for?" I ask Veronica.

She says she doesn't know about Hindu festivals, that she has always been up in the mountains with the Tibetans at this time of year. "But I think they throw water balloons at buses and squirt colored water out of *pitchkarries* at everyone."

"I don't think you and Miss Veronica should leave the hotel, Madam," Gurdip says. "The celebration is a holy festival, but nowadays, it is a misrepresentation of its original form, Madam. Even the Hindus, Madam, lower the grandeur of their Krishna festival by using dirty colors such as ink, tar, coal, diesel oil, and kerosene, which are unwarranted for the occasion, and leave behind unwashable and indelible impressions on the hair, the body, and the clothes. I would recommend staying indoors, Madam."

"Sirdarji is being correct," the desk clerk is swift to interject. "Holi revelers are not remembering that Holi is a holy festival and forcibly besmearing with coloring or ink on others should not be initiated or indulged in. We discourage the use of intoxicants and filthy ways and means around the hotel." His smile beams self-satisfaction and reassurance.

"What to do! There are always unforeseen bewilderments, revelations, adventures, even discomfort and movements of chaos." Quoting Geshe-la or something she has read, Veronica sounds like an adorable fortune cookie. Gurdip and the desk clerk waggle their heads in approval.

"Well," I say to Veronica. "We can wear bath turbans or our Laura Ashley mobcaps and we can buy cotton *kurtas* and pajamas at the Khadi Bhavan." The Khadi Bhavan is a cheap and reliable clothing outlet recommended in the international hippies' *vade mecum*. And though Veronica often finds my tireless erranding after facts and information vexing, now she looks pleased.

"You will be wanting sandalwood paint, dry *gulal*, or *tesu* flower wet color, Madam, if you are going to play Holi." Gurdip wants to make sure we do everything properly. "For the sake of the car, Madam, I would recommend dry paint."

Writing in my notebook, I try to arrange the facts about Holi in tidy parade formation. The Festival of Holi is celebrated annually at the full moon of every March. It begins with the ritual burning of community bonfires on ground that is consecrated by priests performing *puja* and by group chanting and singing. For several days Holika pyres have been in preparation in all areas of New Delhi and Old Delhi—near the India Gate, in Saftarjung, just outside the railway station in Old Delhi, along the Ring Road, in Hauz Khas—surrealistic pyramids of flammables—louvered shutters, wooden cart-wheels, planks, charpoy frames, broken wooden chairs, *jali* screens—piled on top of a circular foundation of dried cow-dung patties, some the size of large casserole lids, some smaller, like the Frisbees Veronica used to throw in Central Park.

"Most of it stolen, I would believe," Gurdip remarks dourly. "The tradition, Madam, is that each contribute so the women can kindle new household fires from the embers of the community's Holika pyre. Frequently, the donations are insufficient. Then the naughty young boys go collecting."

Who was Holika? Why was she burned? What is the reason for the bonfires? What is the meaning of the festival? Mulk can explain. Mulk can tell me. Mulk has left Bombay and will soon be back in Hauz Khas, a village on the outskirts of Delhi. He has telephoned to fix the day and time we shall meet. "Can you believe it? Mulk will be here. We'll see him!" I tell Veronica. O, Joy! Joy! Joy! I'm going to see Mulk again!

I want Veronica to know about Mulk, to understand how special he is as a human being, as my friend. I talk obsessively about him, telling her that he grew up in a Bengali peasant village, that in some miraculous way he managed to go to France to study at the Sorbonne, to England to study at Cambridge, to receive a doctorate in literature and history at the University of London, to write nineteen novels and eight books of essays about literature and the arts. "And he's been the editor of *Marg* since its beginning. It's a superb art magazine, the only major art magazine published in India, and one of the great art magazines of the world!"

Besides proliferating novels like leaves on a mango tree, Mulk has shaped his knowledge about Indian dance, theater, crafts, architecture, poetry to a level that is considered exceptional. "He's an absolute darling," I babble on. "He thinks of himself as an avatar of Krishna, a lover of life and women. He's the eternal childlike spirit. He has incredible vitality. He glows with ideas. He's an extraordinary talker. He's wonderful!"

Mulk has as many interests and projects as a juggler has bowling pins in the air. Deliciously truthful and frank, a man of sensual and moral ardor, he, like his writing, is without artifice. Mischief and affection are as natural to him as erupting is to Old Faithful. He has great good humor, and his writing is as bawdy as Balzac's. Although he has never been able to build up a resistance to the image of himself as Krishna, happily disporting himself with his *gopis*, he is most of all a visionary, paying homage to the past, striking the hard rock of villages and causing culture to spring forth. He makes no arbitrary distinctions among art, architecture, crafts, textiles, dance, theater, literature, feeling very strongly that everything has originally sprung from the village matrix. He has little truck with personal possessions, and gives most of his money away, or spends it to raise money for village projects. He is aware that he possesses a "star quality," the ability to project a unique personality which has never existed before him in India. He's the *éminence grise* of Indian arts, yet age has only ripened his boyish unbending.

I wonder if I have put Veronica off by praising him to excess. Perhaps if I had not gone on, had said something simple such as "He's a darling man who has a passion for Krishna," she would have asked more than "When was he born?"

"In nineteen hundred and five. Calendrical age is not important," I add defensively. "Mulk is always ready to communicate an appetite for life. He's disarmingly unselfconscious. He looks like an imp or a cherub with a great wiry nimbus-like flourish of gray hair. Sort of a Walt Whitman face upside down."

Veronica pushes back the cuticles of her nails. A bad sign.

On the day we are to see him, and just before we reach his place, I say to Veronica, "I hope you like Mulk so we can share him as a friend."

"*Teek*," she says lightly.

An iron gate opens with the muted cry of a seagull. We traverse a path bisecting a garden of roses, red cannas, and snakeplant before we reach a box-like concrete bungalow with a corrugated iron roof and a walled stairway of red-polished steps that lead to a roofed-over veranda. Mulk's studio cottage is as simple as a child's crayon-drawn house with an open-door mouth and a flower-stuck lawn. Local villagers have pitched in to build it, contributing their labor and skills as an expression of communal unity and as an homage to this man who delights in their arts and crafts. After the house and garden were complete, there was a huge party. "Just like an old-fashioned American barn-raising, my dear Leila," Mulk had written me. "And the astonishing part of it is that all the people here are now like my family. It is their house as well as my house, so that the door is always open when I am here, and when I am away, they guard it and take care of it for me."

The door is indeed open, and there is Mulk. After twenty-five years, there he is, my beloved mentor, the older brother I had wanted and never had. I sink into the cushion of his cheek, his hug. The wash of his iodine-colored skin blurs with the red stripes of his shirt, the red of his shorts. I am crying with happiness. Mulk once said that he and I were brethren in the freemasonry of happiness and enthusiasm for life. Now hugging him, nuzzling his warm cheek, embracing this man who remembers me as I had been at twenty-five, hugging this man who now holds my two selves together as Robert would have if he had been alive and if no bitterness had come between us, I feel whole. Mulk had encouraged me, reinforced that part of myself I felt was my best, that part of myself Robert loved the most. Hugging Mulk, I embrace part of myself and part of Robert, the Robert who used to murmur, "Sweet Leelee," as Mulk is now murmuring "Sweet Leila," with the sweetness he and Robert cherished in me, less mine than the sweetness they cherished in themselves, that certain honesty and purity of spirit, that freedom from taint that is, I feel, the core of Veronica's persona as well.

Veronica steeples her hands in a *Namaste* greeting. Mulk kisses her on both cheeks, European style. I see at once from their faces, the smiles in which their eyes play no part, that the chemistry is wrong. Mulk is not a Hindu counterpart of Trijung Rinpoche. He doesn't want to play Grandfather. He wants to be as faun-like, as Pan-like as Krishna. Veronica is not receptive. A silence closes between them like the doors of a vault. I, who had invented an image of us as a loving trio, feel an absurd disposition now towards tears of sheer vexation. I watch as Veronica gracefully absents herself to peer at a bookshelf. "May I read this?" she asks melodiously, extracting a book and then sitting down on a cushion in the far corner of the room and studying it with great care.

Unexpectedly, vexation turns to relief. Not without guilt, I realize that I am secretly pleased to have Mulk all to myself. "Tell me about Holi," I say to him, sitting down on a sofa, patting the *Kalamkari* seat cushion beside me as an invitation for him to sit next to me, which he does. Leaning lazily against his shoulder, I fall back into the intimate bossiness of myself as I was twenty-five years before. "Tell me about Holi. You said on the telephone that it was all topsy-turvies. Untopsy-turvy it for me."

"Don't bully me," he says affectionately, with that familiar Indian distaste for any request to be factual and specific. He relishes the pontifical circumlocutions with which I find it difficult to be patient.

"Who is Holika? Why was she burned? What is the reason for the bonfires? What's Holika's connection with Krishna? What is Holi all about?" I plunge on stubbornly. Mulk surrenders. Holika was a demon princess who was protected from fire by a magic cape, he says. One day, the magic cape blew off her shoulders onto the shoulders of her brother, whom she and her father were always planning to murder by pushing him into a bonfire. At twilight, Holika's father was clawed to death by a creature, part lion, part man, thus fulfilling a prophecy that he wouldn't be destroyed by day or by night, by sword or by knife, by man or by beast. In her grief, Holika stumbled, fell into the blazing fire, and was burned to death.

"Oh, darling, there must be more to it than that," I say.

Of course there is, Mulk continues. It was Vishnu who, in his Krishna-mischievous avatar, had sent the wind to blow off Holika's cape and had caused her to stumble and fall into the fire so that rather than earthly conquest, she could achieve equal spiritual liberation. The demoness Holika thus became entwined with Vishnu and his avatar of Krishna. Mulk pauses to reach for his pipe on the brass tray-table before us. Filling its briarwood bowl with fresh tobacco, he lights it, curling his fingers like tendrils around the bowl. As he talks on, puffing on his pipe, I write in my notebook with the absorption of a schoolgirl cramming for an exam. In the ritual construction of Holika's pyre, everyone participates in the symbolic destruction of world, and of the mighty, the privileged, and the wicked. When the fire burns down, the world is symbolically renewed as the embers are used to re-kindle the household fires in the freshly decorated fire-pits of all the participants. Thus, the ordinary is transformed into the sacred; the wreckage of wood and cloth and dung and straw that blazes into a pyramid of fire symbolizes the sublimation of the individual identity into the larger divine. The old year and old fires are extinguished; the new fires and the new year are born from the ashes of the old. "So, you see, it is the duality," Mulk says, "the double aspect of destruction and creation, of negative and positive, that is so much a part of Hindu theology and of Tantric Buddhism. With the full moon in March, a new life begins." He glances at me. "Like Christmas," he says, "and Easter and the All Fool's Day 'when well-appointed April on the heel of hurrying winter treads.'"

I am delighted to be informed, and my interest seems, in turn, to delight Mulk.

Just as the mind-boggling multiplicity of deities in the Hindu pantheon was caused by the amalgam of the pantheistic Vedic tradition and the local beliefs of tribal India, so the ancient pre-Christian festivals have been subjugated and incorporated into modern religious practice. So a wreath, when brought in from the cold and coupled with candleshine and firelight, is transformed, lifted out of the commonplace as it releases its scent, an odor of primal sanctity that intimates man's connection with the sun and the trees and all things living. Pines and evergreens with their intoxicating resinous incense—aromatic, inspirational, mystical—suggest immortality. Christmas wreaths are a circle, a monogram of God and Nature, suggesting a life that is cyclical, continuous, a Nativity wreath for the birthday of the world.

"That's why you have wreaths of icing on your birthday cakes and wedding cakes, to evoke a sense of joy and exaltation," Mulk says. "Not that your early Christian Church was all that interested in birthday celebrations, for it took four hundred and forty years to get around to setting a date for the Nativity in order to capitalize on the fund of available reverence at the time of the winter solstice, when the earth begins to waken under the kiss of the sun-fire's light."

Warming to his own conversation, he reminds me that the Romans whooped it up with Saturnalia. The Mithraists celebrated *Dies Invicta Solis Natalia*, the birthday of the Unconquerable Sun. The Jews commemorated the cleansing of the temple by Judas Maccabeus after the desecration by lighting candles in a feast of lights and dedication. The Egyptians hung oil lamps outside every house in honor of Osiris, the jolly green giant of vegetation, believing they would serve to guide the spirits of the dead who returned home one night each year around the seventeenth of December. To this day, in Sicily, there are children who are told that it is the dead who bring them presents.

The Norsemen and the Teutonic tribes were great ones for blazing bonfires and human sacrifice. Everyone knew then that death is a fertilizing influence, and when Norsemen were converted by St. Boniface some time around the eighth century, they substituted Yule cakes for human sacrifice, cakes that were wreathed and candlelit, the splendid antecedents of our birth-day cakes.

Dharma, the great wheel of life. Our word Yule came from the Norse *hweol*, which referred to the sun's wheel. In rural parts of Europe, there are people who still push cart-wheels stuffed with blazing straw bounding downhill to imitate the course of the sun and its path. By the sympathetic magic of friction, fires were also kindled to evoke the spirits of romantic dalliance. "And when one speaks of romantic dalliance, one may think of Krishna." Mulk leans his head back on the sofa's rim, puffs on his pipe, looks up at the ceiling. "Krishna, in his maturity, pro-pounded the Bhagavad Gita, all very beautiful and sacred, but what most Hindus love about Krishna is his joyful, simple child-hood and adolescence, when the veil between his divinity and our humanity is least ohpack."

"Ohpack?"

"O-p-a-q-u-e. Ohpack."

I smile at the ectopic Gallicism. I wasn't prepared for it. I remind myself that Mulk did go to the Sorbonne.

Mulk continues, unperturbed. "After the Holika fires have burned out, it is to pierce that veil, to lose oneself in Krishna, to pay homage to Krishna, that one plays Holi."

Holi exaggerates Krishna's childhood mischief into bawdy, riotous behavior. Distinctions of caste and fundamental social values—the precedence of men over women, age over youth, rich over poor, and the privileged over those who have no rank, no position—all are turned topsy-turvy in commemoration of everyone's longing for his own and Krishna's childhood, free of care, beloved and loving, blissfully ignorant of such distinctions.

"In short," Mulk says, drawing a breath, "Holi is a commemoration of the Golden Age of Krishna's divine past when no secular organization of power existed, and in playfully taking the role of another in relation to one's everyday self, each participant learns to play his role anew, with renewed understanding, with more grace and good will, with a reciprocating love."

There is no "in short" when Mulk speaks. "As in all holy days or holidays," he goes on, "Holi is a coming together of people to celebrate their oneness, their commonality in annual mass witness to the enduring power of the past to anneal a people into a belief, a faith, and ultimately, into a culture that is a declaration of man's need to belong to something greater and more ancient than himself. Holi is an occasion for unilateral love to sweep across all customary indifference among separated groups and families, to let lust, simulated or real, sweep aside all established hierarchies of age, sex, caste, power, and wealth in an expression of man's yearning for the divine. Sex and religion, there is always a connection, isn't it?"

Religion as sublimated sex, a mystical sense of oneness, of creation, whether physically or intellectually or spiritually or psychically? Well, of course, but that's only a fraction of religion. What about faith in God? In Christ? It is simpler to deflect Mulk's question by comparing the social implications of Holi with Jesus' Sermon on the Mount, which promises that the meek will inherit the earth at some future time when the social order will be changed. I ask if Holi isn't like the instruction of St. Paul to the Corinthians to become fools for Christ's sake that they may become wise, because God made "foolish the wisdom of the world."

"Ah, but no, my dear Leila," Mulk is quick to reply. "Unlike

Jesus, Krishna does not postpone the reckoning until an ultimate Judgment Day. Krishna decrees it as an annual Mummer's
Day, a Feast of Fools; a medieval carnival with everyone changing places, the fool becoming king for a day, if you will, our
masque of the full moon every March. The Holi of Krishna is
not only a festival of love, but a personal drama that must be
acted out by each participant, each devotee, with joyful passion.
The great themes of world destruction and world renewal,
world pollution followed by world purification, take place not
only on the abstract level, but in the heart and soul of each
participant, like the Eucharist. Like your Communion Service."

"What do I think of Mulk?" Moth-like, Veronica drifts about
the hotel bedroom in a white nightgown. She yawns freshly and
pinkly as a kitten. "Mulk?" she repeats. "Oh, he's all right."

Veiled in sun gauze, Veronica studies her reflection in the
sitting-room mirror. She is heartbreakingly beautiful. The sash
of a lavender dress is cinched around her neat and narrow waist.
I, too, had a small waist as a girl. Aunt Vera had a waist so small
she could fit into the ballgowns stored in the attic at Malahide
that had belonged to James Boswell's wife, Margaret. My
mother often told the story of how her cousin James Talbot,
"who wasn't quite right in the head," had offered Aunt Vera a
croquet box filled with Boswell manuscripts, including the
journal of his tour to the Hebrides. "Oh, goodness me, no,
James, what would I do with all those old papers?" Aunt Vera
had said. "I'd much rather have Margaret's dresses." So James,
"the nitwit," as Mummy alternately referred to both him and
Aunt Vera, opened the attic trunks for Aunt Vera, who transported all their silk and lace and brocade contents back to

America. "And after she had swanned around a few times at parties in them, do you know what she did? She snipped them all up into patchwork skirts and pillow covers that she gave away to friends." Acid triumph boils down with a glitter like lime marmalade in my mother's eyes.

The ankle-length skirt flares above Veronica's child-like pink heels. If I was as beautiful as a girl, I never believed it when people told me so. "Beauty is in the eyes of the beholder," my mother would say when my father would tell me I was "pretty as a speckled pup." "Beauty is as beauty does," the nannies would say, to tell me I had to suffer to be beautiful while they braided my hair or curled it into ringlets while I sat before the green piano practicing scales.

"You look beautiful. You *are* a beauty. The dress is wonderful on you," I say to Veronica.

It was my mother who was really beautiful. People never described her as *attractive*. They said she was *beautiful*. Like a Romney or a Gainsborough, they would say, a true English beauty, like a Greek goddess, a queen, so aristocratic, so regal, so *beautiful*. I remember Robert, in that melodious deep voice of his, saying, "She must have been *very* beautiful when she was a young girl. She is still a wonderful looking woman for a woman of her age. She has a nice voice. She told me she can't sing, but she whistles when she is alone. She whistles in a sort of warbling way. I told her she sounded just like a bird, and she got all flustered." I hear my mother whistling "Beautiful Dreamer" in the lovely vibrato of hers, pulsing and swelling with the sound of birds, a sound that could bring tears to your eyes like the scent of gardenias and hyacinths. And yes, no doubt about it, her beauty was a legend that continued to convince people of the fact well through her eighties. Her appearance, her clothes, and her jewelry were always of great concern to her, though she felt free to cast off her youth and her beauty before my father and me, often using the excuse that she was "too old" to do whatever it was she did not feel like doing. And as for sex, she cast that off as soon as I was born. My birth was too dreadful for her ever to consider going through anything like *that* again. "After you were born," she would say, "I kept myself to myself," and I would hear the words "myself to myself" ratcheting around like pinwheels in my mind. She wore haircurlers, and Frownies—triangular patches of brown sticky-tape paper— between her eyebrows and on the outside corners of her gray-blue-green eyes when she went to bed. In public, she was forever elegant, forever impeccable, her tireless self-discipline of appearance seemingly effortless. I remember her in a pleated white silk dress. "Loveliest of trees, the cherry is now hung with blooms along the bough. / And stands about the woodland ride / Wearing white for Eastertide."

"You *always* are a beauty," I say, as Veronica sits on the bed to cut her toenails with a pair of silver scissors shaped like a stork. The scissors belonged to my grandmother. She used them when she edged handkerchiefs with *point-de-Venise*, and I carry them with me when I travel as I also do the thermometer in a damascened silver tube that my mother used when she was attached to the St. John's Ambulance Brigade in Salonika during World War I.

St. John's Eve, St. John's Day toward the end of June in Scotland. My grandmother loved this festival. St. John, in whose name demons were exorcised, is also the patron saint for the care of the sick and the wounded. It occurs to me that perhaps my mother had joined the St. John's Ambulance Brigade to please my grandmother. I remember Veronica pressing St. John's Wort beneath the covers of *On the Road* and *Dharma Bums*.

"Were you really as smitten with Kerouac as I thought?" I ask her.

She sweeps five minuscule crescents from the bedspread into a Kleenex that she folds several times and drops into the scrap-basket. Then she lies back on a pillow with her hands clasped behind her head. "No, Kerouac was never a hero of mine. Certainly not with all those exhaust-fumy highway dreams of his. Actually, I rather fancied myself as Rima, the Bird Girl."

As I find myself thinking—to my surprise with admiration—of my mother's valor and courage, her endurance of hardship, her abilities as a nurse in that single epoch of her life when she obviously had felt fulfilled, that shining moment which she had so dulled in its repetitive telling that I failed to respond with either interest or appreciation, my memories of Veronica at thirteen also soften. Rima, the Bird Girl, the ethereal child of nature in Hudson's *Green Mansions*. Yes, she would have been a likely heroine for Veronica to twine around her heart like a liana.

"I wanted to be Kipling's *Kim*," I say. "And the Holy Man, too."

"I love Kim. I guess I got into Buddhism because when I was in Rome I wanted someone perfect to love, and there wasn't anyone, and all the relationships with people and work seemed flawed and stained. And then, when I got to Dharamsala, I just found the teachings of Buddhism stunning and the monks so kind and nice."

I don't really comprehend, but I can understand her need for a retreat, her quest for a place that offers a sense of harmony and balance, and the reassuring embrace of people she loves who love her. I know that I find in certain surroundings— archaeological sites, churches, cathedrals, places where even physical sensation has in it something spiritual, as though my flesh no longer has any hold on me—that thrilling peace in which one's mind is alert, one's senses quick to respond. In those moments of bliss, I feel cleansed and pure. I sense being guided from within by something that has sharper vision than my own, and the confusion of life dissolves in a great content- ment. I imagine Veronica felt like that when she left Rome and arrived in Dharamsala.

I want to share this with her, and the one place I know in the Delhi area that has this special spiritual quality is Tughlakabad, a centuries-old citadel city now in ruins. I suggest that we picnic there. The hotel can pack box lunches and fill our thermoses.

"Ask for duffnuts." Veronica reminds me. "Be sure to ask them to put in some duffnuts." She's right. The clerks all look blank when one asks for doughnuts, so duffnuts it is. I give Gurdip a sugar-sprinkled one as we get in the car.

Veronica has said flowers are good omens, and our route is bright with golden *champak*, pink oleanders, the vivacity of cerise bougainvillea. The roses are in bloom in the gardens of the Rashtrapati Bhavan, India's Parliament and residence of its president, the former Viceroy's House of the Raj. Beneath a conifer-like tree by the entrance, two eagles are standing plac- idly. Gurdip brakes the car so that I can look at eagles standing, walking and making quick, darting sorties after lizards. He cannot believe I have never seen an eagle walking on the ground. "They are all-too-common birds in this country, Madam," he tells me politely.

Gurkha guards, wearing paint-box red *achkans*, patrol the parking space in front of the Rashtrapati Bhavan. "Gurkhas!" I exclaim, thrilled to be in the company of Kim again.

Gurdip points to a limousine with a miniature flagpole on its hood. A minister's car, he says. Have I noticed the number on the license plate? "License plates numbered from one to nine belong to the top-ranking fellows in the Gorement, Madam." No one has a license plate with the number ten on it, "because the register in the police station listing names of *goondas* is being numbered ten, Madam."

We stop for a while to walk among roses whose snowiness and creaminess shade into delicacies of pink and blaze into intensities of red and apricot, roses the color of the sun and the moon, roses soft as butter, like silk to the touch, the sheen of their leaves perfection, their scent delicious, their thorns crimson miniatures of tigers' claws. On the entrance gates to the Parliament, entwined motifs of elephants and bells, and the roses, leeks, shamrocks, and thistles of the Raj, are woven in metallic lace, floating, delicate, hidden, obscure, even as I look for the patterns to emerge. Garland-threaders squat in the shade, knotting the heads of roses and jasmine with silver and gold tinsel to create the necklaces people are given as farewell and arrival tokens, stringing and looping marigolds together into great, thick skeins to twirl around the balustrades and archways for festive occasions. We buy necklaces of jasmine buds and flowers to wrap around our necks and wrists, not just for the sensation of their damp, soft coolness, but for their enveloping fragrance. I feel like a voluptuary cocooned in bliss. "It's absolutely tipsying," Veronica says. Sighing with pleasure, she slips a garland over Gurdip's turban, a marine blue one to match the sky. The garland's fragrance mingles with the geranium-like smell of perspiration, a clean, acidic odor of sweat that reminds me of the way my father used to smell when he came in from riding.

Is it the compound of scents or the sense of continuity between Veronica and me that pleases me? It seems as though being together in the back seat of Gurdip's taxi at this particular moment has conspired to produce a certain mystique. My Jungian therapist, puffing softly on his pipe, might reflect on the car as a secondary male sex symbol or as a directed male womb. Mother-in-law Kate might burble about an unconscious desire to be mechanically driven to avoid being emotionally driven.

It is odd that neither Veronica nor I drive—an extension, I suppose, of other aspects of our characters. As I am, she is often overcome by a longing to attach herself to an acolyte destiny, to let someone else take over, lend her passionate purpose, take her out of herself, propel her by meaning other than her own. Perhaps that's why just sitting back in a car, letting someone else do the driving, cope with the traffic, assume responsibility for your safety and getting to where you want to go, is such an abiding satisfaction. That and the fact that being transported in such a little cage, you have no other option than to sit back, look out the window and, disencumbered of demands, duties, and distractions, you can daydream without feeling culpable. So now, as we bowl along past the *charpoy-wallahs* and *mat-wallahs* knotting, weaving, twisting, and braiding their hemp and coir into geometric designs, the intricacies of *jalis* behind them and before them, the shadows cast by these latticed screens shifting dark and light, I daydream, watching drowsily as the dream-cage cars of my childhood roll by in a slow, stately procession: the shiny black Auburn of my primary school years with a running board and gray upholstery banded with blue butterflies, the car Daddy drove us in to Aiken, South Carolina, for a few winter months' stay at Southlea, when I memorized the Burma Shave verses and, at my mother's direction, held up signs lettered THANK YOU or ROAD HOG for the edification of the drivers my father whizzed past; a sporty Plymouth coupé—"Buckskin beej," as Mummy, mocking the car salesman, described its color —with a rumble seat my father heaved his golf bag into before he drove off to play at Meadowbrook, where a hole had been named Burton's folly in his honor. Sometimes I was allowed to climb in next to the leather golf bag and go off with him, and crouch out of sight on the floor when we got there so that he could pretend bewilderment—"Where's Leelee? Where has Leelee gone to?"—and "find" me—"Ah, there you are, old sport. You had your old Dadzo scared stiff thinking you'd fallen out or been carried away by some pooptarara son-of-a-bitch turkey buzzard." Then we would practice putting together on the green in front of the pro shop. There was a gray Studebaker with a sliding roof called a Sunbeam Top, and a maroon Buick, the car my mother learned to drive in and thereafter drove with such tense, nervous concentration that no one dared speak while she was at the wheel. After that, I went away to St. Timothy's, the end of my childhood. The next memorable car was the limousine hired to drive my parents and me to my first wedding, with two white stems of butterfly orchids in chrome vases on either side of the looped gray velvet straps you held to keep yourself from lurching forward when there was a sudden stop.

Gurdip's taxi has chrome vases, too, kept empty because they leak, and fake leather straps I reach for as our speed slackens abruptly. A four-wheeled *ghari* and a two-wheeled *tonga* brisk ahead of us drawn by belled and tasseled black horses, wingless Pegasuses with wild, primitive heads and satiny pelts. We stop to watch waist-high boys fly painted kites on strings that have been dipped in glue and powdered glass to create weapons for aerial combat. A red kite soars into the lovely luminous blue of the sky and, with heads tilted back to watch it, the boys shrill, "*Bo kata! Bo kata!*" It's cut! It's cut!

The city has petered out into a village where women fling rope-strung buckets into a well and haul them up as though they were weightless, filling plastic pails and the lovely, old, tall-necked brass and copper pots, which they place on top of their heads. Their swaying graceful walk is mesmeric. Even the women walking single-file by the roadside balancing enormous burlap-covered puffballs of leaves and sticks for cattle fodder manage to look strangely graceful. In front of every shed-like village house there is a pyramid or a rectangular monument of cow-dung patties, each cake decorated with a handprint or a stick-drawn design of circles, squares, polygons, meanders, spirals.

"It will be a bloody good thing when they lay in water pipes and gas pipes," Gurdip says. "Progress, Madam, we are having a program of progress soon, Madam."

Near the Kutub Minar, the everyday fades out and the flat land is bosomed with the uplifted breasts of Mogul tombs. Deserted for centuries, they sustain an illusion of romance like a

stage set designed to carry the image of peace, quiet, mystery.
Walled, domed, some with *chattris* on each corner of the roof,
the tombs are sepulchres that Moguls built as places of relaxation and pleasure. After their deaths, the sounds of music and
merry-making were silenced, and now there is only the cooing
of the doves in their nests among the weathered plaster carvings
of crumbling pendentives, the remembered sound of the pigeon
loft at Northlea.

"Tombs remain forever with the dust of this earth," Rabin-
dranath Tagore wrote.

> It is death
> That they carefully preserve in a casing of memory,
> But who can hold life?
> The stars claim it: they call it to the sky,
> Invite it to new worlds, to the light
> Of new dawns.
> It breaks
> The knot of memory and runs
> Free along universal tracks.

The lines are from a poem addressed to Shah Jehan, who had
the Taj Mahal built in memory of his queen Mumtaz, a poem
that begins:

> You knew, Emperor of India, Shah Jehan,
> That life, youth, wealth, renown
> All float away down the stream of time.

Of course you knew. The buff and burnt-rose sandstone
foundations of the Kutub Minar were laid in the twelfth century
by Qutb-ud-Din, whose dynasty was succeeded by Tughluk's,
which lasted until your ancestor Timur the Lame invaded India

at the end of the fourteenth century and destroyed Tughlakabad. Your empire, too, is gone. Your armies, whose marching
shook the earth, today have no more weight than the wind-
blown dust on the Delhi road . . .

Tughlakabad's moated, rocky eminence sprawls just ahead, a
vast and wonderful ruin with broken walls and archways where
dark swallows are nesting. High above, accipiters sail in the sky
with a lovely camber to their short, broad wings, turning and
twisting like leaves caught in a whirlpool. On the ground, potsherds are underfoot like shells on a beach, and a tribe of
satanic-faced goats are using the walled fields of withered grass
for pasturage. The desolate beauty of the place is extraordinary.
Unearthly screams of wild peafowl float up from the plain below, and on the sloping ground before us, a lone peacock steps
from behind a fallen column to spread its upper tail coverts and
show its gilded glinting plumes with their unseeing eyes. Lizards
skitter among the rocks. Bats squeak and flitter in the damp and
chilly underground chambers that once were storage rooms,
treasuries, granaries, and slave quarters. Like scraps of torn
umbrellas, they hang above our heads as Veronica and I clamber
down to semi-dark cubicles that, if she weren't with me, would
be almost as frightening to me as the cellar at Northlea had once
been. An elderly *chaukidar* scrambles down to stand beside us.
"See?" he says in a voice like the hoarse falsetto call of a pheasant. He points to runnels in the sandy floor. "In Hindi, *naga*. In
Ingliss is being cobra."

In easy amity, sharing the esthetic of simple forms and designs, we become track- and print-conscious, seeing snake
tracks in the dust; the tracks and scats of a mongoose crossing
the hoof prints of a goat trail; the wavy tracks of lizards; the

prints of crows, peacocks, sparrows; the prints of naked human feet; the prints our own sandals have made along the paths of dust and potsherds. We follow paths that twist through towering, lion-colored gateways and along honey-colored blocks of colossal walls, their archways wisped with silvery grass and lavender-flowered herbs that smell like lemon balm. We have our picnic high on the walls, leaning our backs against a crumbling arch. Looking out on the green savannas beneath us, we can see the peacocks and peahens making their way across the wide expanse, silently, deliberately. When the peacocks scream, it is sudden, for no apparent cause, a sound that rips through the noisy stillness of rock bees humming, cicadas scraping, crows cawing, parakeets chattering, Veronica's and my breathing, and tears a jagged hole in the fabric of our world.

A goat steps neatly, a model of exactness, along a distant path. I remember that Shah Jahan's wine cup had a goat's head for a handle and a chalice made of pearl shell and opalescent jade, all preserved in a state of lustrous perfection in the British Museum. My grandmother took me to see it when I was seven. I would have smashed the glass case if I could have, and stolen the cup. I had never seen any object before that I had wanted so much to own. "Oh, Granny, I wish I were a Mogul and could drink out of a cup like that."

"Nonsense, my precious. Nothing of the sort. That's the last thing you'd want to be. Whatever put that absurd notion in your head? You're a Presbyterian, my darling. A Christian. Not a barbarian or a heathen. I'd have had my mouth washed out with carbolic soap if I'd said a thing like that at your age. Now, come along, and let's see the Elgin Marbles before we go home for tea."

The Elgin Marbles. I expected to see little glass spheres with bewitching colors and designs. Instead—as though the Mogul cup had been the curling-tipped lamp of some interior genie who had said, "You want beauty? Beauty you shall have"—here was another world, a world of stone pale as almonds or winged seeds, cream-colored like chamois, biscuit-colored, the color of raw rice, the color of sand, and people and horses made fast in it—alert, at rest, vital, and still. The wild, romantic emanations of this world of almost unimaginable antiquity swept over me, fecundating my mind, and gave birth to a consciousness of man-made beauty that linked my world to another where gods had ichor coursing in their veins, their carved faces glowing like the flesh of pears, smiles playing around mouths pale as the wool of sheep, gods and goddesses who were larger than earthlings and some who had stepped from pedestals to walk in a procession and were earthling-sized. The heads, arms, and legs broken off of some had left bloodless wounds. There was a man triumphing over a wounded centaur. There were Dionysus, Demeter, and Hermes, easily recognizable, and a centaur pushing a man down and digging his hoofs into the naked man's thigh. It wasn't quite sculpture I was seeing, but people turned to stone, the way Midas had changed trees into gold. And like Pygmalion, I could feel them alive beneath my fingertips until Granny said "Don't touch!" in a voice that all but made me jump out of my own skin. I had no words to say what I felt, to say how this vision of an old world looked to me, and no way to do what I most wanted to do which was to leap into this palpable poem and become part of it. My grandmother tugged me along the Panathenaic procession, past horsemen and chariots, musicians and tray bearers, past Hermes, Dionysus, Demeter, Athena, past Hephaestus hobbling along on a stick.

"Lame, poor man." She towed me along a sculptural procession of horses whose speed increased from a walk to a canter, their tendons, skin folds, veins, and muscles "frozen in a frieze," as she said, waiting to be melted from the spell that had frozen them. Acrobatic hoplites hopped on and off chariots. All I could ask was, "Why are the animals' mouths so alive and the eyes so blind, Granny?"

"Gracious, my treasure, what an interesting observation. Long ago, when they were painted, they must have looked nicer."

Any carving of horses and men with exposed genitalia caused Granny to screen the sculpture from me by turning her back and side-stepping to the next sculpture so that my view was blocked unless I swiveled my head, which I knew enough not to do. Passing these "forbidden" carvings, I felt a rising commotion in my legs, chest, and head, and it seemed that at any moment I might be drawn into the procession and frozen in a long-ago ghost-pale world that my grandmother was only aware of in the details of the shocking parts she was determined I should not get a closer look at.

"Come along, dear, we don't want to be late for tea," Granny said, as she had probably said to my mother when she was a little girl.

Veronica has gone off to feed a goat the remains of our picnic. Now she returns to wipe her hands on the damp towel I have brought along in a plastic bag. She smokes a beedie and says she thinks she'll have a look at the marble-domed mausoleum across the road, at the end of a long, curving causeway. It is Tughlak's grandfather's tomb and faces east toward Mecca. "You'll be all right here, won't you, Mummy, in your little room beneath the arches? I'll be back soon." She brushes the top of my head with her lips and then, graceful and self-reliant as a cat, makes the descent to the lower footpath, turning, when she reaches it, to wave.

Rooms, tombs, wombs, houses of all kinds, are symbolic of women, the feminine aspect of the universe, repositories of wisdom, tradition, and the preservation of cultural heritage. I run the palm of my hand along the rough surface of sun-warmed stone, and look out upon the spreading vastness on either side of the archway. Windows, suggestive of communication, symbolize the possibility of understanding and of passing through to the external and beyond. In the symbolism of dreams, rooms represent the female body, and the displacement from her body to her room reveals itself in the care and attention a woman bestows upon her living space.

My mother seemed besotted to me in her insistence on the right tool for the right job and her gratification that she had rich stores of the right gadgets, the right implements, for everything that seemed unimportant to me at the time. Little ivory shovels to be used only for caviar at parties. Anything else spoils the taste, she said, but when I ran my finger around the emptied tin to secure the few remaining beads, then sucked my finger, I discovered that caviar tasted even better that way. Forks reserved for clams and oysters; spoons to be used only for glass-lined silver jampots; the right soap—gritty oatmeal or translucent Pear's or Yardley's lavender or pink, rose-smelling and rose-stamped soap in the downstairs bathroom for guests' use only and replenished the next day. A precise amount of rosewater in the fingerbowls. The "right" shoes, the "right" handbags and luggage, special stamps for sealing wax with mother-of-pearl handles and the Eliott crest carved on amethyst stampers. "Good" writing paper with raised letters that came in robin's egg–blue boxes, not to be used when I ran out of my own writing paper, as opposed to the everyday paper with flat lettering which I could use, if I asked permission. Never, ever, ever, under any circumstances, could I touch the really special writing paper engraved with the diamond-shaped Eliott lozenge in the shiny purple cardboard boxes sent from London. And never, ever, ever could I touch the music-box that played "Barcarolle" and "The Campbells Are Coming" unless my mother or the clock man was there to see that I didn't overwind the antique mechanism. Every crack, chip, scratch, dent, and sign of wear in a woman's living space and possessions is a tragedy—surface damage to her own body, I reflect, as I remember the fuss and anxiety such damage caused my mother.

How unsure she must have been of herself, her true self, to have been so aware of her looks, so vain, so concerned. If only all that concentrated consideration had been paid to the other arts of living, the qualities of spirit and attitudes of mind that bring out one's best. Instead, my mother had always searched for people she could count on to do this for her. ("Try to be with people who bring out your best, dear," she would say.) And yet, these niceties of hers were no more than a not-all-that-uncommon facet of living well, preserving little grandeurs of bygone times, the way I often do, wanting flowers, wanting everything to be shining clean, and all the silver polished to gleaming perfection, a different facet of Robert's sense of perfectionism and precision that Veronica has inherited to express as her perfect, absolute arrangements of things, her attention to colors and designs; another facet of my grandmother's desire to have everything in its place so that she could reach out and find it in the dark.

Veronica has inherited not only Robert's sense of perfectionism and precision but also my own bent for the often unattainable and perfect, to which both she and I have added interpretations and refinements that thin out like spilled milk to seep into all the cracks and crannies of our lives. Along, needless to say, with all the contrarieties—subtle, blatant, understood. Like the steps of a ritual dance and the dance of life itself, the pattern of stepping back to go forward—"regression in service of the ego," my analyst once explained—is to fall back, to become a child in order to leap forward and to replace hostility with compassion. "*Reculer pour mieux sauter*," he went on, "like a broad jumper, as the French would have it, who must distance himself from the pit, go back along the well-worn track he has come to know so well, then turn, run forward, and gain momentum so that he can make the best possible leap forward." A flame of understanding leaps in my mind.

"Make do, do without," was a phrase I heard my mother repeating to the maids and cooks in response to requests for new knee pads, larger quantities of butter, replacements, fresh supplies. I supposed that this austere command—stingy, mingy, heartless—was of her own devising. As a child, I never realized that her father and mother had been strapped for cash until my grandfather came into the family's Scottish estates, or that my mother married my father in order to be taken care of financially, as he, in his less fulfilled expectancy (that I surmise from letters he wrote to her addressed as "Dear Mummy"), hoped she would take care of him. It was only after my mother died and I was sorting through her papers that I came across these accounts and letters. I see now why it pleased my mother, gave rise to such a rush of elation, for her to be able to give me "the rich toy" in all its dazzling magnificence so that the skimp of her childhood could magically become the largesse of mine. My mother had no way of knowing how much I cherished the seemingly inconsequential green piano that the rich toy replaced. She had no way of knowing that I could only express what I heard in my mind by stroking and drumming on its keys. To my mother, the green piano was probably just a disappointing reminder that I hadn't inherited either her or my grandmother's musical ability; an object to be replaced by another that would be a triumphant reversal of the past rather than a diminishment of it.

My mother was interested in me only when I performed as an idealized version of herself or fulfilled her own unrealized dreams. But why carp about this now? Hadn't I wanted Veronica to live up to an idealized version of myself? "You just wanted me to be a charming angel with a pageboy hairdo," I can hear her snapping at me. "Well, enjoy your images. The real human being before you obviously has no such part in fantasies."

A charming little angel and a good girl, not much difference between the two. My mother was fond of reciting, "Be good, my child, be good, and let who will be clever." My grandmother had probably said that to her, as had generations of Eliott mothers, daughters, and wives before her. The motto inscribed on the banner of the Eliott coat of arms was—what else?—*Soyez sage*. For the first time, with a sense of momentous import, I think of my grandmother, my mother, and myself as *We*, we mothers of daughters, we who wish to be "good."

To feel accepting or understanding about my mother in even

the smallest way, that exasperating, frustrating, remote woman with her reserve of courage and gallantry during the wartime years who later was submerged, propped up as though by the cushions on which she had stitched "Never Explain," "Never Complain," gives me the kind of satisfaction I find in having straightened a picture that has been hung awry, tidied a small drawer. At the same time, I want to cry out for her forgiveness, to disencumber myself of the remorse I feel at knowing I was not the comfort to her I should have been, nor the realization of her thwarted ambitions, hopes, desires—and just what these were she never said, I never knew, never will know, only her beauty, so bright in the flower, so sad in the fruit.

I feel tears behind my eyes, and pick up a stone to throw it down the hill, watching it raise a cloud of dust as it lands and ricochets against a wall. The time, thought, and expense it must have cost my mother to re-do my bedroom as a reward for my having won that schoolgirl prize for neatness which meant nothing to me, but evidently so much to her. Curtains, dressing-table, bedspreads, slipcovers, all new, starched, frilly, and sprigged with pink rosebuds, the room freshly wall-papered with more pink rosebuds, and the rich toy specially French-polished for the occasion of my return from school. "How nice," was all I dutifully said, while I wished the room had been left the way it was or re-done in blue or yellow or checks or stripes—anything other than frilliness.

Giving. Is it true generosity, altruism, a need to make other people feel obligated, or a true pleasure? Veronica and I enjoy giving presents, both of us manifestly enjoying the "getting" by means of identification with the one to whom we give. We are sometimes governed, I imagine, by a need to give to others what we did not get ourselves or what we are inhibited from granting to ourselves. My mother gave me so many things, silver, china, antiques, clothes, a room all done up in frills and rosebuds, the giving of which was the only way she could express her love; my gratitude the only form in which she could receive love from me. We give what we are. We can only give what we have been given, or wish we had been given ourselves. The gifts of things are never as precious as the gifts of thought. The only true gift is a portion of oneself. I wish I could have given my mother more that pleased her. I feel I have never given Veronica enough.

Far away, there is a glimpse of lavender, and I watch as Veronica makes her way toward me past a columned cloister, then disappears behind a wall, and appears again on the path, her hair backlit and seeming to vaporize like the cloud she once wished to be. She sees me watching her, quickens her pace.

"The mausoleum is lovely," she says. "But ouf! I'm thirsty. Any *nimbu pani* left?" I shake the thermos, and as she hears the guggle of assurance, she fetches my plastic-fantastic mug and uses the cap of the thermos as a cup for herself. A plover-like bird, a red-wattled lapwing called a *titeeri*, shrills, "Did he do it, did he do it," and rhesus monkeys lope out of hiding. They are gray, with pronounced supra-orbital ridges which give them an expression of penetrating observation, absurd concentration. Gurdip trudges up the path to check on us, to see if we are "being all right." No dacoits, no *thuggees*, no *goondas* lurking about. He feeds the monkeys the leftovers of his lunch-time *chapattis* and makes the stentorian pronouncement that it is a good thing to feed monkeys. "Hanuman, King of the Monkeys, will bless you," Veronica says in an exaggerated tone, pretending to be serious.

"Monkeys can be trained, Madam, and dressed like little childrens to perform plays by the roadside. Their owners are putting wigs on them. Very comical, I can assure you, Madam."

Gurdip marches down the slope and back to the car. I smoke a beedie in a haze of contentment, feeling as strangely small as you do when you dismount after a long ride on a tall horse. To be in India with Gurdip is to be a child again with a protective, kind giant of nanny, an aspect even of my grandmother, with all the conflicts and ambiguities of mother-daughter relationships weaving a mesh of varicolored filaments in my mind. My grandmother was a product of her upbringing, my mother of hers, I of mine, Veronica of hers. How can I extend the possibilities of truth? How can I do justice to Veronica's and my complexities? It's painful to admit that motherhood arouses hope and terror, painful to admit that one's identity becomes dictated and diminished by others, or that it depends on the diminishment and exploitation of others. Unsanctioned, long-stifled realities begin to stir and assert themselves, caught in a web of my own making. Is Veronica in secret collusion with me, or are we divided? Gurdip makes our path physically easy, but psychically I know I'm in a high-risk situation. Perhaps, just by talking, just by being with Veronica, everything will work out. A weft of pleasure shuttles soothingly across my mind's warp. Rooms, tombs, wombs, looms. I remember Robert and myself watching the Guatemalan women who hitched their looms to trees and themselves to their looms so that the tree, the woman, the weft and warp of the loom, and the lovely woven stuff all became one.

The ruins of Tughlakabad are lightly brushed with the great blurred wings of twilight.

"Do you know, Mum, what they call twilight in India?"

"No, what?"

" 'The hour of cow dust.' I love that phrase. 'The hour of cow dust.' "

The hour of cow dust is like a password of understanding, a perfect phrase, romantic, with the feel of expectancy, the sense of waiting for something to happen, that lovely woven stuff of dreams. And then, as we come skidding and walking down from the ruins along the path where Gurdip has bent back the brambles and the gorse, there, coming along the road in a soft mist of ocher dust, are a large herd of water buffaloes.

"*Bhainsees*," Veronica says. She pronounces the word with the nasal baa of a sheep but with unmistakable affection. "*Bhainsees*. I *love* them."

Some genetic inheritance, some circumstance of birth has provided each buffalo with distinctive horns. Long, raked back, short, curly, some horns sweeping forward and curling inward, others symmetrical. All have halters of hemp strung through their flaring nostrils and knotted behind their heads, a cruel, torturing restriction. Gurdip is quick to tell me that this method assures ease in tethering oxen and *bhainsees*. "I have used the same method myself, Madam, on my farm, Madam, in the Punjab. I am sure the animals they are not hurt or hurting. Your heart is too kind, Madam."

"Thank you, Gurdip Singh."

Even when translated into English, I am forever aware in India of the carefully observed degrees of familiarity and distance, the manifold shadings of deferential respect, the exacting distinctions and elaborate concern with rank, place, degree, and the modulation of tone in vocalization.

Gurdip is an observer of traditional verbal and social niceties, and I feel I almost always let him down by being too brusque when I am scribbling in my notebook, or too friendly, too humble with all my questions. Why is it that I never can enjoy the complacency of being wonderfully correct or the smug confidence that it takes to do and say the Right Thing?

"But, Mum," Veronica says, as though stating a simple fact, "you're too much of an individualist ever to stick to any mannered or restrictive social code *anywhere*. You've always been up front, Mummy. You're one of the lucky people who doesn't have to conform, but who always manages somehow to fit in anywhere, to be right wherever they are. Don't you know that, Mum?"

"Well, no, I don't. But darling Veronica, what a wonderful thing for you to say."

Loyal, supportive, darling, *darling* Elsa Cloud!

The *bhainsees* disappear around a bend in the road. The peacocks are silent, and there is a great quietness. The light in the sky and across the landscape is now a lemony-mauve that gives great clarity to the trees, and to the lion-colored walls and arches of Tughlakabad.

"It's wonderful, isn't it, Mum, the hour of cow dust? So beautiful. So subtle."

Nine

On the eve of Holi, Holika's Eve, Gurdip drives Veronica and me to *Hauz Khas* to see the lighting of a sacred bonfire, to see the pyre, one we have watched being built, go up in flames so that the new year may beget a new life. Villagers hoop the concentric circles of cow-dung patties with protective threads of homespun cotton. Then each layer is quilled with straws. A primitive torch, relayed from a nearby village by several runners, is brought forward by a young man wearing a sleeveless undershirt to set the pyre smoking, smoldering on the inner cakes of dung. Then, with a great whisssh-whoosssh, the flames bound up around a *charpoy*, a shutter, a cart-wheel, brooms, planks and boards, boughs, twigs, cloth, rags, a broken chair. Snapping sparks leap forth with unexpected trajectories.

Like sparks, fragments of other lives whirl upward from one generation to another. "Man is born unto trouble, as the sparks fly upward," says the Book of Job. Is that true? My mother was a positive thinker. I have never before thought that, said that, realized that, but she was. She wanted to believe in Christian

Science, to deny pain, to believe in mind over matter. But once, long after my father's death, on a Father's Day Sunday, she said she would like to go with me to my Presbyterian church. And when it came time to say the Lord's Prayer, without a moment of hesitation she said, "Forgive us our debts as we forgive our debtors"—not the Episcopalian trespasses my father had said, but debts and debtors, the words she had grown up hearing. When my mother died and was cremated, my minister spoke at her memorial service of her courage and gallantry in World War I, and said that death was not an end but the beginning of another life, a greater adventure.

The flames before me sparkle. Curling locks of fire spiral into ephemeral images, a wind-blown mane of fire rising from its man-made mountain, flickering, flashing with lance-points of clear gas-blue, shifting, mobile, yet anchored in the flames. Scenes unreel in my mind: my mother having tea in her bed-room by the fireside, my mother having tea in the living-room by the fireside, her head bent in concentration on the crewel work she is rapidly, rhythmically stitching. Upstairs, down-stairs, I wait to be told to put on another log, to rekindle the fire with pinecones.

I remember the bonfires of autumn leaves at Northlea, the faces around them glowing like apricots. I gaze into the St. John's Eve fires, drawn into the flames and becoming part of them so that I no longer feel encased in my own skin, but wild and whirling and leaping upward. I *am* the leaping fire and the wood-smoke.

Now I am back in that country church, down the path from St. Timothy's, receiving my first communion. I feel transparent, disembodied, as the minister places his hands on my head, and the choir sings, "Breathe on me, Breath of God, 'til I am wholly thine, and all this earthly part of me glows with thy fire divine." I am light as air, cleansed, pure, the confusion of life and people dissolving as I perceive myself lifted up into the sky, into Heaven, with the conviction that I will live for years—maybe forever—loved, protected, watched over. If my mother were in church, I would fling my arms around her and croon, "I love you, I love you." But she is not there to rejoice with me in this moment of melting tendresse, in the sense of unity I feel with God and Love and the World.

No distance seems to separate me from that country church, and from the way I felt cradling Veronica when she was an infant in my arms, and from the way I felt sitting beside my grand-mother, my head resting on a firm, velvet-covered knee, listen-ing to her read psalms from the purple leatherbound Bible that my mother gave to me after Granny died. "Here," she said, rather awkwardly and stiffly. "Maybe you would like the family Bible. It says Stobs Castle on it, and it has my father's coat-of-arms on the bookplate inside." I thought at the time that she disapproved of this Bible because it had belonged to her father or because she was a Christian Scientist and had her own set of matched Bible and reading text. Now I realize that she had been brought up to repress and conceal emotions, that it was not considered "good form," that it was even vulgar, to expose them. She had learned to mask her grief at the loss of her mother and her love for me, to maintain a "stiff upper lip," to not complain and not explain. "Oh, Mummy, I'm so sorry," I say in my mind, hoping that somehow she will hear me wher-ever she is beyond that little dismal urn of ashes.

Fire leaps up as blue as the flames on a Christmas pudding.

Butterfly wings of fire fly into the night. Butterfly emblems of the soul purified by fire, butterflies held close to a candle flame, an image of love in Romanesque art. Hands cupped around flames in the paintings of Georges de la Tour, the painted effect of flame-stained flesh as real as the glow in a jack-o'-lantern. Crimson butterflies wing into the dark, butterflies, the symbol of rebirth. Flames symbolic of purification, flames radiating from the pyre's central point, flames leaping from the navel of the round body of the fire, showering into sparks like comets and fireworks. Hypnotic, mesmeric, this aureole encompassing all of us who watch, the firelight like a wash of divinity on the faces around me.

Holika's pyre burns green, orange, blue, yellow, and red, red, red. Mulk has said that red is the color of blood and life. Red fires. Red food. Red was the color chosen for the food of the ancient gods. Everything red—apples, mullet, lobsters, red berries—was reserved to be eaten at feasts of the dead during the winter solstice, Saturnalia, Yule, Christmas. The alder, the dogwood, and the five-pointed ivy leaf that looked like a goddess's hand were sources of red dye for the ancients who stained their faces scarlet to invoke the strength of the sun and the vibrant sensuality of their youth.

Destruction and renewal, fire followed by riotous revelry and *lila*, the play of the mind, and the divine sport of Krishna, the rites of love. All this lies ahead, yet to be seen and experienced. What will it all be like?

Apollo comes to mind. Apollo, the sun god, the father of the Corybants who danced wildly at the winter solstice. Veronica looked like a Corybant when she danced at the Electric Circus. Apollo, who figured as the child Horus, the solar deity of Egypt, the son of Isis and Osiris, whose fertility image was painted with red dye; Dionysus or Bacchus with his thyrsus-swinging Bacchantes whose revelries marked the new year; and promiscuous Pan with his drunken coterie of Maenads—all the gods of the vine and the sun, they must have their counterparts in the festivities of Holi. All those wonderful ancient gods who harken back to the idealistic conviction of a golden race that lived carefree and labor-free in pre-agricultural times, eating fruits, nuts, and honey, and drinking milk of sheep and goats. They never grew old. They danced. They laughed, and death was no more terrible than sleep. Hesiod had mourned their passing in the seventh century before the birth of Christ. Their spirits survive in Europe as genii of happy rustic retreats, givers of good fortune, upholders of justice, and tree souls whose spirits give trees like the Bo-tree under which Buddha received his Enlightenment a life of their own.

Odin's bonfires, imitating the sun's light and heat, magically encouraging the sun to rekindle its own light as well. Holika's pyres, symbolizing the destruction and renewal of the world, those circular fires, those pyramidal fires. The alchemical fire of transmutation. Truth is error burned up. Norman Brown wrote in *Love's Body* that love is all fire. "As in Augustine, the torments of the damned are part of the felicity of the redeemed. Two cities; which are one city. Eden is a fiery city; just like Hell."

Holi! Holi! Holi! Holy, Holy, Holy, Holy! The jubilation of that hymn, the joy of being able to sing unstammered, unstuttered syllables! Wholly, Wholly, Wholly! Perhaps the fire of this evening is like a flaming monogram of the everlasting God, "who was in the beginning, is now, and ever shall be, world without end."

I reach out for Veronica's hand, cool as an ivy leaf, still dimpled across the knuckles. When she was a baby, her hands with the fingers splayed made me think of stars and starfish. Now I think of ivy leaves, IV, intravenous, scribbles under the skin that record the messages of the blood.

"Are you OK?" she asks. "You sound funny."

"I'm on a high," I say. "Full flight. Anamorphic perspectives. Self-induced Dionysian madness, a connected-thought binge."

"You're just tired, Mummy, it must be the heat," she says kindly. "Do you want to go?"

"No, darling, not yet." Sometimes she reminds me so of her father.

Fires. What *is* it about fires I want to remember? The bonfires of burning leaves in Long Island's cool autumns? The smoking bunches of St. John's Wort in the bonfires of St. John's Eve, protecting the harvests, the land, and everyone and everything on it against demons, devils, witchcraft, and all other evils? Picnic fires on the beach in Jamaica, where Robert played his guitar and we roasted marshmallows for the children and ourselves (the charred, sweet hotness, the scrape of my teeth against the stick when I drew the marshmallow into my mouth, the bubbly crisp brown skin and the melting whiteness, deliciously, burning sweet)?

I had a red kaleidoscope when I was a child, an instant escape, part of the dream world to which I could retreat to see colors and patterns of my own making, and there are many times when my mind whirls around as it does now, wheels on the hub of a moment, mixing thoughts, words, associations into new shapes, new forms of perception. My mind's kaleidoscope is better than my old kaleidoscope. It gives me the fireworks of endlessly rocketing associations that are the Fourth of July pyrotechnics of a soul craving independence from the past. In death and loss, there is always regeneration. Fire, fire, burning bright, in the forests of the night, what immortal hand or eye could fire-rim thy fearful symmetry? O clouds unfold, bring me my chariots of fire.

There was another fire.

Veronica, six months old, is lying on her back in her white basket carrier, wedged between Robert and me in the front seat of our car. We are driving across the Mojave Desert on our way to New York to board a freighter for South Africa, where Robert has been awarded a Fulbright to get his doctorate in geology. In the backseat is Veronica's pale yellow crib with its mesh siding and top, and all the paraphernalia: the bottle sterilizer, the tins of formula, the cloth and disposable diapers, the diaper bag, the bedding, the boxes of baby food jars, the mobile of birds, the cuddly animals; my grandmother's ivory rattle with the silver bells safely pocketed in my leather bag; the tin box of family emergency medical supplies and prescriptions that I hope will never be needed but feel safer having on hand.

Warned that pilferage and stealing are unusually heavy at Durban, where our possessions will be unloaded before they are trucked to the University of the Witwatersrand in Johannesburg, we have decided to take not only our necessaries, but our most cherished possessions with us, stowing them in a U-haul trailer that is hooked, as though it were welded, to the back of our dark blue car.

Robert has packed his collection of treasures: a chamois pouch filled with pearls from the Northern Cook Islands, a repoussé silver bowl from Bangkok; black-lipped pearl shells from the Tuamotus; a heavy gold *guaca* from Costa Rica; a little serving figure meant to work for the dead in the underworld, pinned to a scrap of *tapa* cloth in a shadow-box; a carved tiger's tooth from northern Thailand; silky gold-lipped pearl shells from the Banda Islands; an intricately carved canoe paddle from the Marquesas; the skin of a jaguar he had shot in an Ecuadorean jungle; an ornithological specimen bird of paradise from Indonesia; a bolt of navy blue tribute silk from China; antique sailing charts; six rifles, two pistols, and cartons of ammunition.

My choices: the manuscript of my first book, on which I am working; reference books; family photographs; family treasures. The heavy gold pocket watch with fob and chain and the gold signet ring with a star sapphire that had belonged to my great-grandfather Burton and were so beloved by my father that they had become part of his image. I can look at them and see him. I can touch them, hold them, and feel in magic reversal my baby hand in his warm, strong hand, the pulse of my heart and his.

All my clothes, memories and fantasies of silk, linen, cotton, tweed, and velvet. Schoolgirl sweaters, the Oriental finery of Chinese wedding skirts and silk brocade coats, Indian saris, Siamese silk dresses woven with two colors like the embroidered French gardens of André Le Nôtre so that the purple flickered scarlet, the green flashed blue, and the blue shimmered green. A mink coat given to me by Veronica's godmother. Evening dresses fashioned from Spanish shawls, Moroccan caftans, and Belgian lace, and beaded confections of Mummy's salvaged from the attic trunks in which she had stored her nineteen-twenties' trousseau.

And jewelry boxes. Boxes lined with turquoise silk and covered with Swatow embroidery; an Edwardian purple leather case with three sectioned trays lined with plum velvet and a lid stamped with my grandmother's monogram. A box of tessellated Florentine leather I had bought on my first trip abroad. A robin's egg–blue leather box filled with the delicate gold, pearl, and enamel pins, necklaces, and bracelets of my childhood; tiny coral beads; thread-thin gold chains with lockets; pearl necklaces, enamel and pearl lozenges I had worn on my shoulders to keep the straps of my petticoat from sliding beneath the ribbon-tied sleeves of summer dresses.

A coral leather box for other jewelry I had as a young girl. Horse pins, a rhinestone poodle pin, pearls. A gold charm bracelet clotted and jingling with objects that were evocative of festive occasions, happy experiences, moments of attention that had been of monumental importance at the time, at least a hundred mementos of solid and fragile gold. All my childhood collections—pebbles, seashells, birds' nests, birds' eggs whole and broken, matchbook covers, playing cards, feathers, stamps, postcards, beach glass, foreign coins, letters, Christmas cards —all had disappeared except for the handwritten lists of words whose meanings I looked up in dictionaries that I collected to store in my mind's house. Except for the lists of words, these vanished collections had been supplanted by charms.

A small box of the "real" jewelry I could inventory as "my little diamond horse," "my sapphire ring," "my gold and diamond clip," and there, in the top tray, the blue-beaded hospital identification bracelet that had been attached to Veronica's wrist when she was first brought in for me to see, all swaddled, with a tuft of her hair caught up in an absurd ribboned bow.

A brass chest for the jewelry I had bought on my travels

around the world, that journey I took in my mid-twenties when I had met Robert. Heavy silver and gold-dipped pieces, pearls, coral, turquoise, and pieces set with semi-precious stones. Dramatic, massive and extraordinary adornments that brought to mind souks, markets, bazaars; each piece a memory, an image, a scent, a jingle of another world of which I had wanted to be a part. Reveling in the afterglow of synaesthesia, I could buckle a silver belt and see the naked-tailed rats in a lane in Chiengmai where I had almost stepped on a krait and would have, if I had not been pulled back by a coolie. I fasten a necklace and see again the vista of a beach the color of an ancient bronze mirror, the sampans and junks in Hong Kong's harbor. I put on earrings and hear a muezzin's cry; a bracelet on my wrist brings me to Sri Lanka's Temple of the Tooth and an ocean red with algae and the catamarans surfing into the beach beyond Colombo. I slip on a ring and see mists rising from a gorge in Lebanon. I hold a silver cross in my hand and think of a white-washed church in Santorini, look at a jade necklace and hear a gamelan orchestra playing in Bali, pin on a brooch and hear a child singing a missionary hymn in an up-country lane in the Philippines. I play with toe-rings and feel the heat of India like a lover's embrace. I wear Europe around my neck and wrists and clasp my hair with Asia and let North Africa fall from the lobes of my ears.

There it all is in the trailer and the car, Robert and baby and me to make three in our dark blue heaven.

Robert and I joke and laugh. We talk about what we may expect to find in South Africa. We sing "You Are My Sunshine." Robert is not a church-goer, but he likes to sing the hymns of militant Christianity he learned as a child, hymns like "Onward

Christian Soldiers," "The Battle Hymn of the Republic," "A Mighty Fortress Is Our God," "Glorious Things of Thee Are Spoken." He says he likes the tunes and that the oxygen intake is exhilarating. We sing a missionary hymn Robert first heard in Tahiti, based on an Austrian folk song. The words are simple and the melody is heart-touching.

> Yet never alone is the Christian
> By word, by faith or by prayer.
> For God is a friend unfailing,
> And God is everywhere.

Robert laughs, and reaches with his right arm to draw me closer to him. My hip jounces Veronica's basket, and we both look down at her anxiously. "It's all right. She's sleeping," Robert says.

"I love you," I say to him.

"I love you, too, Leelee," he says to me.

Veronica wakes up. I clasp her tiny, warm hand in my own, taking infinite pleasure in looking at her. Her wisps of hair are like the feathers of a meadowlark's breast.

Robert and I punctuate our conversation with asides to her. "What do you think of *that*, Veronica? Would you like the moon for thimblerig?"

"What does Daddoo's little buttercup-and-fly think about the first star of the evening?"

Veronica smiles, a drop of saliva forming at the corner of her mouth and trickling a patch on her cheek. I blot it with a handkerchief that belonged to my grandmother.

Trucks judder past. Cars speed by. The sun sets and as the sky darkens, I begin to feel cold. Strange reflections of light appear on the windshield. Turning my head to look back, I see

flames behind the rear window. Our U-Haul, with all our cherished possessions, is on fire.

Robert slams on the brakes so sharply that the car lurches to
the side of the road. I pitch forward, hitting my head on the
windshield.

Shouting to me to get out of the car, Robert grabs Veronica's
basket by the handle and swings it over the steering wheel and
through the door. The basket tilts and Veronica's arms fly up as
she slides with her head now wedged against the pillow to the
end of the basket, which is dipping dangerously close to the
ground.

"Get away from the car! Get up on the bank!"

I hear Robert shouting. I do what he says. Veronica's basket
now righted, he sets it down beside me with a bump. Then he
lopes back down the hill and begins kicking the blazing U-Haul,
trying to break it loose from its attachment to the car before
the flames reach the gas tank.

"You'll be killed!" I scream. My voice is coming from the
back of my throat.

Shaking his head, Robert goes on booting the U-Haul like a
madman. By some extraordinary force of strength, he kicks it
loose and sends it toppling off the road onto the desert just as
the flames reach the boxes of ammunition. Shells begin to ex-
plode in intervals of sharp, crackling bursts, detonating like
fireworks, in showering arcs, bullets whining with a nasal metallic sound.

There is a moment when it all seems like a nightmare from
which I can convulsively shiver awake. There is a second when
I feel I can turn off the television, turn off the sound of the
gangster film or the cowboy and Indian shoot-'em-up.

My jaw is quivering. My teeth are chattering. I am terrified that Robert is going to be killed. Fear is like the taste of rust in my mouth.

And then he comes back to stand beside me.

"Well," he says. "The car is saved."

"Damn the car. You could have been killed!" Now that he is safe, I am angry with him for the risk he has taken.

A wind has blown up, and gusts catch glowing scraps of paper and burning clothing and tufts of burning fur that look like bouquets of sparks and send them whirling in the night air above the ghostly desert stretching out on all sides, gray with splotches of cactus and tumbleweed. The trailer casts a circle of pink light so bright that bats appear like swallows out of the night air to dip and circle around it and around Robert and me and Veronica in her basket.

We hear a car in the distance that whooshes past and disappears.

"When the fire dies down, they'll stop to scavenge," Robert says. "Fuck all the good Samaritans out here, the dirty bastards."

Veronica wails. Not a wet-diaper cry, not a cry of discomfort, but a cry of hunger. Leaving Robert to watch over her, I fetch her bottled formula, still lukewarm, from a plastic-lined tote bag that I unzip and zipper again. The familiar sound is comforting.

Now I am standing with Veronica cradled in my arms, feeding her, breathing in the toffee smell of the formula and the sensual smell of punk, listening to the roar of the flames and the crescendo-diminuendo sound—the Doppler effect, Robert calls it—of cars that pass by and disappear. A coyote howls in the distance, an eerie call, a mix of hooting owl and baying dog.

Veronica drinks, making soft slurping sounds as calmly as if she were in my lap in the rocking chair, still in the bedroom of the house we left that morning.

It is cold. I take off my sweater coat and wrap it around Veronica. Robert takes off his tweed jacket and capes it, warm and smelling of sweat and smoke, around my shoulders. He tells me to watch out for snakes. "Rattlers are nasty buggers at night."

The terrible machine-gun tattoo of detonating ammunition has ended, and Robert runs across the road down the slope to the still burning trailer to see if he can rescue anything. He kicks at the trailer, runs backward, runs forward to kick it again, over and over, again and again. He dislodges a box of books that is blazing, and kicks it away from the fire, booting it until it falls apart. I see him bending down to scoop up handfuls of sand, smothering a dozen or so lesser fires of partially burning books.

I think I see a rattlesnake, but it is only a lizard.

There is a strong smell of burning paper, burning resinous wood, singed hair, and a Fourth of July smell of punk that makes me see again the fireworks being ignited by my father on the lawn at Northlea while the gardener, the chauffeur and the butler, who have set up the display and are all more practical and competent than my father, stand by with their wives, who are the laundress, the chambermaid, and the cook. I don't see my mother in this tableau. Because there are mosquitoes, she has probably gone inside the house to watch. I see myself, sitting in a folding wooden armchair, ecstatically twirling a sparkler, swinging my white-sandaled feet, looking down occasionally at them to admire their unfamiliar greenish glimmer in the soft, cool Long Island night. Above, the sky flickers with what I have been told are the Northern Lights, though perhaps they are just the reflection of fireworks elsewhere. Cloud shadows shift across the moon, and the scent of punk, grasses, and herbs fills my nose with invisible particles of pleasure. The scene is very real to me.

To be cold, to be standing shivering by the side of the desert road in California, to be watching the fire in the trailer die down to embers, to be watching Robert poking around the debris with a charred slat from the trailer—I can see where the pale gray part leaves off and the charred part begins—that is unreal, that has the irrationality of a dream. Even Robert, his short-cropped blond hair whitened by the moonlight, his face ruddy with the light of the embers and low-flickering flames, seems like some study in chiaroscuro by Caravaggio, his features made unfamiliar by the shadows of flames that lick up, waver, and die out around him. Only Veronica, asleep now, seems real. I hug her more closely to me, as I watch much of my past disappear in smoke and flying sparks. The tangibles of memories I treasure most have been burned. Except for the mink coat and a few pieces of jewelry, nothing has been insured. But what does that matter? What does anything matter except that we are alive? A diminished self in the desert, I feel myself growing the carapace for a new self in an Old World, a world that I have never seen. I turn my back against the wind and look away from the fire. Veronica is warm in my arms.

I step back now from Holika's pyre, its changing colors hot in my eyes. Distinguishable still are the outer cow-dung patties arranged to overlap each other in concentric circles; a flaming wheel, its spokes and hub; chair legs with their varnish seething, bubbling black. The heat is intense. The villagers around the pyre are shouting Holi! Holi! Holi! and carrying on like demented cheerleaders, rocking back and forth, bending their knees toward the fire as they roar HO, leaning away, heads rolled back, to shout LI, their teeth flashing white, then hidden as they bend forward again to roar HO.

There is another fire to remember, a fire I never saw. My mother instructed the hospital, told doctors, that she must be cremated after her death and though nothing was ever written, she also insisted to the executor of her will, a Burton cousin, that this be done. I was never told about her wishes, which she had never expressed to me, until after they had been carried out.

Why ever did you do it, Mummy? Did you want to be burned the way Indian widows used to be burned on the funeral pyres of their husbands? Was having yourself cremated your way of committing *suttee*? You led such a restricted, constrained life. In death, did you want to be set free, with no more boundaries than a flame's leap and curl, bifurcating taper-caper into the air? Did you want to flame freely, brightly in death, burn into ashes so light and soft you could escape forever from any further imprisonment except in an urn, suggestive in its Grecian form of beauty and truth? Did you set yourself free at last, did you set me free? Watching the Holika fire, I see the Phoenix, like a bird released from your crewel work, soaring from its tight-bound frame in a rocket of fiery feathers, sparks whirling from the light of its body flying away, loosed and free to join the stars.

Now, the out-sticking silhouettes of the charpoy and cartwheels, the brooms, the planks have all lost their shape, their identities disappearing, crumbling, merging, floating up as black leaves in the magic transformation of the fire. Holika's fires will blaze all night, and tomorrow night the embers will be collected to ignite the new household fires. With the heat gusting around my back, my mind melts, my thoughts fuse together. Tears blur the sight of the bonfire, gentle the flames, make them tremble. This is the Key of the Kingdom . . . in that kingdom is . . . town, city, street, lane, bed, basket, flowers . . . of the Kingdom this is the Key. Am I like the medieval traveler who has made a complete circuit of the world without knowing it?

Drops of water slide down my glass and pool on the glass top of the bedside table. We are back at the hotel.

"Do you remember Christmas in Jamaica, all of us singing Silent Night, Holy Night?" I ask Veronica. "I can hear you singing, 'Round yon Vir-i-jen, Muzzer and Child,' and that lullaby for Jesus."

Veronica begins to hum, and then stops, smiling. "Remember Allison singing, 'We will knock you, rock you, sock you'?"

"I thought it was so blasphemous, so sacrilegious, so awful of her. How could she?"

"Oh, Mummy, she was only a little girl," Veronica says.

"I know." I smile. "I suppose it was sort of funny. She was always so much more assertive than you."

"Like you, sometimes, Mummy. Your speedy Western aggressiveness, remember?"

I let the challenge drop. "You made a crèche out of clay and paper and shells," I say. "It was a warm night, and you sang in such a high, clear voice."

Veronica, Allison, Sam, and Bryce home from school with Robert and me, we were all together that Christmas, all one family, six minds that thought alike, I liked to think, six hearts that beat as one, or at least, more or less in unison. "The family, my precious, that's the important thing," my grandmother had said.

Memory keeps us from losing what we think we have lost.

Out of the corner of my eye, I see Veronica rescuing a wasp that has fallen into my glass of iced tea. Very carefully, she lifts the wasp out of the iced tea with a spoon and covers the spoon with a Kleenex. Very carefully, she carries the wasp to the open window and inverts the Kleenex-covered spoon. Finally, she closes the window and turns on the air-conditioning.

I have a strange dream and wake up thinking about fires, music, wounds, trees, dragons, alligators. Outside, I can hear drums being beaten in a wild tattoo. Horns. Laughter. Shouts. Bagpipes. Looking out the window, I see groups of young men running beneath the trees, pelting each other with handfuls of dust. In the near courtyard, a few men are hurling clay pots against a stone wall and cheering when they break. They are the clay pots made and used the year before; breaking them "kills" the old year. Pye dogs are barking and yapping.

It is only six-thirty in the morning, but already breakfast has been laid out in the sitting room. Fresh orange juice, tea, *lassi*, thick toasted slices of bread striped like zebras with the marks of the grill, honey, ham, foil-wrapped butter from Denmark.

I see the breakfast tray. I see Veronica. Suddenly I begin to cry. Terrible, uncontrollable, racking sobs.

"What's the matter, Mummy? What's the matter?" Veronica fetches a cold, wet washcloth wrung out so that it doesn't drip, to wipe my face. She fetches a linen towel to dry my face and my eyes. She fetches a box of Kleenex.

I blow my nose. Abruptly, the spasm of sobbing stops.

It's hard to be logical. There aren't names and emotions for everything. I try to explain to Veronica that Holi, with its theme of destruction and renewal, has set off a volcanic eruption of memories and associations. Chords have been touched in my subconscious. The soothing bandage of time has been torn away from the wounding sense of loss I felt when my father died a week after I told him I was pregnant with Veronica; when I saw my past and part of myself literally going up in smoke, in a desert fire probably caused by a cigarette flipped out the window of a passing truck driver; when I saw the urn containing the ashes I was told were all that was left of my mother.

The past is the fire-breathing dragon I had recurrent nightmares about as a child. But like the plovers on the backs of alligators basking along the banks of the Zambesi, I feel I have picked at the teeth of a monster that has no desire to devour me. I want the fires to die down in my mind, to be extinguished by the restful, the effortless, the commonplace.

Today is the Festival of Holi, the day of playing Holi.

There's a notice in *The Statesman* saying that armed police have been deployed all over the city to maintain law and order, and that regulations have been issued banning the throwing of water or color- and water-filled balloons on "unwilling people or passing vehicles on this day of sexual license, carousing, and merrymaking." Suddenly, we are laughing as we put on our Khadi Bhavan outfits of white draw-stringed pajama-like pants, white cotton tunics, white terry-cloth turbans and Kate Green-

away mobcaps over these. I can see a procession cavorting past
the hotel, a rag-tail, bobtail lot. Young boys are now pelting
each other with dry cow manure and fresh donkey droppings.
An old woman with a turtle's toothless face slings a bucket of
dirty water at an old man's back, then picks up a broom handle
and thwacks him. He runs. She runs after him, thwacking at
him, she yelping, he squawking. Curry-colored dust flies up in
great clouds as children run alongside the woman, cheering her
on. Pandemonium.

The hotel lobby is decorous and relatively quiet. Samesh, the
managing director, is standing behind the front desk as usual,
flanked by clerks. As we approach, he shoots his cuffs and adjusts the perfect knot of his silk tie. He is the sort of man you
know *has* to succeed. A mother's darling, a father's pride. Cour-
teous, intelligent, thoughtful, helpful, Indian movie-star handsome.

Veronica is giggling and being flirtatious with Samesh. Although he is proper and decorous, he plays the little flirty game
with ping-pong timing. Coy, coy, arch, arch, smile, smile, giggle,
giggle. He keeps his distance. Veronica keeps hers. Good shot,
Veronica. Good shot, Samesh. After a nice little rally, the game
is over. We are all smiling and laughing, even the turbaned door-
man who opens the doors for us.

Gurdip, waiting outside, his suit as white as the starch with
which it has been stiffened, his turban the color of a jellaby,
assumes the role of kindly patriarch, somewhat fussy, about to
accompany two granddaughters trick or treating. Just as we
have settled into the taxi, the windows rolled down and the
door still open, out runs Samesh. His face is transformed. His
expression is that of a saucy, impertinent boy with a devilish

grin. Roughly, he swipes an index finger coated with red powdered paint down my cheek, then runs around the side of the
car to do the same to Veronica. She gives a little mewing, tinkling laugh. I'm too surprised, too startled to respond.

In the back roads, men and boys are behaving like deranged
children. They squirt red paint on each other with *pitchkarries*.
They fling mud and manure balls at each other. A face in the
crowd looks as though it might have been painted by Arshile
Gorky. Clothes are as spattered with color and impasto as the
canvases of Jackson Pollock.

A boy, holding his thumb over the top of a bottle of fizzy
Limca, shakes the bottle and moves his thumb, aiming the spray
of foam at Veronica's open window. Veronica, with a seed-
sowing gesture, throws a fistful of powdered paint back at him.
There are shouts of laughter from the onlookers as the paint
blows about the boy's face, making red smudges where it mixes
with perspiration.

Gurdip asks us to close the windows. He doesn't want the
upholstery stained. Shouting *Namaste* and *Holi*, passengers in
passing cars throw paint or siphon it in our direction from
pitchkarries, and the car windows are soon blotched with vermilion as bright as arterial blood. Women chase men and strike at
them with sticks and poles. Gangs of boys and men wrestle on
the sidewalks and pause to lob cow dung at passing trucks. At a
stoplight intersection, a group of men dance, burlesquing vertical copulation, burlesquing Kathakali performances with exaggerated grimaces and eye-rolling.

"It's the *Bhang*, Madam," Gurdip says. "The villagers grind
hemp leaves, Madam, or mash them in a sieve with jaggery, and

dahi, almonds and anise. Highly intoxicating, Madam, this festival drink."

Bhang, pronounced bung, and dung. There must be more to playing Holi than bung and dung.

Veronica leans toward me to put a powdered-paint-coated finger on my cheekbone and slide it down parallel with my nose. "Turn the other side, Mummy," she says, and stripes the left side of my face.

A gang of men and boys run alongside our car. "*Holi! Holi! Holi!*" they shout. Their shouts vibrate with the tension between creation and destruction.

Once more we arrive at Mulk's studio cottage in Hauz Khas. Gurdip mutters about a guard dog he is sure will come lunging out at us, and wields a stout branch he has snapped off a tree to assure our protection. I wonder where the gathering is and worry that we are too early, or too late, and that perhaps everyone has gone off without us. Finally, one of Mulk's casually acquired attendant bearers appears in the dark hallway to lead us to a door at the back of the house that opens onto a large, walled, tree-bordered garden where several dozen people are sitting on the grass. The sounds of an accordion, a harmonica, and some Indian violin-like instruments mingle with the sound of voices and laughter.

I start walking toward the group of people, and then break into a run when I see Mulk in the center of the gathering as speckled and splotched with red dye as an over-ripe banana, a figure no less comic than endearing.

Clasping my hands, Mulk announces me to the gathering as Leila from America. "Welcome Leila, everyone! Oh, this is joyful *Holi* day, when no one gets angry, when all quarrels come to an end and we recover the vision of life's primordial harmony, simple and joyful. Welcome Leila, everyone! Let us all enjoy our *lila*, our divine sport of kings, and our Leila from America!"

Embarrassed to be the center of attention, yet pleased by the applause, I bow and make *Namaste* and beam with what Robert used to call my "banana-in-the-mouth-sidewise" grin. In the background, I see Veronica rolling up her eyes, convulsed with silent laughter. Gurdip, standing near her, furrows his brow. Starched and white and immaculate, as he will remain for the rest of the day, aloof in his Sikhdom that makes no distinctions of caste and therefore needs no occasion to celebrate its disregard, he is enisled in his dignity and disdain for Mulk's puckish Krishna nonsense.

"Ah, the divine comedy of Krishna's annual Day of Judgment! The day of *Holi*, the day we play, the divine holiday when all the social and ritual principles of everyday lives are turned upside down in topsy-turvies!" Mulk carries on exuberantly, gesturing expansively, his white clothes as spattered as a painter's drop cloth, his silver hair blotched, his rubbery terracotta face all measled and streaked with poppy red.

The male guests, impersonating Krishna's fevered eroticism and fluting seductions, perform a comic dance routine which is applauded and cheered by villagers who have climbed up to sit on the garden walls. Some of the village women fetch men a crack over the head as if they were puppets in a Punch and Judy show. Giggling children run about the lawn pelting everyone with fusillades of cookie crumbs, roasted barley seeds, and red dye-powder that floats like a haze, mixing with perspiration, settling in eye corners.

I am given some sweet, almond-flavored *dahi* to drink and am contentedly sipping it when Gurdip comes running to tell me that there is *bhang* in it. Dung? "No, bung. Bung, Madam, bung." Oh dear, *bhang*, bung, the juice of the hemp leaf, liquid marijuana. Already, my mind feels fuzzy. I am beginning to have little sense of where the boundaries of my skin leave off and the air or anything else begin. My mind is blurred, my words are slurred, how absurd.

Veronica comes to sit next to me. "You've got red specks of sleepy dust in your eyes, Mummy," she carols. She wets an edge of her shirt in her mouth, twirls it into a spiral like a turritella shell which she pokes carefully into my eye corners and removes with a flourish to show me the red at its tip.

The color of blood. The color of rejoicing. The color of life itself. *Holi*. Holy. Wholly. I feel a sense of oneness, of melting and floating and flowing into everything. What did some folklorist call it? *Communitas*, switching personal identities in an exultant celebration of role reversals. But he was referring to Hallowe'en, not *Holi*. Veronica and I have switched roles, but that's not the same thing, is it? I remember Mulk saying that children can act any way they wish without fear of punishment on *Holi*, that the servant can play the part of master, the submissive wife can play the role of the domineering husband, the henpecked husband can play the role of the virago wife, tormentors can be safely teased.

Teasing, tease, tea. "Come along, we don't want to be late for tea." The phrase, as my grandmother said it, was a reminder of structure, order, routine, and the promise of delicious things to eat and drink. But the phrase, spoken with an accompanying crease between the eyebrows by a stiff and sour nurse who terrified me with the cautionary advice that if I picked my nose I would have nostrils like tunnels, and if I made a face, and the wind changed, my face would stay that way, called forth in me a bracing force of resistance and tension. There was a kind of dreary cruelty to her that I wanted to keep at arm's length, not because I feared to be its victim in the physical sense, but because I didn't want to be infected with its germs. It allowed nothing to exist without being stepped on, squashed, torn up by the roots, shown to be rotted like an open peach with a disease in its stone. She read me Bible stories every night after my bath. "Faith will move mountains," she assured me. "If you have faith, God will do anything that you ask." I wanted to prove her right.

On an afternoon walk in the woods in back of our property, I decided to ask God to surround her with lions, snarling leopards, and any other animal that bites, as soon as He heard a whistled signal from me. At six, I was not good at whistling, but I thought I could manage the first phrase of "Yankee Doodle." Then, when the nurse was properly terrified, I would advance, with my right arm raised the way I had as an angel in the Christmas pageant, and say, "Shoo! Don't be afraid. There's nothing to be afraid about," and off the animals would slink. An ancient oak tree seemed a likely place to stage this drama, but when I breathily whistled "Yankee Doodle" up to the word "pony," nothing happened. I felt a thump and a rush of heat in my body, as though I were blushing all over. No animals came roaring out of the shadows. I was on my own, all alone. God was not there for me. I didn't believe in God again until my first year at St. Timothy's, when I experienced that mystical change during my first communion.

Had I been an Indian child, I would have played *Holi* instead and been changed for a day into an omnipotent, omniscient being. That's the idea of *Holi*, a change of person, the remaking of oneself in one's own image or an idealized image, an exotic, mad metamorphosis, a moral holiday when the rules are suspended and one is transformed into anything one wants. Children in their imaginings play games like this all the time, and sometimes when they are grown-ups, their child selves remain with them, laughing, experimenting, joking, playing, curious, joyful, eager to learn. My father liked his child self and kept it alive. My grandmother, when I knew her, had put away her child self with her porcelain-headed dolls, which Mummy kept in a trunk in the attic. And since my mother had little sense of play, either, it was rare that anyone ever had time or wanted to play games with me.

Most of the time, I played alone. I liked fitting together the pieces of puzzles, just as I liked the red, cream, and blue sandstone building blocks with their pillars, arches, and turrets because I could construct elaborate buildings that could be made for an hour's pleasure before they had to be dismantled and put away so that my room could be "tidy" by the time I went to bed. I liked the large box which contained the Schoenhut Circus with several dozen performers, each with slotted hands that could be made to hold reins, whips, trapezes, and balancing poles. I liked the creaking sound that the handsome, white-maned, brown-felt-covered rocking horse made when I rocked back and forth in its red leather saddle, my right leg reddening in winter from the heat of the fireplace. Still, I felt foolish "riding" an artificial horse when I had always had a real pony to ride. I felt strangely embarrassed that the attendant nurse or governess should think I was having fun "pretending," since I had no aptitude for "pretending."

Something is pressing forward from the back of my mind to tell Veronica. But when I turn my head, she has vanished. I see her being chatted up by admirers, while an accordionist and a man with a lap piano both sitting cross-legged nearby provide the music for a man dancing as wildly as a statue of Nataraj, or Krishna himself, whirled into life.

I fantasize that my puckish therapist and Robert's mother, Kate, have materialized beside me as guests at the party.

"In all societies," Kate says, "festivals are found, occasions when superego prohibitions are periodically undone, occasions based on a social and biological necessity. Any society that creates chronic dissatisfaction and hardship for its members needs institutions and ceremonial guarantees through which the dammed-up tendencies toward rebellion may be channeled, permitted to express themselves."

My therapist nods his head in agreement. "Yes, quite right," he says. "When the superego is abolished, the powerless are permitted to play at participation, and this enables them to obey for one more year. The good mood that is a correlate of mania, on an intrapsychic basis, of what once took place between chiefs and subjects, becomes internalized and takes place between superegos and egos. In sleep, the ego is submerged nightly into the id from which it arises. In festivals and in mania, the superego may be drawn back into the ego."

The musicians play louder. "Oh, I'm so wonderful, I'm so grand! I'm the leader of a ten-man band," I hum to myself. I feel I know all the secrets of the universe but, for the life of me, I can't figure out what they are. Like the way reading Eliot sometimes used to make me feel. I remember reading, curled up on the leather cushions of a window-seat, about Brahma, the god of creation; Shiva, the god of destruction; Vishnu, the god of preservation, with each of these powers paradoxically containing its opposite. So Vishnu's powers of preservation, for example, involve acts of destruction, his avatars, his varied selves, as capable of bringing the devastation of fire as his Krishna-self could admonish Arjuna on the field of battle, "Not fare well, but fare forward, voyagers."

I loved that line: Not fare well, but fare forward, voyagers. And what was it in *Dry Salvages* that Eliot had written?

> I sometimes wonder if that is what Krishna meant—
> Among other things—or one way of putting the same thing;
> That the future is a faded song, a Royal Rose or a lavender
>   spray
> Of wistful regret for those who are not yet here to regret,
> Pressed between yellow leaves of a book that has never been
>   opened.
> And the way up is the way down, the way forward is the way
>   back.

The week after *Holi* rests in my red-smudged notebook like a watershed, a time of transition. Easter Day has also passed, but while I am getting dressed and having my bath, I continue to sing hymns of renascence with lots of Alleluias.

Pedestrians and bicyclists, wearing the clothes they had worn during *Holi*, look like mobile Easter eggs. Even the *dhobi*'s rigorous stone-pounding fails to remove the resistant mottlings of red and yellow, blue and green. I fold my stained *kameez* and stow it in the bottom of a metal trunk I have bought for storage.

I suppose the *kameez* is unwearable and useless to keep, but I want to keep it, with its red stains as indelible as memories.

In canals and pools, and the water-filled basins of stilled fountains, children float parchment stencils. Filling in the hollow spaces with colored powder, and then removing the cut-outs, called *Sanjhi*, they leave images of Krishna's idyllic childhood and boyhood, his cradle, cows and *gopis* drifting on the water until they feather away like curls of colored smoke.

One afternoon, Mulk drives me to Sultanpur Lake in Haryana State where birds are like a blizzard to the eyes—ducks, teal, cranes, egrets—and vultures' nests are clustered by the dozens in the branches of dead trees. He drives me to Sukhrali village where he has set up a cottage industry to make *mooras*, reed stools shaped like hourglasses. We sit on them beneath the shade of a podded laburnum while the villagers gather around us, squatting on their heels, sitting on stones and tree stumps, all of us striped and amber with the sun's tigerish light, interlaced with shade, while the children flit around us like fish among rocks, asking Mulk for "sweeties." When Mulk bawls them out for asking in English, they grizzle in Hindi until he produces a jute bag filled with fruit, candy, nuts, and raisins.

Then, with the evanescence of a *Sanjhi* image, Mulk is gone. To another village, another state, another project. Darling Mulk, Father India, whose voice and thoughts will always float in pools of silence in my mind.

Part Three

Ten

The hotel porter appears with two teacups filled with paint, black and white, to paint our names on my two fibreboard packing cases and our new metal trunks for which Gurdip has found double padlocks to secure the catches. Veronica will bring one tin trunk. I will bring one packing case. The other case and trunk are already filled and set aside to be stored at the hotel until our return.

The porter copies our names as Veronica has written them for him in capital letters. Alternate expressions of weariness and subjection, concentration and satisfaction settle on his face. His skin is the color of powdered cloves. Patient, humble, intensely eager to serve, for good measure he writes Handle with Care in Hindi on both cases and both trunks. Five hours go by before he completes this task.

Why does the porter remind me of Mr. Green, a Latin teacher I had? Mr. Green loved the Latin language and was delighted to teach it. "*Instruo, instruxi, instructum*," he would say sonorously. "Imagine pulling a kitchen stove toward you. Draw up a range. Draw up, arrange. Get it?" With a stare that glowed like a furnace—the same occasional fierce look of the hotel porter as he paints Veronica's name and mine—Mr. Green wrote with a great deal of squeaky pressure of chalk on the blackboard LABYRINTHUS, and beneath it: *A maze full of intricate passageways*. Then, turning to face us in our chair-connected desks, he announced that this was a word derived from the Greek *labrys*, a double-headed axe. "Perhaps we may assume that it was difficult to decide which edge of the axe to use. Just as it would be complicated for a person in a labyrinth to decide which passageway to take." A quotation, or its paraphrase, comes to mind, that art should serve as the axe for the frozen emotional sea within us. Kafka? I think so. Mr. Green pointed out the relationship between *noise* and *nausea*. He said that *per*, through, and *sona*, sound, when put together as *persona*, meant mask, such as those worn in early stage productions when the spectator could tell whether a play was a tragedy or a comedy by the appearances of the masks. I was fascinated.

Veronica says that body, speech, and mind are interdependent and interrelated. "Speech is between body and mind, hesitating between the mental realm of discrimination, concepts, names, expressible understanding, and the body realm of sound, which is a tangible thing." She reads from an invisible page imprinted in her mind: "Sound is the physical aspect of speech and names, while concepts are the mental aspect. In Eastern thought, all sounds emanate or originate from seed syllables. Sound is related speech. Pitch, rhythm, and volume are important but secondary."

Harmonies when I least deserve them, discords when I least expect them. So much for that subject. I shrug. "I feel like the little boy who went into the library and asked for a book about penguins. . . ."

"And when the librarian came out with a great stack of books, he said, 'That's more about penguins than I want to know,'" Veronica says, finishing the story for me. Her voice has the same affectionate, exasperated, impatient timbre my father's did when he would say to my mother, "Oh, dear, not that old chestnut again," as she embarked on some rambling tale about miscreant maids, clever dogs, or the sound of a stage coach that evaporated in the mist when she opened the window of a family house or a kinsman's castle to look out. (On other occasions, she would remind me that it was bad form to look out windows because it was evidence of undue curiosity, another one of those traits that, like cleverness, should be concealed as deftly as the tailor camouflaged my father's paunch beneath his well-cut coats.)

The porter receives the money I pay him in cupped hands, which he folds together, thumb to thumb, and raises to touch his turban. After he has pocketed the money in his shirt, he does a *mujra* of bowing low and touching his forehead with his right hand three times before backing out of the room. Not the slightest note of resentment or hostility in his deference. I look away uneasily, embarrassed.

Departures, the prospects of new beginnings, unsteady me, and I dawdle on purpose, checking the contents of my LV tote bag and camera bag, tightening the tops of the thermos bottles. I hope we are about to set off on a holiday in which Veronica's love for me and mine for her is such that we can be lifted wholly from regrettable past selves.

Gurdip sees to the loading of the car. Beaming with the bossy joy of managing everything, he repeatedly asks Veronica and me, "So how you are? When is it you are wanting to be going?" Finally, bills, chits, vouchers, tips, receipts are attended to— was there ever such a country for whimsical fiscal paper-work?—and we are on our way to Bharatpur and its sanctuary for migrating birds in an area once used as a duck-shooting preserve by local maharajas. Meenakshi Devi has told us of a day when a royal hunting party bagged more than four thousand ducks of many kinds. She has also told us to be sure to visit nearby Deeg and other attractions, so it will be at least a week before we drive south in Rajasthan to Jaipur and Udaipur, then on to Bangalore and Mysore.

As we follow the path of the Grand Trunk Road and that segment of the old Silk Route which leads from Delhi, looking out the car window, the wind cool in my face, images emerge and wind their way across my mind's landscape. Some are bitten into memory with the graver's tool of concentration on the new and unexpected. Others form a palimpsest, retracing and re-engraving the pleasingly familiar.

A black waterwheel revolves slowly next to the suave white-ness of egrets patrolling the river banks of the Jamuna. Small boys are kyoodling, as Robert would say, in the shade of a huge banyan with aerial roots roping from its branches and dark ground roots writhing away from it in the curry-colored dust. We have left the area of Delhi and crossed the border of Har-yana State. "Much new industry here. Many improvements. Many factories, Madam. Haryana State is the pride of the gore-ment, Madam," Gurdip says.

Palisades of eucalyptus trees with pale, pied, peeling bark

rise high along the road's edge on either side. Their delicate gray-green leaves cast a sun-dappled scrim over the ruins of abandoned mud and plaster villages and over villages with buildings new and alien: prefabricated houses, row after row of small squat concrete boxes with corrugated iron roofs. Then the compounds of factories churning out Rasna soft drinks, Hamam soap, Bata shoes, Tata textiles.

For Gurdip's sake, Veronica and I conceal our excess of distress at this profanation—after all, progress does not have to be ugly—turn away from this brutal, raw ugliness to exchange swift, flickering smiles of sympathy that are overtaken by the knowing, superior smiles of women involved with difficult men. "Deliver me from man's automatism," Veronica murmurs, shielding her mouth with the side of her hand so that Gurdip will not hear.

Gurdip tells us how many thousands of *lakhs*, how many dozens of *crores* more will be earned. It is all true, not a fairytale he is telling. He thrills to thoughts of economic activity. Industry! Progress! Material evolution! Perfection of the human state!

Veronica's eyes take on a peculiar faraway visionary look, much like an expression Robert had, as though he were gazing at some distant frontier. Around the pupil of Robert's right eye was a barely discernible *arcus senilis*, a white crescent prematurely caused from over-exposure to the sun. Veronica's eyes, those deep blue iris Isis eyes, are unmarred. With a subtle half-smile, she escapes into unconscious inaccessibility. Her lips begin to move. She is saying her mantras. She is as fascinating to watch as a cat.

The rows of box-like houses and factories billowing smoke and chemical odors reel past and disappear. The landscape lapses back to fields of greening wheat and plains that stretch away to the horizon. And then here, now, my first *kos minar*. Never having seen one of these old distance markers up close before means having to tell Gurdip to stop the car so that I can go jogging across the field to have a look.

"Watch out, Madam, watch out for the *nagas*, watch out for the rats, watch out for the pye dogs, watch out for the holes, watch out for those field workers, Madam, they may assume you are wanting to rob them," cautions Gurdip.

Veronica stays behind in the car. It's just an old *kos minar*, after all, nothing to see, and it's half a mile away. No thanks. She wants to meditate. "If I can," she adds, with a hint of asperity, a hint of martyrdom, a saintly lilt. If she can, indeed! Now that I have caused an interruption in her thought flow? Oh, Elsa Cloud, you may be as fascinating to watch as a cat, but you can also close up your eye, nose, and ear apertures as effectively as any pangolin. How you tweak me with guilt, pinch me with shame, yet are so earnest, so funny, so lovable, so maddening!

Off Gurdip and I go, kicking up dust. Set on an inward-sloping cube as a base, the *kos minar* is a stubby obelisk with a helmet-shaped top, a monument taller by far than any of the scrub acacia in the field. It suggests an erect phallus about to impregnate the sky.

"It is only a Mogul land-marker, Madam," Gurdip explains as we begin to slow our pace. "Abkar had them built, Madam, every two and one-half miles from Agra to Delhi, and all the way from Delhi to Chandigarh and Kashmir. A good rider could pass as many as sixty a day, Madam, in those bygone times, but now I doubt you could find more than a few dozen of these old things in all of India. Watch out for the goats, Madam."

My eyes on the *kos minar*, I haven't even noticed the goats, but there are a flock of them, brown, gray, white, black, white-and-black, white-and-brown, browsing close by, one of those marvelous chances of pattern and symmetry you find in diagrams of snowflakes and other forms of transcendental geometry. They scatter as we approach, no longer elements of an elegant system, and, in a hollow of arable land, here is a dusty bicycle, a hubble bubble, a bullock cart, and two male field workers. Gurdip barks and roars good-naturedly at them, then translates to me with unction his assurances that we are visitors, not thieves. The men mutter, draw back and watch us with suspicion. There is no thought of their robbing us? They think we might rob *them*? For a moment, it's like *Holi* all over again.

My eyes travel up the stone base of the *kos minar*, up the brick cone with its patches of old plaster, up to where a *coucal*, a jungle crow, black with chestnut wings, is perched on the rounded top. Instead of the *coucal*, I imagine an oil lamp, shielded from the wind with a pierced brass cover, lighting the way at night, a sixteenth-century lighthouse on land.

When one travels, one eats, thinks of food, needs food, wants food, looks for food in a way one never seems to do at home. Having skipped lunch, Veronica and I are now starved. Gurdipji, Gurdipji, what to do? Gurdip enjoys this moment, prolongs it, savors the fare of his own words. "In the gorement's new scheme for tourism development, there are many resthouses, Miss Veronica, Madam. Very new, very clean. All modern conveniences, Miss Veronica. All named after birds, Madam. You are recalling the Rosy Pelican, the same name as the beer, at Sultanpur, Madam? The Sun Bird at Sukrakund, Miss Veronica?

At Hodal, we can stop at the Dabchick. Good meals are being served there. No need to wait dinner until we reach Bharatpur." He swivels his head to smile broadly at us and waggles it by way of taciturn assurance of our assent.

And so we come to the Dabchick, a structure whose harsh, raw look is somewhat softened by the papery magenta of bougainvillea. It is set about by an Anglo-Indian garden of hollyhocks, marigolds, petunias. Scraggly hibiscus stick out pollen-bristling yellow tongues. Shall we sit in the interior dining room with its red and turquoise naugahyde armchairs? No, better to be outside with the skittering bats on an upper terrace where metal chairs scrape against concrete. The waiter, in a frayed and shabby jacket, has dirty fingernails. No matter. They serve beer? Gurdip is all jolly smiles. *Bote atcha!* Before long, he is diving into the meat and mess of his meal. Propping his bearded chin on his elbowed-up left hand, he swabs gravy and secures chunks of vegetables and meat with a *chapatti* folded as a pincer in his right hand. He grunts with contentment. After a long drive, this is the life. *Ohe!*

It is the hour of cow dust, and a flight of ducks flap Veronica's initial across the pearly, paling sky. The silence that is at the center of everything muffles the abrasive chair scrapings but not the cries of peacocks. One streams metallic blue through the garden below, its tail gleaming like the wake of a comet. Tilting back its delicately crested head, it delivers a searing feline shriek, and as the sound echoes, in counterpoint, a gentle sonic wave of the chiming of distant temple bells rolls in.

At nightfall, we are still driving. Past occasional villages where the air is bronze with the glow of kerosene lamps, past stopping places for buses where fires flare in the wood-burning stoves of *chai* shops, Veronica dozes. We stop for tea where the country buses do so that I can have my feet massaged by a *malish-wallah* and my head rubbed until my hair is tangled into a golli-wog's matted frizz.

We are now in Rajasthan, Rajput country, the land of princes, five kilometers from Bharatpur town. Ten minutes later, we arrive at the government tourist lodge for visitors to the Keoldeo Ghana sanctuary for migratory water birds. The stars overhead are like jasmine flowers in the soft darkness of the sky. Orion. Algol and Aldebaran in Taurus. The Corona Borealis. Spica in Virgo. Pollux in Castor . . . Altair and Betelgeuse. Antares and Formalhaut. Where are they, all those lovely stars and constellations? Robert could have pointed to them all in a minute, but I am too tired to search them out. I yearn only for a long, deep soak in a steaming hot bath, but our bedroom's so-called bathroom is a mingy affair with a lavatory, a sink, a dipper, and a feeble shower that splashes directly on the tiled floor and then drains beneath a rug-sized platform of wooden slats.

"The lust for comfort is the murder of the soul," but I'd sell my soul right this minute for hot water forcefully purling into one of those great old footed English porcelain baths manufactured for tall, hefty Colonial types. Hindus, Moslems, the Indian government, whoever is responsible, may consider lounging in your own bathwater unclean, showers preferable. Not I. I no longer have the grace to be amused by the minor inconveniences of travel. *I want a hot bath.* Veronica, as I was at twenty-five, a traveler insouciant about mundane comforts, seeing herself as I once did divested of comfortable concerns and garbed in more becoming cultural canonicals, suggests food. Perseph-

one proffering a sop to Cerberus. With a show of spirited, solicitous humility, she telephones for food, helps me to unpack.

The room boy soon arrives, banging at the door, crashing in
with a tray which he slaps down on a wooden table, making
sure that there is water in the saucers in which each table leg
rests to daunt climbing ants and other insects. His eyes pounce
on us with pleased alertness. How well disposed the gods are to
be hallowing him the hopportunity of practicing Hinglish with
Hinglish-speaking guests. "Ow izzit you fink I yam esspeaking
Hinglish? My pronunciation, that for I hask you, his being gor-
rect?" He is a teacher in Bharatpur town, he says, but he makes
more money as a room boy. So what does he teach his students?

"*Namuck*," he says. "*Namuck* his salt. Salt his being sodium
chloride. *Namuck pani* his being salt water. Salt water his being
sodium chloride hand eyedrochloric hassid, two parts hand
hoxygen. Hand I yam hinstructing my esstudents that garden
his being *bagh*. B for Bumbay, A for effort, G for green, H for
'orse." (Whatever the room boy's local Rajasthani dialect is,
bagh is the Hindi word for garden. I add to the scribblings in my
notebook that gardens are my *bagh*.)

Once started, he is unstoppable. He presses his teachings
upon us until we are desperate. All my fault, of course, for
encouraging him in the first place. We get rid of him finally by
eating what we can of the food, signing the chit, slipping him
an enormous tip, and saying we are terribly tired, would he
excuse us, we are most interested in what he has to say, but we
must sleep. We have to be up before six the next morning to go
out on the marsh to see the birds.

"But his not being henny birdies," he says as he is leaving at
last with our tray. "The hend of the esseason of migration his

being four weeks gone. There his being very few birdies on the
jheel. Pakshi nai."

My heart sinks for the lot of Indian education in Bharatpur
and for the next day's prospects.

"Sweet dreams," Veronica murmurs sleepily.

We have come to the *jheel* through a path in a dense forest of
vaulting, vine-scarfed trees, and it opens before us, a marshy
clearing where there are scattered trees, some soaring tall and
bare and gray from the water, others with a little fling of grassy
land about them, like tiny islands. There is a milky blueness of
dissolving night air, and the marsh throws up a mist. A rowboat
is lying off from a landing stage of broken-down masonry, and
Ranjit, a young, dark-faced boy, hired to be there at dawn, hauls
in the boat and helps Veronica and me into it so that we can sit
side by side in the stern. Then he casts off and poles us away
from the shore.

The water is dark and filmy, with a stony bottom, and the
pole raises clouds of submarine dust. There are tufts of reeds,
floating spreads of white lilies, and mats of pink and mauve-blue
water hyacinths with dragonflies hovering above them, their
tetractine wings finely net-veined like fins, their minnowlike
imprecision of movement and quivering suspensions seeming
more like a performance beneath the water than in the air above
it. The water trembles as we slip through it. Reality melts away
in the blue dimness of the vaporous world of the *jheel*, a phantom world between night and sun, all pearly mist and goblet-
shaped trees, their branching cups twiggy rather than leafy,
light green shimmering cups set on tall shafts of gray that jut
above the mirroring water of a marsh that stretches back to the

horizon. The sound of fish splashing can be heard from a great distance. You can see scintillating arcs, then silvery spray as the fish disappear. A curious metallic pinging, like a repetitive treble note of a xylophone, reveals itself as coming from a woodpecker, scuttling in desultory spurts up the dark bole of a mango tree on the shore behind us. The tree's panicles of upstanding creamy flowers are candelabras of clarity on which I focus my field glasses, catching sight of a *ghileri*, a palm squirrel, twinkling into view on an overhead branch, the chipmunk-like rodent's white stripes on its back said to be the marks of Vishnu's five stroking fingers. Myna birds, invisible in the foliage, salute the dawn with creaky shrieks, and a wild boar with two babies trots out of the shade below, mama jauntily displaying her aggressive superiority, the babies not quite so sure of themselves. As we head toward the center of the *jheel*, water fowl rise and wheel in the moist blue air. Ducks bob like corks close to the far shore, which is edged with deep reeds and fringed with trees that are like puffs of green light. Cormorant-like birds plummet from tree branches into the water as if they had been killed by some unheard, invisible weapon when Ranjit poles the boat not far from them. Although I have the sanctuary's checklist of animals and birds and the definitive Indian bird book by the renowned ornithologist Salim Ali, as well as a pen and a notebook in my tote bag, I am not ready to look at birds. I feel suspended in the delicate mystery of the *jheel* itself, an innocent phantom world of misty quiet and solitude, soothing, sustaining, magical, hushed, the air soft and moist and cool.

Standing in the bow, Ranjit poles us forward, raises his pole with sinewy arms to let us glide ahead, then poles us forward again with a little whispering susurrus of breaking water.

Veronica's face has a semi-abstracted look of wonder, her lips parted, her eyes large, long, bright. The sun is rising now, and the light is palest filtered gold in this world of mist and water lilies, unpeopled except for Veronica, Ranjit, and me.

Like moving pieces of light and shade, antelopes file along the far shore, buff-colored with white bellies and hindparts, the females like large fawns. A male with them breaks from the cover of a bush. He stands for a moment in profile, with his great, annulated, spiraling horns raked back, and I am with Robert in Botswana, known then as Bechuanaland, watching sable antelope larger than these "black buck," but with the same ears, like arum lilies, that go pinky-red when the sun shines through them. All of a sudden, the antelopes flee in bounding leaps with astonishing speed, leaving their shadows on the air behind them. A *nilgai* bull, bluish-gray like a wilde-beeste, has scared them off. The *nilgai* comes stepping into the dun-gold quiet of the tree-fringed shore, its horns plain and unprepossessing, and is unabashed by our presence, staring straight at us and then browsing with no more concern than a *bhainsee*. A *nilgai*, literal translation, a blue cow, is a large Indian antelope with a sheaf of long hair, like a displaced beard, on its throat. Curiouser and curiouser. As I stare through my field glasses, I feel as awed as Alice in Wonderland. A black-capped kingfisher shivers close to the *nilgai*, vibrating its wings like the hummingbirds used to in our Jamaican garden, and then zips like a falling fragment of sapphire into the water and up in a jeweled glitter with a small strip of silver in its bright coral beak. Suddenly the sunshine issues over the *jheel* in a ravishing ocher light, spreading slowly until everything as far as you can see is encompassed in it.

I have always been passionate, besotted by birds, their voices, their songs, their feathers, their wings, the way they move on the ground and in the air, and especially by the birds of my childhood, the birds in the peach tree, and the pigeons in the loft with whom I shared my life. My mother often countered my chronic excitement with an anecdote about having heard a cardinal singing "Radio Keith, Radio Keith," a song so insistent that it prompted her to invest in a stock of the same name which shot up in value and earned enough dividends to pay for an antique gaming table.

If my mother trivialized the beauty and importance of birds, my nurses had not. Storks brought babies. Not a sparrow fell without God's noticing it. Doves surrounded angels somewhere in heaven above the clouds—those castling, extraordinary clouds that formed and re-formed images of animals, boats, human faces, foaming waves, and chimeras with curling tails I could have watched forever if I hadn't been told to stop mooning about and reminded that it was time to do something else. I assumed that birds, like the hidden and then seeable people in the clouds, had a companionable relationship with God, and flew so high that they must glimpse heaven. No doubt about it, birds were special. Watching birds feed, bathe, nest, and fly out of sight, I sensed with the mythologists why one gives wings to all that we endow with supernatural power and freedom. Birds. To see them, hear them, these symbols of human souls, thought, imagination, these emblems of the swiftness of spiritual processes, these dream symbols of longing for what might be lost, these lovely winged creatures that fly among trees and across the face of the sun and moon, swift as a moment of sexual passion, enduring as the spirit.

When I began to burrow into books, reading without any discrimination, growing another self in the world of ideas, the realm of Cloud Cuckoo Land built by birds who entered into a friendly relationship with the gods was as easy to visualize as the pigeon loft above the gardener's garage.

Now the pigeons of my childhood, the pigeons studding the domes of the Moti Masjid in Chandni Chowk, Cloud Seven, Seventh Heaven, Cloud Cuckoo Land, and the birds on the *jheel* all swim together in my mind with Aristophanes' play *The Birds* and their imaginary realm. What was the name of Cloud Cuckoo Land in Greek? *Nephelokokkygia?* A duck quacking as it swims across our wake sounds like that. I make the connection of the Spanish slang word for the male organ "La paloma" and the dove, and the French slang term for the Holy Ghost, "Le pigeon," and see the spiritual connection, the endowment of wings to all that is superior, the Winged Victory, the winged Egyptian sun god, the angels in heaven, Pegasus the winged horse; Athena, Artemis, and Aphrodite. Veronica has told me that Mercury's winged heels are comparable to the special kind of shoes known as "Light Feet" with which Buddhist saints travel through air in Tibetan philosophical scripture.

I was attacked by an enraged catbird when I was a child, a curious child, parting the branches of a hedge of mock orange, seductively sweet-smelling, and finding there a catbird's nest with tiny unfledged birdlings, gaping-mouthed, mouths agape (and when years later I read of *agape*, the love feast of primitive Christians which ended with the "holy kiss," those birds were nested behind my eyes). It was the last sight I remember seeing before there was a piercing shrill, a stab of pain behind my ear, and a parent catbird flapping, shrilling around my head. I felt my skin go hot, then cold. I turned and ran, the bird behind me pecking at my head, shrilling, shrilling, pecking, pecking, the pain anticipated ever greater as I ran screaming across the lawn, this way, that way, toward the birdbath, toward the paddock, toward the playhouse, the catbird whirring, shrilling, pecking whichever way I turned. I clasped my hands behind my head and the pecks pierced the skin on my fingers, a pain my entire body screamed against, fear intensifying pain, pain intensifying fear. As a child, I was not a screamer about physical pain, almost stoical, but then I screamed and screamed. I was so small that the catbird's flight behind me would hardly have been visible in the open, and must have been obscured completely when I ran parallel with the parterre gardens, the hedgerows, and the trees. Perhaps the nurse in charge and the maids thought that I was playing one of my solitary games, or that my screams were a radio turned on somewhere in the house. I ran inside North-lea's kitchen, through the pantry, the dining room, the hallway, pounding up the stairs, rushing to the guestroom where my grandmother was staying on her annual visit. "Let that be a lesson to you," she said. "You should never frighten or disturb baby birds." She wiped my face with her scented lace-edged handkerchief. "You're lucky that it was just a little catbird and not a great big swan. Never let a mother pen or a father cob ever catch you near their cygnets, or then you'll really have some-thing to cry about."

My thoughts go whirling around my head like the hula hoop Veronica long ago set in orbit around her waist. After the cat-bird episode, I don't remember ever feeling afraid of birds. The outcome of my experience was a counterphobic attitude, a mild obsession about birds expressed in impulses to feed them, protect them, watch them, an impelling awareness of them. I remember coaxing Toucan Livecheaper, the bird Robert and I had for a pet in California, down from his perch on the top of a palm tree by waving a chunk of tomato speared on the hook-end of a mop-handle, and calling "Here birdie, here birdie." The nuns across the way in the hospital of Our Lady of the Angels must have thought I was crazy. At the same time in my life, I attached a mobile of familiar birds to Veronica's crib and watched her reach up to play with their plastic forms.

Ranjit poles toward trees mantled in white birds, grassy hummocks iced below in white guano. But even this leisurely gliding is too fast for me. We have to stop so that I can take in the whole scene, see which birds I want to watch closely, just sit there, quiet, in the middle of the *jheel* and *look*.

Ducks bob, dive, up-end, waddle about on mud bunds beneath thorny, podded acacia trees and lantern bushes. Flying high and low are pintails, teal, shovellers, gadwalls, mallards, pigeons, dabchicks, comb ducks, spotbilled ducks, red-crested pochards and tufted pochards. Orangey-brown Brahminy ducks, goose-like, a few grazing at the water's edge, are the "wariest of ducks," according to Salim Ali, and breed and nest in Tibet and Ladakh. Veronica, Ranjit, and I peer at them through my field glasses. But ducks are ducks, and unless they are up-ending in a way that seems almost fulsomely coy, after a while, I see nothing really riveting about ducks.

The jacanas are something else. I adore jacanas.

"You would, Mummy," Veronica says. "They don't just *walk* on the water. They *run* on it." Watching my expression, she catches her lower lip in her teeth, releases it, and giggles.

Winging their way back to breed in Tibet and Ladakh, a skein of bareheaded geese, resonantly honking, fly above us. They leave a few stragglers nearby on an islet and several large gaggles on the marsh bank to our left. Delicately marked with white, gray, and brown, they have pink bills and orange legs. With two black bars striping the napes of their white necks, they remind me of the geese painted on Chinese scrolls and inlaid on Coromandel screens.

I have let Ranjit pole ahead—"*Ahista, ahista* (slowly, slowly) and *teroo, teroo* (wait, wait)"—so that I can look at a colony of gray herons, long-legged, with graceful sloping backs and S-shaped necks; patient, circumspect, the herons Dylan Thomas must have had in mind when he wrote of "heron-priested shores." Veronica hugs herself as she watches the herons in flight. I find myself making the same crossed-armed, self-hugging gesture. A single heron, its neck folded back, crested head drawn in upon powerful shoulders, wings beating in deliberate, steady motions, long legs trailing like twin red streamers, is momentarily silhouetted against the sun. Veronica reaches over the side of the boat to pick a white water lily for me.

"*Teroo, teroo*, Ranjit," I whisper. A pair of Sarus cranes has appeared, the only ones we have seen so far on the *jheel*. Great tall birds, they stand about four-and-one-half feet. They are gray with naked red heads and upper necks and long red legs. Like trumpeter swans, they are said to pair for life. They stride toward us, unafraid. Blacktailed godwits flap away from their path. Ranjit says that during their mating season Sarus cranes attack *bhainsees* and even people if they come near them. He poles rapidly past them, alarming coots which race along the water, half-running, half-flying, before they launch themselves into the golden air. We almost run aground on the island of white-mantled trees we've been heading for. You can hardly see the trees for the storks and their nests. Black-necked, white-necked, white, openbilled, adjutant storks and painted storks, all the varieties listed on the checklist are here. The openbilled storks have bills that look warped and don't close properly. Arching mandibles leave a gap between the upper and lower parts. Salim Ali suggests that the significance and function of this curiously shaped bill may have to do with opening the thick shells of large *Ampullaria* snails found on marshes, the soft body and viscera of which, he says, form a large proportion of the storks' food, but even Salim Ali says no one really knows why the bills of the openbilled storks are the way they are. "It calls for special investigation," he says.

In this extensive heronry, I see two adjutant storks. They look somewhat like the carrion-eating marabou storks of Africa, about four feet tall and ugly. Not just ugly in the dirty, vulture-like way, but really ugly. Ranjit obligingly poles us close so that we can have "a good sense of them." The storks have been marching along with their dirty black, gray, and white backs to us, and now they turn and clatter their mandibles. Their bills are large—long, wide, thick (Salim Ali says "enormous," as he does about the bills of pelicans)—and their clattering is rapid, amazingly loud. They have naked red heads and necks underhung with long, naked, red, flaccid pouches dangling to where their navels would be if they had them.

"If the pouches were more southerly, those storks would be dead-ringers for the flashers I used to see in Central Park," Veronica says in a calm, matter-of-fact tone.

I want to leap out of the boat and stab the two storks, stab them over and over and over again with a sharp knife. All I can see in my mind's eye is the flash of a knife in my hand as I—no, not the flash of a knife, the flash of a cheap mirror that Veronica lifts to break over my head, and the flash of a mirror framed with seashells that I lift to break over hers.

But it is not a knife I feel in my hand. Not a mirror. In my hand is the white water lily Veronica picked for me, the lily, like the *thangka* of the *lila* she painted for me in which defilements are transformed into beatitudes.

Veronica and I lull ourselves by the *jheel* for a week, going out in the boat at dawn, and coming back to shore in time for breakfast; afterwards, Veronica feeds a baby deer—one of the sanctuary's pets—with a nippled baby's milkbottle, and gives it her fingers to suck and lick with its rough black tongue. She feeds it scraps of soft wheat bread, and it follows her about on its loose legs, and when she sits down with her skirt flowering around her, when the fawn kneels to lie down and puts its head in her lap, I think of the way a unicorn lays its head in the lap of the Virgin Mary in the medieval *Dame à la Licorne* tapestries. Symbolic of chastity and also an emblem of the sword or of the word of God, the unicorn is tireless when pursued, yet falls meekly to the ground when it is approached by a virgin, which seems to suggest that it is symbolic of sublimated sex. The deer is *not* a unicorn. It has two horns, twin crescents as fragile and delicate as the wrought-iron filigree in the gates of the Rashtra-pati Bhavan. "But you do remind me of the *Dame à la Licorne*, just the same," I say to Veronica as I lie down on the grass beside her, chevroning an arm over my face to safeguard my eyelids from the sun's white-hot noonday blaze.

"Oh, Mum, why do you always want to think of me as such a goody-goody?" The note of impatience in Veronica's tone re-

solves into a melodious chord of laughter as she tells me that a
kitten she had in Dehra Dun slept just the same way, with a paw
over its face.

I look at my daughter, her creamy brown-rose skin, her good
jaw, her straight nose, her full mouth, and long, straight, corn-
silk hair, and wish that this moment might last forever. Is there
anywhere else a sun as bright, thick-petaled golden flowers
more poignantly perfumed, a fawn's white-spotted pelt that as
I stroke it is like stroking my daughter's mind and my own with
a gentle comb of contentment? Bharatpur. What does it matter
that the avocets have returned to the Great Rann of Kutch and
the great white cranes have emigrated to Siberia and the flocks
of Demoiselle cranes from the African and Asian north have
vanished from the *jheel*? What does it matter that we haven't
sighted the pangolin, the leopard cat, the short-nosed fruit bat,
the long-eared hedgehog, or even the "house mouse" on the
nature reserve's checklist?

The *jheel* with the birds that remain suits me just as it is. We
discover another marsh on the other side of the one we first
boated on. It is separated from it by a forested peninsula which
tails away into a narrow wooded pathway on which we walk for
miles at dusk when parties of purple moor hens, blue-winged
and violet-backed, fly low over the reed beds. At the hour of
cow dust, the *bhainsees* come walking down the path two-by-
two, all dusty, with gnats a moted mandorla around them. Their
eyes are slanted upward, and their variegated horns curl up,
down, flat against their brown-black necks. They file along the
path, many with bells around their dusty necks. They stop and
clumsily slide and scramble down the banks and into the water
for their evening swim. One evening, a flock of snow white

spoonbills is aligned along the bank. They wade in the shallow water, move forward with outstretched necks, swinging their long flat bills which have the shape of large, wooden cooking spoons, black with a yellow tip. They neither fly nor scatter. The flock simply parts to make a single passageway for which the *bhainsees* queue and then swim through. There is something Biblical about the scene. I think of Noah's Ark and Hicks's *Peaceable Kingdom*. To feel pleasure and to be able to share that pleasure is the only antidote to loneliness that I know.

Eleven

Away from the shade, the heat quivers up from the ground. There is a Mogul palace in Bharatpur I'd like to see, turned now into a museum for collections of sculpture and memorabilia of the Maharajas of Bharatpur. "Oof," Veronica grunts. "Do you really want to go?" On principle— the overriding sense of nowness, of living in the present, the Buddhist view—Veronica professes not to care about the past. I argue that without an awareness of the past you can have no sense of the present. The past may become your attic, your cellar, your treasure trove. Accommodating, Veronica says she is not against the *experience* of seeing the museum. So off we drive with Gurdip as our capable chauffeur.

We see women winnowing grain in the fields and walking along the roadside with boyish athletic strides. They no longer glide and float as they do in saris. Saris have vanished and have been replaced by the Rajasthani costume of backless string-tied bodices short enough to leave part of the midriff bare, a great swinging skirt elaborately pleated and tied with a drawstring below the navel, a jacket, and a billowing scarf used as a veil or mantle. (Saris for women, *dhotis* for men, and mantles for monks had been the fashion in India until the arrival of the conquering dynasties of Muslims who brought with them scissors and needles to cut and sew cloth into garments adapted to their equestrian life.) Gorgeous red skirt, deep blue jacket, acidic yellow scarf; orange, blue, magenta; orange, purple, peacock blue; red, black, white; parakeet green, orange, magenta; mustard yellow, lapis lazuli blue—those wonderful, brilliant, risky Indian color combinations are scattered here and there like dabs of vivid impasto on the dusty monochromatic landscape. Thin ankles weighted with carved bands and thick coils of silver. Belled neck chains. Wrist bangles of silver and glass. You can hear them jingling through the open car windows. Some of the women balance globe-shaped pots on their heads, not only one, but often two or three, tiered according to size. As a base, there's a doughnut-shaped ring decorated with cowrie shells and a cowrie-and-mirror-spangled streamer.

I've tried balancing just the ring on my head and have only been able to walk back and forth in our room at the lodge a few times before the ring slides off. How do these Rajasthani women manage with their water pots? How can they walk over rough ground without ever reaching up a hand to steady the pots?

"Too much practice, Madam," Gurdip replies mechanically. "Too much practice."

The colors of the women's clothes continue to fascinate me, and I think again of the *thangka* Veronica painted for me and the colors that represent defilements transformed into beatitudes. Now Veronica draws a diagram like a cross. One color, she says, represents each cardinal point. Red is west. Blue is east. Yellow is south. Green is north. White is in the center. Red, congeneric with the peacock and the lotus, is a sign of power and energy. It represents humor, lust, desire, and craving transformed into compassion and discriminating awareness. Blue, congeneric with lightning bolts and animal life, represents anger transformed into the mirror-like wisdom of equanimity, receptive and reflective at the same time. Compulsive action and ineptitude are transformed into spontaneity, selflessness, and blissful action, all-accomplishing awareness symbolized by green, the color which is favored by warriors, and by crossed bolts of lightning. Yellow, the color of gold and of prosperity, symbolizes pride, closed-mindedness, and stinginess transformed into the impartiality and even-mindedness of discriminating wisdom. White, the color of gods, symbolizes the fascination with the senses, ignorance transformed into panoramic vision.

Blue is my favorite color. In Eastern symbolism blue represents east. The sun rises in the east, and there is the dawning then of the sky's blue. In Western symbolism, east is symbolic of Christ, the Sun in the Universe, while blue is the color of truth, of heavenly love and of heaven itself, the traditional color also of the Virgin Mary's robes. Psychologists claim it is the color of introspection, deliberation, conservatism, favored by people with reflective minds and a predilection for tranquillity.

I chose yellow for Veronica's baby trousseau. In Christian art, yellow is the emblem of the sun and divinity, of revealed truth. Yellow is the sacred color chosen along with maroon for the robes of Buddhist monks, the color of divinity in the paintings of the Renaissance. Psychologically, the preference for yellow, a color which attracts intellectuals and idealists, suggests imagination, a search for self-fulfillment, contemplation and intro-spection, even, as in Eastern symbolism, of discriminating wis-dom.

Red, the color of fire, the color of blood. It is used during Pentecost, which commemorates the coming of the Holy Ghost, and is symbolic of both love and hate, the Church's color for sovereign power and for martyred saints. But it is also the color beloved by carefree extroverts and optimists and activists. Maroon, on the other hand—maroon indicates passion tem-pered by conscience; strength, bravery, ambition tempered by struggle and difficulty. The peacock, in Christian art, symbol-izes immortality and, because of its many-eyed plumes, the "all-seeing" Church. "Why do Buddhists associate the peacock with the color red?" I ask.

"First tell me about green and white," Veronica says.

Is she testing my patience? Green? Green has the universal appeal of nature and symbolizes the triumph of spring over winter, of life over death—psychologically, a sign of balance and normality. In Christian art, the mixture of yellow and blue suggests charity and the regeneration of the soul through good works; it is the color of the Epiphany and of Christ's initiation into the Temple. When Demeter lost Persephone, all the trees of the earth withered, and Demeter's soul and spirit were win-try with grief.

White is the color of light, of innocence and holiness of life. It is worn by Christ after his resurrection. In India, it is the color of mourning.

"White represents peace in the Buddhist tradition," Veron-ica says. "White is the color of the body. The mind is blue. Speech is red. That's why monks wear red or maroon, to remind them always of the words of Lord Buddha." She adds that she had not wanted to tell me before of the association of red with speech because she thought I might find the connection between the color of speech and screaming peacocks ridiculous.

"No more ridiculous than the belief that the flesh of the peacock doesn't decay, and its association, therefore, with immortality. Red speech," I muse. "Fiery words. Red symbolizing lust, transformed into the spermatic word of God, incandescent and unconscious."

"Oh, *Mum!*" Veronica laughs. "You're such a *nut!*"

We have arrived in the small marketplace of Bharatpur. Before us, etiolated in the white sunlight, is the colonnaded palace and its courtyard laid out with quatrefoil pools and fountains. No water comes from the fountains, and the pools are dry. Ring doves flutter about the *chattris* on the four corners of the roof; with sparrows and mynahs, they nest among the cornices and beams of cloistered arches.

The palace, in a state of dignified decay, holds within its walls the remnants of royal living. Vast chambers, a-stammer with light, spinning with birds, are filled with ancient sculpture, some figures so weathered that they are like fetuses in the womb of time. Many of the Hindu and Buddhist figures have smashed faces and broken noses, evidence of the Moguls' iconoclastic fury. A tenth-century sandstone sculpture of Surya, the god of the sun, with his consort and two female personifications of the dawn, remains unharmed, dusty, but intact. A sweeper brushes the main hall's stone floor with a broom of sandalwood twigs. There is the constant soft moaning of the pigeons, the sound of buzzing bees and flies, the hissssssht-hussssssshting of the sweeper's broom. Veronica and I have left our sandals outside and, barefooted, we walk soundlessly through the arched and chambered halls. We are the only visitors.

There is a lovely *hamman*, with *pietra dura* floors patterned with chevrons of flowers. *Jali* windows let in a little light. Sunken octagonal pools for bathing, domed ceilings, dressing rooms with faded frescoed walls from which jut the iron hooks once used to hang lamps and canopies. Serene, peaceful, cool. The museum custodian appears, flustered that he has not seen us arrive, asking us for the admission fee of one rupee each and thrusting upon us a receipt.

We come upon more sculpture of sandstone and red stone of the Gupta's dynasty's mid-period, almost two hundred sculptures in all, deities, devotees, animals, torsos. Broken sculpture, sculpture mutilated by the Moguls, sculpture that has been well-preserved, all just ranged along walls, no glass cases, no attempt at mountings, displays, lighting, no velvet guard ropes; doves, sparrows, swallows perching and flying all about. I try to describe it, try to sum it all up, and scribble in my notebook: cool, mystical, faded grandeur, sad and lovely.

When we return to the courtyard to retrieve our sandals, the custodian tells us there is more to see in another part of the palace. Blinding white light in the courtyard, then the cool shade of the cloisters, then up a two-storey flight of steps, clutching our sandals in our hands. We have come to rooms paneled in dark wood with Victorian lighting fixtures, the former living quarters of one of the late Maharajas of Bharatpur. The wooden floors are covered with strips of threadbare Axminster carpeting that are rough and warm against the soles of my feet, the flooring beneath the runners tilting and uneven. Here and there are dark spaces where bits and pieces of the floor are missing, rotting, chewed through with holes deserted or occupied by rats, mice, snakes or *ghileris* (chipmunks), "all sleeping and not coming out until night-time," the custodian says. Everything to be seen is housed in and on top of Victorian glass cases and glass-fronted cabinets, a gloriously surrealistic hodge-podge and treasure trove.

The first exhibit is labeled NUMISMATICS. Veronica suggests we "skip that, Mummy, shall we?" and in any other museum in the world, I would, but here. . . . And yes, how extraordinary, here are coins in currency when Alexander the Great skirted the Himalayan heights with his Macedonian troops, enjoyed the splendors of rajahs' palaces and recorded his fascination with India's strange animal life—elephants and rhinoceroses, parrots and peacocks, whose likenesses are punched on these rough, round silver coins, the earliest currency of India, mingled in the same case with an American silver dollar, an American fifty-cent piece, a quarter, a dime, a nickel, a penny, the small change of the nineteen-forties, and a fling of third century Gupta gold coins, copper pice, and silver annas and rupees minted by the princely states. In another room, with a hand-painted sign saying ARMOURY SECTION, there are silver- and gold-hilted swords, ivory-handled daggers, iron lances, and shields made from rhinoceros leather side by side with rifles, revolvers, cannons, conch shell carriers for gunpowder, helmets, bamboo bows and arrows, a torpedo shell (the catalogue describes it as "torpedo in the form of Aeroplane for destroying the ship in sea-water bombshell") and leg armor worked with floral designs of gold.

The ARTS, CRAFTS AND INDUSTRY section reveals inkpots, sandalwood sun helmets, ivory-handled fly whisks, hand fans that are like stiffened flags on sticks, a cowrie embellished "pitcher sustainter on head," rosewater sprinklers, antimony cases and boxes, a chart illustrating the nib-making industry of Great Britain, lamps, hookahs, pottery, and an enameled cigarette case.

The attic at Malahide Castle where many of James Boswell's diaries and journals were stored along with the ballgowns of Margaret, his wife, had had this same surrealistic sense of time-warp. On occasion, paintings would be shouldered down the attic stairs to cover the moldy excrescences of paint and plaster on the walls of the downstairs rooms. One of these paintings turned out to be the only family portrait ever painted by Franz Hals. The excitement of its subsequent sale—part of the proceeds were used to glaze the walls of the drawing room a shade of red I remember as the color of tomato soup—appealed to my childhood penchant for the serendipitous, reinforced my conviction that life was filled with surprises and chance rewards in the way that my birthday cakes used to be filled with charms wrapped in oiled paper.

I scribble in my notebook, listing everything, this excerpting from reality, these pure data, this propriety of sheer information a comfort and sustenance to me as I experience the friction of these haphazardly placed objects, their cumulative humor and charm, evocative stimuli filling my heart with nostalgia for all the people and worlds they bring back to life.

CHILDREN SECTION. I am mesmerized, checking items against their catalogue listings. Brass toys representing Ganesha, Brahma, Vishnu, and Hanuman; a Standing European Deity of Bronze [the Virgin Mary], Two Yaks, Elephants with Howdah, Three Lions, Two Scorpions, Four Peacocks, Dancing Pigeon,

Raindeer (sic); Papier Maché toys, Vegetables, Fruits; Black
Marble Snake, Glass Bottles with Toys Inserted Inside; ivory
dice, Wooden Toy Aeroplanes, gramophone electric-driven,
chirping bird in cage, rock salt, cut glass, bottles with letters
written inside, monkey with moving head, lamp in elephant leg,
Persian hanging lamps, Japanese lantern, German lantern, two
sets of ivory pieces for chess game, soapstone models of Taj
Mahal, Kangaru pair (two kangaroos), Christian Deities (crèche
figures), Hindu Musicians, Chawpur Bichat of Beads.

This last consists of eight little beaded beehive shapes on a
game board. The game of chawpur, but what does *bichat* mean?
Why aren't there more details, provenances, descriptions? On
an odd little dwarf figure made of stone, the label is only "Circa?
Find place no known."

"You like the swallows and sparrows flying through and
nesting in the museum," Veronica says. "You can't have that and
expect to have print-out information like the Smithsonian as
well."

How tolerant she is, how sensible, how vexing.

ZOOLOGICAL EXHIBITS: A stuffed crocodile, eight feet long:
"Photo depicting Tibbet yaks"; the jaw of an elephant, the jaw
of a gavial; a "box and teapoy in an elephant leg"; birds' eggs,
human spines and teeth; a "life-sketch of bed-bugs," a "life-
sketch of a mosquito," the fangs of a cobra, stuffed birds beneath bell-jars that are labeled "flower vases"; a stuffed cobra in
striking position; miscellaneous used postage stamps, a drawing
of a train, "fine embroidery in wool depicting a flower pot, done
by a Parsee lady"; a plaster-cast bust of Mahatma Gandhi, a
plaster-cast Buddha, oil paintings done on glass sheets; the
stuffed heads of tigers, panthers, leopards, squirrels, jackals,

deer, an African monkey (stuffed); an Australian sheep (stuffed); "Embroidery specimen depicting Maharaja Kishan Singh shown in a car"; "Marble of Statuette of Mahatma Gandhi."

The unity of art and craft, art and life enchants me. Everything, trivial and profound, is of intrinsic value. Everything is equally honored.

Marvelous miniatures, crowded with incident, packed with significant gesture and detailed symbolism, everything intricately patterned, bespeaking the extraordinary sense of Indian design. Are we in the FINE ARTS section? "No, Mummy, the MISCELLANEOUS section. 'Lady dressing hairs. Elephants fight. Ladies in apartment with blind messenger.'" Veronica reads from the catalogue the titles of some of the paintings on *pipal* leaves. "Butler. Man playing on a *vina*, a Shiva *lingam*. Yogi on a tigerskin. Barber, bangle seller, washerman with iron, tailor, poultry seller, woman dancing, a damsel, a gardener, funeral procession. Rajah, ayah, beggar. Krishna playing Holi. Lovers on Horseback. Lady being dressed."

As we are leaving, I step from the carpet onto the floor and get a splinter in my big toe. Wearily, I sit down on the top stair, hunt through my tote bag, produce a pair of tweezers and a needle. Instant commotion. The custodian, who has been sitting at a roll-top desk presiding over the Visitors' Book, rings a hand bell.

A coolie appears, disappears and re-appears within minutes, jogging up the stairs carrying a pail of steaming water and a clean white rag. Several steps beneath where I am sitting, he sets down the pail, kneels, dips the rag in the water, applies the steaming rag to my toe, gives my rag-covered toe a quick squeeze, moves the cloth: *Atcha*. The head of the splinter is now visible above the skin and easily removed. Another application of the steaming rag, and a pinch of ash from the incense wands burning on the custodian's desk to stop the bleeding. The coolie buckles on my sandals. There. *Atcha!* He wrings out the rag and waves it slowly like a little *punkah* in front of my face and points upward. It is cooler on the roof, he says.

How can this be? Rooftops are hotter, not cooler.

No, no. The coolie grins and makes the motions of appeal a player makes in a game of charades, pleased and pleading. "Yes, Madam," the custodian says, "Hit his being muchly more refreshing on the roof."

Out into the dazzling white heat again. Then up a broad flight of stone stairs to the roof, where there is a columned, domed-ceiling pavilion. The sun is pitiless and, looking at the open-sided pavilion, I wonder what respite *that* is expected to offer. But, miracle of miracles, once beneath the domed ceiling, the temperature drops almost to the point of being chilling. What is so magically cooling about a columned, domed-ceilinged pavilion set on a flat roof so hot that even the coolie, with his thickly callused soles, has to run across it to reach the relief of the pavilion's oasis?

Air currents, wind currents, Veronica suggests, but she knows no more than I do about the secrets of the Mogul architects who have created this miraculous cool spot with the heat wavering up on all sides beyond the columns.

From the rooftop, we can see for miles across a flat dusty landscape. In the foreground are a few bare pipal trees snow-patched with egrets, the bazaar below, the old walls and gate of the Bharatpur fort, and then the open country, with a road meandering through it that tails away toward the horizon, a dusty monochrome with dark splashes of distant trees and bright-colored moving specks of women working in faraway fields.

"*Ram, Ram*," Gurdip salutes us as he says goodnight, and again at dawn, the conventional Oriental time of departure when the air is sure to be cool. We are headed for Fatehpur Sikri along a strip of black macadam that bisects fields of millet and wheat. The bare branches of late-blooming pipal trees are hung with the nests of weaver birds, storks, crows, and herons. From time to time, by a bus stop, ranks of fruit and vegetable *wallahs* sit cross-legged beneath black umbrellas, hookahs beside them, and before them, a bright frieze of melons, oranges, carrots, eggplants, tomatoes, and pyramids of rice and lentils. We stop once to buy oranges and a newspaper spillet of peanuts. Un-roasted, they are soggy and tasteless.

In the sixteenth century, Fatehpur Sikri, The City of Victory, was larger than London. Akbar, the greatest of all the Mogul emperors, required only seven years to have the city built in honor of Sheik Selim Chisti, the Sufi mystic who was his spiritual mentor and who foretold the birth of his three sons. Akbar occupied it as a residence for some fifteen years, then ordered it abandoned, possibly because of his nomadic nature, possibly because of the difficulty of obtaining an adequate supply of water, and moved his court to Lahore. Akbar the Great, grandson of Babur, father of Jehangir, grandfather of Shah Jehan, Akbar, who corresponded with Queen Elizabeth I, who imported rare plants, crossbred dancing doves with acrobatic pigeons, the first ruler to introduce portraiture to Indian art, who received instruction in Christianity from Jesuit priests—natu-

rally, I wanted to see the city he built when I first came to India.
I had read about the Pachisi Court in the shape of a cross where
he played the game with slave girls as the moving pieces, and
when I saw this giant game-board and the rest of what remained
of this extraordinary city all built of royal red-and-white sandstone and marble the color of cream and snow and ivory from
Alwar, Ajmer, and Baroda, I trembled with the excitement of
its romance, mystery, loveliness. Now I want Veronica to see it
as I had and to see it all over again myself.

We pass beneath two of the city's crenellated gateways in the
ruins of red sandstone walls, and drive slowly up a low sandstone ridge toward the royal, deserted city. A white-breasted
eagle, scanning the ground for lizards or field mice, looks up to
stare at us. Beneath the ridge, the landscape stretches to the
horizon, flat, dry, somber, with a grid of sallow bungalows and
a scattering of thorny acacia. Gurdip expatiates on the Mogul's
use of young trees as a means of execution. In a spot where two
saplings grew close together, the heads of the trees were bent to
the ground so that they came together. The victim's legs were
tied one to each tree. The trees were released to spring upright,
and the victim was ripped apart. Gurdip lifts his hands from the
steering wheel, raises them above his turban and claps them
smartly together to demonstrate with what swiftness death occurred. Outside the Diwan-i-Am, the Hall of Public Audience,
there is a massive stone ring. A rogue elephant, rutting, mur-
derous, mad, was tethered "to this very ring, Madam," and all
those who offended Akbar were given to the elephant to gore
and trample.

On a triumphal arch is the inscription: Isa (Jesus) Son of
Mary, on whom be peace, said: The World is a bridge; pass over

it, but build no houses upon it. Who hopes for an hour, hopes for Eternity. The World is an hour; spend it in prayers, for what follows is unseen.

The quotation is of Muslim, not Christian, origin. Akbar's attribution of the saying to Jesus was his way of paying homage to the Jesuit priests who took turns reading the Bible to him during the several years they were honored guests in his palace.

In the inner courtyard of the Jama Masjid is the tomb of Sheik Selim Chisti, and the gatekeeper gives us gray flannel bags to slip over our sandals before we set forth into the dazzling white-hot light bounded by the dark shadows of the halls and pillared corridors of the mosque, the palace, the galleried out-buildings. The tomb of Selim Chisti is in a little domed house of marble, with corbeled brackets and walls of pierced marble screening. Inside, all is dappled with a gentle golden light and violet shadows, and the tomb itself is like a canopied bed, its posts adorned with ribbons, colored string, flower garlands, an ostrich egg, and scraps of cloth brought by childless women who come to pray to Selim Chisti to intercede in their favor. Several dozen women cluster about the mother-of-pearl inlaid bed intoning prayers, and others drift in and out to deposit bunches of flowers on towels that have been spread across the bed to receive these offerings.

By mid-morning, the peace of Fatehpur Sikri has been shat-tered by the arrival of sightseers who have come by the busload to see the Mosque in half an hour and to be plagued in the courtyard by vendors of neon-colored beads, bangles, souve-nirs, and soft drinks. German, French, Russian, and Italian tourists—no Americans, no English—skate behind guides in their gray flannel booties, fall back to take photographs, then quickly skate on to catch up.

We rest in the shade of a majestic gateway before going further. Outside the walls, boys in loin cloths dive into a green-slimed pool to retrieve annas and rupees, and emerge triumphant, arms dripping with ooze, a glinting coin held in a hand glazed with black mud. Veronica says little. She expresses neither enthusiasm nor interest. Is she emulating Buddhist monks who, she has told me, rarely express surprise or curiosity? Or doesn't she feel well? She feels fine, she says.

Away from the massive, pillared stone grandeur of the Mogul past, a watchman dozes on a *charpoy* in the shade of his mud hut's overhanging tin roof. Off to one side of his compound, a mound of cow dung patties has been stacked in the shape of an overturned rowboat. Unlike the dung patties I have become used to seeing, the size of Frisbees or small trays, these are giant medallions, as big as tea-table tops. In place of handprints or simple geometric designs, these have been ornately decorated with braided patterns set at intervals with raised Turk's head knots and dotted triangles. Gurdip appears to think that I'm mad to want to photograph them, while Veronica's expression is that of a dog owner, waiting by a tree while the pet does its duty. I can see she is in no mood to joke or laugh with me. No matter. The Indian gift for giving beauty to commonplace objects charms me. The simplicity of artistically embellished cow dung cakes comes as a relief after exposure to architecture that is massive and immensely intricate. I take my photographs, finish the roll of film, put away the camera, and then am conscious of the path of a wasp, trailing its long yellow legs up my sleeve.

Tote bag in one hand, camera bag in the other, I try to blow the wasp away, but it marches resolutely toward my shoulder. Veronica, beside me now, gently folds the wasp in a tissue of Kleenex and shakes it free to fly into an oleander bush.

Mathura: birthplace of Krishna, the indispensable pilgrimage spot of Hindus. As we drive toward it in the unbroken sunshine, two signposts proclaim the way. One says MATHURA (MUTTRA). Another points to MUTTERER. Mathura is also the site of an important school of Buddhist sculpture founded in the first century A.D. We go at once to the Archaeological Museum, set apart outside the town, housed in a light and airy new building with an open courtyard. The sculpture, some of the best in India, has been mounted along pristine white walls. Two members of the local constabulary, trimly uniformed with visored caps, armed with rifles and holstered revolvers, wave sparrows away from the sculpture with dust cloths. The museum is impregnated with the scent of incense wands burning in a jar at the entrance, the scent of earth and flowers from the courtyard where the clarity of the sun's light makes the roses and champak shine like jewels and enamels their leaves. Here Hellenic Gandhara Buddhas, wavy-haired, long-faced, long-nosed, carved from gray schist, are ranged side by side with the red sandstone Buddhas of Mathura, gentler in their expressions. The sandstone looks as though it would be soft as butter to the touch. There are panels of many figures, women with curving hips, bosoms as round as melons; warriors and gods that rouse the senses like the erotic sculpture at Khajurao and Konarak, that ancient Indian sculpture that makes the skin expectant of contact and embrace, sensual with the plumpness of ripe fruit, the swelling covenant of the seed, impassioned sculpture. Sculpture from Taxila, the capital of the kingdom of Gandhara that fell to Alexander the Great in the fourth century, has a classical, ethereal beauty, an awesome quality of grace and vision. The Mathura sculpture celebrates luxuriance, birth, growth, the mystery of sex and sensuality in a way so compelling that I want to reach out and stroke the figures as though magically to bring life back to life.

Two Indian widows in white, a Hare Krishna fellow with a pigtail, and a beggar bundled in rags who is allowed to sit in the courtyard's sculpture garden but not inside the museum, are the only other visitors. Gurdip says that tourists go to nearby Agra to visit the Taj Mahal and usually don't make the effort to travel on to Mathura. Indians, he adds, are "enjoying more to be talking with each other than regarding old things of the past."

Near the ghats on the western banks of the Jamuna, the cobbled streets with their wandering white cows and crowds of people are too narrow to allow us to drive unless Gurdip presses on the horn continually, blasting progress a few feet at a time. Far simpler to let him back his way out and for Veronica and me to walk the rest of the way between the tall rows of town houses called *havelis* that line the cobbled alleyways. Narrow, three to five storeys high, the *havelis* are wild and whimsical architectural fantasies and follies, with verandahs, pillars, foliated arches, bracketed parapets, cantilevered balconies, bay windows, and elaborate entrances with small doors set into large doors that are strapped with iron and studded with brass. They have walls, ceilings, and lintels inset with domes of stained glass, and in the spaces not covered with intricate carvings, they are painted with floral and geometrical designs and a wild variety of religious and secular scenes.

Combining elements of Pompeiian frescoes, San Blas *molas*, Mogul miniatures, *henta* boards from the Nicobar Islands showing the magic of the white man's possessions, candy-cane and gumdrop gingerbread houses, Dulac's illustrations of fairytale palaces, illustrations from *A Thousand and One Nights*, these *havelis* were built in the eighteenth century for Mathura's aristocratic and well-to-do families. They are painted predominantly in rosy-beige, pink, violet-blue, with chocolate-brown doors and beams. You can imagine nibbling at them for the taste of halvah and cinnamon, cloves and roses, fondant-covered petits-fours, almond-iced gingerbread.

And the inset paintings! All those curling tendrils and serifs, flowers, suns, nailheads, and mirror mosaics setting off paintings of Persian princesses, elephant back hunting scenes, turn-of-the-century trains and ships, portraits of Queen Mary and the Virgin Mary, Queen Victoria in the guise of an Indian matron with a *kumkum* dot daubed in the center of her forehead. And here is Jesus with a crown of thorns! And George V, and red-coated Mogul horsemen with lances raised, riding full tilt above and across a doorway! The door is open, so of course I must go inside. No one will mind, will they? The age of *zenanas* and separate quarters for men and women is past. Indians are extremely hospitable. The tradition of *atithi satkar* (honoring the guest) is still practiced, isn't it? They all have courtyards, anyway, so it isn't as though I would be intruding on anyone's private quarters, is it? What's wrong with having a look inside?

One glance at Veronica's face and I can see she thinks everything is wrong, but in a moment I've already climbed a short flight of stairs, and from a landing, am looking out into a courtyard. Wonderful pierced brass and colored-glass lanterns overhead, frescoes and decorative plaster work surrounding me, and beyond the first courtyard another and yet another! It's like being in an underwater world, all smoky blue-green light filtering in from a stained glass ceiling dome, with the flat white light of the courtyard's open space magnified like sand seen through goggles.

Halfway up the stairs behind me, Veronica tells me that I will be arrested. Will I? Women, holding the *pallau* of their saris over their faces so that only their eyes show, drift into the courtyard. A man in a *dhoti*, shirt, and waistcoat approaches me and I make my *Namaste* and tell him how beautiful everything is, *bahot sundar*, and he is all nods, becks, and wreathed smiles, eager to show me anything I want to see. I look back triumphantly at Veronica and sail ahead into the courtyard where the walls are covered with frescoes of Krishna and Radha and decorated with elaborate plaster-work around the cusped arches of doorways.

In the next courtyard, I catch a glimpse of a woman kneeling as she grinds spices in an old-fashioned mill with a handle on top, and I can see the sun flashing on large circular *thalis* (serving trays) and small brass *katories* (bowls). If I stay a moment longer, Veronica and I will be invited for a meal, and then we won't get away for hours. Veronica glides to my side, all effusive Hindi, gratitude, graceful apologies as she links her arm in mine and propels me back toward the stairs. An exchange of *Namaste*, smiles of farewell, and we are out in the street, and almost running through the crowd of pedestrians.

The tall wooden *havelis* peter out, giving way to buildings of blackened stone with street-level niches for images of Krishna and other deities. Oil lamps smolder among the shadows like glintings of fire opal, casting points of light on brass jars filled with offerings of buffalo curds, *ghee*, and rice, illuminating garlands of marigolds and a mosaic of silver and copper coins. I smell the Jamuna river before I see it, a broad bright sheaf of gray-green water lined with shallow steps that lead to platforms of stone where men and women have gathered to sit and listen to the discourse of gurus. Bare-bottomed children and pye dogs with mangy patches of gray skin trot and stop, turn and run, stop, trot, turn, run, and ever-swirling knee-high carpet that whirls about a litter of water pots, braziers, baskets of food, shawls, and the rolled straw sleeping mats of the pilgrims.

There are boatmen in the river, ferrying people who throw scraps of food at sacred, pale-backed river turtles. There are men swimming and old women in white saris jumping up and down in the water: Krishna's cheerful devotees, firm in the belief that they are now wholly blessed and able to return exalted from this place of pilgrimage to their towns and villages. Men and women emerge dripping from the river and daub their foreheads with vermilion, ocher, and the white ash of burned cow dung. The smell of incense mingles with the smell of the river, a marshy odor, much like the moist earth scent of growth and decaying vegetation of the *jheel* at Bharatpur. Above the water, the air vibrates with the flight of kites and crows and egrets, and from somewhere comes the sound of drums. The heat is immense.

Impatiently, Veronica pulls me away to find Gurdip so that we can continue our drive to the Buddhist temple. Like the merge and flow of patterns in a *shamiani*, there is a merge and

flow of sound and reverence: the shrill quartertones of souvenir
toy flutes, the humming drone of mantras, a humming interrupted by a pause for the audible intaking of hundreds of
breaths then sustained again until the next pause. Children
shriek and skitter underfoot. A phalanx of goats is herded
grunting and bleating across the courtyard, and a group of
young boys walk backward in front of me beseeching me with
comic bravura to take their pictures. Alternately, in the press of
the crowd, I catch hold of Veronica's hand, cling to Gurdip's
arm, or lurch against Veronica as an oncoming dog or child sets
me off balance. Unperturbed, Gurdip strides forward. Veronica
floats along beside him as if she were alone in an empty meadow.

We check our sandals at a stall and pad across the courtyard's
hot stone to a chamber where a group of men are kneeling,
bowing their heads to the floor, and lying face down in the ritual
attitude of prostration, while others are making the sound of
rock bees. Buddhists believe in the spiritual fertility of the repetition of sound, Veronica murmurs. On an altar in a far corner
of the room there is a brass image of the Buddha strewn about
with coins, paper money, flowers. In front of the altar an old
man is sprinkling ashes and yellow powder, lighting wicks floating in dishes of oil, scattering flower petals, and moving brass
bowls and vases from one place to another a few inches away.

"What's that all about?"

"He's doing *puja*, Mummy," Veronica hisses in my ear.

"I thought only Hindus did *puja*."

"Oh, no, Mummy. Buddhists do it, too."

I suppose all devotional acts of consecration and purification
look strange if you don't know what they're about. I tell myself,
as Veronica often has, that Buddhism is more a philosophy than

a religion. This effort at Right Thinking—and it is an effort—is surface skim, a cloak flung over bristling resentment, naked anger. I don't believe what I am saying to myself. *Credunt quod Videre* is one of the three banners above the Eliott coat of arms. I can see my staunchly Presbyterian grandmother pointing it out to me. What would *she* think of this smoke-blackened cavern, which conveys no more sanctity to me than a railway tunnel? What would she make of all those prostrate bodies, humming their way to higher consciousness in steamy semi-darkness with the rank smell of sweat and burning *ghee*?

I feel swaddled, constricted with anger that abrades and burns like Nessus's shirt. Without waiting for Veronica and Gurdip, I hurry outside where the annealing white light instantly withers resentment, and the vendors of trinkets, flutes, and sweets divert me. Mathura is renowned for its candies and sweetmeats. If they can afford to, no one comes to Mathura without buying a sampling. It would be like going to Atlantic City and not buying salt-water taffy, or to Brighton without buying a sack of Brighton rock, or to Lübeck and not buying a marzipan pig. Candy is dandy as a diversion, and the best of what is available in India is arrayed now before me, sequined with flies, dispensed in spillets of newspaper and cornucopias constructed out of pages torn from children's notebooks or from discarded bank papers and other business documents. There is a warm, home-made doughnut smell that I find irresistible. I want to taste everything.

Gur. Large, crumbly brown cakes of unbleached cane sugar.

"Gosh, Mum, not that," Veronica protests. "It'll make your teeth sing and your tummy get hot. Besides, it's hard the way brown sugar gets, so you'll have to suck it."

"The taste is rough," Gurdip says.

One small piece of *gur* is enough.

Pera, said to be Krishna's favorite sweetmeat, is more of a success; a fondant of boiled milk and sugar, flavored with cardamom, rolled into almond-, walnut-, and cashew-centered balls.

There is a preserved quince confection centered with orange-flavored cottage cheese boiled with sugar. Gurdip identifies it as *gulab jamun* without the customary coating of rosewater syrup. I eat several of these.

Now the vendors, up and down the line, produce cardboard boxes, prettily printed with Mogul flower patterns, that they apparently reserve for special customers. I buy one of everything, true to my word, sample everything, and buy boxes of what Gurdip favors for him to take home as a present to his wife.

Barfi, coated with edible, blow-away thin sheets of silver, looks delicious. "It's cottage cheese fried in coconut oil," Veronica says. "*Barfi* is to barf." But the silver *vark* which crunches unpleasantly in my mouth is a coveted status symbol. Gurdip declares that his wife would be delighted to have some.

Rasmullai: cottage cheese (the Indians call it *paneer*) soaked in milk and rosewater, flavored with cardamom, and rolled in chopped pistachio nuts.

Rasgula: a confection made from wheat flour mixed to a paste with boiled milk and sugar, shaped into an egg-like form, fried in *ghee* and then dipped in sugar syrup. Gurdip smiles broadly as I buy boxes of these.

Ladoos: literally sweet balls, made with wheat flour, *gur*, cardamom, and formed into balls the size of lemons, and then sprinkled with *khuskhus* seeds, the favorite food of Ganesh, the Elephant God.

Chikkis: a treat made from sesame seeds; squares made from chick-peas, squares made from almonds.

I stuff myself with the abandon of a child at a birthday party—my own childhood parties, which I can remember with all the clarity of this Indian sunlight. The final seal of pleasure on each was the birthday supper, served in the dining room, with me, the birthday girl, ceremoniously seated in the arm-chair at the head of the table where my father usually sat. The table, concealed until suppertime by curtained glass doors that were opened only after all my guests had been lined up according to height behind me, was always magical with its Jack Horner pie centerpiece, a creation of my Aunt Vera's that comprised a basket covered with ruffled crêpe paper, from which tinted silk and silver ribbons rayed, each attached to a tissue-wrapped present, one for each child. Matching baskets filled with white-sprinkled chocolate non-pareils, gumdrops, and hard candies with chewy centers were placed at each plate, along with a matching, fringe-ended snapper to be torn open after "snapping" to find your fortune. There was also a tin charm, and a tissue paper tricorne the boys usually balled up, dipped in milk, and threw at each other until someone stopped them. At each plate there were "real" crowns, top hats, helmets, caps, inverted cones with pompons, bonnets, fezzes, and turbans to wear, each with an elastic cord to secure it under your chin. There were also small horns attached to a coil of brightly colored paper that unrolled when you blew on the horn, issuing a strangely rude honk, like an animated "raspberry" or Bronx cheer.

For supper, creamed chicken, white rice, and fresh green peas were laid out on silver platters and in vegetable dishes with heavy King's pattern sterling silver serving spoons that were hard to manage. Cornbread muffins or cloverleaf rolls were passed around the table with ridged balls of ice-cold butter that would roll like marbles from one side of your butterplate to the other. Someone would inevitably spill a glass of milk or orange juice that would have to be mopped up, with the maids looking cross while they assured the culprit in cheerful voices not to worry, that it was all right, although everyone knew that it wasn't. This discrepancy between what was said and what was felt was a fact of life with which I grew up, even in the happy lucidity of my birthday parties. But everything would soon be all right again, and the platters of molded ice cream—strawberry roses or fruit ices, or vanilla and chocolate rabbits nested in golden beds of spun sugar that felt hot when it melted in your mouth—would be served. Then the lights would be dimmed, there would be a hush, the pantry door would swing open, and in would come the candlelit cake to the accompaniment of everyone singing "Happy Birthday." I would sit there silent, blushing, grinning, staring at the cake with its rosettes, swags, and inscription piped on to display the cook's artistry. Always it was my absolute favorite, a pound cake flavored with almond essence, with an almond-flavored icing, and a filling between the four layers made from the same icing mixed with raisins and chopped walnuts. When the candles were blown out, one was saved on which to make a wish. In truth I had no wish, only yearning, an undefined desire for something to make me feel complete. As the final candleflame issued its scribble of rising smoke, the smell was like a whiff left over from the Fourth of

July. I would cut the cake with the ivory-handled trowel that my father, on his fifth birthday, had used to lay the cornerstone for Woodbine, the house in which he grew up.

My father used to lead a donkey around on which my party guests and I could ride. Once the donkey pulled a brilliantly painted Sicilian cart, borrowed from one of his friends, in which half a dozen of us could be seated triumphantly, while the remainder lined up, shrieking, "It's my turn next, it's my turn next!" Another time, Daddy yielded his place to a magician wearing a top hat that gleamed like the flanks of my father's dark bay pony. The magician transformed a roll of newspaper with scissors into a tree that reached to the ceiling. He broke an egg into his hat and produced a cake. He waved a wand and suddenly flourished a myriad of silk scarves in marvelous colors. He pulled a birdcage with a live canary in it out of his sleeve. Often there was a clown in a sateen suit with pompoms who cartwheeled around me on the lawn, singing "Happy Birthday, dear Leila," as all the nurses and governesses, ensconced in the shade of the giant maple on white wrought iron seats and white wooden folding chairs looked on.

At other parties as I grew older, there were egg and spoon races, the breathless excitement of treasure hunts, and better yet, the wild confusion of spider webs, endless balls of white cotton string woven by Aunt Vera from the maple tree to the leaden bird-bath cherub and back into the pine grove, where the presents at the end of the strings would be dangling in the boughs. There were blindfolded guessing games, Charlie Chaplin and Rin Tin Tin movies, and Punch and Judy shows.

When the boys were too old for shorts, they were no longer invited because they were sure to throw cake at the table, squirt

milk through straws at the girls, throw puffballs they found on
the lawn at each other, or fight, all of which they did at other
parties as well as my own. By this time, the amply built nurses
with their aureoles of gray hair and the thinner governesses in
their tailored dark suits began to leave their charges at the door,
instead of staying to check out all the presents and gossip about
their employers, and take politely disapproving views of each
others' charges ("My, she's a big girl, isn't she?" "You'll need to
dose him tonight with Syrup of Figs. I think that's his fourth
plate of ice cream").

When the presence of nurses and governesses was no longer
needed at all, the landmark slipped by almost unnoticed, like a
signpost seen from the window of a car. But only a year later I
was a boarder at St. Timothy's. Four years after that, I had
graduated, come out, and was married to Bryce.

"Do you remember your birthday parties in Jamaica?" I ask
Veronica.

"Jamaica?" Veronica repeats vaguely. "Sort of. I remember
eating sugar cane and the milk wagon that came crunching up
the driveway. The driver sometimes gave Sam and me a ride.
And the swimming pool next door, and picnics on the beach."

"Don't you remember your *birthday parties?*"

"Well, sort of, Mummy. There were balloons and lanterns,
weren't there?"

Oh, Elsa Cloud, how could you not remember? Your birthday
parties were like a dream, with pink, lavender, and blue balloons
hung from strings everywhere, beginning from the gateposts up
to the lignum vitae tree where the guinea fowl slept, all around
the topiary bougainvillea bushes framing the house door,
around the porch columns, on the gateposts of the garden lawn,

up to the lime tree and the tulip tree, by the ferns and the back porch which was like an arbor of philodendrons, and around the white wicker furniture with its orange cushions, where your cake would be covered with a tent of stiffened netting until it was time for you to come and blow out the candles. Your Daddoo and I had spent hours decorating the cake—he did the icing, trimming, and writing, and I did the sugar flowers—and he organized the treasure hunt while I spun the spider web and did up all the presents in silver foil. I fixed up Sam's wagon as a cart and hitched it to Billy the kid, and you seemed to have so much fun urging your Daddoo to make Billy "go faster, go faster!"

"Don't you remember all that?"

Veronica raises her shoulders slightly and with elbows at her sides lifts her forearms, turns the palms of her hands outwards in a gesture of amiable helplessness. "I don't remember much, Mum. I was only a child." she says.

Only a child? Had her birthdays not been as magical for her as mine had been for me? Or have all her Buddhist studies and meditations—and what she calls non-attachment—emptied her mind of these cherished childhood memories?

Twelve

Meenakshi has told us that we will be enchanted by the princely palace of Deeg. From Bharatpur, the eastern gateway to Rajasthan, it lies only thirty-two miles away on the western route to Alwar and Jaipur.

Bagwan ki lila. Whatever God wishes. Gurdip and Veronica delight in this play of words on my name. *Bagwan ki lila*, they say, smiling at me with indulgence.

White-washed mud villages, plain mud villages. Village tanks with women on the verges washing clothes. I am convinced that each village we pass must contain some fascinating thing that will only be revealed to me, but at each village where we stop, the circumstances and the scene will vary little. Women in brilliant swinging skirts hurry up from the tank to look at us. Some carry babies with kohl-rimmed eyes, tiny gold earrings pierced through their earlobes, and gold chains, fine as threads, around their necks. Men wearing Holi-stained shirts appear.

With the extraordinary hospitality offered to strangers traveling in India, *chapattis* are given to us, a brass *thali* with a few slices of pale orange melon is produced, a suck on the flexible tube of a hookah is proffered to Gurdip. In return, I pass around extra boxes of Mathura sweets, and give away oranges, felt-tipped pens, bananas, biscuits, magazines, beedies stashed in the car. Gurdip, Veronica, the villagers, and I are all pleased with this exchange.

So here is a courtyard with a charpoy and a stone mortar and pestle. Here is a grindstone worked by a pedal. Here is a bicycle. Scrawny chickens. Scrawny cat. Scrawny pye dog. Here is a chamber of thick mud-brick walls with a U-shaped mud stove and grill and a firepit. On the walls, hanging from pegs, are a wooden yoke and iron cooking utensils. On the floor are large clay jars used for storage, some sealed, some open, filled with millet, pulse, rice. Stone bowls. A stone mortar and pestle not in use takes on the aspect of an art object, primeval sculpture for a fertility rite. A brass bowl filled with curds. Gurdip tells me not to touch anything to do with storing or cooking food, or the food itself, because I will desecrate it with my "unclean presence, if you will forgive my saying so, Madam," and whatever I touch may have to be thrown out. "For the people, Madam, you have no caste, and they are quite superstitious."

Somewhere there is always a twig broom, and everything is swept clean and bare. No clutter, no garbage, everything simple and spare, the jars and pots and charpoys pleasing in their design and simplicity, and the cow dung cakes worked with geometrical designs. Always, too, there is an altar, with a brass image or one of painted clay; a *diwa*, a small oil lamp of baked clay that could pass as an artifact of Greek or Roman antiquity (but "probably made last week," Veronica says) a few wilting field flowers, a few little bowls and jars of clay or brass for the daily *puja*.

I have to see half a dozen of these farm villages to convince myself that this is really the way they all are. The smell of water evaporating in clay pots pervades them as much, I think, as the strength and endurance concentrated on the features of their inhabitants. Gurdip calls these villagers Jats, people of the land, descendants of the people who were settled in the area before the arrival of the Rajput whose chieftains fought the Muslim invaders and the Rajput princes. Many had become Sikhs and joined with the Sikh warriors who finally drove the Moguls out of northeastern Punjab.

"Sikh comes from the Hindu verb, *sikhma*, to learn, Madam, and we Sikhs taught the Jats so well that a Jat farmer named Bandan Singh was made a hereditary Raja by the Mogul emperor, and more than two hundred years ago, it was he, Madam, who founded Bharatpur. The Rajas of Bharatpur were very fine warriors, Madam. You will see their fort in Deeg, Madam, and their palace as well. The maharajas have a nice palace. They lived very nicely, Madam."

As a child in London and in Scotland, I had seen silver-framed photographs of men wearing brocade coats and astonishing turbans with diamond aigrettes, and Granny had read me a letter in which Lord Elgin, James Bruce, the eighth Earl of Elgin, described his state visit as Viceroy to Maharaja Scindia of Gwalior, whose palace contained the largest crystal chandelier in Asia. Gwalior could feed five hundred guests on solid gold plates, and his state banquets were enlivened at dessert time by a solid silver electric train, operated by a button pressed by the prince himself, which made the round of the main banquet table, pulling seven solid silver freight cars carrying chocolates, nuts, bonbons, cigarettes, cigars, brandy, and port. Imagine that!

Some maharajas, my grandmother went on (here she always

twinkled and smiled), had worn diamond eyebrows hooked over their ears like spectacles. I could imagine solid silver howdahs with mahouts waving silver-handled fly whisks of peacock feathers. I could imagine cloth of gold and ropes of pearls as big as marbles. I could imagine the enchanting silver locomotive and cars freighted with chocolates and brandy gliding around the table laden with its service of gold. But diamond eyebrows hooked on like spectacles? No. I was certain Granny was just having her little joke with me.

Gurdip waggles his lime-green turban from side to side. "Oh, yes, Madam." He personally has seen the diamond eyebrows of the Maharajas of Jodphur, which they wore on important occasions of state. Some maharajas, he adds, were also fortunate to have as many as two hundred and fifty motorcars, many of which were gold-plated. Perhaps, some day, Gurdip says, he will come to America, and earn enough money to buy a motorcar like that.

Now the gray-black walls of the moated fortifications of Deeg rise before us, forbidding. The walls are the color of dirty pavement, and projecting all along them are huge, squat, cylindrical towers, ribbed and ridged, sides slightly tapering to shoulders, with a construction, or the remains of one, on top of each. They bear a resemblance to Buddhist *stupas*, or *chortens*, as Veronica says the Tibetans call them, to gigantic domed cake covers, to immense stone ink bottles. The shoulders of some bristle with thorny scrub. All are ringed with holes that are white-bearded with guano, telling of long occupation by doves in place of weaponry.

The interior of the citadel houses several school buildings— I can hear the hum of children within—a Krishna and Radha shrine, and a shrine to Saraswati, goddess of learning. The immense yard consists of hard-packed ocher-colored earth filmed with dust. The heat is such that my teeth feel hot and my watch burns on my left wrist.

In trying to help me with my Rolleiflex, Gurdip accidentally tugs the strap loose, and the camera falls on the hard ground. The light meter is damaged, the film-winding mechanism is no longer operative, and the trustworthy old Rollei on which I've relied for more than twenty-five years is now, for all intents and purposes, useless.

Gurdip is solicitous. He assures me that he knows the court photographer in Jaipur, the personal photographer of Colonel Bhawani Singh, the former Maharaja of Jaipur, who is known as "Bubbles" Jaipur because everyone drank so much champagne at his christening. "And since the royal photographer, Madam, likes photographing ever so much, he has a very good man who can fix your camera when you get to Jaipur. In a few hours, Madam, a day at the most, and your camera will be as fine as new."

"Oh, sure," I say. "Of course." And scuff along, hot, angry, and in no mood at all to be charmed by anything, much less the fort or the palace a few miles away.

Veronica doesn't react well to my anger. Like a bathtub with the plug pulled, I can see her empty herself of feeling.

Stride, stride, stride. Gurdip marches back to the car.

Trudge, trudge, trudge. Scuff, scuff, scuff. Veronica and I follow. The back of Veronica's pale blue dress is dark with perspiration.

Fuming with irritation about a broken camera, upsetting Veronica and Gurdip—what a monster I am! Between the time

Gurdip roars the car away from the fort with a style of driving that gives an impression of speed far beyond the car's capacity, and parks it near the entrance to the gardens surrounding the pleasure palace of the Maharajas of Bharatpur, I am mute, deaf, and blind to everything except my fury.

The avenue of pipal trees at the entrance to the palatial compound is filled with heronries of painted storks, and the massed twiggery of their nests is clumped on every branch. An expression of relief flickers across Veronica's face. She expects me to be diverted by the painted storks and, of course, I am. I look at them as though they were the first painted storks I have ever seen, even though we have seen hundreds of them on the *jheel* and on land. Certainly I have never seen any this close.

Large storks, about four feet tall, with white plumage marked and barred with glistening greenish-black, they blush rosily pink about their wings and shoulders. Their heads are the same poster-paint yellow as their long, heavy beaks, which are neither curved nor sword-like, but a combined irregular form of both. The beaks have the odd appearance of being warped, as if they had been soaked too long in water and not been given a proper chance to dry.

Like the spoonbill, the white ibis, and all storks, the painted storks lack a voice-producing ability and are silent except for the sudden, loud sounds they make, like self-applause, by rapidly clapping their mandibles together. There is an unending commotion, however, of fluttering, rustling, and wing-flapping as the storks take off, are momentarily airborne, and come to roost with folded wings on their frowzy nests.

"You never told me storks brought babies," Veronica says.

I wonder if this is an accusation or an accolade. But no,

Veronica is just curious to know why a stork, of all birds, should be chosen as an infant-carrier.

"Because," I say briskly, "storks announce the coming of spring and therefore came to be associated with the Annunciation. Like cranes, storks are a symbol of vigilance and piety."

"Oh," Veronica says.

The palace turns out to be wonderful. How my father would have enjoyed this! The huge estates and enormous houses of the really rich-rich always delighted him. With a child's enthusiasm, he admired other people's squash courts, racing stables, stud farms, kennels, indoor swimming pools and tennis courts, yachts, Rolls Royces, billiard rooms, and solariums. Happily at ease in the midst of the lavish displays of other people's money, he felt guilty, out of place and awkward in surroundings that were noticeably less comfortable than our own. (My mother, on the other hand, felt envious. She preferred to swan around poorer people who made her feel important and grand.) I, too, loved opulence and grandeur. Taken to visit Woodbine, the place where my father grew up, that gothic Hudson river house set in magnificently landscaped gardens, with its turreted carriage house and arbored viewing gallery by the tennis court overlooking the river, I had thought Northlea regrettably small in comparison. I longed to stay at this place where even the pigeons had marvelous many-storeyed dovecotes decorated with lacy wooden filigree to live in. "But no," my mother said. "It would take a legion of gardeners and servants to keep up, and you know how impossible your father is, dear, about money." Sometime during the Depression of the 1930s, Woodbine was sold and converted into a Catholic retreat.

"You're scowling, Mummy," Veronica says. "Why don't you put on sunglasses?"

The side of the palace along which we approach fronts on a formal garden in the Mogul tradition, with long canals studded with fountain heads for a thousand jets of water. It conveys in an intimate and fragrant manner the Muslim ideas of Paradise, a place to be enjoyed both by the living as a pleasure garden and by the dead as a tomb garden, when the cenotaph would become as ornamental as a pavilion or a gazebo.

Here at Deeg, the garden is laid out precisely as the Koran dictates for a Paradise garden. But this garden is made for the living. Instead of a cenotaph, there is a pillared *baradari*, a pavilion of marble and plaster the color of rich cream, with a dome, cusped archways, and fluted columns in which lotuses replace acanthus leaves in Corinthian capitals. The pavilion shelters a deep pool inset with rows of fountain heads the shape of Persian ewers. About the pavilion and throughout the garden are palms and pomegranate trees, a variety of citrus trees, and a huge and central mango tree—tall, dark green, and glossy. A maze of stone pathways, all order and symmetry, rise above sunken gardens of flowers and flowering shrubs.

Sitting in the marble cool of the *baradari*, Veronica and I lean against the pillars as if we were reclining on the pads and bolsters of silk brocade with which the pavilion would originally have been appointed. Cushioned by contentment, I gaze upon the gentle blue of plumbago, the yellow of champak, the white and gold of lilies. "Smell the jasmine, the frangipani, and the roses," Veronica says. Beyond the rose beds and through an arched trellis of jasmine, I glimpse stands of gracefully fanning lotus, also vital to the horticultural Mogul esthetic. Scurrying lizards make whisperations among oleanders with translucent mauve-pink blossoms, and inquisitive sparrows come to hop around us. A fire-tailed sunbird comes to perch almost within arm's reach. Long, brilliant crimson tail attached to a plump body not much larger than a sparrow's, it has a metallic green crown, a scarlet-and-purple chin and throat veiled with a golden gauze of iridescence, a golden rump and a paler golden belly. I've never seen such an extraordinary bird that close, that still, in all of my life. In India, small birds and animals seem to have no fear of human beings. Perhaps they know they are protected by the Indian policy of non-injury toward birds, animals, and snakes, particularly if they're the *vahana* or vehicle of one of the gods. Veronica says that sometimes, when she is writing letters, a field mouse in search of crumbs will creep fearlessly over her resting arm. A mouse, she says, is Ganesha's *vahana*. Where the animal is, the god is also.

"Oh," I say.

In his *Memoirs*, Babur, the sixteenth-century founder of the Mogul dynasty, fretted that the county of Hindustan was "greatly wanting in charm." Among other things, there were no good horses, no first-rate fruit, no ice, no cold water, no hot baths; no candles, no torches, no candlesticks; no walls to the orchards, no running water in the gardens or the residences. The residences and gardens were constructed all on the same flat plane, he dourly observed, and the residences were without fresh air, regularity, or symmetry. For his gardens, which he ordered cut and dug everywhere he was likely to wish to rest, Babur had insisted upon "suitable borders and parterres in every corner, and in every border rose and narcissus in perfect arrangement." I have read that people who love flowers, and are passionate about them, aspire in relative degree to become children again. Babur regressing to primal narcissism, I suppose an analyst would say. Babur deployed thousands of stonecutters and laborers to lay out symmetrical terraced gardens in the Persian tradition, adorned with water that was skillfully manipulated to run in tiled canals, to cascade into pools, to shower from fountains, to jet as high as the indigenous vines of jasmine. The water would plume above the deep pink shrubs of oleander that had generated from cuttings transported and planted by the armies of Alexander the Great on their line of march along the Indus river eighteen hundred years before. The Mogul machine that churned out violence, despotism, torture, and destruction, bequeathed as well a legacy of opulence, symmetry, and harmony, and this legacy is evident in the calm perfection of Bandan Singh's garden. The Maharajas of Bharatpur had a particular enthusiasm for finials. They are everywhere, gleaming and festive, on the tops of domes, roofs, arches, gables, and yes, even on the haystacks in the fields.

We come upon a great, boat-like pavilion with open sides that have recently been screened with iron mesh and would originally have had embroidered or painted canvas drop curtains to keep out the rain, for this is a pavilion that was only used during the monsoon season. There is a pool inside, and fountains to plume colored sprays of water—a prettily romantic idea, to be sure, but Veronica and I, reminded of Holi, wonder about the consequences to the onlookers of all the splashing dye and tinted mists. Beneath is a chamber containing a channeled and pressurized water course through which large bell-metal balls were set rolling to collide with thunderous clashes to simulate the seasonal thunder of the monsoon.

As Veronica and I are the sole visitors, we attract a guide who offers to demonstrate this eighteenth-century thunder-making mechanism for us by employing the power of small, eager boys rather than the pressurized water to set the bell-metal balls in motion.

No, thank you, we say, no noise. We like being peaceful and quiet.

The guide is irrepressible. He chatters about the huge storage tank on the roof which supplied water for two thousand fountains, and water that circulated through pipes as a cooling system for the palace. He gibbers about a giant stone swing, looted from the Nawabs of Oudh, a colossal stone bed, and monumental marble fountains, all of which he claims the Jat rulers plundered. He informs us that the last ruler, Brijendra Singh, who gave the palace to the state in 1951, had a record-breaking duck shoot in Bharatpur—over six thousand ducks in a single day. *Bas!* I secure our freedom by buying a packet of postcards and tipping the guide with a pay-off that makes Veronica screw up her face in a wincing grimace. "Fifty cents! Mummy, are you out of your mind?"

Away we go to explore a palace with lovely carpets worn threadbare and assemblages of French rococo furniture upholstered in silk with the stuffing of some just beginning to come unstuffed. There are pierced marble screens and latticed windows of purdah galleries, and bays and niches where the Maharanis and women of the *zenana* could look out from their seclusion to see what was happening in the outer world. Meenakshi

has told us several times for emphasis that this custom of veiling
and secluding women was adopted by Hindu India from Muslim
conquerors; the custom does not go far back into the roots of
India. In fact, before the Muslims were entrenched in the country, Rajputani women had boldly ridden into battle, wielding
swords against them.

Pendent from several ceilings are *punkah* fans—rows of faded
silk flounces nailed to a long board swung by a rope to fan the
air. I remember staying in a dak bungalow when I had first come
to India. There had been a *punkah* fan in my room with its rope
strung through a hole in the baseboard. Outside, to my astonishment, a *punkah-wallah* lay on his back, one leg crossed over
the other, as he pulled the rope back and forth with his toes,
during the day when I was in the room and all through the night
while I slept.

Colonnaded and arched verandahs of great elegance give access to vast ground-floor rooms, where the walls and ceiling are
hung with iron rings used for oil lamps, kerosene lamps, elec-
trified globes, crystal chandeliers, and canopies of mosquito
netting suspended above carpeted daises.

There are two stuffed Bengali tigers couchant, dusty and
moth-eaten, in the Diwan-i-Khas where ceremonial durbars
were held and where Brijendra Singh still presides in a life-size
painted photograph mounted on cardboard, showing him dark
of eye and mustache, seated in a chair with arm rests ending in
carved lions' heads. He is dressed in a fitted green brocade coat
and green silk turban clasped with a diamond aigrette and garlanded with pearls. He wears a bib of pearls and his achkan is
cinched with a gold belt through which a jewel-handled gold
dagger with a sickle-shaped blade has been stuck. White churi-

dars, wrinkling above Punjabi shoes with turned up toes like the prows of miniature gondolas, embroidered all over with gold filaments and what look like rubies, sapphires, and emeralds, complete his costume. Around the vaulted ceiling, glass balls—red, green, blue, silver—have been suspended, presumably for the play of color they provide as they rotate in the wind and catch the keen light.

From room to room, capitals broken from ancient pillars are used as door stops for doors of thick, heavy, polished teakwood. In the private drawing-room, an elephant's foot serves to hold a decanter; another has been converted into a humidor. Downstairs, features of the palace resembling grand Venetian palaces and the city palaces of Spain combine harmoniously with Mogul architectural and decorative traditions. Mulk once told me that Hindus never possessed the innate need for extravagance flaunted by the Moguls. I mention this generalization to Veronica. "I suppose so," she says, dismissing the topic. I wish I were better informed or that Mulk was by my side, or Robert, to expatiate.

While downstairs, everything is truly grand, spacious, and airy, upstairs, the palace becomes a mysterious honeycomb of large and small chambers, with little on a level plane.

Marble steps lead alike to balconies, to guest quarters, to the *zenana*, to a door that opens into a dank latrine filled with bats and cobwebs, small animals, and fish bones. It reeks with the odor of human urine, cat excrement, and the unmistakable smell of snakes' nests. Other steps lead down to a room with bolsters and pads for seating about a sunken square inlaid with a checkered board for playing chess or *chaupur*, a *pachisi*-like game. Steps lead up to a bedroom with European-style Art

Deco double beds, dressing-table, and French armoires; and down to an adjacent dressing room with charpoys for personal servants or bodyguards.

Some of the windows are covered with unscreened marble *jalis*. Others are screened with blinds made of split cane, called chicks; some with khuskhus tatties that would have been kept wet to cool the hot winds. Other windows are covered with custom-made quilted navy blue cotton shades that are effective barriers against the glare of the afternoon sun. I lift one of these and look out. Stables, dairies, godowns, servants' quarters, and a sun tank that looks like a smaller replica of the amphitheater of Sukrakund all lie beyond the palace. A series of small family palaces is revealed, and an aviary, a wrought-iron version of a domed parrot cage enlarged to house hundreds of birds that have now disappeared, leaving behind wispy feathers in prismatic colors.

On our way to Alwar, we pass women road-workers chipping rocks into pebble-sized gravel for road repairs.

"Tibetan women do that," Veronica says.

"I could never do that."

"You're lucky you don't have to," Veronica says, as the stifling heat of the steam roller smoothing a patch of treacled tar comes buffeting through the window.

"*Au, au, au*," a shepherd calls out to a herd of goats, waving a bamboo pole at them. The goats are yellowish-gray, with snub noses and spaniel ears. They look rather like Bedlington terriers, more like sheep than goats. "Ow, ow, ow!" the herder cries out to them. Come, come, come!

Hills begin to appear, dry, with rocky outcrops, topped with small fortresses and temples. The grass becomes tussocky. When we slow down by a bus stop with a concrete shelter, a pace of white donkeys, still blotched all over with bright pink Holi paint, give vent to retching brays, a sound that signals, as nothing else does to me, farms and farmland. It is a sound I am so fond of that I ask Gurdip to stop the car so I can feel the braying vibrate through my mind. The owner of the donkeys, a man in a blue *salwar*, *kameez*, and fuchsia turban, is stretched out on the ground beneath the concrete shelter, his hookah beside him.

Approaching Alwar, the hills rise up along the horizon. Was it true, I ask Gurdip, that the last ruler of Alwar, Raja Jay Singh, was so concerned about his hunting preserves, the clockwork *bandobast** of his tiger shoots, that he prohibited the building of roads and railways in his realm, and that he used live children as bait when tiger hunting?

"Oh, yes," Gurdip says. "But His Highness was a fine shot, Madam. Like many of the princes, he could shoot *pice* tossed in the air, so no child ever lost its life when used as bait, and when His Highness went away, Madam, the Gorement was putting in this road and a train track promptly and making a station house in the compound of Vinai Vilas, his city-palace, Madam."

Oh, yes, indeed, that must be the family palace that was deserted by Jay Singh—the maharaja who poured kerosene over misbehaving polo ponies and set them on fire—deserted to build another he never lived in, and yet another with one hundred and five rooms beside the lake that Raja Vinai Singh

---

* *Bandobast*, which is pronounced bundobust and used in English sometimes, means arrangement.

had excavated outside the town. Raja Jay Singh was reported never in public to have removed his silk or chamois gloves, which he wore to avoid touching either cow leather or unclean white skins. What with one thing and another, he provoked a rebellion among his subjects and such a furious quarrel with the British that he was driven into exile in Paris, where he died. "What does the guidebook say about him?" I ask Veronica.

"Nothing much, except that on stately occasions he was always accompanied by a person supporting a gilded umbrella, and that he drove in a gilded carriage two storeys high, holding fifty people, drawn by four of his hunting elephants, accompanied by mace-bearers, peacock-plume bearers, yak-tail bearers, *punkah-wallahs*, spear carriers, men carrying clubs, and ordinary spearmen. And that he had an enormous black bear trained to serve refreshment to his guests. It says that 'this royal pet forgot his manners when a guest grew too friendly and so had to be shot.' Who? The guest or the bear?"

"The bear, Veronicaji," Gurdip sings from the front seat. "We can see the bear all taxidermied in the museum, and a big cup carved out of one first class emerald His Highness drank from on state occasions."

But as it turns out, we can see neither the bear nor the emerald cup. The museum is closed for repairs. No way to see the exceptional collection of Sanskrit, Persian, and Arabian manuscripts or the Babar-namah (the *Memoirs* of Babur) or the Armoury Section that Gurdip wants to see. How he loves swords with ornamented hilts and scabbards! And how too much pleasure it would be, just think of it, to see the shields and swords and daggers of Akbar, Jehangir, Shah Jehan, and Aurungzeb, "inlaid with finest gems, Madam!"

Gurdip says that he will make inquiries about getting in to the museum. And if we want to go up the mountain and see the two miles of ramparts, we will need a police permit and the use of a Jeep. Gurdip says he will find out about that, too.

The landscape of hills bubbling and peaking out of flat land and hills lining the horizon has changed. Now mounded and humped hills surround us, soaring into rocky crags. The primitive Aravalli Hills—Deccan granite, gneiss, syenite, dark slate and masses of rose quartz—the oldest crystalline rocks to be found in India. Strung along the craggy mountain top, the battlements of the medieval fortress grow out of the dark rock.

"You know what your father would have said?" I ask Veronica. "He would have said that he wanted to get up there so badly he could taste it, and he would have been up there like a shot, Jeep or no Jeep, with a geological pick and hammer. Up he would go, and he'd be sure to bring back crystals of pink quartz for you and for me." I can see Robert in my mind's eye, lean and tall, wearing his old safari hat banded with python skin, bounding up and down these Deccan-granite rocks.

It seems odd that Robert should have chosen Death Valley as a place to honeymoon, but it wasn't, not at all. "What are you going to do on your honeymoon?" My son, Bryce, then eight, had asked him.

"When I'm not telling your sweet mother how wonderful she is, I'm going to teach her how to shoot jackrabbits and show her where to find geodes as big as footballs, filled with amethysts," Robert had replied, helping me to settle myself in the front seat of his dark blue car. In the back seat, he stowed what I later came to realize were his inseparables—his geological

pick and hammer, his revolver, his rifle. Death Valley, a Califor-
nian desert patched with encrustations of salt, was enclosed by
mountains that had the look of hammered gold when the sun
rose, and during the day were streaked with greenish blue, lavender, and an apricot glaze. This magical effect was soon discovered to be illusory for, at close range, the foothills were simply
bare, buff-colored rocks grown over with parched grass.

I refused to shoot jackrabbits. I shot instead at fence posts
and cactus. I was pleased to discover that I had a steady hand
and good aim, and that, with little practice or effort, I could
look along the gleam of the barrel and shoot with accuracy.
Robert was a superlative marksman. His superiority and expertise made me feel secure. Pointing across a salt pan or a patch of
desert scrub at a jackrabbit I could not see, he would raise his
rifle and fire. I was full of sensibility. I hoped each time that the
rabbit would escape, would disappear down a hole, would
bound away in time. But no. Robert would lope off, return
holding his prey by its spindly hind legs. He would inspect the
bloodied bullet hole, drop the carcass on the ground, and stride
away looking for the next victim. Before I was even aware of a
warning hiss, he shot a rattlesnake through the head and gave
me the translucent gray rattles. They looked like a slice off a cob
of gray corn, and I put them in a matchbox to keep.

I was glad Robert left the rifle in the car when we searched
for geodes. He knew a hill where they were common. When he
told me what to look for, I found several of these rough, pitted,
bluish-gray ovals of metamorphic rock, each with its interior
cavity filled with crystals of amethyst, a wonderful little world
to itself revealed by a tap of Robert's hammer. Geodes seemed

symbolic to me of the new worlds that my marriage to Robert would reveal.

Later, Robert drove to an outcropping of shale embedded with fossil fish and to a stream where he found a Middle Devonian trilobite in a slab of limestone. He removed it carefully with his pick, made a minutely detailed sketch of it for me, and another of an agave in bloom. At night, before we went to bed, he told me the name of the constellations and the stars in them: Mizar and Alcor, Aldebaran, Capella in Auriga, Arcturus in Bootes, Vega in Lyra, and others which, as he recited their Latin and Arabic names, became an evocative poem to me. One morning, when I was collecting wildflowers to dry in my notebook's pages, Robert delighted me by showing me that the flowers of the larkspur were truly shaped like the hind claw of a lark.

I am roused out of my reverie by Gurdip's return.

There will be no permit. The police chief is on vacation. No *chaukidar*. No amiably disposed museum officials around at this hour in Alwar. Can't see the museum. Can't go by Jeep to the fortress. I know what Robert would say to that, and I let him say it for me in the privacy of my mind. I listen to him fondly. When he was angry or indignant, his words slipped past his calm, scholarly bonds and enjoined outrageous crudities. I used to laugh at his defiance. Now I smile and shrug my own away. Some day, I hope I shall come back to see the *Memoirs* Babur penned, the emerald cup, the jeweled swords of Akbar, Jehangir, and Shah Jehan. There is no end to India's glamorous ghosts.

On our way again, the road climbs and winds between two

wooded hills, with barbed wire fencing off dense forests from the road. Gurdip says that there are many tigers, many leopards, many sambhars in the woods. All we see are langurs, long-tailed, long-haired, long-legged, black-faced, black-pawed, black-eared monkeys with silvery yellow-brown pelts, wide-spaced round eyes, and wistful expressions. Females carry tiny babies clasped by one paw to their breasts. Males and females loop their extravagantly long tails above their backs as they run by the roadside or congregate in chattering troops. Through a clearing, the ruins of an aqueduct leading from Alwar up to Lake Siliserh appear and vanish. Built into a hillside overlooking the lake is the Sariska hunting lodge. Formerly owned by the Alwar rulers, its is now a state-owned hotel. We stop here for food before going on to Jaipur.

Outside the lodge, bees swarm in a quivering, glistening inverted triangle above the brass-studded wooden entrance door and buzz loudly in the garden around a reddish-brown mud hive. Rhesus monkeys, as tame and audacious as those in Tughlakabad, are also out in force, whooshing tree branches as they drop to the ground, shrilling and chittering at us from the garden wall. Always in motion, they are graceful when running or leaping, jerky and fidgety when they come momentarily to rest.

The interior of the former hunting lodge, damp, cool, and moldy-smelling, is lit by a bare bulb off in a corner. It is a weary place, dark and unkempt on the ground floor. There is a marble-topped teak-wood table propped against the wall, its dusty broken leg lying beneath it, spider webs on the Victorian coat rack. We head up a flight of creaking stairs to a landing that opens on a wide balcony with metal chairs and tables. Except for an In-

dian family with a little yappy dog, we have the place to ourselves, and a splendid view of a lake reservoir surrounded by
forested hills. We order tea, buttered toast, fried eggs, fried
sliced potatoes, and melon, sweet and green, from a *khidmutgar*
who presents himself to us, unprepossessing and slovenly in a
frayed and spotted open-necked white shirt, a jacket, and
shabby black trousers.

Dusk begins to settle, and smoke rises from a lakeside village
where a cluster of lights can be seen in the distance. The color
of the trees softens, becoming mauve and misty in the waning
light. The hour of cow dust. A file of white cattle makes its way
along a path toward the distant village, and white egrets fly
across the water toward the far hills. I follow the trails of dragonflies that settle on the rust- and food-stained metal tabletop
and then disappear. A running battle ensues between the yappy
terrior and a rhesus monkey around and about the tables. The
Indian family pays no attention to the dog's barking and rushing
at the monkey, which bares its teeth and leaps up on the balus-
trade and out of the way, then down again for another sortie.
Jackals—or are they ghosts?—wail in the distance.

We stand beneath the marble port-cochère of the Rambagh
Palace, the former residence of the Maharajas of Jaipur, now an
imposingly grand hotel of seventy guestrooms. Gurdip has no
permit to drive in Jaipur state and must return to Delhi.
Though we know this is not a final goodbye—we shall meet
again when I return to Delhi to catch the plane to New York—
our farewell is tearful.

"*Sat Sri Akal*," Gurdip says in a voice choked with emotion and, with a bob of his lime green turban, he settles himself in the car.

"Gurdipji, Gurdipji," I call after him mournfully as he drives the car around the columns and pauses for a moment on the other side of the drive to wave. "Gurdipji, *Sat Sri Akal!*" May the truth be exalted!

Thirteen

First thing the next morning, I get my hair done, luxuriating in all the head- and neck-massaging that accompany the ritual of having one's hair washed by someone else. I have a manicure and a pedicure as well, supplying my own nail polish for my toes. The manicurist, who has a small diamond screwed into her left nostril, asks if I have any spare American cosmetics. Cosmetics are not imported, and the nail polish manufactured in India is "not being of good quality and no pretty or chick colors." Shall I have my legs waxed? Compared with New York prices, Indian prices are giftlike. Why not? A paste of hot sugar-cane syrup mixed with turmeric and lime juice is spread on my legs with a bamboo spatula and left to dry. In the mirror, I see myself with a casque of rollered hair and a quizzical look, but when the paste is shucked, my legs are glabrous and have a softly gleaming finish. *Atcha!* What further concessions to vanity shall I make? Shall I be a voluptuary of pain and have my eyebrows shaped? Why not? In the mirror, I see the small, quick, precise motions of the attendant's hands, long-fingered and the color of sandalwood. Instead of tweezers, she is pulling out stray hairs by looping a thread around each one, sawing the thread back and forth, knotting it and pincering out the hairs with the piece of thread.

"How do you do that?" I ask. "However do you do that?" I ask her to show me, to demonstrate this extraordinary technique in slow motion. I watch her motions attentively as she performs them on the crescent-shaped brows of the hair-washing attendant. I try to imitate her seemingly effortless manipulations. My hands, which Robert used to say were endearingly childlike, yet strong and competent, are incapable, no matter how hard I try, of looping, sawing, and knotting a thread around an eyebrow hair.

Our room at the Rambagh Palace is one of a dozen on the ground floor once used by guests of the late Maharaja Sawai Man Singh II, known as Jai, who was the father of Colonel Bhawani Singh, known as Bubbles, whose photographer is expected to repair my Rolleiflex. It is furnished with Jaipur family possessions. Above the carved rosewood mantelpiece of the fireplace's marble facade is a portrait of Maharaja Sawai Jai Singh, the eponymous eighteenth-century astronomer-builder and ruler of Jaipur. Framed in gilded gesso, his face is as stylized and disdainful as a court card; a likeness reproduced in miniature is in the window of every tourist shop in town. Our beds with handsome mahogany headboards face the fireplace, and above each is a ceiling fan. Veronica says that watching the fan in motion is good for meditation. The high ceiling, the ample dimensions, and the proportions of the room are restful. A squashy dark green leather sofa and club chairs; a round table and cushioned chairs before one of the two long windows, where Veronica and I have space not only for our morning tea tray but for all our books and papers as well; a huge mahogany armoire with shelves, drawers, and mirrored doors; a soft Lahore carpet—what comforts! There is a rosewood dressing table with a triple-folding mirror for the self-absorbed, mirrors for those to whom appearance is everything. In the marble bathroom there is a porcelain bathtub that is luxuriously long, deep, and wide. The room produces in me a different outlook; mentally I change balance. A shell of habitation that conforms to the master setting of wealth narrows the orbit of the world, confers the solace of solipsism.

The heavy mahogany door of our room, thicker than my thumb is long, is like a drawbridge. To close it is to shut out all *tracasseries*. It opens onto a columned marble veranda that looks out upon lush green lawns, marble fountains, stone balustrades, and a rose garden patrolled by peacocks and their obbligato to the order of the day. Garden beds with herbaceous borders and plantings are the sort you would expect to find in an Edinburgh park, a resemblance heightened by the view in the distance of the Moti Doongri, a replica of a fortified Scottish baronial castle lofting from the ridge of a hill, one of the several landmark residences in the area of the Maharajas of Jaipur—the latest of whom evidently had a fondness for Scotland. Mulk told me that anthropologists claim the Rajput rulers were very close to the Scottish Highlanders in temperament and in their clan loyalties, a theory that bemuses me.

There is a pavilion in the hotel compound housing an indoor swimming pool that is the biggest, Veronica says, she has ever seen, with a slide, trapezes, a curving Art Deco bar, leather-cushioned lounge chairs, and a garden outside walled with privet for privacy while sunbathing. Maharaja Sawai Man Singh II obviously shared the Mogul passion for extravagance, the Mogul passion for elaborating on anything that had to do with water.

"*Quel luxe!*" Veronica exclaims, and runs for the diving board. We go outside to read beneath shade trees, spread towels to lie on and sun ourselves. Our skins are soon sun-stained pinky brown, and the towels leave galaxies of red indentations on our bodies. We telephone to have iced coffee, iced tea, and lunch brought to us. A *khidmutgar* appears, wearing a red turban with a crisply starched fan of cloth at one side, bearing a tray of tomato, chicken, and cucumber sandwiches, salad, mango tarts. The Maharani of Jaipur recalls in her book, *A Princess Remembers*, that when the Maharaja was in residence, before he handed over the Rambagh Palace to a private hotel company, there were over four hundred servants in the palace, including eunuch guards for internal messenger duty between men's and women's apartments, and swordsmen and mounted guards at the palace gateways; but not including the groups of boys who were "posted to prevent the many pigeons from settling or causing damage to the buildings"; nor the people in charge of the tents, camp furniture, guns, and other shooting necessities for the *shikars*, nor all the assistants, attendants, bearers, and subordinate bearers; nor the small army of grooms, stable boys, exercisers, and walkers detailed to look after the polo ponies and other horses.

"How wonderful," I say to Veronica, "to be able to live for a while like a Maharani." How wonderful to flake out in the sun and enjoy feeling lazy and self-indulgent, paying for luxuries with money I have earned and have to account for to no one but myself.

I grew up in an era when women were not expected to know about money, and financing went unexplained. And I, true to form, never manage to save any money, yet, believing that luxuries are the only necessities, somehow managed to fly with four hundred and fifty pounds overweight to India. My children, on the other hand, have learned how to save money, manage money, and do all the right things with money. Unlike me, unlike my father.

My father's family were a mix of Dutch and English who had emigrated to America in the nineteenth century, made their money as textile merchants, devoted their lives to the sumptuous comforts of large houses, good food, and wine, the pleasures of the double bed facing windows that looked out on trees, rivers, and lawns which led away to carriage houses and stables. Country life, golf, and above all, horses, were their passions. And, of course, a great concern about the money necessary to maintain their pleasures. "Your father's family were in trade," my mother said in a disparaging tone on many occasions. Lacking romantic history and noble heritage, what they had was money, but according to my mother, my father never had enough, and what he had, he invested unwisely. So had Robert. When the capital which had provided us with comfort and security evaporated in one risky venture after another, our household quivered like a tuning-fork with the tensions and frustrations of financial insecurity. With a terrible clang association, I hear Veronica's bitter reproaches. "How can you expect me to enjoy the pretensions of debutante balls when we don't have any money to enjoy all your blue blood perks with? You don't know the total alienation I feel at school. None of my friends can possibly imagine the sadness I feel, feeling so separate and lonely, the only one with no money."

> This is the Land of Lost Content
> I see it shining plain,
> The happy highways where I went
> And cannot come again.

A. E. Housman. *To an Athlete Dying Young*. My father had died when he was sixty-three. Robert died at fifty-two. My father was the pivot I swung around as a child. My father vouched for me. He said I was "pretty as a speckled pup." Whenever he said, "Good shot, old top," "Well done, old sport," I felt I was all right, someone loved me. And I loved him. And then, Robert. He was the pivot I swung around.

"I loved your father. I miss him," I say to Veronica. "He loved you so much. He used to call you his little buttercup and fly."

"I know. I loved him, too. When he left us to go to the Philippines, I tried to find other men to love, men who would love me, who would make me feel loving and laughing again, but none of them were any good. They didn't have Daddoo's qualities. They didn't do anything interesting. They didn't know anything interesting. I showed them Daddoo's egg-squeezing trick, and they didn't care. They just wanted to find nests for their cocks, nests in me. But I made nests out of their pubic hair."

"For trophies, or what?" As I hear what I am saying, I realize what I am saying. I am screaming silently at myself, *How could you, how could you be so insensitive, so stupid, so dumb, so obtuse, so cruel, so horrible, so totally unresponsive, unreceptive, closed-minded?* Why can't I ever learn to listen, to hear what she is saying? I press the prongs of the lunch fork hard into the palm of my hand. I want to feel them so sharp and hard that my skin will be punctured.

I hear Veronica's voice change as she speaks. "Don't you remember when Bill said you had a hair in your teeth? Can't you imagine how awful I felt? How you betrayed Daddoo when he was away? How betrayed you made me feel?"

Like a moment in a dream when you wish desperately to speak and nothing comes out of your open mouth, I mutely watch her as she gives me a curse-blue look, turns, and walks away.

One man is the same as many. When the man you love leaves you and you wish he had stayed, the idea remains, crazily fixed, that it was you who drove him away, you who caused him to go, something in you, not something in him, that made him leave. Much as I had not wanted to harbor that thought, it had been moored to my mind, anchored there. It was not impossible that Veronica had felt the same, with far less reason. Just as I still feel that I am responsible for my father's untimely death, Veronica could easily have felt she was responsible for her father's flight to the Philippines. One man is the same as many. When the man you love leaves you, he takes with him all that you love about yourself. Without that cherished part of yourself, the drive to love and be loved, a perversion of the true instinct, is so irresistible that you can even be driven to invent someone to love and be loved by. One man is the same as many. I was only doing what

I needed, wanted, was compelled to do, given the nature, temperament, inclinations, and passions of my being. Veronica was doing the same thing with the contributors to her birds' nests. In this primitive cause, we were both as driven as animals by an instinct to give birth again to selves that would be lovable, selves we could learn to love again.

Bill. Bill Leveret. Leveret, a diminutive for the French, *lièvre*, or a hare, a hare in its first year, a woman paramour, a mistress. Robert had been gone a year when Bill Leveret came into my life. Because he played polo, he reminded me of my father and, because a polo helmet looks rather like a 1920s cloche, he reminded me also of my first nanny, the one who had been there one day and disappeared the next. Searching among old photographs, years later, I discovered a photograph of her holding me by my hand to steady me when I was barely walkable. Bill Leveret resembled her, the same dark hair, the same dark eyes. Without Robert, I was conscious of feeling lonely. Bill had just divorced his wife and was on an alcoholic binge. Consciously, I wanted to be loved, needed, wanted. Consciously, he hated himself. A perfect set-up, a classic situation for an emotional regression and a brief, wild, hopelessly mismatched affair to give us both the illusion that we were involving ourselves in compassionate lovemaking. "I don't want to commit adultery," I had said. "I just want to be a child."

One afternoon, I told the children, Veronica included, of course, to meet me at Bill's place so that they and I could then go to my mother's for tea. Bill and I were presentably dressed by the time my children arrived, and I was just about to set off with them when Bill said to me, "You have a hair in your teeth."

A hair in my teeth? Whatever would my mother say? I thought this was hysterically funny. A hair in my teeth. A hare in my teeth. An apt remark from Bill Leveret to his leveret. I laughed shamelessly until tears came. I looked at myself in the vestibule mirror, and sure enough, there was a pubic hair between my front teeth. I removed it, washed my face in cold water, and set off with the children to go to my mother's for tea.

Oh, Elsa Cloud, Elsa Cloud. I can hear your father's voice saying, "The Orphic Egg, the vast egg-shaped world that is under no obligation to conform to our desires." I remember the horror and disgust and shame I felt when I found those pubic hair birds' nests of yours. Whatever did you feel about me? I didn't know you were looking for love. I just thought you were being promiscuous, flirting for fun and frivolity and self-delight or just being seduced and taken advantage of because you, like me, have a somewhat deplorable need to please. But love is something else again. You were looking for a man to *love?* That's so much more difficult that *being* loved. How could I have been so insensitive, so unreceptive, so obtuse, so self-absorbed that I couldn't see how you would think my affair with Bill was a betrayal of your father? You told me the day I was screaming about the birds' nests that you thought you were "frigid." You weren't frigid, you were as numb with shock as I was. You needed love. You gave me love—all those little Valentines, those collages, those beautiful collages when you tried to picture what you couldn't say, just as I used to play how I felt on the green piano—and I said nothing, did nothing you could understand as "love."

I thought you knew how much you were loved. There I was, after all, working from ten in the morning often until midnight holding down two editorial jobs and keeping up with travel writing on the side just so I could pay the school bills above and beyond the scholarship grants you all had to get, just so I could pay for food and clothes for you all, as well as the unending expenses large and small including a full-time housekeeper. I never told you then that Robert had gone through all the capital I had inherited when my father died, as well as the money his father, my grandfather, had left in trust, all of which I turned over to Robert to manage, saying it was "our" money.

Veronica had felt lonely and alienated because she had less money than her classmates? "No money" by comparison? She had once needed money as part of her identity—as I had—and her father had taken that away from her. But he had given her love.

Oh, Elsa Cloud. To be abandoned by your father, and suddenly to have your mother abandon you too, because that's what my working so much of the time must have seemed—a lesser act of abandonment, but an abandonment just the same—a constant reminder that we had "no money" for Christmas, Easter, or summer vacations as a family, the way everyone else you knew did. And all this happening when you were going through a girl's most sensitive and difficult years. Oh, my God, Elsa Cloud, why didn't I see? Why didn't I understand? How could I not? I was just as blind as my mother.

My mother? Why does my mother become an arrow I shoot continually from the bow of my mind, hoping with all my strength to find the feathered hilt of *her* guilt, not my own? She was helping me with the rent, paying for little luxuries here and there, maintaining her lifestyle, lunching at the club and all that.

She didn't see either. We both believed in keeping up appearances, maintaining the pattern of life we had always carried
around the way a flower does its seed.

When I go back to our room, Veronica is there. "I'm sorry," I
say. "I love you." Can she accept my love?

What she says now knocks me for a loop—a silly phrase,
and yet somehow it expresses better than anything else at the
moment how my daughter's words affect me. She says, "Anger
is a weakness, Mummy. Why do you encourage me to be weak
by forgiving so easily?"

"Oh, darling," I say, hugging her. "Oh, darling Elsa Cloud."

"I love you, too," she says, her voice muffled in my neck as I
put my arms around her, kneeling beside the leather chair in
which she is sitting.

Thus we hold out offerings of forgiveness, reassurance,
understanding, comfort. Temporary, incomplete, partial solu-
tions, coaxing a confidence, a rootling of security in ourselves
and each other, like the touch of a green leaf in a cool shade.

Like children having been good, we reward ourselves with
the naughtiness, letting the conversation glide away into the
risible, visible realm of sex. Sex in the abstract. Sex in India,
which has produced the Kamasutra with its lyrical details about
kissing, scratching, biting, and extraordinarily acrobatic forms
of sexual congress even when immersed in water, yet has
stringent laws governing social behavior: kissing-on-the-mouth
scenes forbidden in movies, international hippies arrested for
the indecent behavior of walking in the streets with their arms
around each other, out-of-the-bedroom male-female contact

puritanically regulated. Veronica says everything is explained in
one of her sensational Vishnu comic books. She gets up to fetch
it from the round table, a booklet with a cover picture of a
crocodile biting an elephant's leg. On the back is an advertisement for "Krackjack Biscuits, the Konversation Opener."

Vishnu, the book explains (of whom Krishna is an avatar), is
the second of the Hindu triad. Vishnu descends on earth to
uphold righteousness and to destroy evil, and represents the
male procreative organ, the *lingam*. Lakshmi, his consort, the
goddess of prosperity (whose image can be seen in most shops
and accountants' offices), represents the female procreative organ, the *yoni*. The *yoni* appears in the night sky as the zodiac of
the Milky Way. The zodiac *lingam* moves and rotates the Milky
Way *yoni* like the rhythm of a man and woman making love.

"The love of Vishnu and Lakshmi is said to be universal
movement, the movement of the universe, and the constellations of the zodiac and the Milky Way are their children. Isn't
that a neat explanation, Mum?"

It is indeed. In European traditions, sex and creation are
connected with the agrarian cycle. In India, sex has a celestial
equation. But what about Shiva? I'd always thought that Shiva
was represented by a *lingam*. You see *lingams* in all Shaivite temples. Veronica doesn't want to talk about Shiva. Not while she's
got Vishnu on her mind. She says that Tibetan Buddhists never
go anywhere or do anything important without first consulting
astrologers to find out the right time and what their predictions
are. "They have all sorts of astronomical charts," she says.

Astrological predictions and different forms of divination
seem to me like anamorphic art that's only intelligible if viewed
from an eccentric point of view, like a reflection in a curved

mirror or one seen by an idiosyncratic eye, images and thoughts to be interpreted by the educated guesses of the seer and the subject.

I think vaguely about cerebral-sexual polarities, relieved that Veronica has shifted part of her sexual energy to learning Tibetan grammar, reading Sanskrit, renewing her idealism, her purity of vision, informing me about Eightfold Paths; Four Noble Truths; sixteen, thirty-two, sixty-four Buddhist precepts—all of which she seems easily able to memorize while I can't even remember the Ten Commandments in their proper order.

Veronica summons me back to the realm of the mundane.

"Are you going to have a bath?" she asks. "Or are you going to dine dirty?"

Fourteen

For the first few days in a new place, I like to see as much as I can before the glaze of familiarity sets in, to get a sense of where I am, then look for what lies behind the corners of walls, casually hidden.

Veronica and I sally forth from the oasis of the Rambagh's splendidly green compound, and taxi across the dusty desert to the walled city of Jaipur. When we pass through a tunnel gateway, the city appears like a cardboard facade of ornate buildings picked out in white lattice-work bays—here a vista, there a prospect, as stylized as a Mogul miniature. My immediate impression is of a two-dimensional reproduction of some other city that is the authentic vision of which I am seeing only a copy: another cardboard stand-in, like that of the Maharaja of Bharatpur presiding over the Diwan-i-Khas at Deeg.

The colors of Jaipur are a melting mix of strawberry ice cream, raspberry sherbet, and orange ice. Gridlock car traffic comes as a surprise, but happily, there are almost as many camels as cars in a side street. Camel caravans, camel carts; yellow-toothed, hare-lipped, knobbly-kneed camels with their absurdly supercilious expressions, divested of their dimming zooness; tall odd creatures, loitering along; Biblical beasts, desert beasts; the invariable symbol of the Orient, symbol of St. John the Baptist, bearing a lamb in his arms, eating locusts and honey, and clad in a raiment of camel's hair. St. John took away the sins of the world. What had Gurdip said about *vahanas*? Where the animal is, the god is also.

I close my eyes momentarily against the glare of the sun, and when I open them again I see an explosion of color. Tented bazaars line walls that have gateways high enough for painted elephants with canopied *howdahs* to amble under with plenty of room to spare. It's all part of a joy ride for visitors to Jaipur, organized by the Rajasthan Mounted Sports Association.

Coming upon the Jantar Mantar is a visual jolt. Its constructions appear surrealistic, like a Brobdingnagian geometry set, or perhaps the playground of a child giant, with steps eight storeys tall that soar into the sky like a cinematographic dream sequence. Veronica says that if she didn't know what it was, she'd take it for a collaborative effort of Calder and Dali, Arabs and ancient Romans. More surprising, more romantic, is what this assemblage, in fact, is: the best-preserved of five stone observatories built in the early eighteenth century by Maharaja Jai Singh to revise the calendar and correct the astronomical tables and catalogue of stars.

The showpiece is an equinoctial dial called the Samrat Yantra, flanked on either side by a quadrant of a circle parallel to the plane of its equator. By means of gnomons some fifty yards long, solar time is given with day-to-day variations. The curving walls of the quadrants look like mammoth segments of a peeled iron orange. Astrolabes and sextants are enlarged to gigantic dimensions. Huge bronze and iron circles lie on the ground with hoopoes pecking at the withered grass around them, bobbing their heads with the self-absorbed nonchalance of chickens. There is a concave marble hemisphere to trace the paths of heavenly bodies across the sky, an isosceles triangle of masonry pierced with arches, a labyrinthine construction shaped like a lotus leaf. As I prowl in, around, up, and through these structures, I sense their mysterious, provocative power. There are instruments for the prediction of eclipses, solstices, equinoxes; instruments to read altitudes and azimuths, to ascertain declinations and distances. Squinting her eyes against the sun, Veronica says she understands none of it. No more do I. I wish Robert were here to explain.

We take turns photographing each other standing by zodiac pavilions, Veronica by a bas-relief of a scorpion, symbol of love and romance; me by the Virgo pavilion, with the figure of a woman riding in a boat sculptured in the form of a bird. Veronica says it's Garuda, the solar bird vehicle of Vishnu, slayer of *nagas* (snakes). I think it looks more like the liver-preying eagle Zeus sent to punish Prometheus for stealing the gift of fire from heaven to bring to mankind. To counterbalance the gift of fire, Zeus sent Pandora to earth with her box of evils. "Zeus sounds as vindictive as Shiva," Veronica says. "Stand still, Mummy. Look up at Garuda. Say cheese."

By now, miraculously, my Rolleiflex has been repaired. I had found the former royal photographer sitting at a deal table with his buddies, smoking a hubble bubble and playing *chaupur* in the shade of a tarpaulin strung between a flamboyant tree and a wall along Mizra Ismail street. I explained about the broken winding mechanism, the non-functioning light meter. He scribbled some notes on the back of a used envelope, gave me a receipt, and told me to come back the next day. The cost of the repair would be sixty-four rupees, or about eight dollars. I left wanting to believe Gurdip's prediction. I returned the next day to the same scene. My camera was ready on time and in perfect working order. As lagniappe, the camera case was polished and its worn corners restitched.

In the hyperbolic cultural idiom of Kim, I burble to the photographer in English and Hindi that he has the energy of Babur, the capability of Shah Jehan, the genius of Akbar. He looks at me like a saw-whet owl. "Bubbles was always telling me that I was jolly good," he replies.

To leave the *punkah*-fan cool and air-conditioned chill of the Rambagh and plunge into the day's heat is tiring, if not downright unhealthy. A solicitous *khidmutgar* at the Rambagh tells us the antidote for heat is to drink lots of water and a hot broth redolent with cardamom, coriander, fennel, and cumin, "the besht for don't be feeling the sun."

Veronica grins when I pinch my nostrils shut and swallow my cupful of this brew. "No worse than Tibetan salted tea made with rancid butter," she says. "Try eating mangoes. They have a cooling effect, too."

Thus prepared, we head off to visit the perfume shops, the "utter confusion of the *attar* (pronounced utter) *wallah*," where oils, essences, and blends are contained in cork-stoppered brown and blue bottles. The shops reek of the mustardy, garlicky stink of asafoetida; the cloying sweetness of jasmine oil; the scent of roses; the odor of *rooh khus*, a blend of sandalwood, grass, and the white blossoms of myrtle plants whose leaves are

a source of henna; and musk, from the Sanskrit word for testi-
cle, Veronica explains.

My mother, who had broken her nose as a child and, as a
consequence, had almost no sense of smell, cared deeply about
the bottles and flacons in which perfume was stored. She once
gave me trinkets and junk to sell to the maids from a cardboard
store facade that my governess had made for me. I can feel again
the humiliation and the frightening tremor of wrongness spiraling through me as Mummy's voice rang out after my sales receipts were counted. Exasperated, accusing, her tone was the
same as she used when dismissing servants, "How *could* you sell
all those things for so little? How *could* you? That beautiful La-
lique perfume bottle only had a tiny chip off its stopper." The
container was important to my mother, the thing contained
important to me.

I like the scent of *rooh khus*. The *attar-wallah* says it is the scent
of Indian spring, the time when the flame of the forest tree
becomes covered with red flowers, the color which excites passion; the time when the mango groves are visited by flocks of
koels singing happy love calls; the time when there is music and
the fragrance of flowers in the air, when Radha can only think
of Krishna, and Krishna only of Radha. The attar-wallah produces the cool scent of *chandan*, or sandalwood, to be used in
summer when the peacocks sit in the shade of banana groves
and when the thought of Krishna departing on his travels rends
Radha's heart. He claims that we "beautiful sisters" could encourage passions in the hearts of whatever lovers we wish to
attract if we will permit him to mix special potions for us, just
what the *gopis* would use to attract Krishna. Legendary adultery,
mythic adultery, can the gods do what people cannot? Veronica

says it is more an expression of Tantric duality, the illusory adultery of splitting and fusing. "Like Shiva," she says, "world-splitting, world-spanning. Weren't you listening when your friend Mulk was talking about Shiva, the glorious iconic androgyne? Married to Sati and, after she was dismembered, to Parvathi, and having a fling with Kali? Transcending the violence and aggression of Kali and going back to the harmony and bliss of Parvathi, his good wife? That was the only interesting thing he spoke about with me."

We move on to see the fantasia of the *bandhani* workers, the tyers and dyers who work with the sharp red, yellow, green, and blue colors of the sun dynasty, the colors of the former royal flags of Rajasthan. The city area here is dilapidated, the lime plaster flaking off like dried skin from the sunburned walls, shutters hanging askew by the windows. The frescoes of fighting elephants and legendary scenes of Radha and Krishna, with which Rajasthani houses are decorated to celebrate weddings, are faded and obscured by tattered posters. Women squat on their haunches designing saris in myriad *chunari* patterns of dots, diamonds, and stripes, all by tying hundreds of tiny thread knots around pinches of a sari folded in four.

Taking a white sari length or a length dyed acidic yellow, a woman folds it, drapes the folded material over a ring shaped like a pointed bishop's mitre that she wears on her index finger, ties thread around it, knots the thread, pulls out the mitre-like ring and pokes it again in the cloth, ties thread around it, knots the thread, each set of knots forming a different, intricate pattern.

A man seizes the cloth from her, plunges it into a cauldron of red as bright as arterial blood, and gives the dripping sari to a fellow worker to hang up to dry. When this wrinkled mass of knotted cloth is dry, the knots are unraveled by ripping the folds of material apart, leaving patterns of white or yellow on the red cloth, one dot for each knot.

A spinach green color is added, or a navy blue, by tying more knots before each dying stage, or by protecting a section from a second color by wrapping part of it in a plastic bag for the effect of a colored border. Today's plastic bags replace yesteryear's wax. The process is easier, the effect produced the same. To make the *laharia* designs of strips and chevrons, a sari is rolled lengthways, tied with thread along its length, then dyed and hung up to dry, repeating the process until the patterned effect is achieved with multi-colors.

Symmetry, repetition, alternation of elements, order over randomness, pattern over chaos, space subdivided in a pleasing ration of constancy and variety—the process and the work-manship is extraordinary. Veronica and I watch for an hour, fascinated. Only afterwards does it dawn on me that *bandhani* gives us the word "bandanna."

Both Meenakshi and Mulk had said that if we were interested in textiles, we should drive out to Sanganer to see how block-printing is done. Heading out again into the fiery desert heat, we cross a landscape of sand, thorn-bush, rocky hills, and a few pale green puffs of wild turmeric. Veronica and I settle ourselves on the sheeted upholstery of the car, forego the cups on our *badlas*, and drink straight from the necks of these leaky antique canteens I had bought in the market.

Close to Sanganer, all the land between houses and work-sheds and along the banks of the Saraswati River is tedded with dyed and patterned cloth laid out to dry. Mulk has told me that an ancient involvement with color chemistry, the use of madder and indigo, the presence of calcium and salts in the river water, and the sun's harsh rays give a distinctive quality to the textiles printed in Sanganer and a transforming alchemy to their dominant colors of apricot, rusty-red, and apple-red, black, saffron, and indigo blue.

"Nice," Veronica says, glancing at the finished products displayed on the shelves and counters of a Cottage Industry outlet. "No chemical dyes. Only mood colors, *raga* colors, special colors."

"Yiss," a clerk agrees. "All colors is being surcharged with expression of feelings evoked by the changing seasons and associations with poetry and religion."

Painted cloths intended for use as temple canopies, tent walls, screens to assure privacy in royal palaces, awnings, and hangings have given way to tablecloths, bedspreads, door curtains, tablemats, wraparound skirts, napkins, cushion and bolster covers. Flower patterns, paisleys, scenes from the life of Krishna—*pitchwai* paintings done on handspun cloth, temple art now rendered tourist-saleable—filigree patterns, parades of elephants and camels, geometrical designs, animal and bird motifs range from the commonplace to the extraordinary, all color fast, all done by hand. I address question after question to the craftsmen working by the river, in their houses, and in communal shade. I soon attract the attention of an Indian student here on a visit from the Museum of Textiles in Ahmedabad. Pleased to be of help, he is delighted to show off his expertise.

"First, Madam, you take a length of cloth and soak it in a

solution of cow dung and water overnight, wash it the next morning, let it dry, soak it, wash it, let it dry, and keep on doing this for a week, until the cloth is bleached.

"Then, Madam, you soak the cloth in a solution of water and the powder of a dried pear-shaped fruit called *myrabolan* for its yield of tannin which, combined with iron acetate made by soaking bits of iron in a solution of water and *jaggery*, is a fixative for black coloring, and lends permanency to it. *Myrabolan*, Madam, comes from the Ink Nut tree, *Terminalia chebula*. The kernels of the fruit are being made into ink and black dye.

"For block printing, Madam, the next step is to outline the designs to be printed on the cloth by using a carved teakwood block dipped in the iron acetate solution where black is to be applied, and in a solution of alum as a mordant where red is to be applied. The cloth is then washed to remove the excess gummy coating of alum, derived from roots, bark, and twigs. Next the cloth is stirred around with a stick in boiling water to which madder root and the leaves of a variety of trees have been added as a red dye which is adhering to the parts of the cloth treated with alum."

The student times his speech precisely to the rhythm of my notebook-scribbling. When my magic marker is lifted from the page, he continues.

"The cloth is then removed from the cauldron, wrung out, taken to the river to be washed, and then soaked in a solution of goat dung from which it is taken to be river-washed, then dried, washed again, dried, washed—washed, and dried for a week until the cloth is bleached except for the portions painted with iron acetate and alum which are retaining black designs and red designs.

"If blue, yellow, and green are to be added to the pattern, the cloth now has to be stiffened with starch so that it can be waxed, and is dipped in boiled-rice water, then in a solution of boiled-rice water and *bhainsees'* milk."

"But why milk?" I ask. "What does that do?"

"It gives a whiter, smoother surface, Madam, so that bees-wax can be spread with a bamboo spatula or bamboo stick drawn over the cloth until all the parts to be protected from blue dye are covered."

"And what is the blue dye made of?" I ask.

"Indigo, slaked lime, Fullers earth, cassia seeds, and water, stirred twice a day for a week."

"But what does indigo come from?"

"It is a compound that comes from the wood of a tree and an extract of its leaves which have to be processed with an alkaline solution of Fullers earth and slaked lime before it becomes a blue dye.

"The wax-coated cloth is now dipped in a vat of indigo until the white portions turn the right shade of blue. Then the cloth is spread in the sun so that the blue can oxidize, after which the cloth is dipped into the boiling water to remove the wax. After the wax has been removed, the cloth is washed in a solution of linseed oil, salt, and lime-water; stiffened with boiled-rice water mixed with *bhainsees'* milk; dried in the sun until it is as stiff as canvas. Now yellow can be applied, a yellow dye obtained from boiling the flowers and leaves of *myrabolan*, and green, made by painting the yellow over the indigo. Treating the cloth with *bhainsees'* milk prevents the colors from spreading or running while they are being painted."

While men stir cloth in vats of boiling, steaming dye, two

young girls sit opposite each other, swaying back and forth as they pull on the wooden handle of a stone handmill, grinding wheat into flour. A mound of wheat and a mound of flour as high as their heads is beside them. They sing about wanting a husband as good as Shiva. They beseech golden Gauri to bestow auspicious blessings upon them.

The student of textiles, Veronica, and I walk past them into a shed where the *Kalamkari* workers are. *Kalam*: pen; *kari*: craft or art. The work is done with a pen made from a sliver of bamboo sharpened to a point. The point is split so that a little rag or a cotton or wool ball can be inserted and soaked in the appropriate dye, or in black ink concocted from a mix of water, iron filings, and molasses made from mangled sugar cane. The artist squeezes the dye- or ink-soaked wad and the color flows freely through the bamboo nib.

"Nearing its final stage, Madam," the students says, "the cloth is dipped in a solution of alum and water to render the colors fixed and fast. Sometimes a solution of mango bark is painted over the yellow portions of the pattern for the same purpose. Then the cloth is washed with a solution of water containing lime, salt, and oil, and dried in the sun."

In the Sanganer Cottage Industry outlet's shop, the finished work is sold for a few dollars. The same price as a *bandhani* sari. The same price as an hour's massage by a hotel *malish-wallah*. The same price as an afternoon tea at the Rambagh Palace.

Fifteen

Veronica says she has heard of a factory outside Jaipur where, "for a song," we can buy garnet and jade beads that would make admirable presents for her friends in Dharamsala and Manali. "I know it's almost too hot for even *you* to shop," she adds, that sly minx of a daughter of mine.

We have been swimming in the indoor pool, quitting the pavilion to let the sun dry our bathing suits, returning to swim. It's no use foundering myself with iced tea and the cooling effect of mangoes and mango ice cream spooned up in the air-conditioned dining room of the Rambagh. I ring for the *khidmutgar* to bring the Abominable Brew. Desperately, I drink it down. Two cups of this herbal concoction have me charged with energy.

When we arrive at the establishment of the wholesale dealer of garnet and jade beads, turquoise and lapis lazuli, rose quartz from Rajasthan, bloodstone found in the Aravalli hills, white crystal from the Himalayas, and industrial diamonds from Golconda, Veronica and I giggle about having more beads than we can cope with—beads of perspiration. The dealer introduces us to his wife, who assures us that henna applied to the soles of our feet will keep them cool and make us feel cooler as well. I leave Veronica sitting cross-legged on a cotton-covered floor pad, propped against a cotton-covered bolster, with an electric fan set on the floor between her and the gem dealer. While coolies are summoned to bring trays of semi-precious stones for her inspection, I follow the gem dealer's wife up a flight of concrete stairs, through an interior hallway, across a makeshift ramp, down another flight of stairs, and across a courtyard to the women's quarters, a series of bare, high-ceilinged rooms furnished with little more than floor pads, bolsters, and wooden chests.

She identifies herself as Lakshmi. I identify myself as Leila. She speaks only the local dialect of Jharashahi and speaks it as confidently to me as though I understood every word she is saying, a stream of language that sounds as incomprehensible in my ears as one interminable serpentine word. I speak to her in English, flinging in nouns, verbs, sentences in Hindi, and some-how, by look, gesture, inflection, expression, we communicate our fascination with each other's clothes, jewelry, cosmetics. Here are her hands, hands to be regarded with reverence, for it is the hands which do the work. There is magic in hands and their talismanic imprint. Lakshmi's hands, fingers, palms, and backs, are painted with henna. Not ordinary henna requiring no qualifiers, but henna of a superior quality—*menhadi*—that gives a brighter color. The fragrant blend is made from a variety of myrtle called *rajani* with small, spiky leaves, and a number of these plants are growing in pots in the courtyard.

Menhadi symbolizes prosperity and a wife's perpetual happi-ness with her husband as well as his long and happy life, and

Lakshmi applies it to her hands and feet on all auspicious occasions. Since the festival of Gangaur is soon to take place throughout Rajasthan, *menhadi* is essential. Lakshmi's maid is dispatched to fetch the booklet of *menhadi* patterns, with photographs and drawings of dozens of designs, each for a specific purpose and festival. "You know, it's like being *tiré à quatre épingles*, dressing in one's Sunday best, as Granny used to say," Veronica says. There are designs representing propitious sweetmeats, specific objects, costumes, leaves, flowers, and birds associated with certain festivals. For Gangaur, Lakshmi has not only seen to the baking of sweet cakes called *ghevar*, but she has also applied a special *menhadi* design called *ghevar* to the backs of her hands.

The maid mimes and demonstrates the cumbersome and time-consuming process involved in the preparation of the paste-making. Straining cloths are shown to me, motions of vigorous hand-rubbing are made, trays and bowls are produced. To apply the paste, Lakshmi shows me, she uses a silver wire. Her servants use a matchstick or a tamarind twig. Whatever implement is used, it must be dipped into the *menhadi* paste and lifted out with the paste stringing, like a length of thread, from its tip. The palms are then painted by layering on the design *without the wire or stick ever coming in contact with the skin*! The technique reminds me once more of decorative icing, which is difficult enough, but when I try to imagine how one would manipulate saliva-like thread suspended from a piece of wire— Lakshmi, that simply cannot be done! Had I thought lassoing a stray eyebrow hair difficult? Had I thought inking in or outlining a design by squeezing a wad of dye-soaked cotton through a bamboo nib so that the dye flows onto the cloth difficult? Painting with *menhadi* paste by waving a little wand over the hand to layer on patterns with a thread of henna icing is of absolutely *spectacular* difficulty.

Lakshmi shrugs. Her smile is like a crescent moon. The more viscous the paste, the stickier its syrup, the more smoothly a design can be applied. She shows me that she has two varieties of paste: a fine kind for decorating her palms with intricate and minute designs, and a coarser blend for completely covering her fingertips and the tips of her toes.

Using her gold wrist bangle as a guide, Lakshmi shows me how the circle for the *ghevar* design is made. She has painted the back and palm of her left hand. Her maid has helped her paint her right hand and the soles of her feet. Lakshmi has painted her own insteps. Lakshmi says that *menhadi* possesses the power to strengthen bonds between women. It brings them close together and encourages friendship. Would I like her to demonstrate the art of *menhadi*-painting on the soles of my feet? On the insteps? On my hands?

Of course!

Lakshmi has pots of old paste, pots of new paste. Old leaves don't make as bright a red paste as new leaves. The maid smears the old paste on the soles of my feet, pats them with something gritty. Lakshmi trickles new paste into a floral spray design on my toes: the beginning of the *ghevar* design to celebrate the Festival of Gangaur.

I sit with my feet propped on a low table, glad that I've worn a lace-edged petticoat. LEILA BURTON IS A GOOD GIRL. It's not what people would think if I were run over, dear nannies, it's what they are thinking now as my feet are being painted.

To entertain me, the maid trots out pattern books of Rangavalli designs, an encyclopedic range of geometrical, floral, and figurative decorations used on the threshold of one's home for such occasions as birthdays, marriages, festivals, and the welcoming of friends. Rangavalli designs are made by sprinkling colored powder freehand or by using guidelines of dots and grids. The variations are mind-boggling. These complex designs may only last a day or so before the patterns disintegrate. *Menhadi* designs, however, last from ten to fifteen days, and can be toned up by applying a mixture of powdered lime and mustard oil. A glass vial is given to me by the maid. Then, at a sharp word from Lakshmi, she quickly whisks it away and seals the cork with melted paraffin before returning the vial to me.

A male servant brings us another plateful of *ghevar* cakes— sweet, buttery, crumbly, and spiced with ginger and cardamom. Another male servant, whom I have seen running sugar cane through a mangle in the courtyard, brings us two glasses of chilled *jaggery* juice and more in an exquisite pottery pitcher, its turquoise motifs outlined in deeper shades of blue, its quartz powder like flecks of mica giving the pitcher a sparkling wet shine.

Lakshmi has a calm, friendly face. Her hair, oiled and drawn into a braided knot fastened with gold-belled hairpins at the nape, has a line of red powder along its center parting. While she continues to trickle on *menhadi*, she orders yet another male servant to stand behind me and fan me with a large lollipop of woven palm leaves. Ancient Mogul custom dictates that it is an outrage to exhibit the soles of one's feet. Veronica has told me never to show the soles of my feet. Brahmins don't like it. Buddhists don't like it. But here and now, my feet are the cynosure of all eyes in the room. The maid holds up a mirror to show me the soles of my feet, brick-red with strange little patterns she has made by pressing grains of millet here and there. Giggling, she lifts both ends of her wide, swinging skirt, a *ghagra* she calls it, so that I can admire the skill with which at least twenty yards of blue material have been sewn together in triangular pieces then tied beneath her navel with a draw string. Over her embroidered *choli*, she wears a short scarf. Lakshmi's costume is the same style, but her scarf length is silk, not cotton, the embroidery on her *choli* is done with metallic threads as well as cotton and silk, and her *ghagra* has a silk lining. Wearing a swinging skirt is almost the same thing as wearing one's own *punkah* fan.

I watch with a sort of mindless astonishment the expertise with which Lakshmi finishes patterning my insteps using the color symbolic of sacrificial blood, rebirth, rejuvenation, life. The *tika* she wears on her forehead, as almost all married women do as a sign of good luck in having their husband alive and capable of providing them with suitable status and protection, is a more vivid red. It is made with *kumkum*, a powder of peeled turmeric roots to which spices and lemon juice have been added until the roots are the color of poppies. *Tika* in Hindi, *sindoor* in Bengali, *kumkum* in Maharashtrian, *bindi* in the central provinces of India, the spot of red powder is a feature common to all women in India, an integral part of Hindu culture and way of life. Now I, too, receive a *tika* in the middle of my forehead, applied with a nailhead by Lakshmi as a gesture of goodwill.

While everything has been explained to me in a dumb show, demonstrated, my notebook passed around to be penned with the servants' different scripts, I have been distributing little presents of money, American cigarettes and Bangalore beedies, pic-

ture postcards of New Delhi, Mathura, Fatehpur Sikri, Bharatpur, Deeg, Jaipur. And now I give Lakshmi an extra lipstick in a
pretty case and a mirrored compact she has also admired. I
mime gratitude and admiration for the artwork on my soles and
insteps. Lakshmi and her four servants are all in a splendid
mood, laughing and smiling, as they form a procession to escort
me back to Veronica.

Veronica has heard about a holy place not far from Jaipur and
suggests we go there. The only problem is that she can't remember what the place is called. All she knows is that it's somewhere
beyond the city walls, back in the hills where there's a magical
source of water that never dries up. Veronica says she is sure the
cabdrivers will know where it is, but they haven't a clue. "They
think I'm talking about a monkey temple," she frets, and asks
the next driver and the next and the next.

Monkey temple, what monkey temple? I seem to be better at
eliciting information than Veronica. I'm promptly told the temple is on the road to Galta.

Veronica squeaks with pleasure. Galta, that's the place. Now
she remembers. Galta! Most of the drivers tell us the road is too
rough, but a young driver is willing to take us to an abandoned
palace, its verandah and outbuildings now a temple to Hanuman, the monkey god. Here, black-faced langurs with elegantly
looping tails are fed every afternoon by temple priests and by
Hanuman devotees, who derive merit from dispersing wheat
cakes and carrots to the troops of langurs congregated beyond
the temple, and above it, in the low hills along the dusty dirt
road that leads to Galta.

Looking up, I see kites wheeling in the sky and one flying

with a snake wriggling in its talons. Hanuman, an incarnation of Vishnu. Hanuman, who named all the things of the world, every tree and plant. Hanuman, the red-faced monkey god, who leaped in a single bound from India to Sri Lanka to come to the aid of Righteous Rama, to vanquish Ravanna who had abducted his wife, soft-eyed Sita, born of a field-furrow. Hanuman, Rama's faithful servant who searches for Sita. Banished, lost, discovered, lost, Sita, dying after the "God of Fire incarnate did her stainless virtue prove," says:

> "Spare a daughter's shame and anguish and receive her,
>   Mother Earth! . . .
> Mother Earth! who bore this woman, once again receive thy
>   child!
> If in truth unto my husband I have proved a faithful wife,
> Mother Earth! relieve thy Sita from the burden of this life!"

> Then the earth was rent and parted, and a golden throne
>   arose,
> Held aloft by jeweled Nagas as the leaves enfold the rose.
> And the mother in embraces held her spotless, sinless child
> . . . pure and true and undefiled.
> . . . Fair Sita is no more,
> Lone is Rama's loveless bosom and his days of bliss are o'er.

Poetry, beyond grammar, beyond names in the *Ramayana*, used to bring tears to my eyes when I read it as a little girl, and now there are no words, just hundreds of monkeys and the unworded, unspeakable poetry of the landscape. The ruined palace, now a monkey temple, posited at the foot of a long, steep ridge of hills bleached to the lavender color of the wild onions flowering by the roadside, is mysterious and beautiful with its rooftop *chattris* and storeys of arched windows. From where I stand on a hill of stony sand and bare rock, the palace encompasses all wonder within its ocher and gray walls.

The air is dusty, dry, so hot that my teeth feel hot. Across the foothills, stone and rock and dust give way to drifts of sand and a broad, dry riverbed indented with hoof-marks of cattle and antelope, the trident prints of peacocks, and the pug marks of a tiger. There is no way of knowing how old or how fresh these marks are. There are occasional underground springs here, and patches of mud and stretches of mud and sand that are sun-baked and crackled. Small black and green warblers flitter in the *babul* trees but, in the sun's glare, it hurts my eyes to look at them, even through dark glasses.

The hills narrow to a gorge. The half-deserted town of Galta, with its massive *Surajpol*, its gateway to the sun, forming a crenellated archway to pass through, is revealed. A cylindrical tower. Ruins of tall *havelis*. A palace with paintings on walls of *chunam* plaster smeared in part, scabbed, scuffed, papered over here and there with posters, written over, urinated on, is magical in its dilapidated and deserted beauty. Archways, stairways, columns, latticed bays, and remarkable paintings in unfading reds and yellows. A few old men dressed in white knickers, tunics, and turbans sit about on wooden benches in the square. Tall trees are encircled with platforms of brick and stone at their bases so that one can sit in the shade. Children. There are always children, and here four small girls are squatting in the dust playing a game with pebbles and a ball that looks like the game of jacks. *Ghota*, they tell me it is called. There are langurs in the trees, a few goats and calves, bullocks, and a pye dog in the square.

I am content to sit on a stone platform under a tree in this strange dream-like place. I like to sit mindless, looking at the wall paintings and figure drawings, watching the children play. Veronica wants to walk up the rock-jut crags into which flights of steps have been laid because here, in Galta, there is a miracle. Water flows unceasingly from a cleft in a rock high above the town, water that gushes down the crags and is channeled into a series of tanks, each within a temple. Veronica wants to join the ranks of the pilgrims and the holy men performing oblations in the temples, bathing in the tanks, or just standing around gazing at the miracle of water.

Oh, Elsa Cloud, sometimes you seem so tiresome in your holier-than-thou attitude, particularly when it involves climbing mountains and leaving behind the mystery of a beautiful old town. I don't know which is more irritating, your reverence, or the fact that I don't share this feeling with you. But just as you are whole-hearted in your spiritual pursuits, I am whole-hearted in my determination not to miss anything. So all right, let's go.

I hold out my hands and let Veronica pull me to my feet. It's an effort for me even to walk to where the stairs begin. When we reach the first tank, I can see that the tanks and temples are both latter-day constructions. Where earlier rock pools and original temples must have been there are now square concrete tanks as large as Olympic-sized swimming pools and as deep as wells. A cat has fallen into the first pool, and there is a great flurry as everyone rushes about hunting for a bucket to tie to a rope that is lowered to haul up the cat which has managed to remain afloat in deep water some forty feet beneath the walkway at the pool's edge. There is no way that the bucket is going to be lowered beneath the cat and brought up with the cat inside. That much is obvious.

Will the cat drown? What will happen? Why doesn't someone just dive in and rescue the cat?

Surprisingly, as the bottom of the bucket touches the surface
of the water, the cat claws at its side, and with extraordinary
cooperation between the man lowering the bucket and the cat,
the cat succeeds in grasping the rim of the bucket and manages
to hold on until the bucket is hauled to the top of the pool's
edge. The cat does not release its hold until the bucket has been
swung back against the bordering rock-face, at which point the
cat drops to the ground and streaks off to the safety of the
temple enclosure.

An extraordinary rescue operation. The view of the town
below, the rock-jut crags and distant hills crowned with battlemented forts, is as dramatic and romantic as an early Turner
lithograph. Veronica hurries me along because, she says sternly,
the holy men want to undress and bathe and she is sure it will
embarrass them if they see me watching from the stairs.

I manage to climb the steps leading to the second tank and
temple and the third, but that is as far as I can manage before
the going gets too rough and the steps narrow and dwindle away
to mere footholds. From there, the rock ascends steeply to a
narrow ledge that winds around to a cave temple. The aspect
really is frightening to me, dizzying to contemplate and dangerous. I beg Veronica not to go any further, but away she goes. I
sit on the steps and pray that she will return safely, as pilgrims
and goats walk up and down past her and me.

By the time Veronica comes skipping down the stairs, safely
returned from an expedition to a cave that she has not found of
any great interest, the afternoon light has begun to fade. Night
falls with the suddenness it does in the Far East. The stairs up

the gorge have been illuminated, but the town is mostly dark, lit only by fires in the tea stalls set up to accommodate pilgrims and the glow of lamps in a few habitations still occupied in the little town.

Veronica tells me gleefully that I was right. The pathway really had been dangerous. She had nearly lost her footing several times. "But I just clawed on to the rocks the way the cat clawed on to the bucket," she says.

Amber is my idea for a day's outing. The Aravalli hills cleave. High on an escarpment to the northwest is the Jaigarh Fort. Its battlemented ramparts descend from the summit, bridge the rocky gorge, and ascend the hills to the northeast. According to stories circulating in Jaipur, everyone's national debt could be paid and then some if the treasures hidden in the Fort could be located and sold. The ancient capital of Amber, and its palace, reflected in a lake, are embraced by massive walls, protected by the Fort and its watchtowers on the summit above. I hear the word Amber in my mind, like a lump of topaz-colored resin, but the local pronunciation is "arm-hair," "Ah-mair." Ah, mère, O mother of the Mogul Rajasthani world!

The place is empty and marvelous. Veronica and I see a choir of ourselves in the convex mirrors of Shish Mahal, a chamber of mirrored hemispheres the size of pingpong balls sliced in two, set in the walls and ceiling of a chapel-like room, in which a single lighted match or the flame from my cigarette lighter creates the effect of a starlit night. An Indian tour guide calls out *Au! Au! Au!* Ow! Ow! Ow! (Come! Come! Come!), in the same tone as a goatherd, to a group of Indian tourists who creep along behind him, too intimidated, almost, to speak.

Veronica takes a folded kerchief from her cloth shoulder bag, a square pocket of striped material made from the same hand-woven fabric, she tells me, that Tibetan women use for aprons. With the woven cloth, she gently plucks yet another wasp from my sleeve. Her gesture is reminiscent of her childhood rituals. Veronica delighted in childhood rituals, knocking on wood, holding her breath and saying "Rabbit, rabbit" whenever we drove past a graveyard. These and other conjurations against bad luck and misfortune, and the fervor with which she had believed in them, seem to have united forces with the Buddhist precept to protect and preserve all life. I've now made a habit of dousing myself with Cutter's insect repellent so that I won't offend Veronica as I used to by swatting flies and mosquitoes. I let her take care of the wasps.

Veronica gazes at the inlaid mosaics of filigreed ivory and rosewood, at the inlays of mirror and glass. "It all looks so festive, so like party-time," she says lightly.

Outside the palace, we look at the twin silver doors, their panels carved with a variety of deities and their *vahanas*, that open into a temple to Kali, the tutelary deity of the rulers of Jaipur. Four-armed, black-faced, garlanded with skulls, her tongue protruding, her long teeth bared, fearsome Kali is one of the aspects in which Shakti, the Mother Goddess, is worshipped. The black *naga*, the snake of Kali, twines around the white tree of Shiva. Kali is worshipped as power, power which is creative, her gracious aspect, and power which is destructive, her terrifying aspect. Besides Kali, Shakti, the Divine Mother has many forms and many names, including Lakshmi, Parvathi, Durga, Sarasvati, all of whom are divided into the dual aspects of male and female.

Shiva, the androgyne, the erotic ascetic, is eternally linked with Shakti. There's a lot of duality, androgyny, incest, and adultery in Hinduism, the play of the animus and the anima, not so much a matter of morality or the lack of it, but of duality, of good and evil, black and white, male and female, incorporated in one self, a matter of splitting and fusing the skeleton and sinews. A matter of paradoxes.

From Veronica's comic books I've learned that in order to amass power to create sexually, Shiva had to become an ascetic on a Himalayan mountaintop. Shiva and Vishnu combine. The Milky Way becomes the Ganges, a river woman who flows from Shiva's head. Shiva is the male principle, the father god, a destroyer who also creates, sustains, and obscures by his power of illusion, and offers grace to the suffering world. Shiva is the dancing Nataraj, dancing with dead Sati in his arms while Vishnu angrily dismembers her. Shiva of the sacred phallic *lingam* cut off the head of the son Parvathi made for him with her tears and menstrual blood, and replaced his son's head with that of an elephant, beloved Ganesha. Parvathi was furious with Shiva for mutilating her son whom she had made all by herself yet who was part of Shiva as well. For Parvathi is as much a part of Shiva as Shiva is of Parvathi. The image of the *lingam* resting in the *yoni*—Shiva's *lingam* in Parvathi's *yoni*—is a constant reminder of their union.

Legend has it that Kali knew Shiva wanted to sleep with Parvathi, but Parvathi was refusing to sleep with Shiva to punish him for one of his many misdeeds. Kali changed herself into a demon who pretended to be Parvathi and began to make love with Shiva. Kali placed teeth inside her vagina as sharp as thunderbolts. The real Parvathi changed herself into a snake and

turned Shiva's cock into a sword with which Shiva killed the
demon Kali. Then Parvathi sloughed her snakeskin and her
good self returned to Shiva as Gauri, the golden one, while her
black, angry self rode off on a lion. Shiva is the supreme cosmic
consciousness. Shakti, who also takes the names and forms of
Parvathi and Kali, is the female principle and the supreme primordial energy. Shiva and Shakti, the supreme male and female
principles, are inseparably connected. They are the substance
and drama of the world. Kali, the cosmic energy, dances eternally on the breast of Shiva, the cosmic consciousness.

At Amber, Kali appears in another guise, one of her terrifying ones. She sits, her black body shriveled, her breasts pendu-
lous, her fingers elongated into talons, her necklace of skulls
drooping over her crossed legs. "I've never thought much about
the Hindu idea of horrible old Mum," I say to Veronica. Oh,
haven't I just, I say to myself. What's more, I've given Veronica
cause to identify horrible old Mum with me.

"Buddhism, the kind practiced by Tibetans, has a particular
love and reverence for the mother's love," Veronica says soothingly. "Tibetans feel that a mother's love for her children has no
rewards or ulterior motive, and so no gain can be gotten. Love
just flows out from the mother and that in itself brings the
mother happiness."

"Oh," I say, warming to Tibetan Buddhism.

We slowly walk back to the entrance gate, where gaudily
painted elephants with *howdahs* wait to carry tourists up the
long ridged ramp to the palace—the caryatids and telamons of
the universe fallen to the sad estate of four-footed taxis, scribbled over with graffiti.

Perhaps it is because I feel I have gotten nowhere in all my notebooks, perhaps it is because back in our room at the Rambagh, I catch a glimpse of myself in the triple mirrors of the dressing-table, but somehow I know I am in for a fit of the blues.

I stare at myself in the mirror. I look at a photograph in my wallet of Robert and myself. My face that smiles out from the photograph and Robert's face with its candid expression are like peat-preserved bodies that archaeologists have excavated from bogs—relics of life, relics of death. When women grow old and lose their looks, they're often given the reassurance that they are ageless. Translated: you may look awful, but at least you remain young in spirit.

"You still look beautiful and young," Veronica says, reading my mind.

When she was a little girl and Allison said, "Mummy, you look like a princess—an old princess," Veronica had laughed. She was more honest then.

I lie on the bed, propping my right foot on my raised left knee examining the patterns on my sole and instep. Somehow, I feel like a jigsaw puzzle with pieces missing or a cup with a missing handle—not quite whole. I don't know what it is. My silent voice jibbers crazily. Boris Godunov. An *oeuf* is as good as a feast. Lay on, Macduff. What's good enough for Boris is good enough for me. What was the point of that opera? Gregory pretending to be Dimitri. Kali pretending to be Parvathi. I'm Parvathi-stricken. Baroque.

"I feel like an empty bottle," I say to Veronica. "Can you funnel optimism into me? Instant optimism, that's what I need."

What I crave is optimism, warmth, happiness. *Happiness?* my silent voice echoes. That's the way a Frenchwoman described her married life, and as she said it, it sounded like "Ah, penis." Erase that. Change to "The *pen* is mightier than the sword." A pen is a female swan. My grandmother told me that. Not an eagle, not Garuda, but a swan, sacred to Venus. Virgo, dear God, what a sign to be born under. Apollo's swan hauls his chariot over the waters by night. The ambivalent swan, its long serpentine neck, masculine; its rounded silky body, feminine, chaste, immaculately white as Shiva's tree. Shiva's tree, kiss-coiled by Kali.

Sixteen

On the way to the airport to catch the plane from Jaipur to Udaipur, the open taxi windows let in the smell of dust, a whiff of wild turmeric, the song of a bulbul, and the soft, early morning desert light that outlines Veronica's sunburned profile in my peripheral vision. We stop at a crossroad to buy crisp-crusted gingery *ghevar* cakes, and politely address the old biddy selling them as Mataji. Honorable Mother smiles. Her mouth opens, her lips widen across broken, betel-brown teeth in a smile that yet is radiantly sweet, fleeting, and she begins to speak about the festival of Gangaur, her eyes as bright as if she had just seen a miracle. When I tell her in Hindi that we are on our way "to see Gangaur, to go away, Udaipur," she reaches out to put her fingers on my hand, and smiles again.

The air is fresh and pearly. I note in my journal that many men bicycle side by side, holding hands. We eat our *ghevar* cakes, carefully sip orange juice from our *badlas*, and then we're at the airport. Here, an obviously rich departing group is garlanded with red and white roses, the men wearing turbans twirled and

tied to one side with their European-style business suits. The
women wearing iridescent blue, green and pink shot silk saris
gleam and glint with pearls and diamonds. Three local minstrels
have grouped themselves between the women and men to play
ravanhathas, stringed instruments with coconut shell halves as
resonators, and belled bows providing a tinkling percussion.
Every once in a while, a passerby drops a coin in their alms
basket. The garlanded men talk, laugh, gesticulate in fellowship.
The women, in the convention of wallflowers at a dance, put up
a show of intense interest in what the other women are saying,
but all the time watch the men surreptitiously.

Our plane is called. I eye it warily. It is a very small plane.
Soon after we board, a stewardess in a sari passes around trays
of pineapple juice and gingersnaps. We bump and lurch along
for an hour or so and finally land in flat desert country, picked
out with scrub and euphorbia. The car I have arranged for is
there to meet us. The driver's name is Bhaice. He is twenty-
three, quiet, pleasant.

We drive away past the ruins of the thick walls and tunnel
gates of Chittor, and Chittorgarh, the fortresses of Chittor, the
old capital of the dynastic maharanas of Mewar, who reigned in
the Aravalli hills long before the time of the Muslim conquest.
In one of the crenellated walls a stone Ganesha is enshrined in a
niche, splashed with red and yellow dye, streaked with offertory
dribbles of curds and *ghee*. Bhaice brakes the car so I can photograph the guardian deity whose trunk is curved to remove
obstacles, whose worshipers propitiate him affectionately at the
start of a ritual or the beginning of a journey. I put our last *ghevar*
cake by his side, where sparrows will be sure to find it.

Then we are on our way again, past Jain temples and out into a green and pastoral landscape checkered with low gray stone walls and great high stone walls with white bullocks beside them turning water wheels. The *ghagra*, that glorious *punkah* fan of a swinging skirt, has disappeared. Women are wearing saris again.

As with forest birds which rarely see each other and make and maintain contact almost exclusively by their voices, there are times when Veronica and I talk constantly. Now we chatter, interrupting each other, laughing, discussing the vagaries of language, word meanings, word origins, the endearing things Veronica used to say as a child. "When you talked about your dreams," I say, "you said you saw them in your pillow. When I talked about soft music, you asked what hard music was. You called a pig's snout his 'snort,' and the part in your hair, a road. You called meringues 'brangs.' "

"Oh, Mum," Veronica says, "you're *so* funny."

Then we fall silent, gazing at the colors of a botanical garden on the fringe of Udaipur, the brilliance of bougainvillea, the blue-mauve of jacaranda, strollers in orange turbans and crimson saris, a group of young girls wearing saris in paint-box colors who are picking flowers and filling up their brass pots with them.

"For Gangaur festival," Bhaice says, pointing out an architectural folly called Queen Victoria's Palace. The statue of the queen in the center of a rose garden has been replaced by a statue of Mahatma Gandhi. Both Mummy and Granny had told me never to refer to Gandhi as Mahatma Gandhi, but to say Mr. Gandhi. Why? "Because houghmagandie, lassie, is the act of creation," a Scottish chambermaid blushingly explained. Her explanation, incomprehensible to me years ago, is suddenly clear. Well, hurrah for houghmagandie, and hurrah for Gangaur and the mother goddess Gauri and a good man with whom to share one's life.

Gangaur is a local festival, a women's festival that follows Holi and lasts for eighteen days, I scribble in my notebook, reading back what I've written to Veronica. Like Easter, it is a celebration of the vernal equinox, when Holika, who has been burned in effigy in the bonfires of Holi, is resurrected in the aspect of Gauri or Parvathi. Tomorrow, on the last day of the festival, images of Gauri will be carried through the streets in procession—Holika reborn in a doll's body, beautifully dressed, symbolic of the new harvest of the land—along with images of her consort Shiva, in his aspect of Issar or Gan. Because this is a women's festival, images of Shiva-Issar-Gan are always shorter than the meter's height prescribed for figurines of Holika-Parvathi-Gauri. The procession ends at Lake Pichola—a spring-fed man-made basin built in the fourteenth century to catch the monsoon's rains—where the images of Gan and Gauri are given a ceremonial bath. The flowers we have seen the young girls collecting will be offered tomorrow to Gauri.

"Ah, then Gangaur corresponds to Dakini Day in the Tibetan lunar calendar, which takes place ten days after the full moon in May, also a *Shakti* day, a women's day," Veronica says in her waltz-of-the-flowers voice. "Dakinis represent the kind of spirited inspiration which cuts through mental dullness and selfishness. Rather like the Muses. But instead of dolls, dakinis are represented as images or paintings of women who can *fly*." An inspirational festival, she says. She suggests that if we are going to be up early for the procession, we might as well have a nap before we change for dinner. "Or are we going to dine dirty?" She smiles teasingly.

To dine dirty is a phrase, much in use during the days of the British Raj, that means not to change for dinner. My grand-mother used it and I, too, sometimes, in a joking way—yet seriously enough for Veronica to play it back to me so repeti-tively that I'm tired of being taunted with it.

We are staying at the Lake Palace, more than three hundred years old, a former royal retreat, now freshly renovated as a hotel, set on four acres of rock in the middle of Lake Pichola. The water lapping beneath our window is light green, with moving pads of water hyacinths and lilies that make psychedelic reflections on our ceiling. At sunset, the City Palace across the lake turns from etiolated white to rose-peach. Thousands of green parrots fly overhead, winging their way back to their nesting sites in the ruins of the old Jag Mandir palace far away on the other side of the lake.

I wake the next morning to what I think is the sound of drums. It turns out to be the sound of *dhobis* pounding dirty laundry against the steps of the *dhobi-ghats*.

The festival day of Gangaur restores to me the excitement of the grand occasions and seasonal holidays of my childhood, dates marked by presents, flowers, traditional cakes, special fra-grances. I hug Veronica before I have my bath. I hug Veronica after I have my bath. I don my most becoming dress and weight my neck and arms with gold-dipped silver Indian jewelry (which Indians never fail to admire and believe to be solid gold rather than silver in impressive masquerade). I clown around the room, dancing, laughing, clashing, and jingling. Mummy had said more than once she couldn't understand where I had got my peasant hands, my peasant feet, my "Mediterranean temperament." Now my daughter asks, "How manic can you be?" She rolls up her eyes, grimacing with the same exasperation my mother expressed, but I notice that she has put on her most becoming blue Laura Ashley dress and fished through the bureau drawer for the lapis lazuli ring we bought in Chandni Chowk.

We have breakfast outside in the rose garden where a fountain splashes into a pool in which small orange fish swim beneath scattered pads of lotus. Lotus-land, lotus-land, such lotus-eaters we are, propped not on beds of amaranth and moly, but on cushioned wooden chairs called by the waiters "long-sleevers" because of their long armrests. They have detachable leg-rests and stands for our coffee cups attached to their sides. There is a cushioned brass swing in the loggia, and after breakfast we settle in to it, pushing it slowly back and forth with our sandaled toes. More beautiful by far than the *menhadi* designs on my insteps are the patterns spun by light filtering through filigreed screens along ground floor corridors, crocheted marble walls sculptured to look like bedspreads of six-petaled flowers tightly stretched to dry in the sun which cast rondelles of brilliant light on white marble floors. The sky is pink with the rising sun, and thousands upon thousands of green parrots are now leaving their nesting places in Jag Mandir and flying towards the town. I am dizzied with delight.

We walk from the loggia, its slender carved columns adjacent to our groundfloor room, to a stone terrace, then down steep steps to a waiting launch that takes us ashore to dock in the shadow of the City Palace. Bhaice, waiting for us, drives us around to the entrance of the palace through the Hathi Pol, or Elephant Gate. We pass along a main street crowded with little shops selling antiques and curios, ivory and sandalwood chess sets, marionettes, portable shrines of Krishna, brass and bronze images, carved wooden printing blocks, *pitchwai* paintings, and a glorious fling of jewelry.

Iron shutters roll up and shops open to take advantage of the morning cool. If a shop is closed, all you have to do is bang on the door and shout *koyi hai* (is anybody there?) and pretty soon someone will come to open the door. Bhaice says he'll bang on doors for us, but we tell him no, not now, not today. We want to go as quickly as possible to the Jagdish Temple where we'll have the best view of the procession.

In a few minutes we arrive at an immense Indo-Saracenic pile with a seemingly interminable flight of steps leading to the open terrace of its platform, which is massed with carvings and figures of gods, goddesses, and elephants sculptured from gray stone. Conscious of my camera and totebag, and the *badlas* and box lunches Veronica and I are carrying, I pause, wondering if it's really all right, not sacrilegious, to make use of such an awesome temple as a grandstand and picnic spot. But Bhaice says it's the best sitting place in town, so up we go, with large-eyed, smiling girl-children minnowing around us, wistful and appealing. Their quick, coaxing voices nibble at us with pleas and questions:

Where is it you are coming from?
Andiamo?
Quel age a vous?
Buon giorno.

Bon jour.
Baksheesh.
Bon Bon.
One rupee?
Buona sera.
Ciao.
What country are you coming from?
American coin for collection?
Menhadi. Bahot Sundar!
Lire?
Francs?
Sweeties?
Beedies?

Large, dark, uncomprehending eyes. Beautiful smiles. Beautiful uplifted faces. Even Veronica, as skilled at deflecting beggars as she is the conversational gambits of lonely tourists, finds the children beguiling. I find them irresistible. When we reach the platform, they help us remove our sandals and skip before us to point out Garuda and Krishna and hold up earthenware lamps beneath the chins of certain sculptures so we can see how the light makes their lips curve in gentle smiles. They run to get us strips of coconut matting so we can sit at the top of the flight of stairs leading to the platform without getting our dresses dusty, and they sit on either side of us so that people walking up the stairs won't step on our skirts or brush against us. A child who can be no more than five, seeing me struggling with the complex of camera straps and sunglasses and reading glasses attached to ribbons around my neck, shyly reaches up, unties my glasses, reties them, unbuckles the Rolleiflex from its strap and re-buckles it with such swift expertise that I am astonished. When I was five, I couldn't even tie a shoelace!

A holy man reclining in the shade of a stone elephant smiles at us and at them. We give him a few coins, and one of the children gives him a coin we have given her and then comes back to us and holds out her little hennaed palm for another.

Opposite us, facing the steps of the Jagdish Temple, is a towering red sandstone archway, and through it, the procession passes. Women in brilliant gold-embroidered saris in vibrant shades of scarlet, deep green, lemon-yellow. Women in silver-embroidered saris in pastel shades of violet, rose, honey, green, apricot, azure. Women in cerise, dandelion yellow, emerald, vermilion. On platforms raised above sari-shawled heads they carry wooden or terracotta images of Gauri costumed in saris, mostly red, pink, yellow, sparkling with sequins and glass jewels, wreathed in flowers, while girl children, some not much taller than the figurines, walk beside them carrying images of Gan and Gauri. The crowd seethes in an access of good will. There are occasional camels with bulging panniers and families riding on their backs, and a few caparisoned elephants guided by mahouts wearing fanning turbans of poppy-colored muslin, with families seated behind them in *howdahs* garlanded with marigolds and golden champak. There are bands of musicians, and children holding green paper parrots on sticks, little boys whirling ratcheted noisemakers, little boys tooting tin horns and blowing whistles, balloon sellers carrying huge bouquets of helium-filled balloons in hot pinks, acid greens, and sun yellows; and men playing bagpipes, be-ribboned and covered with various tartans; and wonderful jugglers, juggling with oranges and sticks and balls. Happy, spirited, beautiful, the processional pageantry continues through the morning and early afternoon.

Then, before the religious ceremonies by the lake begin, the crowds disperse to eat and to buy souvenirs.

The girl children tell us there is a fairground down by the *ghats* where they specially want to go and where we'll be able to have a good view of the Gauri *puja*, and where we will see the women dancing the *Ghoomer* and where we can buy sweeties and ice cream. They'll show us. They know the way. *Au! Au! Au!* Ow! Ow! Ow! It's very near. The square just below the Jagdish Temple is where the fair is, and the *ghats* are just a square beyond that. *Au! Au! Au!* Ow! Ow! Ow!

Down from the heights of the temple, around the corner, tall cream and ivory houses and archways are decorated with lively paintings of horses and elephants, scenes from the epic and heroic tales of ancient Rajputana. The children know all the stories. Rana Pratap, a *kshatriya* (warrior) hero, Shiva, Krishna; an elephant bearing the royal Mewar tutelary deity Eklingji; Rama, Parvathi in the form of Shakti riding a lion; Indra lord of the heavens, Surya the sun, Agni the fire, Varuna the wind—I hear the names in the trilling words pouring from the children. We pass a woman giving her brass-caged parrot a bath. We watch for a moment while a woman sitting in a doorway applies *menhadi* patterns to the feet of another, a freehand composition of greater intricacy than the patterns on my feet. We compare designs, exchange pleasantries, while the girls escorting us wait, giggling, smiling, laughing, whispering.

Gangaur is a day of abundance, and how lucky the girls are to have found Veronica and me. They know we'll be generous and pay for lots of sweeties, ice cream and rides and, of course, that's what we do. They race for the merry-go-round with its wonderful old wooden horses and shriek with joy as they swing high overhead on the ferris wheel. They lap up their ice cream without spilling any on their dresses.

Every shop in the square displays a figure of Gauri, each of her wooden fingers ringed and tipped with *menhadi*, her red *tika* often spangled, her mantle embroidered with gold and silver thread, her Mewari finery fresh, bright, and charming. All around us are mounds of fruit on split bamboo trays to be offered to Gauri, and old-fashioned toys and little wooden figures of animals, people, birds, fish that we buy for the children and for ourselves.

When we hear the sound of drums, horns, and stringed instruments in the distance, the children come to steer us through a gathering crowd into the square by the *ghats* where no men except the priests who are already there performing *puja*, are allowed. Our entourage of girl sprites finds us a place on a balcony to watch from as the square is cleared and women float forward to dance to the accompaniment of a small orchestra of drums and stringed instruments that for a little while drowns out the sound of the oncoming processional band. No folk ballet was ever as lovely—the lake shimmering green-blue beyond the white square with its delicately colored wall paintings, the women whirling and swaying, their deep pink, light pink, red, orange, blue saris flaring. The ivory and cream walls turn golden as the sun slides down in the sky and the dancers draw back to make room for a tightly grouped procession of women carrying images of Gauri. They sing hymns in praise of her, their voices raised above the tremendous din of the processional band, and then suddenly the voices are *a capella*, a sound as pure, clear, and joyous as Easter Alleluias. The images are then carried to the *ghats* and down the steps to the lake for the ceremonial baths. The square is now filled with women of all ages, some with babies in their arms, children by the hand. A few high-prowed boats filled with flowers and women carrying images of Gauri glide into the lake, poled toward some unknown destination by men standing in the prows like gondolieri. The golden light, and the groups of cinnamon-skinned women in their gauze and silk saris of hues that form pattern after pattern of drifting beauty, are mesmeric.

Before Gauri in the form of Parvathi, there was Sati, Shiva's first wife, who immolated herself when Shiva was not invited to her father's sacrificial feast. Sati, whose name means true, good, pure, symbolizing the quintessential quality of a good wife who can neither bear to live if her husband is insulted nor outlive him if he dies, survives in the eponymous term, more commonly spelled *suttee*, meaning the immolation of widows, a practice forbidden under British government and now practically obsolete. When Shiva learned that Sati had killed herself, he took up her body in his arms and danced in grief, harassing the world with his tears until Vishnu chopped the corpse into pieces. Where the *yoni* fell, Shiva went in the form of a *lingam* and peace was re-established in the universe. Love is all fire, so heaven and hell are the same place, the torments of the damned part of the felicity of the redeemed. The custom of *suttee* may be obsolete, but the idea and the idealism remain.

In *Love's Body*, Norman Brown, quoting from the Upanishads as well as synthesizing the philosophies of Blake and Reik, wrote: "A fiery consummation. Not suspense, but end-pleasure; not partial sacrifice (castration), but total holocaust. It is as fire that sex and war and eating and sacrifice are one. 'Woman, verily, O Gautama, is a sacrificial fire. In this case the sexual organ is the fuel: when one invites, the smoke; the vulva, the flame; when one inserts, the coals: the sexual pleasure, the sparks. In this fire the gods offer semen. From this oblation arises the fetus.' Sex and war and the Last Judgment—'the Loins, the place of the Last Judgment.' The word consummation refers both to the burning of the world and the sacred marriage."

Love. In India, the strange duality of the ascetic and the erotic is glorified in the worship of Shiva. Shiva, the anti-social ascetic on the mountaintop of Kailasa saves his seed so that he can be wildly erotic when he descends to earth. That's the way the gods live. Ordinary mortals in India apparently think marriage is not a matter of love, but of status, physical appearance, and money—how much the prospective husband earns, the size of the dowry the prospective bride can offer. The wife merges with her husband, lives through him, suffers with him. She is not considered too weak, too empty to live her own life, nor is she considered to be exploiting her husband in gaining success, power, prestige through him. This is the role of a good wife: to feed and nurture her husband, to provide him with sons who will take care of him in his old age, to be his servant. He is expected to fulfill all the expectations of her life and to take responsibility for all good and evil that befalls them. Successful manipulation of him is her predominant task. After the wedding, her own family, by custom, takes second place to his. Her mother is supplanted in importance by her mother-in-law.

Love. Conjugal love. Romantic love. God's love. The first love a child knows is the protective, nurturing love of its mother. Later the father's love is the bridge from the mother to the world, drawing the child out just as the sun draws moisture from the earth and the clouds send it back as life-giving rain. Veronica was deprived of that. Her father abandoned us when she was a child. Suddenly, I am standing again in that strange moonscape that is Iceland, hearing Veronica say in a voice like the sighing of pines in the wind, "I want to be the sea, the jungle, or else a cloud." And I hear beyond her speech, beyond her words, the longing to know her direction in life, to be different from me, separate from me and superior in every way possible to me, or am I imagining her feelings about me to be the same as mine once were about my mother?

The only way my mother could show her love for me was to give me material objects; the only way she could receive love from me was to receive my pleasure in those objects. My offered gratitude when she gave me the "rich toy" was probably as inadequate for her as her gratitude was for me for the pomander balls I had cramped and dented the cushion of my index finger making, for the bouquets of wild flowers I picked for her. "That's nice, dear," she said, and forgot to put them in water.

Loving and being loved are psychologically different. I've read that a person who becomes loved no longer feels the urgent desire to love. My desire to love was always urgent. I loved birds, trees, flowers, clouds, sunsets, the smell of horses, the little black spire of a Siamese kitten's tail. I loved Kim and the Holy Man. I loved my grandmother. My grandmother's ideal of a good and wonderful idealized self was God, and what my grandmother admired, I admired, too. God was everything, until I met Robert, and then God and Robert and Veronica all became inseparable, all mine to love. I could escape what I didn't like about myself and become enthralled by them. The emotions of love, the inspirations of religion, the creative power of Michelangelo and Shakespeare all are ways of filling the soul with delight, to be blessed vessels of a supernatural power beyond one's grasp—"Ah, but a man's reach should exceed his grasp, or what's a heaven for?" I always felt a drive for self-perfection that I could love in someone or something else. Veronica longed for "someone perfect to love," a man to be as perfect as her father, a man to draw her out from a self-enclosing world into another world. Just as my mother had done for me, I gave Veronica things—molten maternal love is a lava flow of things—instead of what she wanted. I remember her words "How can you say you love me, Mummy, if you don't do what I want you to do?"

My mind circles like a carousel, the need to learn, understand, explain riding around and around, the spirit of my grandmother on one side, the spirit of Robert on the other, holding out brass rings of comprehension I reach for and miss.

We are back at the Lake Palace. Snuggling into a goose-down pillow with a rose silk comforter rustling in my ears, I feel myself drifting away. Sleep that "knits up the ravell'd sleeve of care . . . balm of hurt minds . . ." is around me now. The purling water of the lake carries me in a boat floating toward another shore where Shiva is dancing with my father, my grandmother, and Robert, who is limp as a rag doll he is holding in his arms with the feathers flying from its stuffing like snowflakes whirling in a glass ball, falling slowly to rest on a tree and a castle. Thoughts streak across the drowsing landscape of my mind with the force-filled clarity of lightning. I hear once more the story my mother used to tell—"that old chestnut again," my father would say impatiently when she got to the part about herself as an infant wrapped in a shawl at the foot of her Papa's and Mama's double bed. "And there I was, swaddled in a shawl on top of the *rose-pink counterpane*, with Mama lying back on the pillows, when Papa came bounding into the room, inflamed with desire . . . Determined to have his way with Mama, Papa flung the counterpane to the floor in the frenzy of his excitement, hurled it into a corner, and leaped between the sheets to make the animal with two backs." The thick layers of down had muffled my mother's cries, but had not prevented "contusions and a concussion."

"The *pink counterpane*," she had always said with careful emphasis, the *pink counterpane*, in italics, "thrown on the floor, hurled into a corner." And suddenly the enormity of that pun, the inversion, the reversal of meaning, seems clear to me. No wonder Mummy was so possessive about me, so determined that my love for her should be exclusive that she dismissed any nurse for whom I showed affection or who showed affection for me. In drawing me closer she had pushed me away, perpetuating the pain of her childhood in the circumstances of mine. And Veronica? Have all the clumsy misunderstandings about love and sex for which I faulted my mother been repeated in other ways with my daughter? The rose-pink counterpane whispers and rustles, the last sound I hear as I fall asleep.

The dream-like setting of the Lake Palace and the dream-like vision of Udaipur lull Veronica and me into passing days of sybaritic simplicity, comfort, pleasure. Wakened by the *dhobis'* morning tattoo, we swim in a small deep pool we have all to ourselves and, climbing out of it, have breakfast brought to us, read books, write letters in the shade of a mango tree.

We picnic with palm squirrels sharing our sandwiches at the Sehelion ki Bara gardens where, just as Meenakshi described them, black stone *chattris* topped with pewter doves surround one pool, while another is guarded by four life-size stone elephants, the vehicles of Indra, lord of the heavens. The fountains in both pools are turned on full force, and the cold spray combined with the scorching heat of the midday sun is so delicious that Veronica and I let ourselves get soaked just for the pleasure of shivering for a few minutes in the daytime as we often do at night.

I am content just to wander around the peaceful town, rambling through rose gardens, and searching through dusty little shops packed with the beautiful and the curious. There are scalloped arches everywhere, the sight and sound of water always somewhere, and now that Gangaur has passed, no crowds.

Across the lake the walls of the City Palace with their rows of arched windows are like flattened columbaria, the Colosseum unfurled, a meandering convolution of four palaces fortressed and enclosed as one.

The palace is maze-like, labyrinthine, the largest in Rajasthan. It is built on the crest of a ridge, with part of it against a cliff face, and extended with terraces supported on huge archways, all up and down. In one chamber, a tree grows straight through the ceiling into a roofed-over terrace above, where it has thrust through one *chattri* and branched into another. Marble, virtually the only building material for floors and walls, tilts underfoot. Walls have been masked in decorative plasterwork, mirror mosaics, frescoes, inlays in geometric and floral patterns, and insets of stained glass, an architectural detail like an element in a stage set. In an eighteenth-century chamber covered with blue-and-white Delft tiles depicting biblical scenes, there is a stained glass window which records images of Krishna and Radha. Elsewhere, walls appear to be hung with pages from an illuminated Oriental Book of Hours, but these turn out to be mosaics worked in shards of colored glass, and gemstones in cloisonné bas-relief.

Veronica and I wander through a courtyard where elephant fights used to take place, their huge stalls now used as storage space for an antiquated Rolls Royce with a Humber body, a tiger cage, a brass house that could have served as a fountain or a hot-water shower, a weighing seat with a brass chair in which a Maharaja had sat to balance his weight against a largesse of silver coins to be tossed to the poor, the frame of a harp with most of its strings missing and a label saying it was from Stüttgart, a grand piano with an open top exposing a wild tangle of broken wires and attachments, a lacquered silver-plated coach, several gilded *howdahs, ambabadis* with double-peaked canopies and tattered red silk curtains, all dusty fragments of the lives of recent Mewar rulers, the descendants of the sun who once ruled a tenth of India.

To get out of the palace, we have to follow a tour guide whose stock in trade seems to be to ask how many tigers there are in a painting of leopards. He explains the joke tiresomely in English and a dozen other languages, including "Sweetish" for Veronica, who is often thought to be Scandinavian. Italians in the group ogle Veronica and me and murmur passionate endearments. Veronica, suddenly haughty and grand, replies to them in Tibetan, which foxes everyone.

On our last night in Udaipur before we fly south to Bangalore, there is to be a "puppet" show on the roof of the Lake

Palace at half-past eight. We take our places under a dark blue velvet sky. The air is silky and caressing, cool, but not chilly. There is a vast fling of stars and a full moon, with fruit-bats silhouetted against it in flickering arcs. Mystery and romance compound with the scent of water and the firelight of the torchères with which the low-walled roof is lit. Veronica and I seat ourselves, cross-legged and expectant.

A fat, jolly, bearded old man, standing behind the stage and manipulating the strings, introduces the characters one by one:

> A snake charmer without a snake;
> A postman on a recalcitrant camel;
> A maharaja, standing up to dance on his horse and
>   brandishing flaming torches (real flames);
> A pink-costumed dancer;
> Palace guards;
> An angry maharaja, lopping off his enemy's head with a
>   scimitar;
> A drummer.

In their costumes of brocade and shimmering silk, the figures are whimsical, humorous, and charming.

The marionette master's young wife is seated on the roof, stage left. While the play is acted, she sings, speaks the dialogue, and drums on a *tabla*, her drumming coordinated with that of the marionette drummer, who is seated in front of the curtain and above her mantled head.

Rajasthan is renowned for its marionettes, and what we are seeing is a traveling theater of Rajput folk legends. I am bewildered, unable to follow the dialogue, but the action has great vivacity and humor. I am mesmerized by the frightening twisting of a cobra that has appeared on stage, so lifelike that when it strikes the wicked maharaja, I gasp audibly. Veronica laughs and puts her arm around my shoulder. "It's all right, Mummy," she says in the tone of a mother soothing a frightened child.

The marionette master's wife is wonderful. She does strong male voices, sweet women's voices, amiable peasant voices, voices with many nuances. The marionette master is a wizard at reproducing the prance of a horse, the knock-kneed gait of a camel, and the arm movements of the energetic drummer.

When the performance is over, the characters make *mujras* to the audience. The messages they sign with their fingers and the positions of their hands prompt enthusiastic acknowledgement from the audience. The cobra bites its tail to become an ourobouros and lets the snake charmer tap it like a hoop around the stage. We applaud wildly. The marionettes have taken on such a life of their own that it's difficult to accept the death of an illusion as I watch them being folded up, wrapped in cloth and laid in layers in a tin trunk.

Seventeen

On the way to Bangalore from the airport, I notice flame-of-the-forest trees in bloom, gul mohur trees flowering lemon-bright, palms, eucalyptus, iron-red earth. A sweep of grassland that reminds me of the high veldt in South Africa and the same quality of light gives a distinctiveness to everything: the clarity of a mazarine sky; a billboard saying VISIT NATESAN'S ANTIQARTS, ANTIQUES, HANDICRAFTS, BATIKS; another heralding BANGALORE THE GARDEN CITY; another advertising HAPPY-GAY-LUCKY FASHIONS; red-tiled roofs, goats, oxen, a child standing by a bus stop selling white and yellow flowers wrapped in wet leaves; a sign saying CHRIST THE KING; another sign saying HYDRAULIC PRESSING WORKS; a sign above a store in town saying HIGGINBOTHAM'S STATIONERY. And then the taxi pulls up in front of the modern, air-conditioned Ashoka Hotel.

"Very American," Veronica says, sounding pleased, looking around the lobby.

Once we're ensconced in our motel-like room, I flop on the bed with a copy of the *Deccan Herald*.

"Thought for the day," I read. " 'Humility is the true cure for many a needles heartache.' I adore 'needles heartache.' " I lie on my back, my feet propped up on pillows. The *menhadi* patterns are barely visible. "Do you want to see a movie in English, Kannada, Tamil, Telegu, Hindi, or Malayalam?" I ask. "We've got a choice of twenty-six movies in six languages."

We go to see Satyajit Ray's *Shadranj ki Kilari* in Hindi, a marvelous film, preceded by fifteen minutes of commercials, including one in which an Indian gentleman absent-mindedly stubs out his cigarette on his wife's hand.

"Bangalore, literally, 'the city of bengalu,' a kind of bean, has a space research center founded by the philanthropic Tata family; the remains of a fort built by Huder Ali, a Muslim ruler of the eighteenth century; a boating lake, a children's park, several mosques, a Maharaja's palace, many factories. Does this interest you?" I ask Veronica, reading from a guidebook over our breakfast coffee.

"Does it interest you?"

"Well, I don't want to be here and miss anything," I reply. "There's also the Lal Bagh Botanical Garden, the Government Museum and adjacent Venkatappa Art Gallery, the Russel Fruit and Vegetable Market. It doesn't sound like much, but something might turn out to be wonderful." I can hear my own doubtful optimism—hopeful, but skeptical. "Expect the best, but prepare for the worst."

"Granny used to say that," Veronica says reproachfully. She begins to stir lazily about the room, straightening her books and mine, closing the lids of our tin trunks. She picks up my camera. "Are you going to take it?"

"No."

"Good." Veronica puts the Rolleiflex back on the bureau top. "Here are your sunglasses. Have you got your reading glasses?"

"Yes, thank you, darling."

"Are we coming back or are we going to be out all day?"

"Out."

"You drank an awful lot of coffee this morning."

"Don't worry. I've been to the loo."

"Well, but don't wear underpants. Just in case."

She means just in case there isn't a "decent" bathroom, and I have to make do with one of the hole-in-the-sloping-cement-floor affairs which are found in public places. To stand or squat, to pull down underpants and hold on to them to keep them from slipping to the wet floor, to pull up my skirt and bunch it around my waist—that I can manage. But I never can manage the smell. I get the dry heaves. Veronica thinks if I use my other hand to pinch my nostrils together, my "princess and the pee problem," as she calls it, will be a lot easier. I ignore her advice not to wear underpants.

In the British-built, early Victorian Russel Market, along the arcades of a building as long as Buckingham Palace which overflows into a mass of tented stalls in the building's courtyard, dozens of garland-threaders are stringing jasmine, tuberoses, and an orange flower called *kanakamarum* in perfumed serpentines along counters covered with wet newspaper. Bangalore matrons are buying vegetables: *brinjals* (eggplant), ladies' fingers (okra), a tropical kind of squash called cho-cho that I remember eating in Jamaica, tomatoes, beans, beets, onions, cucumbers, green chilies, peas, potatoes, carrots, cabbages, cauliflowers, yams. Herbs, spices, and spice compounds—all sorts of special *masala* mixes. Pepper corns. Roots of ginger. Turmeric. Cloves. Coconuts. Butterfruit or yellow rose apples, as some people call them—a specialty of Bangalore—which taste of pears and roses and are so delicious that I buy two kilos of them, and another kilo of mangoes. The air is rich with the smell of smoke and food grilling and frying on braziers, of ripe fruit and cabbages and flowers. Like the city of Bangalore, the market is spacious, clean, easy to find one's way in, but unlike the city, the market throbs with human intensity: haggling buyers, wheedling sellers, and *seths*, the hustlers who will negotiate anything for a price. Men, women, and children are hawking cheap pens, toys, lottery tickets, peacock feathers, soft drinks, shoelaces, spools of thread, religious images, mirrors framed in plastic, padlocks, and brass bells. A *seth* asks us if we want to buy a gold watch. Veronica says she doesn't need a watch. I say I already have one. By one of the exits, I see a sign saying LADIES URINLAS.

Veronica fusses when she sees me emerge from it with my face blotched and my eyes red and watery. She is sure I'm going to "burst a blood vessel one of these days" if I'm not careful.

"Is there no might, no majesty?" Robert used to say whenever he felt his dignity or his self-esteem threatened. I smile as I hear my voice echoing his. When I'm alone in my apartment in New York, I do just what my mother and grandmother always did: close the bathroom door and turn on the water taps in the basin. Out of habit, I do the same in our Indian hotel rooms. Veronica knows I'm very private about such things. Unfazed, she says that maybe the only solution in public loos is for her to come and hold my nose for me. I sustain the illusion that at times, she is I, and by simple transposition, that I am my daughter. I remember pinching her nostrils together to help her swallow the codliver oil the pediatrician recommended she take daily in South Africa.

Forget the past, live in the present. Veronica is always stress-
ing the Buddhist values of single-pointedness of mind, of living
in the present. I hope she has replaced codliver oil with vitamins. Oh, yes, she says, she takes vitamins and Tibetan herbal
medicine, and sometimes other Ayurvedic medicine as well. If
there's an Ayurvedic medicine stall in the market, maybe it
would be a good idea to buy some asafoetida. "If I held *that* to
your nose, Mummy, then it would be impossible to smell anything else."

I can't stand the smell of asafoetida either, but I'm always
game for Ayurvedic pharmacies and stalls, and by now I've
looked at so many of them that I can recognize some of the
remedies at a glance. Practitioners of Ayurveda have told me
that foods with a sweet taste have a cooling action—mangoes,
jams, marmalade, puddings are guaranteed to depress internal
heat, blood pressure, and general metabolism, as well as lessen
the tendency of fatigue, nervous tension, red eyes, and hemor-
rhaging. Now that I think of it, my bamboo basket filled with
mangoes and yellow rose apples is in itself a store of delicious
medicine, much more attractive in appearance than the contents of the Ayurvedic dispensary which we find not far from
the LADIES URINLAS.

Here there are chilies, ginger, and pepper for the effect of
increasing the body's internal heat and decreasing "body muci-
lage"; molasses and rose leaves arranged in alternating layers in
a tightly covered glass jar, cooling, soothing, and excellent for
constipation and piles; garlic in sesame oil for chronic disorders
of the ear; white onion crushed with a little *gur* (jaggery) to
alleviate fatigue; equal parts of *hing* (asafoetida) and camphor
rubbed together with honey into pills recommended for fits of

hysteria and abdominal colic; *tulsi* (basil), betel leaf, fresh ginger, *fudina* (mint), and something unidentifiable called *vasaka* to mix with honey for an infallible cough remedy; *chai-ka-masala*, a combination of black pepper, cinnamon, cloves, and cardamom to be taken with tea to keep the body free from infections; a distillation of basil for the relief of malarial fevers; dried powdered coriander to be mixed with water and used as an eyewash for the cure of conjunctivitis; bottles of black pepper and honey to promote digestion and tone up the appetite; *zira* (cumin seeds), which also promotes digestion, is beneficial to the heart, and is recommended as an "appetizer" to tone sluggish appetites; *adrak* (ginger), useful for relieving colds, coughs, anorexia, indigestion, gas; *dhaniya* (coriander) is cooling, soothing, and calming, a carminative and another "appetizer"; *lashan* (garlic) powdered and dried, for the relief of facial paralysis, sciatica, rheumatic pains and backaches; equal parts of cardamom, *ghee*, and molasses to be taken with milk to nourish the brain, rejuvenate the body, and serve as an efficacious aphrodisiac; a compound of dried figs, shelled almonds, shelled pistachios, cardamom, sugar, saffron, and *ghee* made from cow's milk, recommended as a more nutritious aphrodisiac mixture, two spoonsful to be taken in the morning—more costly a tonic than fried onions taken daily with a little honey "on an empty stomach for three to six weeks," but "is getting better results," the dispensing pharmacist tells me. He also says that basil, essence of camphor, and peppermint in equal quantities, and a little tincture of cardamom—five or six drops—added to a cupful of water, taken three or four times a day, will provide relief from nausea, vomiting, diarrhea, dysentery, abdominal colic, gastroenteritis. A few drops of this mixture every hour with a cupful of water are "most curative" during attacks of cholera, while a few drops on absorbent cotton applied to a mosquito or a scorpion bite will provide instant relief.

The Karnataka Government Museum and the newly built Venkatappa Art Gallery—admission tickets twenty pice each —turn out to be a magnificent five cents' worth of instruction and entertainment. Here in the gallery are previews of what we will soon see for ourselves in Ootacamund: landscapes of the mystical Nilgiri Hills and paintings of the town's Church, its Library, and a garden. Some of the paintings remind me of the English countryside, others of Scottish borderland terrain. Like a caterpillar laying down a trail of silk, I feel I am connected by a silken lifeline to Scotland, kept aloft midair by the silk of memory, and now blown sidewise into the branch of another tree of thought. Graphic arts, fine arts, and the decorative arts of nature flow from paintings of Ootacamund, to a twelfth-century moon-breasted woman with outthrust hip, to delicate formations of rock crystals from the hills and coral from the coast, to the pattern of white spots on the pelt of a forest *chital*, a camouflage that even now from the distance of the museum's corridor looks like a sun-dappled log.

From Bangalore we'll drive to Hassan—then to Halebid and to Belur, to Mercara and to Mysore.

Byllakuppe is on the way to Mysore, and Veronica wants to stop there. "There's a *Gompa* there, Mummy," she says. A *Gompa* is a Tibetan temple-monastery-school complex. Fine. Of course. All hotel arrangements have been booked ahead, something I never bother about in Europe, something I always do in India. I've hired another car and a driver named Balan.

Balan comes to meet us wearing a clean, starched white uniform. Deferential, he stows away our luggage efficiently. He doesn't speak Hindi. He speaks Kannada, Malayalam, and just enough English not to speak it with a sing-song accent.

"We go Hassan," he says in a questioning tone as he opens the door of the car for us.

"Hassan," Veronica says, nodding and smiling.

"Hassan," I say, nodding and smiling.

We set off from Bangalore at half-past seven on a Saturday morning.

Veronica closes her eyes, touches her thumbs and first two fingers together, and moves her lips silently. She could be chanting the repetitive Jesus prayer of J. D. Salinger's heroine Franny, the prayer Franny claimed would endow the person who says it with Christ-consciousness. As I look at Veronica, I think of myself as Franny's awful beau: dull, thick, obtuse.

Oh, Elsa Cloud, I remember once you wrote me that my love for your Daddoo came to mean more to me than just love. It became a symbol of fulfillment so that every time I felt something was missing he would come to my thoughts, an answer to my yearning. More often, I think I feel this way about you.

Frustrated in my loneliness, I look out the windows, scribble in my notebook. Red earth. Red-tiled roofs. Locusts and cicadas zinging. Yellow houses. White mosques. Flame-of-the-forest trees. Lantana, a rambling, prickly shrub with multicolored orange and red flowers. They scent the air with an odor of black currants mixed with the smell of invisible woodsmoke. White flowers, yellow flowers, pink flowers, clouds of lavender-blue jacaranda.

The road runs through a corridor of tamarind trees. Enormous banyans appear like earth-mothering guardians at the occasional crossroad. Flocks of goats and black-faced sheep. Feathery fans of bamboo. Herds of oxen with horns like devils' ears, triangular horns pointed straight up. It is all peaceful and pastoral, an almost unpeopled landscape, until we come to the first village on the way.

The village is made up of long, low mud-brick buildings with doors and windows decorated with mango leaves. An arbor of mango leaves, a gazebo of mango leaves, and flowers strewn about like confetti indicate that a wedding has recently taken place. Men in white *longhis* stand by the roadside offering green coconuts for sale. A woman with a double nose-ring sits beneath a banyan tree, using a black umbrella to protect herself from its falling fruit, which are the size and shape of figs, green and reddish. Between the idea from that marvelous Marvell poem—"What wondrous life is this I lead! Ripe apples drop about my head"—and the reality, falls the shadow of a black umbrella and the patient resignation in the expression of the woman's face.

The landscape is suddenly dotted with anthills, red cones tall as an oxen's back rising up from flat fields that give way to the vivid green of rice paddies. Nothing in the world is as freshly green as a rice paddy, not even a Scottish lawn after a morning shower. Before I can stop Balan, we have zipped through the villages of Gotikere and Kunigal. Then we are passing anthills again, and a field of sugarcane.

When we reach a town called Magadilipalya, I insist on stopping. There is a white mosque here, too, a Saturday market with mounds of watermelons and green coconuts, and rhesus monkeys everywhere. Veronica emerges from her cocoon of medi-

tation and is glad to get out of the car. We buy oranges and
finger bananas, peel them, eat them, rinse our hands at the
market's water pump. Balan, to whom I have given money to
buy a snack, buys nothing, does nothing except stand by the car
shooing monkeys away. Veronica buys a green coconut, drinks
its contents, makes use of a slice of the coconut as a scoop to
hollow out the inside meat, some of which she eats, some of
which she offers me. What we can't eat, we toss to the monkeys.
We rinse our hands again, shake them dry. "Nothing much
here," Veronica says. I agree, and thinking how absurd it is that
I should agree, we return to the car.

I hold Veronica's left hand with my right and both of us look
out the car windows. Men carrying black umbrellas as sun-
shades walk across bare and rocky fields. Through the stands of
coconut palms, flycatchers twist and turn, some blue, some
brown. There are spectacular birds with long, ribbonlike tail
feathers. Some make harsh and grating cries, others utter pleasing trills. Sunbirds, glinting purple, flashing yellow, patched
with scarlet, flit restlessly through fronds of palms. Kites swim
in the vaulting sky. Blue, high-wheeled carts trundle along the
road, and occasional buses honk us to the side of the narrow
road. It's a vast, flat, barren landscape with lots of rocks and
remarkably few people.

Suddenly, we hear the sound of drums with a loud accompaniment of horns and shrilling flutes. A sign says *Chindarayha-
patua*. Ahead are people from miles around and the commotion
of an oxen sale. For every person there is a rhesus monkey and
at least two oxen, standing, lying down, walking about on the
dusty red earth, their ribs pushing against their pelts like fire-
grates. We stop, the only car in this pulsing mass of people,

oxen and monkeys, crows, sparrows, and pye dogs. Men, most dressed in shirts, shorts, *longhis*, and head wrappings rather than proper turbans hunker in the shade of eucalyptus trees where a listless market is being conducted, and beyond, beneath black umbrellas stuck upright in the dusty earth and burlap canopies propped on poles. There is little color. Women are wearing mostly faded blue and faded yellow saris. The men are wearing mostly white, faded blue, faded yellow.

"Poor people," Balan says. "But they are feeding monkeys coconuts, too." Is it pride with which he says this, or is it his way of lessening what he anticipates is a painful revelation for Veronica and me? "Hanuman, Lord of the monkeys, will bless you." I remember Veronica saying this jokingly at Tughlakabad. Does Balan want to assure us that we aren't the only ones blessed by Hanuman today? Whatever his intentions, I feel a nip of shame and guilt. I can't distinguish what I'm responsible for and what can't be helped.

When we get back in the car, Veronica tells me my mind creates problems, invents problems just so I won't be bored.

"What do you mean, *bored?*"

"The mind doesn't want to be relaxed or be contented. It enjoys problems. It creates situations of suffering, depression, longing, anger, irritation, helplessness, frustration in order to entertain itself, to protect itself from boredom."

"That's the way Buddhists think?"

"Everyone thinks like that. Buddhists know, of course, that you don't *have* to think like that. That's essential Buddha dharma." The impatience of her mood shifts, her voice changes. "Maybe you're a meditator like me, Mum. There's a Buddhist proverb which says that the ordinary person experiences the sufferings of life like a hair in his eye." She smiles, a good sign, as we roll on across a landscape that alternates fields of sugarcane with bare, rocky stretches of scrub and aloes and the miracle of rice paddies. I haven't a clue where we are, for Balan has taken us from Bangalore on a route in which nothing is indicated on the map.

Hassan springs out of nowhere—a sudden oasis of huge banyans and feathery casuarinas, a rushing stream. The village gives me the sense of a small New England mill-town. As we pull in the driveway of the Hassan Motel, we are escorted by an elderly man flourishing a coconut shell banjo with a cobra skin-covered soundbox. He prances along beside us, playing "Mademoiselle from Armentières" and singing its chorus, "Eeenky-deenky Parlay Voo."

The man hovers by our sides as we struggle with the luggage and the process of checking in, pressing on us his white pasteboard business cards, snipped at the corners and printed with purple ink: Syed Husein, Magician, Channapattana, Hassan Talok, Hasan District, Karnataka State.

Do we want to see him perform magic tricks? He tells us he has performed in Mysore, Madras, Umrica, Switz, German, and Franchayzee.

"India's answer to pay television," Veronica says with an ascerbic smile.

"Tell him, darling, *after* we get the luggage in the room."

"*You* tell him, Mummy. He speaks English," Veronica wearily retorts.

Seconds later, I comply and she relents. We chorus simultaneously, "*After* we get the luggage in the room."

We wash. The dust on our faces and hands becomes mud on

the towels. I'm tired, yet Syed Husein's waiting presence tugs me from our room, with Veronica trailing after me. Syed, having exacted payment in advance, goes into an act that is astonishing. He exhales smoke, then opens his mouth to show us a tiny bonfire on his tongue which he apparently swallows. From a shabby little cloth bag containing wooden cups and buttons, a piece of silk and a few tin trinkets, he performs sleight-of-hand feats and illusions of great skill and charm, all the time keeping up an incomprehensible patter and baring a few yellow tooth-stumps in an idiot's grin. He produces a small rat or a large mouse from behind his neck—it is too quick to see which—for now smoke curls from his ears and there is fire again in his mouth. And then he is gone in a twinkling of the eye. We hear him playing "Mademoiselle from Armentières" in the garden.

Veronica and I dine on tomato soup made with coconut juice, dry chicken tandoor with too much *masala*, and then go to sleep for ten hours. We wake to the sound of a radio blaring outside our ground-floor window.

Mulk's enthusiasm for the splendid twelfth-century shrines built by the Hoysala Dynasty has been largely for the sexual energy of the female sculptures. I hear him apostrophizing, "Oh, moon-breasted, swan-waisted, elephant-hipped beauties!" He has told us that we should visit the shrines in Halebid and Belur.

" '*Poy*, Sala!' or '*Hoy*, Sala! (Strike, Sala!),' " his followers shouted to Sala, legendary head of the Hoysala Dynasty, as they urged him to kill a menacing tiger. King Sala struck the tiger, felled him with a single blow, and this heroic act became the emblem and the rallying cry of the Dynasty. So, " '*Poy*, Sala, *Hoy*,

Sala!' off we go, on the Deccan Plateau!" I hear myself sounding
overly hearty—Mummy, the falsely jovial parental educator,
exuding the prescriptive parental enthusiasm which jets from
me when I'm not sure Veronica will like something I think will
be good for us both to see.

Brick kilns, a roadside stall selling coconuts, and then, just
like that, as though it had been let down from the sky and
deposited intact, is Halebid temple, set in a small park bannered
brightly with flame-of-the-forest trees whose fallen petals
fringe the park tank with vermilion. The temple is a low building of gray stone, a central pillared hall built on a layered star-
shaped platform. The stone is chloritic schist, hard as granite,
extremely difficult to carve, and the wonder of the temple is
that it is carved throughout with intricate reliefs, friezes of
elephants, lions, horses, human figures, complex floral and decorative designs. The minute elaboration of detail, the play of
light and shade, the variety of the sculptured walls, pavilions,
canopies, doorways, sanctuaries, and pillars are thrilling. There
is a wild, sensual beauty about the sculpture, bodily health and
solidity overlaid with masses of jewelry, homage to vigorous
volumes of flesh caught in rhythmic motion.

Owing to the iconoclastic fury of invading Moslems, some of
the sculpture has been mutilated. Ganesh has suffered the most,
his trunk savaged in sculpture after sculpture. Did the Moslems
think of the trunk as a phallic symbol and try to render the
genial god impotent?

Inside one pavilion is a central sculpture of a magnificent
stone bull, Shiva's beloved *nandi*. Unlike the two guardian bulls
at the temple entrance, this *nandi* is decked with garlands and
necklaces of stone, and rests on folded legs braceleted at both

hoof and joint. His head is crowned with jeweled ornaments, and his face has such a peculiar expression of bewilderment that I find it endearing. There are Shaivite *lingams* placed conspicuously throughout the pavilion, each meaningful masculine brag shaped like a solid upside-down U, the word made steel-like, flesh of stone. Asked by Brahma to create and having seen that the universe was full, Shiva tore off his *lingam*, sacrificing his own personal sensuality for the sake of the fertility of the universe. His *lingam* was a destructive fire until it was placed under control, its fiery power worshipped as a flame, the *lingam* taking on life and becoming sexually active without being re-joined to Shiva's body, a part of Shiva yet not a part, depersonalized, iconized. What had Mulk told me? Shiva is not rendered asexual, but extends his sexuality to the sages and to the whole universe. The true Shaivite yogi can, like Shiva, draw up his seed not only in chastity but in sexuality as well. Loss of seed is loss of the power aroused by sexual stimulation. Seed stirred sexually can be likened to steam in a boiler, controlled, no longer random, a channeling of creative life forces to the brain. I remember Joseph Cornell telling me he was afraid that if he ever made love, he would lose his creativity. He told me a story about a French writer who, every time he succumbed to erotic temptation, would rush into the garden moaning, "*J'ai perdu un livre.*" There can be no creation without mortality. In myths and legends, Joseph said, this is the terror and attraction of love, that it equates with death.

When I first came to India, the same age as Veronica is now, all the monumental genitalia sensuously carved in sandstone and granite in delicate shades of honey, pink, and cocoa brown; all those melon-and-mango shaped breasts, all those permutations of sexual activity, all those arching backs and dazzling erections made me flush, blush, laugh with surprise. It all seemed like one vast sculptural blue movie, until Mulk explained that the sculpture's symbolism was really more cosmic than sexual. "Sculpture of explicit sensuality derives from the female principle of Shakti," he said, "and wound its way into the traditions of Tantric Buddhist art." I whisk out this fig-leaf phrase now as I do whenever anyone takes a close look at the gilded iconographical statue of Hevajira I have in my New York apartment. Hevajira, a guardian deity in his sixteen-armed manifestation, with eight faces and four legs, is embracing his Dakini in divine and mystical love, and stepping on four copulating forms of *Mara*, Tantric Buddhist demons who try to make men prefer earthly life with all its attachments rather than the path toward enlightenment and emancipation from its fetters. The Dakini is the personification of wisdom, emancipated from the self, permeated by the true nature of the world. Mulk said that Hevajira was an extension of the Shaivite beliefs, that the Shiva *lingam* is the pivot and axis of all cosmic energy, but that energy is born only when the male and female principles in Shiva unite. The female principle exists within Shiva as well as outside of him in the form of his wife and consort, under whichever guise she is known: Shakti, Parvathi, Kali, Sati, Gauri.

On my first trip to India, I couldn't understand why there should be such a plethora of erotic stone nudity when the only live nudity to be seen was among celibate holy men and beyond-the-pale international sunbathers. Could Alexander the Great have had anything to do with this? The heroic nudity of Greek athletes who took part in games at religious festivals? I asked

Mulk if the Indians were like the Etruscans who felt that Greek heroic nudity could be expressed in paintings and sculpture, but not adopted as a custom in daily life. Could Alexander, when he marched through India in the fourth century B.C. have brought with him the idea of heroic nudity? Had the attire of Greek women been the inspiration behind the sari, draped in the manner of chitons and himations.

"You think *we* copied the robes and mantles of the ancient Greeks?" Mulk looked astonished. "Balderdash, my dear Leila, it was *quite* the other way around."

Outside the Halebid temple, young boys with primitive stringed instruments play tunes that sound like squeaky Irish jigs and, from time to time, recognizable snatches from "Danny Boy." Where did they learn those songs? Who taught them those songs? The boys look at me blankly. They know the melodies. They have *always* heard them. They shrug. *Everyone* in their village knows them, they say.

Women dressed in saris and carrying iron pots on their heads ask us for chocolates. Chocolates? Outside of big cities, wherever can you expect to find chocolates in India? Chocolates! Veronica laughs at the absurdity, and the Indian women smile wistfully. Chocolates, they say, chocolates, chocolates, chocolates, chanting mournfully as they walk away. Lizards, the color of autumn leaves, burnt orange, yellow, and brown, skitter out of their path.

We were well-advised by Mulk to come to Halebid first, for it is a haunting prelude to the grand-scale orchestration of Belur, where we are now headed. On our way, whitewashed road-markers appear at crossroads like clusters of gravestones, and from a distance along the tree-shaded roadside, whitewashed temples with pillars and cornices have the look of Greek architecture, small Palladian villas. Close up, they are easily recognizable as Shaivite temples, each with its roof-top guardian stone *nandi*. Vendors sit around the steps below selling dark green jackfruit the size of footballs, the outer skins prickly, the inner flesh orange. Some of the vendors have used jackfruit seeds to make mosaic pictures, mounted on wood, of *lingams, nandis*, and temples. We come upon a bus which has toppled into a harvested rice paddy that is now a marshland of pink lotus. The bus is listing to one side at a forty-five-degree angle. Passengers are scrambling about in the mud and among the lotuses. No one has been seriously hurt, but the spectacle has drawn a crowd of onlookers. Already there are food sellers on the scene. How did they know? How could they have gotten here so quickly? Did they just happen to be passing by on the road when the accident occurred?

"Why do you ask so many questions?" Veronica demands. "What does it matter?"

"What's wrong with asking questions? I like to understand and know about things. What's wrong with asking questions?" Bryce used to say a good offense was a good defense. Nurses used to remind me that curiosity killed the cat. Veronica makes me feel childish, flat as the landscape.

I subside into silence, saying nothing, looking out the car widows and seeing nothing, until we reach Belur. Around the temple, scruffy stalls and one-room shops rent cameras and novelty binoculars with almost no magnifying power, and sell cheap toys and packets of gaudily tinted postcards. A snake charmer, seated beneath the shade of a banyan, is playing a

bamboo violin, and we are just in time to see an image of
Vishnu, dressed in gold, carried on a palanquin, and shaded
from the sun by a silver umbrella. Vishnu has emerged from the
temple, accompanied by a band of drum players, bell ringers,
horn blowers. The sound is deafening, until the procession
marches away.

Veronica and I leave our footgear at the great tower of the
temple entrance. Passengers who have disembarked from the
Hassan-Chikmalagur bus and buses from Bangalore and Mangalore are also taking off their sandals. How temple *chaukidars*
manage to keep track of which footgear belongs to whom, and
why no one ever seems to walk away with someone else's look-
alike sandals is one of India's minor mysteries. With all the
ubiquitous paperwork in this country, the fact that there is no
exchange of receipts, no form of duplicate checks issued by
temple shoe guardians is another puzzlement. I voice no questions. My sneakers, the sturdiest I could find in L. L. Bean's
catalogue, are unique. The *chaukidar* regards them with an
expression of curiosity and approval.

"*Namaste*, begging your pardon, can I refuse to acquaint you
with the heavenly beauty of our temple? It is a piece of Eden on
earth. How can I miss the golden opportunity of guiding you
madams? It is my duty and service." Attaching obsequiousness
to his voice, the guide who has descended upon us manages to
suggest that he is our intimate friend and the most humble and
obedient of servants. I tighten my lips and shake my head, but
the guide doggedly continues his inquiries and finally secures a
quartet of bus passengers.

The courtyard with arcaded walls is immense. It contains a
central pillared sanctuary built on a stellate platform, other

buildings, and free-standing sculpture of elephants and a horse. The stone paving of the temple compound is hot on the soles of my feet. Four young women are talking by a square concrete well. One draws water and fills two terracotta jars. The four women are as graceful and lovely as the princesses of Ajanta. Mulk had told me when I first saw the cave paintings there that I would always remember them, and I always have. Now, bare-footed at Belur, I look at the princesses in their bright cotton saris, and see the coconut palms like photographs of dark green fireworks beyond the temple walls, their fronds exploding in the bluest of blue skies.

The sculpture of the temple has romance and nostalgia in common: a reminder to viewers of an age of exuberant personal ornamentation, spiritual confidence, and self-assurance. The Hoysala sculptors paid homage to the idea of creativity as symbolized by round-breasted, slender-waisted, wide-hipped women, which they carved in a remarkable series of bracket figures. Mulk told me this and now I tell Veronica. Sharing my fieldglasses, we tilt back our heads to look up at goddesses meditating, a woman with a parrot on her arm, figures dancing, goddesses and women in moments of dalliance, women as mothers, paramours, wives, warriors, attendants to the gods, a woman contemplating her face in a mirror, women telling for-tunes, a woman dressing her hair, a woman aiming an arrow, a woman playing on a flute, a woman beating a drum, and another poised to strike a monkey tugging at her sari, a woman eating a mango, a curious image of a woman with a mustache and a beard.

"The twelfth-century version of the *Mujer Barbuda* we saw in Toledo," Veronica says.

"That looked more like a man with breasts. *This* looks more like a woman with a beard."

She agrees. We move past gods, demon kings, Surya, Shiva, Arjuna, Brahma, and a woman shaking a scorpion out of her sari. "This one is either symbolic of an exorcism of lust, represented by the scorpion, or else it's just the sort of thing I used to worry about in Africa and Jamaica. But I don't think there are as many scorpions here as there were there," I add.

"I wish my birth sign didn't symbolize lust," Veronica says.

In a dark, pillared hallway there is an altar to Shiva, presided over by a priest in a white *longhi* to whom people are giving coconuts, finger bananas and garlands of flowers to be blessed. The priest sanctifies the fruits and flowers and then returns them. Then he changes the pitch of his chanting. Dipping two fingers of his right hand in a brass pot, he sprinkles yellow water on the outstretched hands of the people surrounding him at the altar.

"Hold out your hands, Mummy. Don't be rude. It's only saffron water," Veronica whispers furiously to me. "Then put it on your forehead or your head."

I see that this is what everyone else is doing, and meekly hold out my hands to have them sprinkled, but I feel like a double fraud and a blasphemer as I pat my hands on my hair. Outside, a man has prostrated himself on the courtyard pavement as he faces the temple. A woman, who I suppose is his wife, pushes a tiny child toward him. The child flops on the ground beside his father.

Returning from Belur to Hassan, Balan takes us by way of Belgola, and its twin hills, Chandragiri and Indragiri. *Giri* is the

Sanskrit word for hill, *chandra*, the moon. On the summit of the hill named in honor of Indra, lord of the heavens, visible for miles around, there is a five-storey granite statue of Gomateshvara, a Jain saint. As we arrive at the foot of the Indragiri, a party of naked Jain holy men, sturdy and muscular, carrying fans of peacock feathers, and perspiring pilgrims in both white and orange robes, have set off to climb to the peak-top temple and statue. By the time we have driven up the hill and back, all I can see are the followers, orange and white spots, moving up the boulder-strewn hillside. At the top is the massive granite statue—so stylized in its male nudity that it is no more sensual than a colossal armature—and by comparison so small, by comparison so terribly real, the holy men and their followers —the enormous and bloodless looking down upon the tiny warm and living.

Eighteen

From the province of Hassan to the province of Coorg, all
part of Karnataka state, is a seventy-two-mile drive,
nothing at all, just a little distance on the map from a
gray patch to a yellow patch. Karnataka is bordered on the west
by the state of Kerala and the Arabian Sea, and on the south by
the state of Tamil Nadu and the Indian Ocean. But as we head
west toward Coorg, the road climbs into hills wooded with tall
teak trees, their greenish-white bark distinctive. We rise into
another world, cool, fresh, and green with coffee plantations,
ferns, white flowers, misty hills, teak forests.

In India, few people move. Once settled on the land, unless
forcibly driven away by a stronger power, they stay, and their
descendants and their descendants' children after them. Indians
are neither nomads by nature nor travelers by instinct. Circumstances force some to intermix with their conquerors, to inter-
marry. Among dark-skinned Dravidian faces, I see a few lighter
complexioned ones with thin, aquiline features. "Kogada peo-
ples," Balan says, Coorgi clansmen of the highlands. Descendants of the former rajas of Coorg, they still regard descendants

of other tribes, formerly their slaves and menials, today mostly farmers and artisans, as their social and intellectual inferiors. It amuses me to remember that this is just as the Scottish highlanders in Boswell's time (and ours) looked down on members of the Border clans.

We stop for the night in Mercara, the provincial capital of Coorg, a hill station four thousand feet above sea level. It is a charming mix of narrow eighteenth-century streets, *havelis* with fretwork porticoes, Hindu temples, Muslim mosques, Anglican and Catholic churches, nineteenth-century British cannons and cannonballs polished with shoe-blacking (I can tell by the smell and because my finger leaves a silvery imprint and comes away smudged), cusped archways, enormous stone statues of elephants; plus black velvet fezzes, crocheted woolly berets, turbans, and bare heads crossing in front of us all at the same time.

In the morning, with the mist rising from the valley and the air chill and foggy, I walk for a while along a road just outside of town, listening to the brook's rushing susurrus and the glottal burbling of tree frogs giving way to the early morning chorus of birdsong, the fanfaronade of roosters for miles around, and the chime of Mercara's church bells. I am myself in India, and an eight-year-old child walking in Scotland, wondering why the sheep are silent. I don't want to leave the highlands of Coorg. But after our breakfast tea, brought with a pitcher of hot milk topped with a wrinkled skin and a bowl of coarse-grained grayish sugar crystals with a wasp making the rounds of its rim, we set off again, on our way now to Mysore.

We rumble down from blue hills to the rice paddies in the valley, continuing along the Deccan plain to Kashalnaggar and

Byllakuppe, and then on to Mysore. The Cauvery River, the so-called Ganges of the South, rises in Kashalnaggar, and the idea of Kashalnaggar had formed in my mind as a settlement on the banks of a river as broad as the Mississippi. Not so. Kashalnaggar is an Indian market town, and if the Cauvery rises here, I see no sign of it at all. Nor do I see a Byllakuppe signpost anywhere. Balan, Veronica, and I ask for directions to Byllakuppe and receive vague answers, arms waved to the south, fingers pointed eastward.

Then, two Buddhist monks appear, walking ahead of us.

"*Tashidelek, tashidelek*," Veronica calls out excitedly, and tells Balan to stop the car.

The monks turn grave, incurious faces toward us.

Veronica, with a clear and lilting voice, speaks to them in Tibetan which, as she speaks it, in rhythm and intonation, sounds somewhat like Japanese. I hear the word Byllakuppe, and Veronica turns to tell me that the monks are on their way there. She asks if we can give them a lift. Of course. Veronica goes on talking with them.

If I were a Buddhist monk walking along in an Indian market town, and a girl with long yellow hair leaned out of a car window and addressed me in Tibetan, I wouldn't just stand there, look solemn, and express no surprise. But I'm not a Buddhist monk, and I recall Veronica saying something about Tibetans and especially lamas being secretive about their private lives and rarely expressing surprise at *anything*. What else had she said? That Tibetans can be too polite. That some kinds of politeness are definitely intended to keep a distance. That sometimes the distance is friendly, allowing a more subtle and low-key communication to take place. That sometimes the distance is

intended to alienate or to test because of suspicion. That Tibetans aren't obsessed by the necessity of keeping up conversation.
That being with Tibetans can be quite refreshing, not simply
because they're not hysterical, but because they're not speedy.
That being speedy is a form of aggression. "That's what I find,
anyway." I hear her say this in some past conversation with me,
using the same tone she is now using with the monks.

They respond to her in low, resonating voices. Smiles, sweet
as a child's, light up their faces as they move slowly toward the
car, wrapped in their voluminous maroon robes. On my mind's
screen, there flashes an image of monks in Bangkok. They are
enfolded in robes of tangerine cotton. As I remember them,
their faces look sere and dry. Perhaps in the tourney between
flesh and spirit, there is always a clear expression of saintliness
in the faces of the truly dedicated religious ones, a look of inner
radiance, serenity, joy. The monks I remember in Thailand
seemed frail and wispy creatures to me, ascetics, dry and scholarly. These Tibetan monks, like European monks, have a more
substantial look. They are large men, so bulky in their robes
that I wonder if there is enough room for them in the back seat.

Veronica gets out of the car, opening first one rear door, and
then moving to the other side of the car to open the other door
so that the monks can each sit beside me if I edge forward to
make room for them. As she presents me to the monks, intro-
ducing them in such a way as to sound as though she were giving
both them and me a delicious treat, I feel a surge of feeling, a
precipitation toward her.

Oh, Elsa Cloud, my darling daughter, my dear, darling angel,
Elsa Cloud!

I cross my legs, balancing my ankle on my knee. Veronica

immediately hisses at me. "Don't point your feet at them. Don't show the soles of your sneakers. They won't like it."

I quickly put both of my feet on either side of the drive shaft ridge.

The monks look at Veronica and me with nothing in their expressions to cramp or darken the human spirit. How extraordinary to be seated between two Tibetan monks! How unexpected! I feel like a book, supported by two firm and solid bookends. Just as I did when I met Trijung Rinpoche, the junior tutor of the Dalai Lama, I experience a feeling of *darshan*, a silent blessing.

I listen to the two monks, Thupten and Choden, telling Veronica the way to Byllakuppe, directions which she then relays to Balan. Like Trijung, the monks have an extraordinary way of sanctifying the space around them with their presence, their being, their outer and inner silence, their serenity and inner strength. Am I imagining this? Exaggerating? No. Just as some people can come into a room and agitate you at once, while others can project an exhilarating aura, the monks bestow an intensification of calm and relaxation. At the same time, I feel a rush of ingenuous pleasure at this romantic surprise, a retrieval, perhaps, of my encounter at the age of ten or eleven with a real Indian in a real turban aboard the Queen Mary.

Tibetans, I am seated between two Tibetans, I keep telling myself, as we jounce along a dusty side road. Tibet, not so long ago, a magical never-never land, remote, austere, encompassed by mountains, the highest country in the world, a country whose people claim descent from the six strong and courageous children born to a monkey, a reincarnation of Chenresig, divine protector of Tibet, the Lord who looks down with compassion; and an ogress, a reincarnation of Green Tara, a powerful, compassionate female deity. Tibet, an Asiatic *Graustark*, a country for so long accessible only in dreams.

As a schoolgirl, I had delivered a paper about Tibet in a current events class. "A peaceful, semi-feudal theocracy, with a sparse and scattered population estimated at six million, of which at least one quarter are celibate monks and lamas housed in monasteries that also serve as schools . . . about one hundred and fifty are families of the landed aristocracy . . . the remainder of the people are farmers, traders, nomads." Pause here for a slide picture of the Dalai Lama, a round-faced child in richly embroidered robes, wearing a fur-trimmed hat like an upside-down tulip, and an expression of sweetness and intelligence rare in a four-year-old child. I remember mentioning that fluffy white yak tails, packed by caravan to India, were exported to America for Santa Claus beards; that female yaks were called *dris*; that it was a Tibetan custom to open one's mouth and stick out one's tongue as a sign of respectful salutation to one's superior, a greeting, for example, of a beggar to a merchant. Pause for laughter and a few younger children in the back row sticking out their tongues at each other and giggling. Then more slides of Tibetan houses, artifacts, costumed people, temples, a typical schoolgirl's talk, the compilation of what Robert liked to call gee-whiz facts and illustrations.

Now I try to breathe in the real Tibet from the scent of the dusty woolen robes of the monks on either side of me. Instead of Indian dust, I imagine I am inhaling oxygen-thin Himalayan air, air from the Roof of the World—another cliché I belabored in my schoolgirl recitatif, conflating the idea of the Roof of the World with an attic in which wonderful treasures, venerable crafts, hallowed traditions were stored.

Dare I smoke a beedie? Inhale the burning-leaf scent of reality? I pinch the fleshy part of my thumb at its base, a childhood ritual that prevents me from doing what I want to do, forces me to concentrate, and the pinch brings with it an image of the Potala Palace in Lhasa, dazzling, enormous, its gilded roofs and gold-painted pinnacles momentarily as clear as the Kodachrome slide I showed my boarding-school audience, which pops up in my mind effortlessly now like a slice of toast in a toaster. Where is memory bred, in the heart or in the head? Wake up to nowness, I tell myself, the panoramic nowness Veronica is always talking about.

I look out the window and see neat little bungalows painted in Easter egg colors—pink, green, blue, yellow—and above them, all around, pennants strung across trees and rooftops. They remind me of the tails of kites Robert and I used to tie with cuttings from old sheets, sun-faded pennants in gray-whites and pastels, but these have printing on them.

"Prayer flags, Mummy," Veronica says. They are printed with the mystical mantra *Om mani padme hum*, dedicated to Chenre-sig, the Great Compassionate One, of which all Dalai Lamas are an incarnation, carrying supplication to protecting deities, to all the cardinal points of heaven. "*Om mani padme hum*, the jewel in the heart of the lotus. Everyone knows that, Mummy. The expression of the worshipful heart."

The expression of the worshipful heart. From Tibet, the Roof of the World, to Byllakuppe on the scorching Deccan plain. All I know is that Byllakuppe is a settlement of Tibetans who fled from their homeland after an unsuccessful uprising against the Chinese Communists in 1959, and who are now trying to rebuild their way of life on land generously given to them by the Indian government.

Why pretend to phony worldliness? I've read about prayer flags, but this is the first time I've ever *seen* them, "and they *do* look like the scraps of cloth your Daddoo and I used to tie on the tails of kites for you, Sam, Allison, and Bryce to fly," I say, suddenly, inexplicably, at the point of tears.

The monks shift toward me, almost imperceptibly, the wool of their robes and their arms beneath them pressing gently against my arms in their wrist-length sleeves. The corners of the monks' mouths lift fractionally upward. I look into Choden's dark brown eyes and into Thupten's dark brown eyes behind his rimless spectacles. Their expressions are kind, gentle, loving. The car stops. We have arrived at Byllakuppe.

Choden and Thupten loom large before me, their maroon robes rearranged now so that their right arms are bared, exposing a high-necked saffron under-robe. They appear to take pleasure in leading us calmly, slowly, with never a wasted motion, never an idle gesture, around the grounds of the settlement. Veronica tells me that when the refugees first arrived in India, most of them made the equivalent of fifteen cents a day as road-workers, and lived on radishes and *tsampa* (barley meal).

Instead of the dazzling sprawl of the Potala Palace, here is a neat, clean, stucco bungalow with a polished red porch—the sacred color not as vivid as the color Trijung Rinpoche's socks had been, more the color of a red apple. The bungalow is ready and waiting for the arrival of His Holiness, the Dalai Lama, who came once, but who may never come again, or who may appear

any week for another visit. The windows are closed. The outer
doors are unlocked for us. As we enter, the house smells freshly
aired, is cool, aromatic. It seems such a poignant sign of reverence that all the rooms are immaculate, everything clean and
polished, and that there are bowls of zinnias and marigolds set
about on tables and on the bedroom bureau. A monk is hosing
the flowers in the garden outside, and a young man, wearing a
T-shirt and faded tan trousers, is raking the gravel pathways.

Beyond the hedges of the garden, you can see the temple in
the distance. No great or grand temple, but a box-like concrete
structure ornamented with pillars and a frieze painted turquoise, red, green, and white, carnival bright, the colors blur-
ring into the air at their edges, like strokes of watercolor laid
on wet paper, like colors seen through tears. From the temple
comes the sound of rock bees humming, a bagpipe's drone,
wind in a tunnel—yet it is none of these. The sound inhales
me, draws me into it. A purring, flattened crescendo, with the
low register and the high register audible in a continuous resonance, the deep sound deeper than the bass notes of a tuba,
the high sound reed-like, moaning and melancholy, the dual
sounds pleached, plaited together, sustained for what seems
several minutes, interrupted for a second, then continuing until
that almost indiscernible interruption, continuing again in a vibrating hum—AHHHHHH OHHHHHH Mmmmmmmmm—
AHHHHHHH OHHHHH Mmmmmmmmmm.

"That's the monks chanting," Veronica says.

Chanting. *Per sona*, through sound. All sounds emanate or
originate from seed syllables. Tibetan Buddhists believe that the
power embodied in certain sounds can set up inner vibrations
which will open the mind to "higher consciousness," "higher

experiences." Is this why the sound of a mother's voice, a father's voice, the voice of a lover, the voice of a child also prompt
inner vibrations, the minuscule echo of the Gospel of St. John?
In the beginning was the Word and the Word was with God,
and the Word was God. Freud said that we must refrain from
uniting with words in order to unite with the word made flesh.
Seed syllables. The spermatic word. I hear that blissful groan of
copulation.

Choden and Thupten explain to Veronica, who translates for
me, that through years of artistic training and meditation on
selflessness, choirs of monks have developed the ability to create
a multi-harmonic voice so that each monk is able to sound a
single note with up to three octaves of overtone resonance.
Monks used to chant like this for days, Choden and Thupten
remember. In Byllakuppe, a place concerned with dairy and
poultry farms, orchards, crops of cereal grass and maize, carpet
weaving and agricultural cooperatives, teaching and instructing
students of all ages, the monks have less time to set aside for
their rituals, their mantras, their prayers, their blessings—less
time, but *enough* time, they assure Veronica.

Listening intently, aurally staring, I peer through the open
doorway of the temple. Hundreds of gilded images of the Buddha are crowded on the floor, reflecting the flames of hundreds
of little lamps. I see parallel rows of maroon-and-saffron-robed
monks with heads shaved to shadowed helmets. The monks are
seated cross-legged facing each other, and from each mouth
comes this extraordinary sound, the deep basso profundo and
the high note at the same time, one voice split into male and
female registers, two halves of one thought, a sound so extraordinary that part of me becomes part of the sound and the rest

of me feels as simplified as an espaliered tree. For a magic moment, the deepest religious feelings I have ever felt or sensed are expressed outside of me by monks of another culture, another religion, another language, another voice. This moment of revelation, spiritual re-discovery, this transitory feeling of one world eliding into another, is interrupted when Veronica tells me that the lamps burn butter, not oil or kerosene.

Bhainsee butter, not *dri* butter, the butter from a female yak. I take out my pen and notebook from my LV tote bag and record these details as I linger in the temple doorway. The sacrificial lamps whose undying flames once lit shrines in every tent, hut, house, shop, and temple in Tibet before the Communist occupation, now illuminate this temple in India, this cave-like, nave-like temple. In a corner, trays of bread have been set out for the evening meal.

To see Buddhism practiced, to hear Buddhism practiced, to feel the devotion again that I have felt in certain churches, certain cathedrals, is an epiphany, the sort that produces a longing to express the inexpressible. I follow Veronica and Choden and Thupten down the temple stairs. Ahead of us, instead of the great Sera University in Lhasa, is a simple one-storeyed schoolhouse with open windows through which I can see and hear novice monks, some no older than five or six, chanting their lessons. This sound, innocent, earnest, enthusiastic, is so endearing that I want to rush in and hug them all. Instead, I follow Veronica and the two monks away from the religious compound to the secular part of the settlement.

There are twenty villages on Byllakuppe's fifty-five hundred acres, where out of a jungle, ten thousand or so refugees have carved a way of life for themselves. They are sustained by religious devotion and by subsistence rations of fifteen to twenty cents a day given them by the government of India or earned by road construction work. Veronica says that Tibetans get more value out of the little money they have than anyone else she has seen anywhere. "These are *settled* refugees," she adds.

Tibetan women appear, their shiny black hair falling in plaits or coiled in braids around their heads. They wear what look like pinafores of multi-colored striped material, and most of them are adorned with ornaments of coral or turquoise in their hair, around their necks, on their fingers and wrists. Everyone is smiling, cheerful, welcoming. We pass a small carpet-weaving establishment, then neat rows of cottages, each with its own vegetable and flower garden. Strung from tree to tree, from rooftop to rooftop, prayer flags snap in the wind. Everywhere there is a sense of order, of good health and good will.

As I look at passing monks and lay Tibetans, my first impression, formed at the Ashoka Hotel in New Delhi—that Tibetans have faces that might be American Indian, Mongolian, Indonesian, Chinese, Burmese, Eskimo, Filipino—seems as fatuous to me now as it did then, but no less true. There is no definitive Tibetan look except for a pleasant and serene cast of expression, and a way of moving without wasted gestures or motion. Even children no taller than my waist seem to have a degree of this inner control, this concentration on whatever it is they happen to be doing. Nothing seems to disturb their parents' poise, to unsettle their capacity for absorption, their deftness of movement. Other than the most discreet of passing glances, they betray no interest in us.

An English-speaking monk has been summoned to meet us, a tall man with steel-rimmed spectacles. During the construction of the buildings and the clearing of the forest, he tells me that over a dozen of the refugee settlers were trampled by wild elephants, more were killed by snakebite, accidents, illnesses. Now, with the help of their government in exile in Dharamsala and by their own efforts, they have joined the economic middle class, and their children are housed and schooled in the traditions of their homeland.

I troop along with the monks and Veronica to a reception hall where we are to have Tibetan tea. "Brick tea," Veronica murmurs. "Terrible stuff, churned with salt, milk, and *bhainsee* butter. You'll hate it."

I know about brick tea, embossed tiles of tea leaves compressed between two wooden stamps, an old Chinese and Central Asian method of preparing tea so that it would be simpler to transport by camel and horse over the Mongolian plateau to Russia. But I have never tasted it. "Depending on the amount of milk, salt, or butter added, you can drink the real thing or *eat* it." Veronica grins wickedly. "Just gulp it down, it's better that way."

The sunlight is so bright that when I enter the hall I can make out only low banquettes covered with Tibetan rugs, and carved chests before them that serve as tables for bowls of flowers. The monks motion us to be seated as they seat themselves. Uncertain of how to address them, bemused and rather bewildered, I try to keep a straight face as my eyes meet Veronica's.

The milk-salt-butter tea, served in lidded cups, is a chooey-booey mess. I gulp it down, regardless. There are also *momos*, little ravioli-like things of chopped meat and onions in envelopes of dough. I eat them, too. They're not bad.

From somewhere in the monastery comes the sound of baby

monks repeating their lessons and the sound again of the chanting of mantras. *Om mani padme hum.* The jewel in the heart of
the lotus is the expression of the essential worshipful heart of
Tibetan life and devotional practice, mindful of the great wheel
of Dharma, the Universal Law, set in motion by Lord Buddha
and kept in motion by means of mechanistic and repetitive
invocations and circumambulations of temples and holy places.
Like memories, like the great flow and current of life itself,
like rebirth. No one and nothing ever dies as long as it lives in
memory.

The monks tell me about the Tibet of their childhood before
the 1950 occupation by the Chinese Communists. They point
to photographs on the wall and describe memories more vivid
in their minds. Lime-washed *chortens*, monuments commemo-
rating the heart of Buddha, sometimes also built to honor high
lamas and family members, dazzling white with gilded pinnacles, chiseled with the mystical mantra. Narrow stony paths
across the mountains where there were no roads to offend the
earth spirits, nor any wheeled carts, bicycles, buses, cars, or
trains. The only means of travel or transport, they tell me, were
horses, yaks, mules, *dzos* (crosses between yaks and cows),
hand-carried palanquins, and river trips along the Brahmaputra
in coracles made of yak skin stretched across a rectangular willow frame.

Magnificent pageants with gorgeously costumed musicians
and masked dancers who whirled and turned cartwheels in
stylized ballets to the deep roar of long horns, drums, trumpets,
cymbals. Oh, yes, they said, before the Chinese came, they re-
joiced in seasonal religious festivals where there was the drama
and excitement of folk opera, and dances where the dancers

wore costumes whose brilliant embroidery symbolized "non-dualistic wisdom of bliss and emptiness" and protection from evil influences. Music. Oh, yes, oh, yes, they said, there was always music. Beautifully carved conch-shell horns banded with silver; deeply resonant horns called *dungchen*, so long that two men had to carry them; bugles, trumpets, silvery-toned bells, and drums to convey joyful tidings.

And there were festive battles with kites whose strings had been dipped in broken glass. And fireworks, acrobats, dancing bears, snake charmers, storytellers, pigeon races. And tournaments where archers stood upright on galloping horses to loose arrows at painted targets. And wrestling matches. And competitions to judge the merits of intricate sculptures made of butter tinted in different colors. At Lhasa, they said, everyone marveled at the annual spectacle of the two enormous sacred banners, brilliantly painted with finely detailed religious scenes, that took fifty monks to lift and to lower from the upper ramparts of the Potala to cover the greater part of the building's southern foundation walls. Just as religion was the root of Tibetan life, they said, so were religious festivals the framework of the year's pleasures, a time in which to make merry, dance, sing, play dice, and founder oneself on mild barley beer called *chang*.

And food, there was always enough so that not even the poorest beggar went hungry. Always *tsampa*, roasted barley or chickpeas ground to powder, baked into bread or mixed with buttered tea to form a stiff porridge, and regular supplements of fish, meat, dried crumbled cheese, *momos* like the ones we are eating, and green tea boiled with a pinch of carbonate of soda and churned with salt and *dri* butter, even better than the tea we are now drinking. Veronica smiles at me and I manage to smile, too, despite the sour, terrible taste in my mouth.

The monks tell me about the Jokhang temple in Lhasa and of other great temples and the monastic universities of Drepung, Sera, and Ganden near Lhasa, and Tashilungpo near Shigatse, hung with *thangkas* and filled with brass, bronze, and gold images, ornamented with jewels, the skillful and resplendent workmanship of thirteen centuries. They tell me of iron- and silverwork as delicate as cobwebs.

They tell me of the Potala Palace, thirteen long white storeys high, and the vast halls it contains for ceremonial occasions, of its richly carved and painted chapels and the cenotaphs, plated with gold and studded with precious stones, of early Dalai Lamas.

They tell me of libraries stacked with thousands of enormous volumes, some of which weighed as much as eighty pounds, recording centuries of Tibetan culture: liturgical works, metaphysical treatises, spiritual poems, lyrical poems, the verses of Milarepa, political and historical chronologies, with illuminations of the scriptures written in inks made of powdered gold, silver, iron, copper, conch shell, and turquoise, the pages often separated with miniature *thangkas* mounted on brocade. As in pre-Gutenberg times, each word had been carved, letter by letter, on a wooden printing block. The loose, rectangular pages, laboriously made from reed fibers or the bark of trees, are printed on both sides and sandwiched between wooden covers, then wrapped with dust-covers of yellow and red silk and, occasionally, white silk.

"Come," the monks said. "We will show you." And they lead

us away to a large room where pages of handmade paper in rectangular strips are pinned to dry, like washing on a line. "We still make books as we did in Lhasa," they say, and I am awed.

Oh, yes. In Tibet, there was no outlet for spending money impulsively on ephemeral enjoyments, no cheap machine-made, large-scale production of anything. And since few possessions are needed for comfort, all possessions, even those of people with modest or meager means, had intrinsic value, and were made by craftsmen steeped in the traditions of artistic conscience, workmen who fulfilled the need to beautify common things. Everything was made in accordance with the criteria of honored traditions: the small rugs that were made to fit between the columns that supported the ceilings of houses; the carved, painted, and gilded wardrobes, chests, and low tea tables; the braziers for warming teapots; the teapots; the teacups, lidded and often fitted with raised stands. Whether a cup was crafted of wood, or wood chased with brass or silver, or of jade or solid gold, it was durable, well made, and pleasing to the eye, as were the tent pegs, knives, stirrups, bridles, and saddle rugs of the nomads.

Now more monks join us, showing us drawings and paintings made on handmade rice paper by Tibetan children born in Byllakuppe. There are lotuses and temples, women in Tibetan costumes milking *dris*, drawings of the Sera monastery here in Byllakuppe, drawings of Buddha, drawings of Indian birds, drawings of Mother Teresa and Mahatma Gandhi portrayed with reverence to their saintliness and homage to their good works, each accompanied by a card which has printed on its overleaf, "In aid of Tibetan Children's Educations."

They produce photographs of friends and families, worn

sepia-toned pictures invested now with memories they recall with such emotion that I can see apple and peach orchards patrolled by musters of iridescent-necked peacocks, and walled gardens bedded with sky-blue poppies, lavender aquilegia, white roses, and yellow daisies almost as large as sunflowers. I see also tame musk deer browsing by fish ponds, and Brahminy ducks switching their tails contentedly beneath the stone walls in the spring and summer.

Ah, yes. Tibet, the lost paradise of nature and beauty and simplicity. No telephones. No electricity, either, the monks tell me, other than the motor generator in the Potala Palace, a generator that was always breaking down, to the satisfaction of the teenaged Dalai Lama who, fascinated with things mechanical, enjoyed having an excuse to take the generator to pieces.

Without the telephone, without communication except by relays of mail-runners, jingling with bells, who jogged across vast distances or, when weather and terrain permitted, carried mail and other necessaries on sturdy mountain ponies, also festooned with bells—no wonder Tibetans were such a self-contained people, not given to small talk and conversation. They had grown up accustomed to interior dialogue and independent of the need for input from other sources. It was, as Veronica has told me, refreshing to be with them.

The Abbot of Sera in Byllakuppe is interested in what Veronica tells him of her studies in Dharamsala. He would like to examine her concerning what she has learned about tolerance and compassion. Since they will carry on their dialogue in Tibetan, Veronica and the elderly abbot closet themselves in the reception room, while I wander off in the company of a group of maroon-robed monks of different ages, some of whom had

fled Tibet with their families after the unsuccessful uprising in
1959, some of whom had been born in Lhasa before or during
the Chinese occupation, some of whom had only recently escaped. They all read, write, and speak English with varying
degrees of fluency and understanding. They have acquired English since they have come to India, they say; English is taught
at all settlements for Tibetan refugees here. They speak the
language haltingly, simply, slowly, but astonishingly, with none
of the sing-song Indian intonation.

On the wall of the room in which we have gathered, I notice
a poster quoting a statement by the Dalai Lama: "The tragedy
of Tibet is that a whole race, a people, strongly opposed to
foreign domination, has been subjugated, oppressed, and gob-
bled up by China."

Eager to enlarge upon this statement, eager to practice their
English, eager to tell me about what they have lived through
and experienced, the monks explain that in September of 1949,
the Chinese People's Liberation Army marched to annex Tibet.
Promising to help the Tibetan people develop their education,
agriculture and animal husbandry, industry and commerce, and
generally improve their standard of living, the PLA solemnly
pledged that there would be freedom of religious belief and
worship for all regions of Tibet; that lamaseries and temples
would be protected; that the Tibetans, whose culture and language were different from those of the Chinese, would be free
to follow their time-honored customs and traditions. Having
promised Utopia, they delivered death and destruction, followed, after the unsuccessful uprising of the Tibetans in 1959,
by atrocities which aimed at the assimilation and eradication of
the Tibetan race.

One monk told me that he had seen his mother and father swaddled in cotton, crucified, and burnt alive. Another told of his grandfather, a high lama, forced to eat bowlsful of human and animal excrement. Another told of public trials in which each member of the crowd was ordered to kick the victim's teeth, pull out the victim's hair, pull the victim's nose until it was broken, or pull the victim's ears to the point of tearing them from his or her head.

They described how food and clothing allotments were doled out on the basis of work points earned by slave labor and how no provisions were made for children under the age of seven, or for the disabled, sick or aged. Tibetans, who had slaved for the work points necessary for minimal clothing and had still managed to put up prayer flags, saw the Chinese Communists tear down and burn these sacrificial scraps symbolizing their faith.

Religious monuments were smashed. Small shrines were smashed. All religious objects and articles, including prayer beads and the portable shrines Tibetans wore around their necks or shoulders, were taken away from them and carted off to be sold to the tourist trade in Peking. Temples were torn down or converted into warehouses or other municipal buildings. Historically and intrinsically valuable images were sent to antique shops. Clay images were ground into powder and made into bricks specifically intended for the construction of latrines. Ancient scriptures were shredded into pulp for newsprint, or flagrantly used by the Chinese for toilet paper, the padding of boot soles, the kindling of fires. The wooden blocks used for printing the earliest known Aryan writings—the religious, historical, and political chronologies; the epic histories of Mongolians and the Romans; the sacred Buddhist and Tantric texts—were made into handles for farm implements; hammered into chairs, benches, and planking for floors; or burned as fuel.

The Chinese Communists showed contempt for Tibetan script and banned Tibetan songs and dances. Tibetans were forced to sing Chinese songs, wear Chinese dress, practice Chinese customs, and to speak "Tibetan-Chinese Friendship language," a mixture of Tibetan and Chinese which was comparable, at worst, to pidgin English, and at best to a patois of common parlance.

Celebrations of seasonal fairs and religious festivals were banned. Children and young people were drilled to report anyone, including their parents and members of their family, who disagreed with or opposed Communist policies in any way. The Chinese liberation of Tibet, the monks said, was "like putting on a wet leather cap: as time passes, it becomes tighter and tighter until it kills the person wearing it."

Food rations for Tibetan communes dwindled until many Tibetans kept alive by foraging for herbs, berries, grasses. Steeped in the Buddhist tradition of nonviolence, Tibetans helplessly watched the Communists kill herds of deer and mountain sheep, leopards, and other wild game for their musk, meat, skins, and pelts. They watched their children being forced to kill migrating birds, small wild animals, dogs, and cats, not only because these were regarded as enemies of the harvest as well as free-loading consumers of food, but also, the monks said, to train children to show no compassion for living creatures.

Thousands starved. Mothers were known to slit their wrists

in order to give their blood to nourish their children. Life, as
the Tibetans had known it, had vanished and been replaced by
torment, torture, and destruction. Like the Brahmaputra River,
which rises in Tibet, the only instance of a river flowing in an
opposite direction of what it once did, while still occupying the
same bed, the current of life in Tibet had been reversed. It had
taken millions of years for this to happen with the Brahmaputra,
but less than thirty years for the change to take place in Tibet.

I find this information shattering. Tears streaming down my
face, I hug the monks closest to me. What bravery they have,
what courage, what faith, what loyalty to the country they have
managed to escape. Riding on horses or yaks, or just walking
out eighteen hundred miles across rivers and plateaus and over
the Himalayas, they brought whatever treasures they could
with them—in most cases, their children, and very little else.

There is another poster which states: "The cause of our
people will prevail because no matter how ruthless the Chinese
are, and how powerful their physical might may appear to be,
the human spirit cannot be vanquished by force alone."

The invincibility of the human spirit, *that* is what is important. To have suffered and witnessed torment, torture, and destruction and still to believe in the invincibility of the human
spirit, *that* is what endears the Tibetans to me. That, and the
faces of the aspirant baby monks who are now gathering on the
verandah, enamel mugs and plates in hand, waiting to be served
their evening meal. For a moment, their maroon robes, their
shaved heads, and their solemn mien distort their reality, give
them the look of homunculi, or dwarfs. But no, the moment
their teacher's back is turned, they stare at me with mischievous
dark eyes, smiling, giggling, and free-spirited, irresistibly lov-

able because they appear so openly ready to love, to have fun, to play. One of them runs across the dusty path and up the steps to give me a hug that is strong enough to last a lifetime. Then, embarrassed, he runs away.

A monk in his late twenties, identifying himself as Jhamchoe, tells me by way of explanation for this impulsive show of affection that the child, like himself, had lost both his mother and his sisters, and that all of his family had been killed. Unlike the other baby monks born in Byllakuppe, this child had been sent to Byllakuppe, rather than to one of the Tibetan villages set up throughout India for orphaned children, because he was considered to have a special inclination for the spiritual and scholarly life. Smiling a Bodhisattva smile that shines impartially on me and upon the back of the baby monk, Jhamchoe shows me a photograph of one of his uncles wearing the eponymous yellow hat of the Gelugpa order, which bears an extraordinary resemblance to the shining brass helmets with panaches worn by the soldiers of Alexander the Great, who had marched at least as far as Kashmir in the early part of the fourth century before Christ. He tells me that each of the thousand and eighteen woolen threads with which these priestly hats are woven represents a reincarnation of Buddhas yet to be born. Someday, he says, he hopes he will pass all the examinations necessary for him to be able to wear such a hat, which symbolizes the full development of wisdom, compassion, and power, and the attainment of Buddahood. I like the idea that costumes represent the collective history of a country and the thought that the memory of Alexander should be preserved in the hat of a Buddhist lama.

Jhamchoe disappears and soon reappears with a basket filled with coarsely crumbled dried milk cheese. *Dri* cheese, he tells me, offering me the basket, some of the supply he has carried out from Tibet.

What a gift to give me! I have no words to thank him. Trying to keep the tears from my eyes, I embrace him with the same sudden fervor with which the baby monk hugged me.

The sun pours down, its rays scalding in this tropical Tibetan enclave, torturing, surely, to these gentle people from the land on top of the world, one more torture, even in this land of their refuge.

Veronica appears at that very moment in the doorway of the verandah and is suddenly at my side. "Please don't hug the monks, Mummy," she says in a fierce whisper. "They won't like it."

"It's all right," Jhamchoe says, taking my hand. "She is my sister. She is my mother."

The Abbot of the Sera Gompa at Byllakuppe gives Veronica and me *kataks*, ceremonial white scarves representing purity of mind and speech, as he and the other monks gather on the verandah of the communal hall to see us on our way again. The baby monks, who have been shushed and told to behave by their teachers, stand momentarily grave and impassive. But soon they twitch irrepressibly into smiles, and then shouts of *tashidelek*, *tashidelek*, an all-purpose salutation of greeting and farewell that Veronica tells me is untranslatable into English.

"You asked what a *gompa* means," she says as we drive away, showing off more of her knowledge as she consults a lexicon she has compiled of Tibetan words and phrases. I am being unfair. She really isn't "showing off." When your daughter knows more than you do, resentment precedes pride in her accomplishments, I tell myself. I suppose I find it hard to accept that there is so much my daughter can teach me that I don't know, and am interested in knowing.

"*Gompa* means a solitary place, wilderness, a waved-leaf fig tree. Hence, a hermitage, so-called on account of its original situation in earlier times in lonely places abounding in Bodhi trees. Later on, these hermitages became converted into monasteries. Monasteries in later times assumed the size of large castles and collections of dwelling houses with the estates belonging to the monasteries used for the support of monks. So a *gompa* means a school for reading, writing, debate, prayer, history, logic, philosophy, astronomy, medicine, and so on, as well as a residence for monks."

"I liked the monks," I say. "That's why I hugged them. That's why they hugged me."

Veronica reflects that it seems impossible, but is true, that the love one receives from others comes from one's own heart, one's own mind.

"Yes," I say, "there's an old proverb that love begets love."

Veronica is silent. Silence can also be a form of conversation.

For a while, we continue to drive through the estates of Byllakuppe, seeing the tilled land, the sleek Swiss cows, and prayer flags everywhere printed with the eight Buddhist symbols of happy augury.

"Here," Veronica says with tender authority, "let me draw them for you in your notebook."

Even though the road is not smooth, she draws small, neat, stylized pictures. The lidded vase, which holds the elixir of life and symbolizes fulfillment and immortality. The arabesque, or knot, which symbolizes longevity and eternity. The pair of fish, like the yin and yang, which symbolize duality, harmony, fertility. The lotus, blooming from the mud with its beauty, which symbolizes purity and compassion. The umbrella, which is a symbol of protection. The conch shell, as resonant as a trumpet or a seashell held to the ear, which symbolizes the propagation of the *dharma*. The octagonal wheel of the law, which is the original symbol of Buddhist teaching. The banner, which is symbolic of the victory of good over evil.

There is time to see the land become dry and the earth red, time to see villagers husking tiny grains of millet by the roadside, time to notice fields of sugarcane, rice paddies, the loveliness of *gul mohur* trees. Then it is dark, and we fall asleep, waking only at the roar of the Krishnarajasagar Dam just outside Mysore and the glare of the bright lights of a causeway across the Cauvery River.

Nineteen

Mysore, city of silk and sandalwood, coiled around by the Cauvery, curls beneath the foot of a hill topped with a temple. Both the hill and the temple are named for the goddess Kali of Chamundi, the city's maternal deity, who saved the town from destruction by a demon. Flaunting the extravagance of its evening suit of lights, the *lingam*-like side of Chamundi hill flashes WELCOME on and off from an electrically lit billboard. The thousand ancient steps carved in the hill leading up to the temple are illuminated by the headlights of motor traffic, conferring a softening grace on the intensities of the temple's Hoysala architecture. Beyond a giant statue of the vanquished demon, who flourishes a sword in one hand and a snake in the other, is a colossal reclining *Nandi*. Shiva's bell-and-flower wreathed *vahana*, carved from a single boulder, is so massive, so huge that when Veronica and I come in the daytime to sit beside it on its platform, our heads barely reach above the *Nandi's* left hoof.

Somnolent on the hillside, the great rockhewn *Nandi* is blackened with the smoke of *puja* ceremonies. A child priest offers us *prasad*, a handful of consecrated jasmine blossoms. As we scatter these among the stone figures, the child priest sings a hymn about Shiva, lord of dancers, destroyer of demons; Shiva who is man, who is woman; the dark blue bird and the green parrot with red eyes; Shiva who is the cloud with lightning in its womb; Shiva who has no beginning and is everywhere, from whom all worlds are born. "Shiva!" his voice shivers in exaltation. "Shiva the Embodied One, my kin, my flesh, heart within my flesh, image within my heart, my all-bestowing tree, my vision, my eye, pupil of my eye, image seen in that pupil!"

A woman with red, black, and yellow wool plaited in her long braid of hair, tasseled and tinkling with bells, kneels devoutly to stroke the genitals of the *Nandi*. She may be barren, she may hope for fertility, she may hope to be blessed with a son.

I look at the *Nandi* and see the minotaur of my childhood, no longer frightening, come to rest.

Veronica says the *Nandi* reminds her of a holiday she once spent in Crete, in a village near Knossos, where she could never wander in the thyme-scented hills without shepherds following her. "When they found I wasn't available," she says, "they just stuck a sheep's hindlegs inside their boot-tops, and used the sheep instead."

Below us, the Mysore traffic hums like a top.

"You used to tell me I should be glad that men desired me, found me attractive," Veronica says softly. The soft voice of the serpent.

"Well, I didn't want you to be like me, accepting the first marriage proposal that came along. I wanted you to have confidence in yourself, to love yourself, to know you were beautiful and desirable."

"Did you think it was wonderful when Bill Leveret was sitting on the sofa with you and he turned around and pointed to me and said, 'I want *her.*' Weren't you sorry, then? Weren't you jealous?"

"I wasn't jealous. You were only thirteen." I couldn't imagine Veronica's sexuality. I had yet to discover the pubic hair birds' nests. When I was fifteen, two years older than she at the time, I hadn't known the meaning of that Coney Island button, "You can play with my doggy, but leave my pussy alone." Bill Leveret was a man in his thirties trying to pretend he was a sixteen-year-old, or perhaps indulging in the fantasy of wanting to bed both mother and daughter.

Something nags at me, like the first bar of a tune of which you can't remember the rest. I am on the promenade deck of the Queen Mary, a white lifesaver with that name on it roped to a bulkhead behind me. My chin is in the vise of my hands, bare elbows propped on a teak railing that is slimy-gritty with salt. I am gazing at the seemingly infinite horizon when someone comes to stand further along toward the bow. I turn to stare at him if he were under glass, a specimen under a slide. Gray-bearded, his face the color of tea with a generous pour of milk, and topped with a maroon turban crisscrossed in front, he is the first live Indian I have ever seen.

Appreciatively, inquisitively, I edge toward him. He turns, looks down at me, smiles. I am shy. I stutter, so adoring and admiring, I suppose, that I fawn around him, gibbering about

Kipling, listening to his every response with passionate attention, telling him I long to go to India, asking him idiotic questions. He says he has many photographs of India. Would I like to see them? They are in an album in his cabin.

I pinch the idea in my mind, testing it like a plum for its ripeness. Never talk with strangers. Never go anywhere with anyone you don't know. But an Indian, a real live Indian who was willing to show me photographs of India? Surely, Mummy wouldn't be cross about that? So I follow this Indian in a turban to his tiny cabin in Tourist Class. He shows me pictures of the *terai*, the plains country below the Himalayas, he explains, and pictures of Punjabi women in saris posed before wells worked by bullocks. Here is Mr. Singh, my host, standing beneath a banyan tree with aerial roots, Mr. Singh wearing a topee, Mr. Singh standing on a verandah curtained with chicks ("Not chicky birdies, *chicks*—esscreens of sblit reed sbringled viz vawter to cool the hot vinds dat be blowing in."). Picture after picture. Elephants, palaces, camels, temples, parrots, and palm trees, each pleasure spreads to the limits of the spent one like a wave foaming in to shore.

When the thick black album is finally closed, Mr. Singh produces a little pair of drums he calls a *tabla* and shows me how to tap them with my fingertips and slap them with the heel of my hand. I realize that the afternoon is wearing on, that it's almost tea-time, and that I should, as Granny and Mummy always say, delay not upon the order of my going. Reluctantly, I say goodbye, curtsey—a few months short of my thirteenth birthday, I am still curtseying—and find my way back to the First Class stairway and the A Deck where our cabins are.

And there, of course, is my mother, shivering with hysterics that go right into me so that I am all gooseflesh, trembling, teeth-jittering, cold. Where have I been? Everyone thought I had fallen overboard. She had asked the captain to stop the ship and send out lifeboats. They are about to ring all the alarm bells. Oh, the problems I have caused. I will have to go and apologize to the captain. Everyone has been frantic, *frenzied*. How could I? Why had I? Why hadn't I? My mother's voice stabs through me. "Did he touch you? Did he touch you?" I tell her that I shook his hand goodbye.

"Jealous?" I say again to Veronica. "No, I wasn't jealous. It never occurred to me that I had any reason to be."

"Oh," Veronica says. "I thought Bill felt I'd be better in bed than you."

How could she have thought that? "He didn't make a pass at you, did he?"

"No. But I never encouraged him to."

"What you're saying is that had you encouraged him, he would have gone to bed with you?"

"Sure. I've never met a man who didn't want to go to bed with me. Did you, when you were younger?"

"I don't know," I say. "Times were different." It occurs to me suddenly that whatever her reasons, my mother managed to protect me far better than I have protected Veronica.

When I was married, I was inviolate, monogamous, a one-man woman. Between marriages, passion held the seeds of destruction, the terrible fear of abandonment, the mind-deranging threat of loss. There was no such thing as developing passion. It was always enveloping, instant, the moth's desire for the flame.

A look, some unspoken communication of eyes and voice would seize me, capture me. The attraction would be wild and intense. The death of the ego is implicit in such a passion. The source of the attraction that, if I let myself pass beyond the boundaries of my self, my will, my identity, at first exhilarating and yearned for, to merge with the consciousness of another, locking into the mind as well as the body of another, would become the cause of an obsessive dependency that could only lead to grief, anguish, despair. I knew this. I feared emotional enslavement, as well as physical abandonment.

My mother loathed Bill Leveret. She said he looked like the Devil Incarnate. Actually, he looked very much like the nurse who looked after me until I was almost two, the nurse who disappeared one day and whom I never saw again. "Where's Bill?" I remember screaming, when he told me to meet him at his apartment and didn't show up, a scream that came absolutely unbidden, worse than any primal scream, a shriek of anguish. My therapist said later that I wasn't screaming for Bill, that I had bottled up that scream all those years and finally shrieked the pain I couldn't release as a child.

Veronica thinks I am exaggerating, dramatizing. "I never got men mixed up with *you*," she says.

Our room at the Krishnarajasagar Hotel, high-ceilinged, at least three times the size of an ordinary room, is furnished in the style of Europe's comfortable nineteen-thirties. At night, the illuminated gardens beyond the French doors have an aspect of the Prater. From tea-time until late at night, the hotel's orchestra plays Strauss waltzes, echoing afternoon concerts on Cunard liners, dinner music I fell asleep to on long-ago vacations in the

Adirondacks, clutching a pillow embroidered, "I pine fir yew and balsam too." In the morning, the dining room, with its whiffs of furniture polish, frying fish and bacon, could be Brighton, or Rhodesia before it was called Zimbabwe. It is only when I am seated, turbaned waiters hovering around me like waltzing mice, starched white napkins plumped into empty water goblets and furled like elephants' heads, that I have any sense that an Indian city is only a few minutes' drive away.

Mysore, a guidebook says, is a tourist paradise, a garden city, and more. "We welcome you as a Litterateur, Archaeologist, Anthropologist, Numismatist, Scientist, Geographer, Technologist, Epigraphist, Mineralogist, Sericulturalist, Speech Therapist, Bibliopole." A Bibliopole. Maybe I should write that after my occupation in my passport. In a state of hubris, I once wrote "Writer" and it was changed to "Waiter." As the sunlight streams in through the dining room's stained glass windows, turning the water in our goblets into red wine, we head out to see the offerings of this "tourist paradise, garden city, and more."

Our first stop is the Amba Vilas palace of Mysore's Wadiyar dynasty. The Mysore city palace of the Wadiyars is by far the most dazzling we have seen, with "thousand pillar" halls; golden walls; intricate lattices; delicate inlay; carved, sculpted, gilded ceilings reflected on corridors of marble and porphyry that glow pink, green, amber. The finials and domes of its exterior are covered with eighteen-carat gold. The enormous throne, cushioned with crimson velvet, is solid gold, carved in a fine and florid style. In the courtyard, with its triumphal gateway, there are platoons of palace guards who sporadically chase away minstrels playing stringed instruments with soundboxes covered in cobra skin. Vendors selling python skins, cobra skins, sandalwood boxes, and carved elephants clamorously besiege and beseech all who pass through the triumphal archway. "Elephant, elephant, elephant! Cheapy, cheapy, cheapy! *Hathi, hathi, hathi!*"

In the recent past, Mysore was renowned for its *Kheddas*, its round-ups of herds of wild elephants that would be domesticated and trained to perform chores, and would march in the October *Dassera* procession, in celebration of King Rama's victory over the forces of evil. Mysore is still famous for the extravagance of this observance, and the festivities bring to the capital and its palace musicians, dancers, painters, storytellers, puppeteers, archers, jugglers, acrobats, and horsemen. "Sabu, elephant boy, rode Mysore elephant. Elephant, elephant, elephant! *Hathi, hathi, hathi!* Cheapy, cheapy, cheapy!"

The entreaties of vendors at the palace also shrill outside other local residences of the Wadiyars, where in cool, drawn-curtain interiors, gazelle-legged tables of rosewood and sandalwood, inlaid with ivory, stand browsing among ebony chairs carved in the shape of peacocks, and the walls are hung with images of ceremonial *durbars*, *shikars*, after-the-*shikar* celebrations, polo matches, *Dassera* processions, and other religious and secular occasions of import. As Veronica and I look in absorptive stillness at one cornucopia of riches after another amassed by the maharajas and their families, their houses seem like the nests bower birds build as part of their courtship ritual, surrogate ornamentation to beguile and fascinate. The duller the plumage, the fancier the bower is an observation true of bower birds, but is it applicable to the Wadiyar rulers? I examine a wall hanging embroidered all over with the iridescent backs of cantharides beetles. I look at rock crystal cups jeweled with rubies and emeralds. I ask Veronica to identify the musical instruments—*veenas*, *serenghis*, *oudhs*, *sitars*. I gaze at the captions on the oil paintings and lithographs: Late His Highness Krishnaraja Wadiyar III in European Durbar. Late His Highness Krishnaraja Wadiyar IV in Wedding Durbar. His Highness Sri Jayachamaraja Wadiyar in childhood installation robes. Shiva *lingam* worshiped by Late His Highness Krishnaraja Wadiyar III. Late His Highness Chamaraja Wadiyar in his Birthday Procession. Group photo of His Highness Sri Jayachamaraja Wadiyar Maharaja of Mysore with His Holiness Swami Shivananda, in the Divine Life Society Ananda Kutira, March 13, 1952.

Mysore, "a smiling city," as the guidebooks claim, reveals daily evidence that a succession of rulers has succeeded in making the state progressive and prosperous. I list admirable medical colleges; a university; technological institutes; manifestly flourishing arts, industry, commerce; many cultural and educational organizations; hospitals; pleasing parks; public libraries; well-stocked bookstores; temples; a well-attended church. I send Gurdip postcards of Mysore's modern sugar factory, sandalwood oil factory, silk factory, cotton mills. Veronica reminds me to mention the Mangalore Ganesh Beedie factory, which the guidebooks don't usually include in their listing of Mysore's attractions. Scribble, scribble, scribble.

Of the five hundred and sixty-two former princely states, Mysore was among the top five. Each princely state was graded according to the number of guns ceremonially fired to salute its ruler. The top five states rated a twenty-one-gun salute. Each prince with more than eleven guns had one vote in the Chamber of Princes. I note that one hundred and twenty-seven states qualified to share only twelve votes, and that there were four hundred and thirteen princes who had no guns at all and who had to remain silent in the assembly of their more grandly cannonaded brethren. Now I understand why the Wadiyars are often referred to as "great guns," or "big shots," a nineteenth-century development of the phrase that my father sometimes used, applying it to the very rich, and to people who played better polo or golf than he did.

But the Wadiyars are forever eclipsed in my mind by Tippoo Sultan, an eighteenth-century ruler known as the Tiger of Mysore. Tippoo, whose name means tiger in Kanarese, had a passion for tigers, extending his obsession for the emblem of Mysore and its early capital of Seringapatam to everything around him. His golden throne was built in the shape of a rampant tiger, richly illuminated with stripes and Arabic verses, its canopy fringed with pearls, its railing set with ten small tiger heads inlaid with precious stones. Some of his weapons were inscribed with a tiger's face formed by an arrangement of Arabic characters, and the hilts of swords were fashioned into tigers' heads as were the muzzles of his cannon. His mortars were in the form of crouching tigers. Tiger stripes were incorporated in many of his turbans, and in the jackets worn by his palace guards and his infantrymen. Tigers were chained in the private square in front of his palace in Seringapatam, "an insulated metropolis," described as "the richest, most convenient, and beautiful spot possessed . . . by any native Prince in India." Persian scholars have discovered among Tippoo's memoirs that he even dreamed of tigers. But it is his music box tiger, captured by the British at the fall of Seringapatam, in 1799 that first stamped an indelible imprint on the walls of my mind's house.

It is a moment that the child who dwells within my time-altered body can still remember in all its original intensity.

Unearthly roars and growls mixed with groans and shrieks of pain—that was how I first heard it in the Victoria and Albert Museum, where I had come with my grandmother after visiting the Elgin Marbles at the British Museum. I thought a wild animal had escaped from the Regent's Park Zoo. I was too frightened to scream. I hated myself for being frightened, wished I were as brave as Kim protecting his Holy Man, as fearless as Hercules and Alexander. God was my grandmother's confidant. God would save us, wouldn't He? I flung my right arm around my grandmother's substantial waist, buried my face in the folds of her blue cashmere cloak and wailed, "Granny, Granny, save me! I don't want to die!"

"Don't be absurd, child." My grandmother shook me loose. "It's only Tippoo Sultan's music box tiger." She took my hand and led me down a corridor to an extraordinary effigy, not life-sized, but seeming to be, of a prostrate employee of the British East India Company being mauled by a tiger.

I study the silent figures. The man is pink-faced. He wears a black, broad-brimmed hat trimmed with olive green; a high-collared, fitted tunic in Chinese red, embroidered with silver flowers, with gilded cuffs and collar; short blue breeches; white stockings; and black shoes. The tiger is crouched over him, its claws digging into his thighs and chest, its jaws open, its white muzzle with black whisker spots pressed against the right side of its victim's cheek and neck. The tiger is orange with stripes stylized in the shape of olive-green mango leaves with black-painted incised centers, each leaf having the aspects of eye,

mouth, and leaf, a painted pelt as inexorably cruel and devour-
ing as the jungle I imagined where Shere Khan carried off a man
at twilight and meant to kill Mowgli until Mowgli herded buffaloes into the terrible charge "against which no tiger can hope
to stand." I walk around this wooden tiger and see that its tail is
precisely barred, curving downward, taut as a snake about to
strike, above a protruding anal passage which (I know better
than to point out to my grandmother) is in the shape of a Valentine heart.

The white kid-skinned-gloved hand of my grandmother un-
does the clasp of her crocodile bag, disappears inside, rustles
about, appears with a copper coin which she drops into a slot
beside the music box. She grasps the brass handle of a mahogany
arm pull, pushes it backward, releases it. The music box comes
to life. The man's left arm waves in an oscillating motion between his mouth and the tiger's ear, the motion ingeniously
gauged to shade the tone and pitch of the screams and groans
from a brass pipe I can see in his open mouth, while simultaneously from a grill-like vent in the tiger's left side come the
terrible, savage roars and growls of a Bengal tiger at its kill. In
the world of my mother and grandmother, anything sexual,
visceral, or violent is unmentionable, unspeakable. Perhaps it is
for this reason, or perhaps to overcome my original fear of the
furious roars of the tiger and the shrieks of its victim, that I
clamor for more coins, and squander my allowance to listen to
the roars of the Man-Tiger-Organ. "Such a little sadist," a uniformed museum attendant remarks.

"Oh, no," I retort with an innocent, boastful confidence of
being. "I'm a happiest."

My grandmother, to whom I look up questioningly, shakes her head, mouths silently to me. "You shouldn't speak to strangers or answer back." Aloud, she says, "Come along, dear, you don't want to be late for tea."

Bryce wore a shoulder patch with a tiger on it, the emblem of his Army tank division before he became involved with an Army unit of Psychological Warfare. The first night we slept in twin Army beds hooked together, he scratched a mark with his Army knife on his side of the bed for every time he had an orgasm. I was fascinated to see him have an erection. "Oh, do it again!" I kept exclaiming, clapping my hands, applauding him. Later, he used to say, standing before the mirror, admiring the press of his uniform, that "next to a good fuck, a good shit is best." He would ask me to tie him down on the bed after dinner, tickle him with a feather, and ride him like a bucking bronco. It was around this time, pointing at a woman (as Bill Leveret pointed later at Veronica)—this woman, dressed in a red sheath with a cool look that reminded me of Marlene Dietrich—that Bryce said, "I *like* her." His freedom of expression and behavior bewildered me, but I accepted him as the index, infinitely superior to me because he knew more, had read more, and could usually remember more precisely than I could just what he had read. He was right when he told me over and over again that I was like Browning's *Last Duchess*, with a heart too soon made glad, too easily impressed, smiling at everyone and everything she saw, her looks going everywhere. As he recited the lines with a smile of condescension, I thought of my mother who told me not to smile so much.

Robert liked me to smile. Because he also seemed to me as

intrepid a hunter as Major Jim Corbett, I gave him a volume of Corbett's tales about tracking and the man-eating tigers of Kumaon in the Himalayan foothills. Someday, he said, we would go to India together, when Veronica was older. I smiled what he called my lateral banana smile, a smile like a banana in my mouth sidewise.

Veronica and I are both smiling now when we reach Seringapatam and Tippoo Sultan's summer palace, the Dariya Daulat, its interior walls covered with paintings of flowers and murals of battles. We look at Tippoo's private mosque, and at the pigeons and swallows flying in and out of small open windows in the mosque's minaret. We look at the ruins of an old fort, the stones of its walls the texture of fossilized sponges. We slog across a marshy plain where the battle of Seringapatam was fought, when the British won and Tippoo was killed. We look at dank underground prisons where a guide says many British prisoners were tortured, strangled, impaled, thrown to tigers, poisoned, or succumbed to starvation and fever. We look at faded paintings of British soldiers being castrated and decapitated.

Before his death in 1799, Tippoo Sultan made Mysore the strongest power in India, a rallying point for Indian hopes and aspirations, and a constant challenge to the British. Tippoo, a bronze plaque says, claimed it was better to live one year as a tiger than a thousand as a sheep. The spot where he was killed is marked with a plain gray slab of stone inscribed "Better to die like a soldier than to live a miserable life dependent on the infidels on the list of their pensioned rajas and nabobs." The British, of course, were the infidels to whom he refers, and the guide hardly needs to tell us, as he does, that Tippoo was a brave enemy of the British and their East India Company. Tippoo's Man-Tiger-Organ is a strange and glamorous testimony of his Anglophobia. In *Cap and Bells*, Keats wrote about "that little buzzing noise" which "Comes from a play-thing of the Emperor's choice, From a Man-Tiger-Organ, prettiest of his toys."

As I walk with Veronica, our arms linked, across the muddy battlefield of Seringapatam, another incident in my childhood flies up in my mind like a startled bird.

I see myself carrying a large, fine-meshed sieve, simple as a round Shaker box, filled with kernels of corn to feed to the pigeons in the loft. Meandering as I skip along the pine-bordered path from Northlea's latticed kitchen yard to the pigeon loft above the gardener's garage and tool shed, I whistle "Some talk of Alexander and some of Hercules," a tune in praise of British grenadiers. I climb the ladder into the pigeon loft, one hand on the railing, one hand clutching the sieve filled with kernels—larger, coarser than popping corn, each grain shaped like a baby-tooth. "Pidgies, pidgies, don't be scared. I love you, I love you," I croon to those plump birds with their amber-button eyes, the variations in the color of their plumage an unfailing fascination. Flapping their wings as though they are clapping their hands with delight, the pigeons fly around me, settle on the floor beneath their straw-filled orange-crate nests, and greedily pick up the corn. I am needed. I am loved. When the corn is gone, down the ladder I go, empty sieve in hand.

I see myself pedaling the wheel of the knife-sharpening grinder to the left of the ladder beneath the pigeon loft. I'm sitting on its bicycle seat, wearing a navy blue cotton halter and white shorts, pedaling, pedaling, mindlessly sharpening a stick, listening to the sound it makes against the wheel's whir, imagining myself a hunter sharpening a spear. I can smell the pigeons above, hear their cooing and fluttering, inhale the scent of woodshavings and damp earth in the room below. I can smell my own sweat, pungent as marigolds and geraniums, feel it trickling down my arms and in the creases where my legs join my body. The creaking sound of the wheel is like the creaking sound of the rocking horse I have long since outgrown, the sound it made as I sat on its red leather saddle, rocking mindlessly back and forth, up and down in front of the fireplace in my nursery.

Then I see Karl the gardener come into the shed. Beautiful Karl, like a golden giant. I am used to watching him in the garden, to seeing the sun glinting on the golden hairs of his arms, turning the drops of his sweat into melting glass jewels, while he digs up weeds.

Sometimes he hands me a sun-warmed tomato to eat or a strawberry from beneath a net that keeps the starlings and the crows away. Sometimes, when it is hot, he sprays my legs and sneakers with a hose.

He comes to stand behind my back as I am pedaling. He puts his hands on my shoulders and begins to rub my neck the way Aunt Vera does when she wants me to go to sleep, but it feels different when Karl does it. I shiver inside, shudder with pleasure. The places I am too embarrassed to name for myself, what my mother calls my shocking parts, feel strange and throbbing. Karl slips his hands beneath my arms to my breasts, which have just begun to point up in little pyramids like anthills. He rubs where my nipples are and I can feel his body pressing against my bottom and back. I feel something is wrong, but what? I stop pedaling, and all I can hear is Karl's breath, and the pigeons' soft moaning and the sound of a horsefly buzzing. I scramble off the saddle of the knife-sharpening wheel and run out the door, crunching across the gravel driveway, racing up the path between the pines, through the open wood gate into the kitchen courtyard, pounding up the gray-painted stairs to the kitchen porch, through the kitchen's screen door, hearing it slam behind me, through the kitchen, the pantry, and up the back stairs through the hall to my room. *Something is wrong*, I want to tell someone, but there is no one to tell.

My mother perceived me as being constantly threatened by rapacious men from whom it was her duty to protect me, and yet when I was in real danger, physically, psychically, she saw nothing, and I had no words to tell her, no way of asking for help. And what of me, my grown-up Mummy self? Unless Veronica mentioned some specific incident, I was apparently insouciant about protecting her from sexual encounters. I overlooked my capacity for sexual arousal and remembered only my innocence at the same age and considered Veronica's virginity similarly protected. Even when I discovered this was not the way it was, I thought of her as somehow armored against the unwelcome attentions of men; that she might provoke them by games of attraction, rejection, seduction didn't occur to me because it was something I hadn't done. And so, for all my good intentions, I was no more help to Veronica than my mother was to me.

Maybe it would have been better for both of us if I had seen Veronica as a sexual competitor. Maybe then I would have been aware of her sensuality. But I was enthralled by her grace, her beauty, her charm, by the way she sang, painted, drew pictures, played the guitar. At the same time, I hoped she would respect, admire, and delight in me, laugh at my jokes, be warm, intimate, and loving, be as sharing with me as I wanted to be with her. When I was tired, I hoped she would rub my back as my Aunt Vera used to do, as my father did for my mother, as I would do when Veronica was tired or sick. But she didn't. "I'm not your nursemaid," she said, and then took infinite care to stitch felt pouches for the twelve thumb-sized ceramic sculptures of the carved figures of the Zodiac she gave me as a birthday present.

At fifteen she wrote, "Loving is being often very jealous . . . the key to much of my misery and all of my happiness . . . sometimes terribly upsetting . . . being someplace faraway and quiet with you . . . very intense . . . to be meditated upon . . . *la fleur de ma vie* . . . a feeling of great security . . . the fitting together of both of our natures . . . having a shoulder to lean on . . . worrying about you and waiting for you to come home . . . celestial and magic . . . mysterious and often elusive . . ."

Walking along, side by side, Veronica has begun to whisper her mantras. I look at her. Where is the impassioned young girl who wrote that poem? For whom was it written? Her father? She now seems almost without emotion. In her ritual Buddhist nonattachment, I see my mother's coldness all over again. Birth links birth in an endless chain. Patterns of behavior are repeated from generation to generation. *Mea culpa. Mea culpa.*

That night, Veronica and I stand before the open French doors of our room, gazing out upon the allée of the Brindavan Gardens: topiary trees and plumes of water are illuminated with changing rainbow colors, avenues of poplars are garlanded with twinkling lights like elongated Christmas trees, the sound of the dam's waterfall is like the distant rumbling of a train. The terrace exhales the retained heat of the day, and the scent of jasmine and roses, cumin and sandalwood is released into the night air. Veronica has returned from dinner, sated with caviar, lobster, asparagus with hollandaise, ice cream, and champagne, dancing at the hotel discothèque, and a late snack of pizza. She clasps her hands behind her head, pulling her elbows back. "Ah, this rich mix of unaccustomed sensual pleasures has made me feel sleepy-byes." She stretches her arms horizontally, lets them fall to her sides. "Now what I'd like is to see an Ingmar Bergman film, listen to Bach, eat shad roe, an artichoke vinaigrette, and a great big bowl of fresh raspberries with heavy cream, and go for a swim."

"Have some fruit." I pick up a small reddish-skinned banana from the basket that is re-filled every evening and set on the table between our beds with a thermos of iced water. "Have a *chiku* or a pomegranate or a tangerine or a banana." Veronica examines the fruit bowl. Pushing the bananas to one side with her finger, pushing away the cocoa-colored *chikus*, she selects a pomegranate, reaches for the fruit knife.

Her teeth, milk white in the room's dim light, close on a segment of pomegranate. She has peeled the rosy skin from the fruit, and it lies like an arabesque on a plate by her side, with a heap of seeds, sloe-black and shiny.

"You can puncture a hole in one end of a pomegranate and just suck out the juice," she says. "But I like the seeds."

"You and Persephone." Pluto held Persephone prisoner in the underworld for as many months as the number of pomegranate seeds she had eaten, and after this time, Pluto and Zeus decreed that she could return to earth, and her return would herald the beginning of spring.

Veronica slices another chunk from the pomegranate, symbol of rejuvenation and eternal life. Patting her mouth with a napkin, she says that Lord Buddha is often shown holding a pomegranate, a fertility symbol, suggesting an abundance of sons.

"In the 'Song of Songs,' Solomon compares his beloved to a 'park of pomegranates.' Do you suppose that's why?" I ask. "Or do you think it's got something to do with the Latin *ponum granatum*, apple of many seeds, the many facets to her character that symbolized rebirth and renewal of his spirit?"

"Gosh, I don't know. It's a nice thought. It's *grenada* in Spanish, *grenade* in French, *anar* in Hindi. I remember Solomon saying that the cheeks of his beloved were like a pomegranate split open. I thought that was a funny image, ruby red and seedy. But you know what, Mum?"

"What?"

"You've got non-attachment all wrong."

I wait for Veronica to deliver some ascetic, austere Buddhist doctrine. Instead, she surprises me.

"Non-attachment or detachment in the Buddhist sense has nothing to do with being isolated, indifferent, intellectually aloof, distant, above everything, not caring or not loving, or not emotional, or acting wise, or anything like that," she says in her good-humored, lilting, musical voice. Having finished eating the pomegranate, she washes her hands and puts her sandals out in the hall to be polished. She undresses slowly, carefully, dropping her underwear into a pile for the hotel laundry, hanging up her skirt, adding her T-shirt to the laundry pile. "Non-attachment doesn't mean you have to be poor, or not live luxuriously, or not enjoy life or sensual pleasures, or that you have to live like a monk or a nun," she says. She opens a drawer, lifts out a white cotton nightgown, shakes it free of its folds, and says how wonderful it is that the drawers don't stick the way they do in Dharamsala after the monsoon.

"The actual meaning of detachment," she says, "is the understanding that comes when you know about yourself and the world. You know that people, things, places are impermanent. The world changes, the mind changes."

I tamp out a beedie and lace the fingers of both my hands together in a childhood hand-game, bringing up my thumbs to make doors, my index fingers to make a steeple. *This is a church, this is a steeple, open the door and see all the people.* I used to hear it as "see all the peep-holes," the way the stars looked like tiny holes in the dark blue shade pulled across the sky. Now I study the triangle of my steepling index fingers. Is it a steeple like an obelisk, a symbol of a sunbeam?

"The way one sees the world depends on one's opinion of it. The world as one knows it depends on one's perception of it." Veronica's voice affects me as though I were listening to a choir of boy sopranos with a bowl of lilies of the valley beside me.

Perceptions change from moment to moment. The Buddhist sense of detachment doesn't come by talking about it. It comes from contemplating the impermanence of everything, even thoughts, by practicing meditation. The whole network of one's senses, memories, knowledge, understanding, and perceptions is changing every second. If one's mind is undergoing change all the time, naturally one's perceptions will be changing.

"Nothing is final forever," she concludes. I pull my hands apart, reach out to clasp her hand.

Twenty

Ootacamund is ninety-five miles from Mysore. We are on our way again. Sunbirds, with bodies blue as Egyptian faience and heads velvety purple as clematis, flicker about the roadside bushes of orange lantana. Ferruginous earth. *Bhainsees* wallowing among water lilies of a village tank. Cactus. With a jiggling pen, I record the landscape as it reels by. Wayside temples with oleanders. Peacocks. Many monkeys.

Hills begin to mound like clouds on the horizon, and by early afternoon we reach the Bandipur wildlife sanctuary and deer forest. We see a white-spotted deer, a flying squirrel, and two elephants tethered as a tourist attraction outside the gamekeeper's lodge. Balan says there are many tigers around. We see no trace of them, but langurs are out in force. At the end of the road through the forest there is a sign flanked by feathery mimosa trees filled with canary-bright blossoms. END OF KARNATAKA, it says. WELCOME TAMIL NADU.

Now the hills rise around us, their crests misted in clouds, and the earth becomes the color of cinnamon, then dark as chocolate. Bamboo, which thrives in acid soil, appears in occasional clumps and soon in groves. Lantana flares along a corridor of blue-green tamarind trees that traces the path of the road. The air cools, and coffee estates begin, untidy bushes beneath stands of eucalyptus, the bark peeling from their tall, straight trunks and the canopy of their leaves marvelously aromatic. The eucalyptus of the Indian plains is almost scentless. You forget what it is until you crush a leaf in your hands. Here, in the cool of the rising hills, it is as if an entire forest of eucalyptus leaves has been crushed by a hand reaching down from heaven. The rounded hills of the Nilgiris really are blue.

" *Nila* is Sanskrit for blue, Mummy. *Giri* is Sanskrit for hills or mountains," Veronica says patiently. "I remember Daddy telling me that hills are blue because the sun extracts oleo-resins from the trees and holds them in the air, or something like that." She says the Himalayas are not as blue as Nicholas Roerich painted them, not as blue as the Nilgiris. Blue is the color of interior life. Blue is my favorite color, the color Nicholas Roerich swept across his canvases. I take great pleasure in quoting William Gass: "Whether slick light sharp high bright thin quick sour new and cool or low deep sweet thick dark soft slow smooth heavy old and warm: blue moves easily among them all, and all profoundly qualify our states of feeling."

It is the hour of cow dust. White-winged insects speckle the windshield with pointillist patterns. The pale trunks of areca palms appear and reappear, tall and columnar among the coffee bushes. Then the coffee plantations give way to tidy tea estates, expanses of glossy-leafed bushes sheltered by silver oak "nurse trees," which shade them and grip the soil with their roots. The foliage of the oaks is feathery like that of casuarinas and mimosas, and their trunks are so tall and straight that you have to look up, up, up to see the first leafing branch.

Scotsmen were the first Europeans to settle in the Nilgiris, to plant tea and set the mountains in order with Presbyterian determination, and there are still Scottish names here on estate markers: Armstrongs from the Borders, Stuarts from the Highlands. As we ascend higher and higher, the air turns misty and bracingly chilly. We weave around hairpin bends, past a temple honoring horses, and a monkeys' sleeping tree in which monkeys are rapidly moving about, getting ready to settle for the night. Pedestrians appear along the road wearing woolen turbans, scarves, and coats. We pass a lake dam with a weir and flume, and now there are moors and undulating fields with coppices of trees turning mauve as the light fades; a tiny train puffing clouds of white steam; a few little villages with spired churches. Jerseys, Holsteins, sheep, horses, long-legged colts, a lake, primroses, lilies by the roadside, a patch of road carpeted with the brilliance of fallen mimosa blossoms, and then the dark falls swiftly as a curtain, and the lights twinkle on.

We arrive finally at the Savoy Hotel. The manager leads us to a little cottage, comprised of an entrance hall, sitting room/bedroom, dressing room, and bath. The floorboards tilt, the bathtub has ball-and-claw feet, the curtains are flowered chintz, the pictures on the wall are of the English countryside in the nineteenth century. There is a white ironstone chamber pot behind the closed door of the bedside nightstand.

Our bedsheets are cold and damp, and there is a pervasive smell of dampness in all the rooms except the bathroom, which smells of Dettol, the way some bathrooms do in English country inns. Veronica and I light a fire in the sitting room, filling it with smoke, blackening our hands with soot as we try to adjust the damper.

We fill the bathtub with steaming hot water, unpack, chatter about, and are astonished when there is a knock at the door and a turbaned houseboy delivers a tea tray. As I slather hot buttered scones with Nilgiri honey, thick as heather honey but with a tang of eucalyptus, stuff ravenously, and drink tea which really does taste the way I remember tea tasting in England and Scotland, I can't believe I'm in India. There's even a cake of Pears' soap in a slatted soap-holder hooked over the rim of the bathtub, and two red rubber hot-water bottles hanging behind the bathroom door.

Waking to the sound of roosters crowing and donkeys braying, self-congratulatory that I've brought along wool skirts and sweaters, I hare out of our cottage into a dew-wet morning and a world of roses, hollyhocks, pinks, daisies, delphiniums, alyssum, columbines, nasturtiums, and the deep sapphiric blue of lobelia. Jacarandas shade an aviary of budgerigars; the hotel manager, in a shapeless, sensible tweed jacket and skirt and matching puce pullover, is feeding them bread and seeds.

"I call them my Donald Budgerigars," she tells me in a Yorkshire accent. Donald Budge, tennis champion during the late nineteen-thirties. It takes me a moment to remember.

A sweep of sweet peas in pastel colors, seen from a distance, reminds me so poignantly of those in the gardens at Northlea that I tremble at their gentle beauty. "It's been so long since I've seen sweet peas," I say, drifting toward them and back to childhood, back to Northlea.

It was always the exterior of the house, the outside, the glorious expanse of lawns, trees, flowers that I loved best. There was the main garden hedged high in a great rectangle with boxwood, an arch of white lattice, and a gate at either end.

There were gravel paths edged with diagonally set bricks that lay in even, sharp, triangular points that ran along the sides of carefully tended beds of flowers and vegetables. The spires of hollyhocks at the end of the garden were at a precise right angle with the stables, the garage, and the place where the gardening equipment was stored.

Not far from the latticed kitchen courtyard and the laundry-yard was the best part of the cutting garden. The beds of pinks and carnations, and the delphiniums, white, purple, light and dark blue, are what I remember most clearly. Also, the sweet peas staked on poles and wire netting, the cabbages, lettuce, and carrots, and the beans, peas, tomatoes and corn on the other side.

Away from the main garden, there were crescent-shaped beds of peonies on the lawn, large ruffled pink ones and white ones. The image of my mother dead-heading these herself is as clear as though she were within arm's length. Snip-snap with the secaturs, just like the red-legged scissor-man who cut off Conrad's thumbs in *Struwwelpeter*. She used to make a dramatic show of picking off the rose bugs and giving them "the cosmos treatment," as she called it, dropping them into a milk-bottle half-filled with kerosene.

Ootacamund. Everyone calls it Ooty. The archetypal British hill station. Even Mollie Panter-Downes's *Ooty Preserved* has not prepared me for this place. Trying to be organized, I note that Ooty is eleven degrees north of the equator and 7378 feet above sea level in the Nilgiri range of South India.

Welcome to the Blue Hills. Veronica thrusts a guidebook into my hands. It is she, now, who becomes the enthusiastic sightseer. She wants to see the Ooty of a BBC documentary that captured her imagination. So now it is quick into the car and off across the hills, dales, and woods that are so like England and Scotland. We stop at a lake in a setting of pine-covered hills, its clear blue water brightly dowered with sculls and pedalos, row boats, and motor boats with tinsel wakes. Children in billed, black velvet riding caps ride Shetland ponies on the ocher-rose paths along the shore. Mares, foals, sleek chestnut stallions, and woolly white sheep graze in fields near the Kandel Cross, a Roman Catholic shrine of the Lord Crucified. Here we find sculptural representations of the fourteen stations of the cross, and signs directing pilgrims to a relic of the True Cross. A former footman of the Maharaja of Mysore, attendant at the shrine, tells us that he will pray to St. Anthony for Missy and Madam, that even if he doesn't have any money he will beg for enough to buy a candle for us. When Veronica isn't looking, I give him enough to keep the candelabras blazing for a month.

As we journey into town, we learn that today is Mariamma, a local Indian festival honoring the red lotus lady of South India. Mariamma is celebrated in the streets of Ooty with screeching horns, dancing, thundering drums. Men with gongs and drums hung around their left shoulders are roiling forth from the lanes, slam-crashing and ka-BOOM-BOOM-BOOM-ing all along the main street. An elderly man has a costumed, chained monkey which performs acrobatic tricks and jumps in and out of a hoop of fire. Men and women in spangled costumes twirl slowly in looping patterns, their expressions lifeless as painted dolls, while other dancers spin in dizzying circles around them. I, who usually love brass bands and circuses, street fairs and festivals, find the noise and commotion strangely intrusive in the British village atmosphere.

When the festival of Mariamma is past, Veronica and I return to town for a shopping excursion. With its Tudor facade cafés, its rambling one- and two-storeyed buildings, the scarlet pillars of its mailboxes, the smartly uniformed policemen directing traffic from circular mounds, and the trim roundabouts paisleyed with flowers, there is a strong sense of time warp in Ooty, the preservation of a resort from a vanished epoch.

From a junction called Charing Cross, one road leads to the Gymkhana Golf Club and another to Missionary Hill, the third to the Race Course, the fourth to the Botanical Gardens. There is Commissioners Road, where I stock up on tins of biscuits and freshly baked bread at Mahan's. There is Commercial Road where the Nilgiri Seed Depot is located, a large, dark room, filled with sacks and barrels and baskets of what are labeled vegetable, flower, green-manuring, cover-crop, and tree seeds. Acacia, bamboo, eucalyptus, silver oak, poinciana, jacaranda, spathodea, pine, mahogany, casuarina exquisitfolia, cassia, cedrus deodars. I collect little brown paper bags of each, imagine them all flourishing in terracotta pots on my kitchen windowsill in New York. I hold the seeds loose in my hand, smell the smell of Ooty's red earth, its black earth, the fragrance of eucalyptus which reminds me of Africa and Robert.

The principal color of the buildings in the town and its environs is a sort of port-wine shade. The library is this color. The racetrack pavilion with its spires and cupolas is this color. Have all the stones and bricks been dyed to resemble red shale, or have they been painted and weathered to this lovely hue? Most of the shops in town have their dark red facades trimmed with white; all are within view of a tall fountain, all have silver oaks and pines as a backdrop. As we go from Higginbotham's where there are books and stationery supplies, to Spender's, where you can buy Aertex shirts and toothpaste and hairpins and eau de cologne and red currant jelly and children's tin lunch boxes, "strawberry boys" squatting on the sidewalk call out their wares. How can we resist strawberries? In the cool misty air of Ooty, what germs can harm us? I buy several baskets of strawberries, and Veronica and I nibble on the unwashed, sweetly tart fruit.

In a store exhibiting Kerala handcrafts, I buy eucalyptus oil, thick and dark as treacle; embroidered tea towels; children's wooden building blocks with Tamil lettering; and some tiny clay birds from Udaipur that have found their way into this jumble of Kerala artifacts. There is a section devoted to Nilgiri products: Nilgiri tea, which comes in a paper packet stamped "High Grown Tea"; *Cinfresh*, an antiseptic floor wash; *Cinomos* and *Cinspray* insect repellents, and other medicinal and pharmaceutical quinine products made from the cinchona trees that grow high on the hillsides; camphor oil; Gaultheria oil, an all-purpose pain-reliever; oil of citronella; geranium oil for scenting the bath; various kinds of eucalyptus oil; and the edible nests of swifts, from which bird's-nest soup is made by a few Chinese restaurateurs in the vicinity.

Veronica asks the shopkeeper if Elfrieda Gay, "a dear old spinster and artist," whom she saw featured on the BBC documentary, is still alive and well. Indeed she is, we are told, and we can find her in residence at the Lady Willingdon Home for Elderly Indian and European Ladies. Lady Willingdon was a Vicereine who left an impressive track of hospitals, hostels, hotels, clubs, and other buildings named in her honor from one end of the Indian subcontinent to the other, and the Lady Willingdon Home is not difficult to find. It comprises a string of

concrete bungalows fronted with gardens, bounded with black
wrought iron fencing ribboning down a hillside.

Balan parks the car, and Veronica and I walk past a high wall
covered with a tangled mat of orange trumpet flowers and *Pas-
siflora*, passion flowers, so called because their parts symbolize
Christ's passion: the corona the crown of thorns, the ten sepals
and petals the apostles minus Peter and Judas, and the flower
itself, red, purple, and white, the wounds of Christ; a tropical
jungle flower used by sixteenth-century missionaries to instruct
"the heathens." Large and fanciful in appearance, the flowers
could inspire awe in the mind of any simple soul; certainly they
have always astonished me. Veronica says she remembers a
passion-flower vine covering an archway in our garden in Jamaica.

"Do you? I started it from seed," I say as we begin to walk
down a steep incline toward the bungalows. "Elfrieda Gay can't
be all that old if she climbs up and down this path once a day," I
add breathlessly, slipping and sliding along a trail terraced at
intervals with level landings that have become eroded and
muddy from rains so recent that there are still puddles. The
trail must cascade like a waterfall during the monsoon.

At the bottom of the footpath, there is a broader path which
leads past the row of bungalows. We begin to search for Miss
Gay's nameplate, find it midway down the row. I unlatch the
squeaky iron gate to her garden, and we make our way to her
front door. I ring the doorbell, the old-fashioned, one-toned
kind that really rings. There is the sound of footsteps, and a
rather querulous voice asking, "Who is it? Who is it?"

Miss Gay opens the door. An elfin creature, no larger than a
ten-year-old girl, she is bandy-legged, merry-faced, and fair as

the flesh of a pear. Her blue eyes are considerably enlarged behind her rimless spectacles. Eighty-nine years old, she was born in Mussoorie of a German father and an English-Scottish mother, and has lived in Ooty for more than forty years, working as an artist and art teacher. Her gray hair is sparse and has receded so that her forehead is abnormally high, its measure the same as that from her wispy eyebrows to her firm chin. She is wearing a baggy gray flannel suit, a belted navy blue pullover beneath her open jacket, a string of lapis lazuli beads, navy blue lisle stockings, and sturdy brown leather oxfords.

"My, I must look a sight," she says, patting her hairnetted hair. "The place is a shambles," she says. "My *ayah* hasn't been in, but she'll wallow by tomorrow for sure, complaining of a stomach ache."

Appearing not at all surprised that we have come unannounced to visit her, Miss Gay also seems delighted to see us. She wants to have a connection with America, she says, she likes to be in touch with America. She flips through a pile of drawings and produces several sketches of Indian fashions in shoes and jewelry she did for an American newspaper in the nineteen-thirties. She has forgotten its name. "I never know the names of things," she says. "I'll forget my own name in a minute."

She shows us the two rooms in which she lives, along with the kitchen, and patters all the while about the high cost of living and the problems of having a hypochondriacal *ayah*. The concrete-walled rooms are small, and are cluttered with books, papers, drawing and painting materials, and furniture that is too large for the space. A bentwood rocking chair, surrounded by stacks of books and tin boxes, takes up an entire corner, and a sofa that also does for a bed fills the whole length of a wall. Framed prints of paintings by Renoir, Gauguin, Van Gogh, and

Turner are hung on the white walls, interspersed with calendars advertising kitchen soap or illustrated with photographs of German and Scottish landscapes. Miss Gay unearths stacks of her own drawings and paintings to show us. We study her portraits of Europeans and Indians, her water-color landscapes of Tamil Nadu, the Nilgiri Hills, and Ooty. All are like pretty pastel postcards.

Thank heavens, Miss Gay is too occupied showing us her work to notice Veronica's expression. I think of e.e. cummings's line, "Miss Gay had nothing to say to the animals, and the animals had nothing to say to Miss Gay," and ask Miss Gay if she would be willing to part with a sketch of a Toda *mund*, a temple in the nearby tribal village, and if so, for how much she would consider selling it.

"It *is* a pet, isn't it?" Miss Gay says, holding up the picture and squinting at it. "D'you think ten bob would be too much?"

Ten shillings? A dollar-fifty? Heavens, no, I say. I insist on giving her ten dollars for the sketch, eight hundred rupees. I'd feel guilty offering her any less. She is delighted to have the extra money because sweaters and blouses "cost the earth" in Ooty. You can see right away that Miss Gay cares very much about keeping up appearances.

She tells us that she leads an active social life, that she and Miss Guthrie, Miss Wells, Mrs. Dow, who is a widow, and Mrs. Hill all meet at the Ooty Club once a week for a game of bridge. Miss Guthrie, who ran the Willingdon House Hotel for Lady Willingdon in the old days, is now its owner. Miss Guthrie owns several racehorses which "have won many major races." Miss Guthrie has a car and a Tamil driver and often transports Miss Gay about Ooty, although Miss Gay says that she is quite capable of walking "everywhere." Mrs. Hill is the Club secretary. There are meetings to attend, such as the Culture Circle at the Indian Union Club, where the lectures are "very interestin'." There is the cinema. A shipment of new books arrives every month at Higginbotham's and the library is well stocked. There is the annual Flower Show and the Dog Show, and even if the famous Ooty Hunt is no more, there are, "well, horse shows and such." And there are now film factories and the new fishery and a great deal of industry coming to Ooty. Miss Gay is rather vague about what all these new factories are, but she knows there are many of them, recently built and under construction.

We invite Miss Gay to have lunch with us at the Savoy, but she invites us instead to the Ooty Club, an impressive Palladian-style building with a pillared portico. Inside, the decor is all pale yellow and white, the walls in most rooms covered with the heads of African and Indian game, some mounted on mahogany plaques, some just appearing to poke through the walls. *Nilgai*, wild boar, tiger, leopard, wildebeest, sable antelope, mountain sheep, small and great antelope, gazelles of many varieties, zebra, lions, masks of hill jackals: extravagant testimony to British marksmanship and enthusiasm for the hunt. The ivory crescents of elephant tusks flank a fireplace. A few members of the European community in the Nilgiris are having a peg in the mahogany-paneled bar. Perhaps they are planters from the tea estates or involved with the new film factory. Miss Gay doesn't recognize them.

We seat ourselves in comfortable chintz-covered armchairs in the drawing room, which is empty except for us. No one at the writing tables, no one on the down-filled sofas, no one leafing through the airmail editions of London newspapers or through the *Illustrated London News*, *Vogue*, the *Queen*, or *Tatler*, all laid out on a long table behind the central sofa. When Miss Gay rings, tapping her finger on top of one of those silver-plated contraptions that remain mechanically reliable for decades, a servant in a crisp white uniform and scarlet turban comes to take our orders. Since Miss Gay manages to survive on the pittance of her pension, she is appreciative of the few tots of sherry, to which I, with my tourist drink permit, am entitled. She wraps up the peanuts and potato chips we are served in a paper napkin which she folds like a cornucopia. "Every bit helps," she explains with no trace of self-pity.

At the Ooty Club, traditions are maintained *de rigeur*, and Miss Gay has appropriated the peanuts adroitly while the *khidmutgar* is out of sight. When he comes back unexpectedly, she smiles. "For the birds," she says, raising her voice. "They are so fond of treats."

"Perhaps they are liking some biscuits, too, Madam?" the *khidmutgar* rejoins, offering her a plastic bag of Huntley & Palmer digestive biscuits.

"Thank you, Vilendra," Miss Gay says. "Very thoughtful of you."

In India, perhaps as nowhere else, there still exists a devotion and compassion between master and servant, servant and master. Even though Miss Gay keeps up a running commentary about the shortcomings of her *ayah*, it is clear that she is as devoted to the *ayah* as her *ayah* is to her, just as it is clear that Vilendra will always have on hand for Miss Gay a little something "for the birds." It is understood also that, as visitors, our bill will be puffed with extra charges that we will be expected not to notice or carp about.

Miss Gay leads us on a tour of the paneled dining room with

its framed photographs of club members in a variety of poses: mounted on their horses and ponies enjoying the hunt, in evening clothes at dinners and balls, in tennis whites, in masquerade costumes, at garden parties in the Indian sunshine. There is an unmistakable expression of rectitude and incorruptibility in the faces of the men and women in the pictures, evidence of the punctilious observance of outdated etiquette and attention to bygone standards. We progress to the reading room, the bridge room, and the billiard room where, even though the cloth on the billiard table is faded, everything is beautifully kept up, everything in the Victorian tradition of "running a good show."

British Victorians were inclined to be contemptuous of other cultures, and often took it for granted that any custom different from their own was wrong, barbarous, or even wicked. The standards of their youth—honor, decency, truthfulness, cleanliness, doing everything "properly"—were those they adhered to, and a century later, among the dwindling old guard European community ambered in the hill station preserve of Ooty, these standards remain.

The night before we are to leave Ooty to begin our journey to the Himalayas, our doorbell rings. It is Jhamchoe, the young monk we met in Byllakuppe, the monk whose family have all been killed by the Chinese Communists, the monk who gave me a basket of dried Tibetan cheese he had carried from Lhasa, the monk who assured Veronica it was all right for me to hug him because I was "his sister, his mother."

He has come to Ooty, as many do, for health reasons. The months he has spent at Byllakuppe, the change in altitude, and the heat have weakened his constitution, he tells us. He has a bad cough, difficulty sleeping, and feels "too tired" all the time, but a few weeks in Ooty and he will be "A-1" again. He smiles. His dark eyes shine at us from behind his rimless spectacles. The vaccination mark on his upper right arm shows as a pale, puckered asterisk beneath the short saffron sleeve of his under-dress. He is glad he has found us. From a large square shoulder bag of purple silk and saffron, he brings forth a parcel for me done up in brown wrapping paper. It contains two *pangdens*, Tibetan aprons striped with many colors, the material tightly woven and as sturdy as lightweight canvas. I am thrilled to have them, of course, and I sit on the sofa, smoothing the material across my knees, stroking its stripes, admiring the colors. Currents of affection pass between Jhamchoe and me.

Veronica, who has removed the granny glasses I often tease her for wearing as a shield against her burdensome beauty, telephones for tea, sandwiches, strawberries, and we eat before the crackling fire. Then Jhamchoe, sitting very straight on the far end of the sofa, shyly produces a thin rectangular something wrapped in a yellow hand towel. His special present for me, he says, and slowly unfolds the towel to reveal a book, hand-printed on handmade paper, a stack of long rectangular pages with lettering on both sides. It is a book written by His Holiness, the Dalai Lama, he explains, a book he has carried with him all the way from Lhasa, and now he would like me to have it because I was "such great help" to him when I was in Bylla-kuppe, giving him money to further his education, so that he, too, might someday ascend in rank, might wear the yellow hat.

"But it was nothing, *nothing*," I say. I don't deserve the book. I can't accept the book, can't take the book away from him.

"He wants you to have it, Mum," Veronica says. Jhamchoe

looks at her. She looks at him. "He wouldn't give it to you if he didn't want you to have it." Jhamchoe nods his agreement.

I am all exuberant gratitude and idiotic questions. What does the book say? Will he read a few lines of it and translate them? Is this really and truly a book that the Dalai Lama wrote? How wonderful! Wonderful Jhamchoe! Now I have something to talk about with His Holiness! Oh, thank you, thank you! Like a seaside marker, Jhamchoe is drenched in my waves of enthusiasm, and sits there, unchanged, except for a tremulous smile which relaxes at last into a wide grin of genuine pleasure. Veronica looks horrified when I move closer to Jhamchoe, hug him, and again ask him to read from the book that His Holiness has written. I can feel her stifled indignation at what I know she considers unseemly behavior. But Jhamchoe doesn't seem to mind that I have ignored all those carefully calibrated degrees of familiarity by which distance and respect would seem to be synonymous. If monkhood stamps Jhamchoe's personality with certain characteristics—solemnity, a noticeable lack of gaiety, curiosity, humor—he nonetheless shares a sense of kinship with me which overrides our personal differences. I can see that Veronica finds this sudden friendship unexpected, preposterous, but Jhamchoe is no bromide masquerading in a monk's robe. He is a kind, generous human being, wholehearted, sincere. Why shouldn't I like him? Why shouldn't he like me?

When Jhamchoe returns the next morning to say goodbye to us before we set off on our return to New Delhi, I photograph him wrapped in his maroon robe, standing before a tapestry of plants and brightly colored flowers.

Part Four

Twenty-One

Back in New Delhi, Veronica and I go to the station to board a train for Pathankot in the Punjab. This is the first lap of our journey to Manali and Dharamsala, the places in the Himalayas where Veronica parted from my world and found what?—I still don't know.

Our meeting with Jhamchoe has been strangely unsettling, a revelation of the threatening undertow beneath the smooth surface waters of Veronica's and my companionability. I had thought I was finally doing everything right. Traveling with Veronica, I had come to be infused with good feelings of closeness, warmth, communication—mother and daughter united harmoniously. Now, confronted once more with the prospect of physical dislocation, I feel myself emotionally dislocated, assailed by fears and doubts.

Yet Veronica shows no resentment of me. She doesn't sulk. She doesn't glare. She sends out no signals of a sunny-centered daisy turned bristling, no semiotics of a *ne touche pas* attitude. There is not even a flicker of a pitying smile to be bestowed on the sad ignorance of poor old Mum, poor benighted old Mum

who loves her so but just doesn't have a clue, not . . . a . . . clue,
about *anything*.

And I? I in my misery of anxiety feel like a caterpillar, all
hunched up, preparing to move. With our carry-alls, a fibreboard packing case, and our tin trunks set down, with Gurdip
once more our faithful guardian, we sit on the trunks, enisled
in a world—Veronica's world?—of family encampments, vendors, beggars, pye dogs, and a mass of sleeping people, rolled in
blankets like cocoons. Their heads are covered, while their feet,
sandaled or wrapped in rags, protrude like stubby antennae.
Two little boys standing close to us are peeing on each other's
toes.

When the train comes rushing through the tunnel, there is a
wild to-do about finding the sleeper. I can't read the signs, can't
see the numbers. The make-way shouts of the porters, the rack-
eting of the vendors of *pooris* and tea with their vats of boiling
water and the screaming hiss of steam, plus a cacophony of yells,
wails, and cries are a dizzying craziness until Gurdip pulls Veronica and me up into our compartment. Wood-paneled, with
a window equipped with glass, screening, and wooden louvers,
it consists of two berths, a stainless steel washbasin, a closeted
toilet, wall lamps. The sheets are pulled tight on the berths,
the mattresses and pillows are hard and thin, the blankets are
frayed. There is no dining car on the overnight trip from Delhi
to Pathankot.

"*Pas mal*," Veronica says. Then glancing at me, adds, "It's not
the greatest, but it beats the bus."

I have brought a thermos of hot coffee and one of chilled
orange juice. I have brought sandwiches, mangoes, *chikus*, bananas, biscuits, washcloths, towels, napkins, insect repellent,

hand fans, a cake of wild hyacinth soap, guidebooks, maps, a bottle of cologne, a flashlight, extra batteries for it, emergency medical supplies, my notebook, and magic markers. If there is a breakdown or a delay, I am prepared. The pure data of the list are reassuring. The sound of the train's wheels, the rocking motion are a gentle soporific. Sleep comes easily.

I wake up at five to see the sunrise from the train window. The farmland of the Punjab is flat and covered with the geometrics of conical haystacks, rectangular mud huts, and the domes of mosques rising above crenellated walled squares. All is pale buff, ocher, rose, with the dark red of the huts and the walls and the deep dark green of the trees cast against an opaline sky. I open the window. The morning air is fresh, deliciously cool. The landscape fans away to the horizon.

As scheduled, at six forty-five on the dot, we arrive at Pathankot, fifteen kilometers from the border of Pakistan and about a half-day's train journey from Chinese-occupied Tibet. It pleases me to locate our whereabouts on the map, steadies me before the nerve-straining brouhaha of actually setting foot on new ground. When we do, it's as though my life depended on getting Veronica, myself, and our baggage out of the train and onto the station platform. Once that is accomplished, with mutual hysteria on the part of the coolies and myself, I feel dazed, dimly aware of the commotion around me. Passengers are rushing from the train to buy tea and newspapers; uniformed bearers are jogging back and forth from the train to the station café, carrying breakfast trays aboard; there is a mass exodus from the second-class coaches to the water spigots, where passengers wash and engage in vigorous tooth-brushing before the train sets off again.

Since Gurdip has never driven in the Kangra or Kulu districts of Himachal Pradesh State and has no license to drive there, we are to be met by a driver-courier named Parvin Sarin, a partner in an establishment based on Chandigarh called Himachal Trek 'n' Tour. It sounds appalling, and when a somewhat Spanish-looking fellow pitches up, wearing a gray business suit and a Humphrey Bogart hat ("Call me Parvi"), I become guarded, impatient, hard-to-please. Veronica becomes a compensating angel of sweetness and light. Amiably, Mr. Sarin leads us to the station café. I hang up my cardigan on a curlicue of a Victorian hat stand. Mr. Sarin hangs up his hat on an adjacent brass hook. He orders buttered toast and tea, a small basket of jungle apricots, a plate of anise seeds, mango juice. "Mangoes bring happiness and good fortune," he says. He places my LV tote bag on a chair where it won't fall over. He adjusts the speed of the *punkah* fan so that the fan whirs pleasantly above the table. He is polite but firm with the *khidmutgar*. He speaks excellent English. When I ask what the Punjabi word is for anise seeds, he replies "*saunf.*" And those? I ask, pointing to the apricots. "*Lungart,*" he replies with a smile, and I am won. Here is a man who is informative but not garrulous, knowledgeable but not didactic.

When we leave the café, chewing seeds of anise to freshen our mouths and, as Parvin says, to aid our digestions, we come upon a group of *paharis* (hill people) by the station exit. They have lengths of rope coiled around their middles and woolen caps on their heads like the kind children wear in Central Park in winter. They have an air of independence, of being their own masters. Their strength and endurance are phenomenal, Parvin says, and they quickly shoulder our tin trunks as if they were filled with feathers and stow them and the rest of our baggage in the black Mercedes that is now "ours."

The carts are different here. *Ikkas*, Parvin calls them, primitive hand-hewn affairs of sand-colored wood, with a palisade of poles for sides, splayed outward above a platform resting on either low, solid wooden wheels or high spoked ones. In the early morning, they cast long shadows, on their way to furnish the station-market with a glorious mix of brass cooking bowls, terracotta jars, tomatoes, melons, coconuts, purple *brinjals* (eggplants), gourds, cauliflower spilling from wicker cornucopias, bundles of spinach leaves, and multi-storeyed chicken coops crammed with white hens and crowing roosters. *Gujjars*, Muslim shepherds from Kashmir and Afghanistan in turbans, shirts and *longhis*, and *Gaddis*, Hindu shepherds in turbans, inverted pot-like headgear, tunics and breeches, are looking over the produce. Taller than the *paharis*, their features less aquiline, they appear strong, ageless, tireless. I fantasize a shipwreck in which I'd be washed to the shores of a desert island with the shepherds and Veronica. They would take care of us, know how to build shelters, how to get food. Am I romanticizing them? "The Lord is my shepherd, I shall not want. He maketh me to lie down in green pastures; he leadeth me beside the still waters. He restoreth my soul."

Pathankot is just a single main street, with a row of old arcaded buildings on the station side and a row of modern flat-roofed structures on the other. Standing in front of the station, you can look to either side and see "the country." In between the few ugly structures across the way is a large grass-tufted square where elephants have been housed in a dilapidated tent belonging to an itinerant carnival. Now, as we watch, the elephants begin to march out, led and mounted by mahouts. Half a dozen beasts, each with a foreleg chained to a handler, shuffle their great, round feet, swaying slowly in a mud-gray enfilade to the west. I watch as their bulking, flaccid haunches diminish, and their waving, bony tails fringed with an absurd tuft of hair disappear.

After a glimpse of Pathankot, we set off in the Mercedes for Nurpur. I expect Veronica to murmur "*Quel luxe*," but she doesn't. For a while the road runs parallel to the Chakki River, which has dried up to an olive green stream that flows almost imperceptibly past bushy islands and sparse woodlands of tall trees. Collared ring doves fly up from the road. We pass an *ikka* filled with lucerne, a pale green wisping cattle fodder that forms a lovely plump hummock inside the cart, and a herd of bone-thin *bhainsees* chivvied along the roadside by Muslim nomads.

The houses which appear on either side of the road—different from any I have seen in India before—are set apart by land and trees, some within calling range of each other, some separated by easy walking distances. Two-storeyed, with the second storey set back so that the first storey has its own partial roof of slate shingles, the houses are made of brick or hand-cut stone, with small windows. Each has its setting of trees; its bright orange-and-deep-crimson or delicate mauve-and-purple lantana shrub, rambling and prickly, with leaves of bright, clear green; its shed or stable; its citrus trees; its bougainvillea and oleander; its tall, dark, spreading mango tree. Purple ageratums and *bhang* (marijuana) cover the roadside verge and banks. Morning glories, like vines of Amazonian butterflies, are flung over a few houses, sometimes garlanding a hedgerow.

There is an occasional mud hut, its rough texture of mud

and straw imprinted with the magical potency of a white-washed hand to be accorded reverence for all the work it does with such skill and such simple tools. This talismanic hand is as indelible as the hand of my grandmother on the door of her room that lives in my mind's house, a replica of the silver hand with a flared lace cuff that formed the handle of a letter-opener she always used. The handprint as an act of faith was anterior to the Apostles' Creed, and must have carried with it, to an intensified degree, the same thrill I felt as a child standing beside my father in church, holding his hand as I said the words, feeling but not understanding them.

We continue on our way, Parvin not speaking unless spoken to, Veronica and I quiet, too. And then, suddenly, around a wooded curve, I have my first sight of the snow-capped Dhauladar, the White Mountain Range, the foothills of the Outer Himalayas. They glisten silvery and glorious, their fanning glaciers and mantle of snow sparkling before the backdrop of the blue morning sky. They rise on the horizon behind the smoky violet ridges of the Shiwalik hills across a plain shimmering with tasseled wheat on which trees appear, by some trick of light, like the silhouettes of tall-stemmed goblets. The sky, the Dhauladar, the Shiwalik hills, the plain of wheat, the dark symmetrical trees are a vast and magical panorama.

We have passed the boundaries of the Punjab and are now in the Kangra Valley. For the remainder of our journey, the road will be a corridor leading to scenically splendid settings that impart a sense of the numinous, the mystical, that offer the tantalizing possibility of merging one's self into a total harmony that is love, or joy, or God as a pervasive life-force in the world. Is that what you have found here, Elsa Cloud? A strange and powerful mood of exaltation, of serenity, of responsiveness, so open and creative that you could feel one with the universe? To experience delight in the landscape is to experience an aspect of God, of perfection beyond the boundaries of self, within the boundaries of self, intimations of immortality. Is that what you feel, Elsa Cloud? It's what I feel, but all I can manage to say is, "Oh, how beautiful!"

We slow down to cross a bridge over the Chakki River, and on a road shaded by dark-branched feathery-foliaged trees ("*Shisham trees*," Parvin says, before I can even ask), and embraced by orchards of mangoes and oranges, we come across a caravansary with a barber and an ear-cleaner plying their trades in the courtyard. A dozen pack-camels are lying about in the shade, batting their wiry eyelashes to keep the gnats, the midges, the large black flies and tigerish wasps at bay. They make curious, blubbering noises, grinding their iron bits with a continuous motion of their jaws, baring their yellow rectangular teeth, their coated, flabby tongues lolling between hare-lips. Their pelts, gritty as doormats, have a sour odor. Their spindly forelegs, folded beneath them, are thrust forward like beggars' legs amputated at the knees.

Almost invariably, artists and illustrators portray camels in profile. I suddenly understand why. Seen from the front, a camel's nose is a bulbous, rubbery snout with its upper lip sliding forward beneath it, pouching over its teeth, bulging above its shorter lower lip in such a way that as I squint, I no longer see an animal that looks anything like the way I expect a camel in profile to look full face. What I see is some other creature, something like a sea serpent or a dog-faced dinosaur.

In the distance, to the northwest, where the hills are green, there is a mauve explosion of jacaranda, and I can see a fling of buildings on a hilltop. It is the fort and the town of Nurpur, the "abode of light," a name derived from the name of the Mogul Emperor Nuruddin Jehangir, for whose wife the Taj Mahal was constructed.

Nurpur, the sixteenth-century capital of a former Rajput state, has been ruled by the hill rajas, conquered by the Moguls, ceded to the Afghans, besieged by the Sikhs, governed by the British, and settled by Kashmiri weavers who weave the incredible "ring shawls," or *pashmina* (goats' hair of the finest, silkiest quality) *shahtooshes*, shawls so soft and light you can draw them through a ring. Nurpur sounds romantic and wonderful to me, but Parvin says that it's not much, "just a little old hill town with a nice Krishna temple and a fort, and a good rest house nearby."

Like Babur who complained about India's "flatness," I rejoice in peaks and valleys, and all hill towns, no matter how nondescript, appeal to me. Among the buildings on either side of a narrow alley ranging down a steep hillside, I find a jeweler's cubbyhole. It turns out to be the only place in the entire Kangra Valley where you can still buy a carved, dome-like silver hair ornament known as a *chauk*. On the back wall, I can see the nests of swallows whose oscillating chittering is maintained *con brio* as the jeweler pongs a greenish-blue marble into the top of a *chauk* I have excitedly bargained for. Parvin believes that Veronica and I are the only Westerners, the only Europeans, surely the only Americans the townspeople have ever seen, and the women crowd around us to touch our clothes and Veronica's honey-colored hair for good luck.

Within the compound of Nurpur's ruins is a government

high-school with perhaps two hundred young boys pooled beneath shade trees. Voices in a parrot-chorus chant the numbers
and atomic weights of chemical elements, while an instructor
points with a stick to a blackboard chalked with the word
ISOTOPS.

When we approach, it is as if an invisible cage door has been
opened. The boys leap to their feet and run toward us. Seeing
my camera, those closest to us ask to be photographed. Some
make funny faces and wave their arms to attract attention, and
there is a clamor at the decibel level of jackhammers, until two
teachers, like shepherd and collie, herd the boys back beneath
the trees so that I can take several proper group photographs to
send them later. I think of the village school-teacher-turned-
roomboy who talked our ears off at the government rest-house
in Bharatpur. I remember Mahatma Gandhi's plans for a "Basic
Education" system in which young children would be taught
everything through manual activity, and would never be told
any fact until their curiosity had already been aroused by it. I
wave goodbye to the boys and their teachers, glad I have escaped
before anyone can ask me for a definition of isotopes.

Parvin, thirsting for *hooch* (the Punjabi term for a mixed
drink), whisks us away for a meal at the rest house, a British
colonial construction of uncertain vintage. It is a solid, plain,
no-nonsense sort of place built to endure in a solid, plain, functional sort of way. Because of frequent moves, British civil servants adopted the idea of portable gardens in the form of potted
plants, an odd variety of which are visible here. In the *terai*, the
plains country below the Himalayas, and in the *mofussil*, the
remote up-country stations, potted plants continue to be a pas-
sionately observed convention among the resident Indians. The

Moguls must be shuddering in their tombs at the sight of all these potted snake plants and cacti, all these red-painted verandahs and window sills put into service as stands for eyesores.

Parvin explains away the ugliness of these plants by saying that they are badly cared for and need pruning. Red paint is more expensive than whitewash, he says, a symbol of affluence. I can hear Mulk responding that "Affluence and good taste are not always the closest of companions."

I look away at the glistening Dhauladar. From above, a mountain grows wider, like the inverted tree whose roots grow up towards heaven while its foliage points downward, expressing multiplicity, involution, materialization, the universe in expansion. Perhaps this is why Eliade says that "the peak of the cosmic mountain is not only the highest point on earth, it is also the earth's navel, the point where creation had its beginning," its root, as Cirlot points out. The Dhauladar sparkles with ice and snow.

Veronica says that Himachal Pradesh glosses roughly as the Land of the Snows. As archaic as the sixth sense, as primitive as animals, as informed as scholars of body language, as sophisticated as electronic waves and the circuitry of computers, Veronica and I can both transmit feelings and thoughts which the other can receive, consciously or unconsciously. Now she is telling me more than she is saying. I unfold a map, and she says, "See? We're in the district of Kangra in the *state* of Himachal Pradesh. We're in the *Outer* Himalayas." I am the daughter of my daughter. She is my teacher.

Parvin says that Kangra really means *kan gara*, ear shapers. During the rule of the Sikhs and the Moguls, he explains, a common form of punishment for criminals and unfaithful wives

was to cut off their ears and noses, and for centuries, Kangra
has been a center for plastic surgery. A British traveler in the
mid-nineteenth century described the procedure. The patient
is rendered senseless with a quantity of wine, *bhang*, or opium.
"They [the surgeons] then tap the skin of the forehead above
the nose, until a sort of blister rises, from which a piece of skin
of the proper shape is then cut and immediately applied as a
nose, sewed on and supported with pieces of cotton."

Parvin says that leeches were used, as they are today, to suck
out stagnant blood. "Ear restoration was more successful than
noses, however." He also tells us that in Nagarkot in Kangra
there is a temple of Vajreshwari Devi, the supreme force of
Shakti, which is held in great esteem by worshipers and pilgrims
who still cut out their tongues and offer them in homage to the
Devi. "The tongue is an organ with great regenerative power,"
Parvin says, "and some re-growth often takes place. Still, the
Devi has many devotees who can no longer speak."

Punishing mutilation, self-mutilation, distorted expressions
of blocked sexuality; I think of the priests who castrated themselves in order to dedicate themselves to God, their emascula-
tion a means of entering into a great, protecting union. The
thought wings away, leaving its cold talons in my mind.

"Norbu had the most beautiful pink tongue," Veronica says,
tightening and curling her lips as Robert used to do when he
was mulling over something in his mind. "He was my precious
and beloved dog-friend. I babied him like a child, and in return,
he was sweet and loving to everyone. He slept on my bed, ate
what I ate, followed me wherever I went. Most of the people in
the Manali bazaar knew his name more than mine."

And then, one afternoon, he drifted away from her.

"The next morning, I saw his carcass all ripped up, lying on the town garbage dump." He had been attacked and killed by a lammergeier or some other bird of prey, possibly by other dogs, perhaps even by a jackal. No one had seen what happened. She closes her eyes, lights a beedie, leans her head against the back-seat window ledge. "I always say prayers for his well-being. It was painful to have to learn the poignancy and truth of imper-manence, to have to learn through hurt to love without posses-siveness."

She says that to live well is to die well, that from the day you are born, you have to die, that the beginning of death is birth. She says there is no more reason to fear death than to be afraid of going to sleep, that the two are similar, and that anyway, one is born again. I say that I always feel that every day is like a little life, that sleep is a uterine regression, and that no one really dies as long as he is remembered. She says again that her grief for Norbu is as impermanent as everything else, and I wonder if she, as I am, is remembering Robert.

She goes on. "Norbu used to play so happily in the long grass in the orchards, and then come back, all dew-wet, and curl up next to me, getting his silky white-and-red hairs all over my blankets and on the rug. The empty space left by a dead friend, even a dead dog friend, is so definitely empty that it's better not to miss anybody. It's better just to generate an in-the-present warmth for him and wishes for his well-being."

"Yes," I say, wanting for a moment to leap out of the car and run and run and run and shriek out pain and anger and grief like a Maenad, but I look out at the mountains, the mothering, magical mountains, and I feel my emotions subsiding, sliding down my throat, swallowed, gone, leaving only an ache behind my tongue.

Twenty-Two

As we spiral down from Nurpur on our way to the government-owned *dak* bungalow at Kotla, we come to a place called Trilokpur, the place of the Three Realms. It is an Indian equivalent of a "rest area," a watering spot where drivers of lorries and buses pull in to let their radiators cool off, and where travelers wash and eat, refill their water bottles and canteens from a wayside spring. On one side of the road is a *chai* shop with a wood-burning stove and a grill mounted on a cement block. Covered with a roof of thatch, and covered again with a sheet of faded canvas, the stall exhales spicy, garlic-scented fumes, alluring scents of cheese *pakoras*, *samosas*, and *parothas* browning in *ghee*, of kebabs sizzling on skewers, of wood smoke. On the other side of the road, icy mountain water spurtles from the crevices of a rocky limestone cliff, then pools in a ditch and runs off, making a long, dark, jagged shape beneath the *shisham* trees. Craggy, wild, with bushes exploding in lush green from the boulders and rocks, this is one of those extraordinary places, remarkable, yet as familiar as the landscapes in the genre of Poussin, Turner and the adventuresome Victorians.

There are caves above the bright racing water; the figures of two fishermen with rods and long-poled nets crouch before the dark holes. Beneath them, a man is swimming in the rapids, fighting the swirling currents, holding on to a rock every few minutes to catch his breath.

It is not just the wonders of nature that have attracted us, but man-made marvels as well. The cliff face and the boulders below have been carved with figures of crowned kings, spear-carrying warriors, Shiva, Ganesha with his trunk broken by image-shattering Moguls. A splendid *nandi*, partially covered with green-gray lichen, rests on a ledge carved with foot-holds. The swimmer struggles unsuccessfully to grasp onto them, finally managing to catch hold of a branch and swing himself out of the water. Now, belly down, arms outstretched, he lies there, his lean naked body slick and sparkling in the sun.

From the road, a slippery, inclined walkway carved from the cliff leads to a cave temple where stalagmites are worshipped as *lingams* of Shiva. The temple has been there "always," Parvin says. The road has "always" been there, too, the track of the old silk route now broadened, macadamized, "a fine two-lane road," on which two buses can safely pass.

Inside the cave temple, brass votive lamps are garlanded by withering mountain flowers. Stalagmites rise to meet stalactites, their inverted images. The wet reflections of flickering flames and the attendant white-robed priest give the place the dream-like quality of an Edmund Dulac illustration, the strange sensuality of a Fuseli painting. It is so cold I shiver. The smoke of the sandalwood incense tickles my nose like snuff as Veronica and I cup our hands to receive a few grains of rice, *prasad* from the priest in exchange for the coins we have given him.

"*Basmati* rice," Veronica says later in the car. "From the Dun Valley, the best."

Parvin says he has ordered a "slap-up luncheon" for us in Kotla: *basmati* rice cooked with coconut meat, cloves, and cardamom pods, as well as *pancha dal*, which is five different kinds of *dal*: *masoor dal*, *urad dal*, *mung dal*, *chana dal*, and *toor dal* all cooked in one pot with ginger, onion, lemon, *garam masala*, turmeric, shredded coconut, and mustard seeds.

"And *murghi*," the *khidmutgar* tells us when we arrive at the government's *dak* bungalow. I watch him as he stalks the perimeter of the room with an insect spray gun—ssshhhttt, ssshhhttt, ssshhhttt—just as in the advertisement of my childhood: "Quick, Henry, the Flit!" Frowning, Veronica leaves the room.

"She's a Buddhist," I tell Parvin. He tells the *khidmutgar* to stop spraying.

I go outside to find Veronica. I watch as she picks a broad blade of grass, holds it between both thumbs, and then blows hard to make it shriek. Robert taught her that trick. I could never do it. I think of Frederick Leighton's painting "Return of Persephone," showing Demeter with both arms reaching out to her daughter who, poised at a cave's entrance, is about to leap into them. Impulsively, I reach out my arms to Veronica.

She stops blowing on the blade of grass. "What are you doing?" she asks. "Stretching? You look funny."

I just wanted to hug her. I think of birds in mirrored cages singing love songs to companions who are only reflections of themselves. It takes an effort to smile at her. In response, her expression seems somewhat dazed and distrustful, but she kisses me lightly on the cheek, and we go in for lunch.

The government's *dak* bungalow, an archetypal up-country bungalow dating back to the Anglo-Indian architecture of the late Victorian era, is one of many posited at strategic points throughout India. It is built facing the northeast, the coolest aspect, and the rooms are high-ceilinged and large in order to remain cool during the hot weather. There is a verandah, a sitting room flanked by two bedroom suites and a bathroom, a dark, old mess of a pantry, a separate shed in back which serves as a kitchen, a back verandah facing a hillside and a scatter of firewood, chickens (I suppose our lunchtime *murghi* had been running about with them only a few hours before), chicken coops, broken bottles, rusty tins, and oil drums. ("Mummy would have it all cleaned up in a day, and turned into a rock garden in a month," Veronica tells Parvin.)

Inside, the walls are timber framework plastered over with earth mixed with cow dung, then whitewashed. Beneath the galvanized iron roof, burlap sacking, also whitewashed, forms the ceilings which bulge, stir, ripple. ("Snakes?" I ask. "More likely mice, Mummy," Veronica replies. "Dust," Parvin says. "The wind.") There are kerosene lamps and an old-fashioned telephone, one of those sturdy black daffodils with the receiver, like a pendant black datura flower, hooked to its stem. The furniture is all makeshift, junky, tumbledown. There are cobwebs in every corner, floor to ceiling, cobwebbed windows. So why is everything bolted, padlocked, and guarded by a brute of a mongrel dog? Parvin says it's the custom. "There are bandits in the hills, *goondas* and *thuggees* in the mountains, along the roads." He says this in the same matter-of-fact tone he uses to tell me that *piku* is the word for the head ring that women wear for pot-carrying, *ikka* the word for carts. Instead of the scimitar-like *kukree* beneath the front seat Gurdip hid for protection, Parvin carries a pistol and boxes of bullets in the glove compartment.

We are on a road that coils around the Shiwalik hills above the Kangra Valley. The central Himalayan landscape is a vast terrain of rolling downs and moorland with gray granitic boulders half-buried in the soil, some patchily covered with turf, some bare and splashed over with mold that is dark as dried blood, some streaked with lichen that is an eye-piercing yellow. The giant cobbles covering the valley like beach stones are the moraine of the Dhauladar's glaciers. From Cambrian times to the Eocene, all this land was under Tethys, or the Central Mediterranean Sea, which extended from the present Mediterranean to the heart of China. With parental didacticism, I inform Veronica that in the beginning of the Eocene period, a volcanic eruption of Deccan lavas poured forth cubic miles of molten rock which re-shaped the world, caused seas to form new continents, gave rise to the sedimentary and crystalline Himalayas. Later, upheavals pushed the mountains forward, crumpling and folding them. Unimpressed, she gazes out at the window.

Far below, the valley is traversed by a broad water-course, one of many that have their source in the snow-melt of the Dhauladar. The stream in the water-course glistens darkly, thin as a whipsnake across the valley. In another month, Veronica says, when the monsoon rains begin, the little stream will turn into a raging torrent. The monsoon, she croons, the monsoon, the monsoon.

I will be gone when the monsoon comes, back in New York. Time is running out, leaking, rushing away. Veronica and I will be parted again. The thought makes me tremble. My vision trembles, too, as tears well in my eyes. I reach for my sunglasses and a beedie. Nothing has been settled, nothing has been resolved. Or has it? Am I pursued by a specter of unattainable and unnecessary perfection? Why does it sometimes seem that Veronica and I both do the opposite of whatever the other desires? Why, when Jhamchoe drew close to me did I sense that Veronica was jealous, afraid that I would encroach on the people and ideas that she considers *hers*? I like to share friends and ideas, and have others share friends and ideas with me. Now that I'm traveling Veronica's terrain, I have the feeling she wants to keep me away.

I won't let her. I try to coax her back. "Your Daddoo told me that the Quaternary period is divided into the Pleistocene or Ice Age, and the Holocene or Recent, a mere ten thousand years," I say. Acquiring and imparting information is my way of meditation, a paradoxical task, a therapeutic dialysis, emptying the mind and refilling it with information to pour into a notebook. The process of writing, the pressure of the pen forming large letters and small, underlining, circling, listing, numbering, scribbling, scrawling, compressing myself in order to expand, hunching myself up like a caterpillar before I move forward, is a restraint for what I can't cope with and a release for what I can. "He told me that as I was quoting Ts'en Shen's 'When the ten thousand things have been seen in their unity, we return to the beginning and remain where we have always been.' The Age of Man is so tiny a division in the geological time scale that some geologists regard it as a mere subdivision of the preceding Tertiary. But not Robert. He idolized Leakey and Dart, and regarded the Age of Man as a total fascination."

"But he didn't like people all that much," Veronica says. "Just us. He liked nature and ideas and looking at the way an ant can carry a leaf of grass. He told me that." She looks at me, challenging me with an expression instantly recognizable as Daddy-loved-me-more-than-you-and-told-me-things-he-didn't-tell-you. Electra is revealed in the pitch of her voice, her flickering smile. It is a cast of countenance I suddenly realize must have been my own when I spoke with my mother about my father.

Maybe Robert did love Veronica more than he did me, for she was his child, part of him in a way I never could be, and perhaps that was the way my father felt about me. I loved Robert, but I love Veronica more. A friend once asked me if I were in a shipwreck and could save only one person, who would I save, Robert or Veronica. Veronica, I replied. Veronica, of course. My friend was surprised. She would unhesitatingly save her husband, she said. She could always have more babies. I don't think she loved her husband more than I loved Robert, it's just that I love Veronica more than anyone, because she is both Robert and me, the child born of the love we had when there was just the simplicity of love and the richness of anticipating a lifetime of happiness together.

In his *Tour to the Hebrides*, Boswell mentions how "Dr. Johnson's heart was cheered by the sight of a road marked with cartwheels. . . . It gave us a pleasure similar to that which a traveler feels when, whilst wandering on what he fears is a desert island, he perceives the print of human feet." When we stop in a hamlet with a few houses, Bozzy's observation recurs to me.

The houses are double-storeyed, with columned verandahs set high off the ground, and doors and lintels of dark wood with Jacobean-style carvings. "Nothing," Veronica assures me, in comparison to the carving and fretwork in the Kulu Valley, where "the winters really are snowbound and everyone whittles as a pastime." These carvings appear more the work of an artist than an amateur whittler to me, but neither Veronica nor Parvin is much impressed by folk art. Veronica says she has seen too much of it to care about it anymore, while Parvin condescends to the folkways of "peasants."

There are paintings, too, around the doors and on the walls beside them to celebrate a marriage, to welcome a bride to her new house. Unlike the wall frescoes in Rajasthan, these paintings have borders of vines, flowers, insects, and the paintings themselves—all with a lovely freshness of life—are noticeably different in style. Here, Krishna, Radha, and other gods and goddesses have round faces, with eyes gently delineated, noses slightly upturned. In paintings of elephants, leopards, tigers, parrots, partridge, pheasant, ibex, musk deer, black bears, cobras, monkeys, panthers, turtles, dogs, fish, sheep, goats—each animal has an individual character, an essence so reverently caricatured that as I look at this marvelous bestiary, I feel I am experiencing each animal as it really is, not just as it appears to be. A goat smiles inanely, a watching dog grins knowingly, a snow leopard playfully bats at a butterfly. A panther tenses a sharp-clawed paw to scoop a turtle out of a stream, and in some magical way, that paw is not only tensed, but already flashing forward. You know the turtle won't escape. You know a monkey is about to tweak the tail of a kingfisher, warning it to fly away before it is eaten by a snake.

Parvin shrugs. He says the paintings are "typical of Kangra art," a style of Rajput painting developed in the eighteenth century when Hindu artists were commissioned by the rajas of the eastern hill states to decorate their temples and palaces.

Their manner of painting was "more free, more curvaceous than that of Mogul artists, and the same style applies to the folk art which it has become." The blue paint is no longer made with lapis lazuli, but with indigo, and the green is no longer powdered vertigris. When mixed with white, however, the greens and blues still look much the way the greens and blues look in the old paintings. Reds are made with cinnabar and an indigenous clay called *hurmachi*, the familiar tawny Indian red. Yellow is made from pulverized yellow river clay, and black is prepared from burnt coconut shell or from the soot of mustard oil burned in earthenware lamps.

Veronica says that the Tibetans use only minerals ground to a powder with millstones for their *thangka* paints.

"The *lila* thangka you did for me is my most treasured possession," I say. Veronica allows me to put my arm around her waist.

There are hill ponies tethered to the columns of verandahs, the first I've seen, with furry pelts, long manes, and flowing tails, short-legged, sturdy, obviously well-cared for and healthy. When Parvin stops the car so that I can photograph them, a chestnut foal with a white diamond blaze comes to lick the salty residue of perspiration from my arms before it returns to the more satisfying nourishment of its mother. While Veronica and I are stroking and feeding the hill ponies, small boys wearing gold stud earrings and gold nose screws laugh at their reflections on the shiny black doors of the Mercedes.

The climate has changed. It is still brilliantly sunny, but cool, and the awesome landscape is freshened with masses of wild roses—clear pinks, white, and deep red. The flamboyant blossoms of the silver-trunked silk cotton trees are beginning to show the tender green fingers of their fruit. Some of the trees have been cut, or their branches lopped off for fuel and fodder, but unscathed groves remain—dark-tiered pines, bamboo, *pipal* trees with fluttering heart-shaped leaves, *shisham* trees with hay pitched to dry among their lower light-green foliage, large dark mango trees gleaming with ripening fruit. Lantana and ageratums brighten the roadside. Hill ponies and sheep graze among gray boulders. The landscape, with its hills and the great white Dhauladar range, is pure and pastoral, as sparsely furnished as an Indian house.

Parvin suddenly swerves to avoid driving over a *jatu-tona*, a pattern of rice laid out on the road to exorcise evil spirits. "A non-observant driver who crosses over the pattern takes on the problem," Parvin explains. Like a banana peel tossed in front of an unsuspecting pedestrian? Veronica and I find this practical joke hilarious, as well as the disarray of bags, baskets, books, and maps that results from Parvin's maneuver. Parvin is indignant, yet triumphant that he has outwitted the jokesters. "There. See? *They* did it, that wedding party, the louses," he crows, speeding to catch up with them.

Looking ahead, I see a bride with an ornamental gold nose ring peering out from the curtains of a double-pointed red-tented palanquin, mounted on two poles and shouldered by six young men. Probably the bride's brothers, Parvin says, carrying her from her house to the house of her bridegroom. He is all smiles again. "May you bathe in milk, blossom in sons," he says as we pull alongside them, blessing the small, solemn twelve-year-old bride arrayed in crimson silk, weighted with gold. Her nose ring, like a crescent moon, almost covers one side of her face. Gleefully, Parvin tells the men that we have evaded their *jatu-tona*.

Grinning like naughty boys, they hold out their free hands to accept our gifts of oranges and plastic bags filled with nuts and raisins. They have walked about five miles so far and have twenty or more to go before they reach their destination in Kangra. Mid-May is the wedding season, and this day, deemed astrologically suitable according to the horoscopes of both the bride and groom, seems to be an auspicious day for other wedding couples as well. We will see several more festive red-tented palanquins proceeding along the road, and more the next day, some with brides who look far younger than Veronica was when she was fêted as the Mermaid Princess in Nova Scotia.

Far away, shepherds known as *Gaddis* (pronounced to rhyme with buddies) herd their sheep close to the boulder and stone banks of a water course. The sheep are beautiful at a distance, like clusters of white stars along the pale expanse of land. Close-up, barrel-fat and baaing, they bring back the Celtic and Calvinist sound of Scotland to me. The *Gaddis* are shepherds whose ancestors migrated from the Gangetic plains of the Punjab some three centuries ago to escape the oppression of their Muslim rulers. Refusing to accept Islam, they fled for sanctuary to the forests in Chamba and Kangra, on either side of the Dhauladar range. Now they move freely from Kangra to Chamba when the passes are not snowbound, and often have homes in both territories. You can see rows of their box-like wood and stone houses in forest clearings, at altitudes Parvin estimates as about four thousand feet on the Kangra side, eight thousand feet on the Chamba side. The Great White Mountain range, the Dhauladar, is the *Gaddis'* Mother Mountain. Shiva, they say, lives on the lower slopes of the range during the winter, and on Kailash peak, the loftiest pinnacle in the region, from April to September. During these months, the *Gaddis* migrate from their winter pastures to their summer pastures in Lahaul, a land of wild magnificence that lies across the peaks and passes of the Inner Himalayas. The *Gaddis* will have to travel for a month or more before they reach Lahaul, whose isolated valleys are at altitudes of about fifteen thousand feet and whose mountains have an average height of nineteen thousand feet. Lahaul was once a part of southwestern Tibet and remained a tributary of Lhasa for centuries until it came under Indian jurisdiction.

Veronica says that she has trekked in Lahaul. Once, the hill pony she had borrowed shied at a shadow, threw her off in the middle of a stream, and galloped back to its owner. Alone, wet and cold, she tried to make her way back to Manali, but after a day became so sick and feverish that she would have died if she hadn't been rescued by seven Tibetan novice monks making a pilgrimage. "Baby monks," she calls them, about ten years old, who carried her to a cave, wrapped her in their sheepskin blankets, fed her tea and *tsampa*, doctored her with herbal remedies, nursed her back to health. They made a stretcher for her and, sometimes walking with her, sometimes carrying her in the stretcher, they accompanied her on the journey back to "civilization," to Manali. "I felt like Snow White with the Seven Dwarfs," she says.

"You never told me about that."

"Why should I? You'd have been worried sick."

I suppose it's better to be worried sick now, with Veronica sitting all healthy and rosy beside me. Veronica says it is. Parvin says it's amazing what the young can survive.

We drive up alongside a family group of *Gaddis*: Father, Mother, Older Son, Younger Son. Shaken by Veronica's story, I welcome the distraction of photographing them, sharing for a moment their aura, their presence, seeing the *Gaddis* as good omens, good shepherds, some primitive part of me wanting to receive a blessing from them.

The Older Son, olive-skinned, sun-browned, tall, could pass as a Greek *evzone*. He wears the traditional *Gaddi chola*, a full, loose tunic of handspun white wool, secured below his waist with yards of black woolen rope wound around him many times. He has a lamb cradled in the pouch of his *chola*, a floppy-eared, russet-colored animal I mistake at first for some sort of dog. Besides the newborn lamb, he shows me that his *chola* also contains a draw-stringed leather pouch, extra clothes, food, and other necessaries.

I marvel aloud at the utility of this garment.

"The Tibetan layman's *chuba* is the same idea," Veronica says in a what-a-simpleton-you-are tone of voice.

"But I haven't seen *chubas*, and this is my first *chola*," I retort in defense.

The Older Son shows me how he can unfold his white peaked cap, embroidered with red and green wool, and pull it over his ears like a bonnet. Veronica gives us a look that says as plainly as if she had spoken the words out loud that she thinks we are both behaving idiotically. The Older Son and I refuse to be perturbed. He points with obvious pride to his out-sized, clumsily made *chapplees*, the ubiquitous Indian sandal of crisscrossed leather straps buckled behind the ankle. He has fashioned them himself of pale untanned leather and they are comically bulky. Yet he strides in them with the grace of indomitable maleness and radiant good health.

The Older Son wears a silver ring on the fourth finger of his left hand, but why on earth has he painted his fingernails with nail-polish? He flashes a marvelous smile when Parvin, who is acting as our interpreter, poses this question, and glances at his left hand resting on the lamb's furry flank. He likes the color, he says, because it matches the color of tree rhododendrons, and it cost him "too much rupees" in the bazaar, this bottle of polish he produces from the depths of his *chola*, this bottle with its clever little brush inside. "Isn't it wonderful? Isn't the rose-purple color wonderful?"

Parvin, the sophisticated city dweller, smiles paternally, waggling his head in agreement, pretending astonishment at the little brush attached to the bottle-cap.

The Younger Son, with a silver bangle on his right wrist, has the alert intelligence of a street urchin, swift at comprehending the situation. His *chola*, probably his older brother's cast-off, is ragged, its sleeves so long for him that he has turned them up to his elbows. He squats on the road holding a stout stick, and laughs as one of the family's flock of sheep butts him on his backside. He swivels to hug the sheep, stands up, straddles the sheep, and pretends to ride it so that I can photograph him doing so. He clowns to receive attention, and we all smile with indulgence, his brother, Parvin, his father, his mother, and I.

Parvin says that *Gaddi* women are noted for their beauty, and the Mother must have been lovely as a girl, for she has fine features and a graceful way of moving. Her woolen dress of rose

paisley with woven insets of brown-flowered panels has a voluminous, long pleated skirt. The lovely effect of its handspun
wool and its soft, muted vegetable dyes is offset by the harsh
blue aniline dye of her gauze *pattu*, a shawl she wears over her
head and shoulders which droops on one side almost to the
ground. She stiffens at the sight of my camera pointed in her
direction, casts off her grace and strength, and becomes sullen,
staring, frozen. She clasps her husband's hand, squints in the
sun. After the camera's click, she relaxes, smiles, and adjusts her
pattu, folding it in such a way that it is almost an attractive
complement to her costume.

The Father, however, is a natural subject. He is handsome,
upright, elderly, and his fierce singularity is mingled with good
humor. He is wearing a khaki woolen shirt over a pair of khaki
shorts cut so short that where the fly-seam ends his hard, sturdy
thighs begin. Except for the cherub faces in his knees, he has
the well-muscled legs of a gymnast. Around his neck he wears a
string of *rudraksha* beads, the nutmeg-like seeds of which are
considered a manifestation of the gods. He carries a stout walking stick. His eyes are brown, his mustache and eyebrows are a
ginger color, and his skin so fair that he could be mistaken for a
sun-burned Celt. He has a great slash of a scar above his left
eyebrow.

Parvin is less interested in the Father's face than he is in the
Father's bulging white turban. Perhaps, Parvin says, the old man
is one of the *Gaddis* who has never cut his hair. Sometimes they
weight their hair, extend it by plaiting in lambs' wool. Sometimes, it is said, their hair reaches right down to the ground.
"Let's see," Parvin says to me, and waggishly asks the old man
to show us his hair.

I cringe at the arrogance of Parvin's request, at this dreadful, touristy intrusion on the old man's privacy, but the Father doesn't give a hoot. He unwinds his turban to reveal an equally inflated turban of hair.

Parvin is beside himself. If only the old man will undo his hair for us! He fishes a rupee from his pocket, which he proffers with a smile. From the consideration he gives to every rupee he dispenses or tells me I shall have to dispense for petrol, food, or accommodations, I know that the coin he offers to the old man is real money, serious money, something quite different from what he thinks of as my American-exchanged-dollar money. What I am about to see is An Event. A Happening. Thank heavens Veronica, who so objects to any aggressive curiosity on my part, has gone off down the road and isn't around to witness my complicity. But dear God, here she comes. Parvin has run down the road to fetch her, and is now running back.

I feel Veronica beside me like a blown-up balloon, huffed with indignation, swollen with outrage. I can feel myself fluttering about her like a frightened bird. I can feel Parvin brimming over with excitement, his whole being like a trembling meniscus. The Older Son and the Mother are strangely still. Even the Younger Son is in a state of suspended motion. The Father has us all in his power. He stands there like a giant with his great turban of hair, and only he is calm, assured. This is no ordinary occasion. A certain ceremony must be observed. Roles suddenly have been reversed. It is the Father now who tells Parvin what to do. His name is Sri Ram Kaur: Parvin must write this down and perhaps I can also take a photograph of him and Parvin, and Parvin can take a photograph of him standing with Veronica and me, and here is the address where the photographs should be sent. Sri Ram Kaur, he repeats, the village head man from Lambh, a village which is serviced by the post office of Holi in the *thesil* of Bharmaur, a temple town in the Pangi Valley in the Chamba area of Himachal Pradesh.

I imagine our photographs carried in sackloads on the top of a bus, carted off from a depot in an ox-drawn *ikka* and then hand-carried or bicycled to yet another destination and finally delivered up a sheep trail to a box-like house in a forest clearing. Like Miniver Cheevy, I'm almost set dancing at the romance of it all. A post-office called Holi! I can hear Veronica taking deep breaths and know without looking at her that she has narrowed her eyes against the sun and is making an effort not to scowl. Parvin is still carefully writing out the address that I have scribbled in my notebook.

And now, finally, the moment has come. Like some latter-day Rapunzel of another gender, Sri Ram Kaur removes the pins from his great turban of hair. Several dozen plaits swing loose, fall to the ground and cover his dusty bare toes. Parvin gasps as his camera clicks and whirs. More than two meters of hair, over six feet of hair, possibly even six-and-a-half feet of hair, all real, no sheeps' wool plaited in it at all! And no weights! What a privilege to see! Never in his life has he seen anything like this!

Without his turban, standing there with what looks like a hawser unraveled on either side of his head, this fierce old giant of a *Gaddi*, Sri Ram Kaur, the village head man from Lambh, looks shrunken, slightly freakish. I am impatient now for him to do up his hair again and become his former romantic self. I sympathize with Veronica. Perhaps she would be happier if she went for a walk, I suggest, or sat in the car, because now Parvin has taken over again, asking the family questions, translating their replies for me to write in my notebook.

"Don't you want me around when you're being Mummy the Anthropologist?"

"I just thought you—" I begin, then give up trying to explain. Of course, I say, I want her to stay. So she stands at my side, holding the pages down in my notebook when the wind gets under them.

Parvin, in a burst of uncharacteristic garrulity, spouts platitudes and generalities about the virtues of the *Gaddis*. "A simple people of Aryan descent, crime is almost unknown among them. Whatever they tell you, you can take for the gospel truth."

When they reach Lahaul, they say, they will "sleep out," rolled in blankets with their flocks, sometimes pulling their sheep over them and piling them on top of each other for warmth. "Sheep are better than goats," the Younger Son says. "Goats are bonier and have tongues that lick more, tickle more." The Older Son says they light fires to keep the leopards at bay. If they use up their matches, it's simple to strike a piece of flint against a rock and catch the sparks in dried flowers or withered leaves. The Mother says they use pine cones to build fires inside circles of piled-up stones to boil water for tea, to cook, to set their bonfires at night. "And to light a hookah," the Father says. "It is good to smoke after a meal, to sit with one's back against a tree."

Parvin knows my style. He leaps to ask about the kinds of trees, but Veronica is already ahead of him. "Tamarisk, deodar, willow, walnut, spruce, pine," she says. I try not to laugh because that makes my writing worse. My grandmother, trotting me around the British Museum, used to show me samples of Emily Bronte's tiny, neat script as a model. It is uncanny how close Veronica's handwriting comes to replicating that model script. I, on the other hand, scrawl at the best of times.

Now, hurrying to catch up, I scribble as the Older Son says, "When the winds are like arrows of ice, there are always rock shelters where the bears go and for us to go where the bears are not."

Father Ram Kaur says that on festive occasions the men join hands and dance in a ring, while the women watch. They sing their "old songs." They play the flute, the drums, and the Indian bagpipes (which have two drones instead of three like the Scottish). They drink their home-made beer. "And get very drunk and wild," the Mother adds.

Dionysian revels. All male folk-dancing. The *evzone*-like costume. The Greek face of the Older Son, and his delight in the rose-purple color of rhododendrons, native to Macedon and Greece, the seeds of which Hercules, Dionysus, and Alexander are said to have brought to India. Coincidence, or the perpetuation of ancestral memories? A little knowledge is a dangerous thing, an *ignis fatuus*, I say to Veronica, "but I do like knowing about the derivations of words, the root of customs, the origins of things."

"As if I didn't know that!" she says, crossing her arms. "But aren't you done yet? I don't think this is all that riveting." Her voice trills with impatience.

"I'd like to hear more about their songs, and then we'll go. All right?"

Parvin, glancing from Veronica to me, says that the *Gaddis* express in their songs a gift for poetry unlike any other hill tribe of the Punjab Himalayas.

"Oh, sure," Veronica mutters so that only I can hear.

Parvin is probably exaggerating. My expression betrays me, I know, because he assures me that *really*, it is true. "Just listen to this," he says, tilting back his head, looking off to his left, the way one does when trying to remember. He thumps his Humphrey Bogart hat more securely on his head. "Just listen to this," he says again. And then, in a voice as oddly and beautifully rough-edged as a young boy's, he sings the words to a melody that uses only five notes, a pentatonic scale, an air sweetly keening as the wind, a song that blows around us like spindrift.

> If the husband dies,
> One may wander;
> If the lover dies,
> How can you live?
> If a blanket is torn,
> One may put on a patch,
> If the sky is torn,
> How can you sew it?

He asks the Mother if she knows the song. She favors him with a swift glance. Her lips part in a flash of white teeth. She hums the tune. Yes, she knows the song. "That's why the sky is patched with clouds," she says.

Twenty-Three

Heralding our approach to the town of Kangra, the roadside is blazoned with white billboards lettered in black. "Signs of civilization," Veronica says, her mouth turning down at its corners.

TIME IS GOLD, DO NOT FRITTER IT AWAY

DELAY BREEDS CORRUPTION

WORK LIKE A HORSE, LIVE LIKE A HERMIT

WHAT IS HURRY? TALK LESS, WORK MORE

WORK HARD, TALK LESS

NO SUBSTITUTE FOR HARD WORK

WORK IS WORSHIP

NICE TO BE IMPORTANT, MORE IMPORTANT TO BE NICE

COURTESY KEEPS EVERYONE HAPPY

MANY RELIGIONS, ONE NATION, LET US BE PROUD OF IT

LIVE AND LET LIVE, A CHANCE TAKEN IS AN ACCIDENT

RECKLESS DRIVERS KILL AND DIE, LEAVING ALL BEHIND TO CRY

I chant the slogans aloud as we pass them, a child-self again on the way to South Carolina, singing out the Burma-Shave signs.

In the valley, barley and wheat are sown together and alternate with a patchwork of maize, flax, linseed, peas, safflower, lentils, all ribboned with irrigation ditches, tinsel trappings in the sun. There are scatters of two-storey homesteads, half-hidden by encircling groves of fruit trees. Mangoes and medlars. Mulberry and peach trees. Pomegranates, limes, guavas, quinces, oranges, and the yellow plums that are called *aluchas*. Apples. Not cherries.

"Cherries grow wild," Parvin says. "Walnuts grow in the upper hill villages, along with medicinal trees and shrubs." I look in the direction of his moving, pointing, outstretched arm. I become obsessively interested in photographing the patterns of terraced wheat fields. I am drawn to their rippling green, wave-like embankments, and their gradients crisscrossed with goatpaths winding around gray rocks, with here and there a patch of mud, crazed and crackled into contrapuntal patterns darkly incised on the pale earth. Like music, the patterns evoke a mysterious emotional response in me, a graphic toccata and fugue that make me quiver with pleasure, that engage me in a visual copulation with nature. The ever-changing play of sunshine and clouds on the peaks of the snow range of the Dhaula-dar kiss my mind, make me want to hug the landscape, incorporate it within my being. I try to capture it through the camera's eye, to make the memory of the moment a tangible treasure.

Kangra, still sometimes referred to by its ancient name of Nagarkot, Kangra, the town of the ear-shapers, dates back in recorded history to the tenth century. The old town was destroyed in the Great Valley Earthquake of 1905, and has been rebuilt in functional British Colonial style, enlivened here and

there with decorative arpeggios of masonry erected by Italian
prisoners during World War II. A fountain with a Mediterranean air, a building facade, and benches constructed with chips
of marble are instantly remarkable in an accretion of plain-
looking banks and shops, a post-office and a library, two movie
houses. Himachal police, spruce in yellow and purple turbans
and brass-buttoned tunics, direct vehicle traffic at intersections.
Away from the main street, the town is a warren of lanes and
alleys winding to and from a canvas-canopied bazaar, where you
can buy furniture dusters made of peacock feathers, incense
sticks, locally woven woolen blankets, and *chenna*, *dal* roasted in
a pan with sand, then shaken in a coarsely meshed sieve. Veronica says it tastes "just as good as popcorn." I munch a spilletful
of puffed grain with gritty burned bits and sample the local ice
cream which is spooned from a barrel covered with newspaper
and burlap onto a *tung* tree's broad leaf, and tastes of roses and
almonds. Scattered about the bazaar, NO HURRY, NO WORRY
signs stuck on poles caution against what?—speedy Indian
aggression?

The town occupies a hill overlooking the Banganga torrent,
a great rush of water roaring through a steep-faced, narrow
gorge. Rising sheer above the river, crowning a precipitous
rock, is Kangra's ancient Rajput fort, which dominates the surrounding valley lands. Parvin says that there has been no period
in the history of India when the vast landscape spread around
us did not see infiltrations, invasions and onslaughts from without and within, constant disruption, fighting factions, battered
principalities, bitter struggles between disparate elements.
There are as many ruined fortresses in the area as there are
Shaivite temples. The Kangra Fort, seat of power of the Rajas of

Kangra, dates back to the thirteenth century and the heroic splendor of feudal India—"a very nice fort," Parvin says, coaxingly. I had hoped to be spared from a tour de forts, but Parvin will be hurt if we decline. Ah well, just one more delay before we get to Manali.

The Kangra Fort is accessible only by a narrow strip of land guarded by a series of gates named after its conquerors. Jehangir. Ranjit Singh who became Maharaja of Punjab when he was a boy, who consolidated an Empire stretching from the Sutlej River on the south to Afghanistan on the north, from Kashmir and Ladakh on the east, to the Sind in the west. The British. Fierce, far-off battles, a life alien but accessible.

The Fort reminds me of militant Christianity. I think of the hymn, "A Mighty Fortress is Our God." A bulwark never failing. Music dissolves interior pressures. I hum the hymn as I look at the Fort. "There is no more easy comfort in religion than in a *tête-à-tête* with oneself," I say to Veronica, the words coming unbidden, spoken before I even knew I was thinking them.

"Do you want to hear a Buddhist joke?" she asks. "A psychiatrist is talking with a crazy man and asks him why he thinks he is God. And the crazy man replies, 'Because every time I say my prayers, I find I'm talking to myself.' "

It's not all that funny a joke, but we laugh as if it were. Maybe our laughter is just a release of hostility, like baring one's teeth in a smile to show that one isn't going to snarl.

We look at the Fort, whiskered with grass. How massive it is. It must be like climbing up a labyrinth within its walls to get to the top. Veronica walks ahead of me, striding up an inner incline which leads to the summit. Parvin is whistling somewhere up ahead. I look at Veronica's mane of hair swinging across her

shoulders. Abundant hair is a symbol of procreation and regeneration. How terrible it would be if I were twenty-five again,
and had so much before me to learn, so much anguish to suffer
through. At fifty, there is the possibility that I have all the pleasure of youth stored within me, and the possibility that I may
grow younger as I grow older. I touch the stones tufted with
grass and lichen, touching history, touching the past embattled
centuries.

At the summit, the Fort placed between two rivers is like the
tawny pupil of an eye high above the valley. I have never seen a
fort as beautiful. High, high on a hill, sprawled golden in the
sun, with the lizards darting across the sun-warmed stones, and
the valley green, green below, bisected by the twin rivers, dotted
with houses, sprinkled with tiny specks of sheep and goats, it is
an arrangement designed by a child, a Peaceable Kingdom. Veronica and I sit side by side against a ruined wall, sheltered by
the tentacle roots of a *pipal* tree. Like me, I know that Veronica
is hearing, but not listening to what Parvin is saying about the
Fort's dimensions, the number of its bastions. Like Buddha, I
think, smiling at the incongruity of the thought, I have received
enlightenment. For a moment, Veronica rests her cool hand
lightly on top of mine. Both of us are silent.

As we pass a railway station in Palampur, a one-street town of
dilapidated Victorian and derelict eighteenth-century *havelis*, a
man wearing a white tunic and a turban shaped like an inverted
flowerpot with its saucer askew, brandishes his scimitar men-
acingly at us. Parvin whips the car away, tires screeching, then
tells us there's no cause for alarm. The man is just one of sixty
thousand "crazy followers" of a Sikh guru called Sri Namdhari

who believes that the end of the world is imminent and that the only refuge for true believers is one of the islands in Riwalser Lake near Mandi where the guru was born and where his sect is centered. But why there? Because the guru is a holy man and that's where he was born, Parvin says patiently, adding that some of Sri Namdhari's followers are "werry wy-o-lent people, not at all like other Sikhs. They do not take kindly to Westerners for World Wars One and Two. Except the Italian prisoners of war. They sang nice songs and were werry clever at carving marble." Everyone liked them, Parvin says. "*Funiculi! Funicula! Bravo! Va bene!*" He smiles at us in the mirror above the dashboard.

Like pebbles resting in the sieve of memory, what I can recall of our journey from Kangra to Mandi are small incidents, complete in themselves, esthetic gratifications, curiosities, a psychic and symbolic travelogue, perhaps, for I was in one of those moods where you see and hear only what you want to. Veronica and I hardly spoke at all of anything memorable, although our interior voices were constantly speaking to each other, and it wasn't until we had left Mandi and were on the last leg of our journey to Manali that she spoke in detail about her life there.

From Mandi to Manali is a ninety-seven-kilometer drive. *Sic transit gloria* Mandi. Unlike Gurdip, whose driving style conferred an impression of speed beyond his car's capacity, Parvin is a cautious driver, easing the Mercedes around Mandi's gates along the course of the Beas River, through dark forests. The Dhauladar's snowy peaks disappear and are replaced with the low but steep hills of the Great Himalayas. At Pandoh, a suspension bridge leads to a narrow, unpaved road that is carved out of a mountain. We now have a cliff rising above us on our left and another on our right, "our" side of the road, which drops off into the churning white depths of the Beas River gorge. From Pandoh to Aut, a distance of about fifteen kilometers, we have to cover "a rough stretch," Parvin says. It looks horrifying to me. "Nice horror," Parvin says soothingly. "Fun, like a roller coaster." Little does he know that horror movies and roller coasters never had any appeal to me.

At every twist and turn of this tortuous dusty road, Parvin sounds the horn and, for a while, thankfully, there is no answering sound, no sound at all except for the wind and the crunch of our wheels on the stony roadbed. Parvin ventures on a quavering flight of song. And then, far away, I see a bus coming toward us. Parvin finds a place to park on the side of the road, so close to the edge of the gorge that I fling myself to the left side of the car where Veronica is huddled, and have my hand on the door-handle, ready to roll out of the car and pull her with me to safety in case we topple over the edge. After all, there have been landslides here, and who knows how secure the edge of the road really is? Parvin says that he *thinks* we are safe. The bus comes nearer, nearer, closer, closer. I squeak with terror and clutch Veronica's hand. "I love you," I say. "I love you, I love you." Then the bus is gone, juddering past us by such a narrow margin I feel we have "traded paint," as Robert would have said.

"Oh, thank you, God, thank you, God, thank you, God." But this is only the first of many horrors. The road has crumbled away in sections, and in others, the stones and boulders that we can hear crashing down the mountain fall behind us or in front of us and scatter shale across the track. We stop so that *Gaddis* and their flocks of sheep and goats can make their way around us. The higher the ribbon of track is, looping and coiling in its switchbacks, the more terrible our situation appears. Is this our last moment on earth? Can we make it around this angle of road? And the next, and the next?

A car coming in the opposite direction pulls over into a shallow cave in the mountainside and waits for us to pass him, and even then, we are perilously close to the edge of a precipice. But I'm not ready to die yet, I keep thinking. Not now, not in this awesome gorge with the mountains closing in on either side and the water down below churning green and white.

We descend. Finally, we descend. The track broadens, and we are safe. Unbelievably, incredibly safe. On solid ground at last. The mountains still rise on both sides of us, but we are on eye level with the Beas once again. "Oh, thank you, God, thank you, God, thank you, God."

"On to Kulu and Manali," Parvin says.

"Better there than Heaven," I say.

Veronica giggles. "If Saint Peter let me in the Gate, I'm sure I'd trip over the threshold and have my halo fall off and go rolling down Heaven's main street into the gutter."

Oh, Elsa Cloud, what an extraordinary remark for you to make. I'm aware every moment of our shadow selves, the unconscious made conscious, your theologically naive, childlike associations with Christianity, and my own. Meditation also figures in Christianity. If there were Trappist nuns as well as Trappist monks, would you have become one, Elsa Cloud? As soon as the question occurs to me, I answer it for myself. No.

"You won't trip over the threshold at Heaven's Gate," I say softly and dreamily, the way one speaks when one is drowsy, eyes closed. "You'll just float on through like a lovely cloud haloed by the sun."

"You mean the way clouds look at sunset, as if a miracle were about to happen?"

"You bet."

"The clouds look like that in Dharamsala and Manali," Veronica says. "At Abo Rinpoche's Gompa there, the lamas often talk about the Tibetan views on dying. You can die when your own lifespan has been exhausted, or when your merit has been exhausted, or you can die if you're in an accident. It is important not to be angry when you die, because the method by which you release your soul from your body influences the next rebirth. If one conducts one's lifetime now in a good manner, this will be beneficial to the next one. When one is able to keep impermanence in mind—seeing that the very nature of things is to disintegrate—then one will most likely not be shocked by happenings and events, and one's attachment to this lifetime becomes weaker."

"Well, I certainly was shocked by that road," I say perversely, as though I were incapable of understanding Veronica's dissertation on the Tibetan views of dying. I don't suppose I am, really. It's just that I like things which endure, and dislike the idea of impermanence. Life is more precious after one has been on the verge of losing it, and I luxuriate in being alive, eagerly on the lookout for signs of the earth's marvels and miracles.

We are now in the Kulu Valley, the end of the habitable world, as it used to be called, the Valley of the Gods, a valley fifty miles in length and no more than a mile wide in most sections, bisected by the Beas. From the base of the mountains on either side of the valley, terraced land slopes gently to the banks of the river, irrigated and planted with wheat, corn, rice, and orchards of apples, plums, pears, peaches, cherries, apri-

cots. There are groves of walnut trees, islands in the river covered with alders, and avenues of alders along the road, interspersed with elms, poplars, and deodars. There are glades of
horse chestnuts, buttercups, and iris in the meadows.

Here in the village of Kotgarh, a Pennsylvanian named Samuel Stokes settled in 1912. He married a *pahari* woman, became
a Hindu, and introduced Red and Golden Delicious apples from
America which are now grown on a large estate managed by his
son. A temple on a hilltop has been erected as a memorial to
Samuel Stokes from Pennsylvania. "You see?" I say, pointing to
the temple. "America isn't all neon and naugahyde."

"Of course," Veronica says. She smiles amiably. "There are a
lot of times when I wish I were lying on one of your big, soft
beds watching something good on TV, or snacking in the
kitchen, or going to a museum or a party."

Is this all Veronica remembers of New York? It seems such a
tiny life.

One lives more by the body in India, Veronica goes on. She
says she is sensitive, perhaps overly so, to every physical change
because, with the little money she lives on, there are only primitive, mechanical means to alter the situation, "like the fan I
rent when in Dehra Dun." Difficulties, she says, become simply
curiosities, and eventually amusing, the juicy entertainments
one shares with people, instead of magazines, television, movies.

My daughter, the would-be ascetic, in a pale blue long-
sleeved, sashed dress. She talks of diamond, sapphire, emerald
mornings, when the air is clear and the sky deep blue. She talks
about stunning yellow orioles, lavender morning glories in the
hedges and tropical orange trumpet flowers growing over verandah arbors. She talks about having seen a silvery gray snake

about two and a half feet long. She reminisces about Trah-Trah (Tibetan for calico), a cat she had in Dehra Dun, Trah-Trah who was always having kittens. "One day, Trah-Trah had half her ear bitten off by a dog, and I didn't know how to help her. Physical sickness is so pitiful, but being unhappy about pain just increases the tensions and doesn't make it go away does it?"

No, I say.

She says she loved all the things I sent her. "Blue was the perfect color for a down coat because it was a layman's color. Greens and browns are considered colors only for married women; red, yellow and purple are for the *sangha*, the spiritual community of monks, nuns, married lamas, and *yoginis*. And the nylon cloth was wonderful because fleas and lice couldn't get through it. I experimented putting a dog's flea collar around my thigh overnight, but the next morning there was a white scar where the skin had been bleached by the poison. The scar lasted six months, so I've learned to be patient with the seasonal itches of the lice and the chiggers and the great little Manali nipper called '*snooru*' that comes with the rains." She says that deworming herself every few months is simply routine.

"Tell me more about Manali," I say.

"What season?" Veronica asks. "Summer, fall, winter, spring?"

"Autumn," I say, "That's when both of our birthdays are."

In autumn, Veronica says, the skies get gray and a real winter wind blows the leaves off the apple trees. The apples have been harvested and she dries slices for her winter muesli. The corn is drying on the slate rooftops. "Country rats come into my house at night and bash around looking for goodies to store away for the long, cold months. I told you how a rat once tried to pinch my opal ring. And that's when I go out and walk in the hills and pick the wild herbs and rosehips." Autumn is when she experiments with cooking, she says, because the cold weather excites her appetite. "I can make hot vichyssoise, lentil soup, *chapattis*, *dal* barley, wheat, rice, pulse, millet, maize, lentils. I know how to cook all of them for vegetables, soups, salads, porridge. Lots of vitamins and minerals. It's amazing what I can cook on two kerosene stoves." She says her landlady keeps cows and brings her creamy fresh milk, and that they chat about the price of things, "like the price of sugar, which is sixteen times as much this year as it was last." She says her landlady's hands are cracked from the cold, and she gives her some of the lanolin handcream I send. She says she likes watching the snow line creeping down the mountains. Last year, in the late fall, she says, she went for a walk up the mountain. The local hunter who guided her insisted on taking out his shotgun every time a pheasant or quail whirred through the branches of the deodars. She'd cry out, "Don't shoot. *Om mani padme hum!*" expecting a screech and a thud of bird-flesh, but to her relief and his fury, all the quail and the pheasant escaped. There were fox tracks, bears' tracks, and pine-martins in the juniper bushes above the tree line, and magnificent alpine meadows that made her want to sing "The hills are alive with the sound of music!" at the top of her lungs. At the peak, about thirteen thousand feet high, she could see for hundreds of miles. "The north was all snow mountains of different shapes, some all pinnacles like a Gothic cathedral and others like *stupas*. There was Humpta Pass, and in the south, the view of Kulu. We camped out at night and froze, but I didn't mind."

I'm a warm weather person. Bouts of malaria have thinned

my blood. I hate the cold. Veronica knows this. She gives me an almost exultant glance of pleasure as she goes on. "I love the winter," she says. In Dehra Dun and Manali, the cold season sometimes brings weeks of no kerosene which she uses for cooking, and often days of no electricity in the town. "But somehow, there is always a way around these botherations, and sharing the tiresome aspect of things is the basis of a friendly exchange of negativity with the neighbors, who are all in the same boat."

In the winter, Veronica says, she has a little cast-iron wood-burning stove to use at night, and she leaves the door of it open so that she has more light to write by. "There's an indescribably peaceful whiteness about winter," she goes on, "and the mornings are deliciously dark and cold and white. Sometimes, it snows as much as three feet in the morning, sometimes more on the north-facing slopes and in places where there is wind. Did I tell you I learned to ski last winter?"

No, but this is no great surprise. I remember photographs of her suspended from a glider-kite and her descent to ski on water, easily able to keep her balance.

"Well, as I was coming back home after a bath at the hot springs—we'll pass it just before we get to Manali—and was walking through a village called Koshla which looked like a Bruegel painting come alive, a well-known man about the hills called Tarachand was there with skis he had bought in Germany, and he said, 'You want to try skiing?' And it was great! Many near misses into apple trees, of course, because the ski run went through an orchard and paddy field, but the children kept yelling 'Shabash!', you know, Hindi for 'well done,' every time I hit the snow."

A couple of weeks later she and a group of boys from the bazaar went up to a place high in the mountains where there was a log cabin and a long ski run with no trees. "All around in the craggy peaks you could hear the boom and whoosh of small avalanches, and there were Himalayan vultures, lammergeiers, and a golden eagle tearing pieces of flesh off a stillborn goat. That's where I really learned to ski. When I returned home, Norbu, my dog, Norbu, was licking snowflakes off his fur, curled up next to the *tandoor*, and I remember tossing in a few wood chips, and then, just like that, in a couple of hours, a heat wave set in, and all the snow melted into rivulets. The ferns started coming out, and the jonquils. I felt like T. S. Eliot. It was cruel. No, no, no, bring back oblivion! And then the snow returned, and there was peace again."

Binding me in the spell of her pleasure, she tells me how lovely life is in Manali, how friendly, but such a difference, she exclaims, between February and March! In February, it is very cold and there is a pattern. Snow one day, clear one day, overcast one day. And then snow again. Black crows perch on the bare apple trees. In February the Tibetans celebrate *Losar*, the New Year, and everyone takes a week's break from the strict daily schedule for parties, with lots of *chang*—rice beer—and *arak*— "you know, the really hard stuff, like pernod" and delicious, indigestible edibles. And they have ritual dances symbolizing The Path you discover in realizing your enlightenment. "Oh, Mum, it's such a warm, spirited time—emotionally that is, not the weather." She looks at me, her eyes long, wide, brilliant.

She says the thing she misses the most is running water. "I try to catch every drop that falls from the sky in buckets and barrels, and just heat up snow in winter." There isn't a gutter on the roof of her house, she says, and when the snow begins to melt on the deodars, "you should see me running after the fattest trickles as they fall from my roof. It's a sweat, but when I put the bucket down and stop for a breath, I look at the view of the valley which is so beautiful, especially when it turns all golden and lovely in the late afternoon."

Spring in Manali is all crystal blue and filled with bird song, Veronica says, and butterflies everywhere. The terraced fields at the foot of the mountains turn yellow as the mustard crop ripens. The mint sprouts along the irrigation streams, and she collects mushrooms under the pine trees, and drumstick ferns, which you eat like broccoli or asparagus. "March is when the plum blossoms do their popcorn act," she says. March is when everything is gay and fresh with asphodels, and the alpine meadows are covered in strawberries that smell delectable when you crush them underfoot. Deep crimson and orange poppies bloom, miniatures, with leaves like strawberry leaves, ridged and spiny, and yellow watercups grow by the snow-melt streams as far as the eye can see. The air is moist with evaporating dew and fresh with clear sunlight. The little birds amuse her, she says, with their "funny way of moving their bodies, all speedy and blinky." She used to worry that "a whiny little cat that adopted me" would catch them. "But all she did was to bring in dead rats and leave them on the porch. I love animals, but I can see why Buddhists say that theirs is the realm of stupidity, endlessly killing each other, sincere, but humorless, unable to grasp a situation three-dimensionally."

Veronica says that mountain-climbing is even better in spring than it is in early winter. Last spring she climbed to a lake at an altitude of some fourteen thousand feet and saw pheasant-like monal birds and black bears. Trekking into the mountain pastures and uplands, she says, she saw at least a dozen wild ibex, "an animal that hunters and nature preservationists came from all over the world to see," as well as snowy langurs and rare mountain birds. "So many spring flowers, and the trees with their pale green leaves, all the walnut, birch, maple, wild cherry, golden oak in bud, and I even found some rhubarb on an alpine precipice and brought it back and made spicy rhubarb jam from a recipe in *The Joy of Cooking*."

She says this is a wonderful cookbook because it tells her how to prepare Morel mushrooms and how to parboil and eliminate the oxalic acid from the wild buckwheat leaves, the wood sorrel, the fiddlehead ferns, and the lambs' quarters that grow around the apple trees in the orchards. "But I have to admit that when it comes to sweets and cookies, I go cross-eyed with desire; it takes too much willpower, almost, to keep from munching on the page of the recipe."

She talks in an impassioned voice, raptly, as women often talk about their lovers. "I like the rough-edged feel of the land and my garden in the spring," she says. "It's as if nature were always slipping out of a cultivator's fingers. The lizards nip the budding heads off the French beans, what they call 'prass beans' in Manali, and strange little plants come up where I'm sure I have planted spinach and pumpkin. I always plant spinach and pumpkin first, because they're easy, and then go on to flowers and broccoli." She says that springtime is when the landlady brings her punnets of white truffles. In Manali, the white variety is "less common, really 'super.'"

She tells me that the previous spring, there had been a nest of baby yellow-cheeked mountain tits on her verandah wall.

One day she came out of her room, and there was a four-foot-long tan snake at the foot of the verandah. "He was sitting straight up, still as a doorknob, like a cobra, except that they really only have grass snakes and rat snakes and a few vipers in Manali. He must have eaten the baby tits because they just disappeared."

I remember running to hug Veronica one summer in Rhode Island and feeling her stomach squirming horridly against my own. I remember shrieking as she produced a small black milk snake from beneath her T-shirt, drawing the snake up by its head through the neck of her shirt. That was the summer before she was the Mermaid Princess in the parade at the camp in Nova Scotia.

She tells me that in April and May, lots of people come up from the plains to Manali, families from the Punjab, families from Bombay. The weather is clear, warm, blue. Crickets zing in the orchards; barley, wheat, and cherries ripen. In July there is the verdure and mists of the monsoon, and a dramatic ripening of all the fruit. The plums turn from innocent green to purple and crimson, the apricots are gold, and the apples, each a different shade of red, look like Christmas decorations. By the beginning of August, thanks to *The Joy of Cooking*, she has apple pie, apple betty, apple crumble, apple fritters, apple jam, apple-sauce, apple pancakes, dried apples, and spiced apples practically coming out of her ears. That's the time when the coolies are hired en masse to heft crates of apples to the bazaar to be taken by truck to Delhi. "It's a yearly Manali ritual of packers, pickers, crow scarers, sprayers, contractors—a huge bustle. The trees look so decorated and satisfying before the harvest that I always feel a sense of loss when the orchards are back to their ordinary green."

The monsoon, she says is a lovely season. The cool breezes bring "ghosts of cloud pieces in through my windows with the smell of ferns." Then she pauses, looking down as she loosely knots a white woolen cardigan around her shoulders. "Well, it's good you won't be in Manali when the rain arrives. You might like to see the fish come squiggling out of the mud to swim again, but the monsoon brings mosquitoes and invisible skin-biters, and spiders as big as my hand." She spreads out her long, tan fingers. "Huge, black, hairy night-lurkers," she says. "They hang around my walls near the candles or lamps, which are usually by my bed, and when I shine the flashlight on them their eyes all sparkle, all eight or more." She says she used to think lice were pretty disgusting but now, with familiarity, she has come to think of them as funny. "They're so tiny, and quick. When Norbu used to lie in my lap, chewing on a crabapple, I'd see them on him, and the moment I did, they'd jump off of him onto me."

"But I wasn't always so cool and nonchalant," she says. She recalls the time when she first went to Dehra Dun. She was living in a snug little leak-proof house with a corrugated metal roof, "like a large tool shed with windows," and a cistern out back where she doused herself a couple of times a day, "almost as good as swimming." Her mental image of America then still scared her a bit, "so speedy and aggressive," and she thought how nice it was to live in her little house near the forest. She believes that the Dehra Dun forest is the largest in India, "mostly skinny *sal* trees with those big leaves the Indians put together to make their 'paper plates,' and elephants and tigers, believe it or not." At night, "the king of the local hyenas used to scream just like some horror movie person being murdered, and then howl with insane laughter, actually so awful that it was silly, like a joke." For months, there was a Tibetan yogi who was doing the practice called *chöd*, offering his body in visualization to all beings in the world who are hungry and want to eat it. "If the practitioner is brave enough, like this yogi, he goes to the place where bodies of the dead are burned or cut up and he practices *chöd* there at night. The burning ground was only a few hundred yards from my house, and the combination of the yogi's shrieks—I guess the visualization became pretty life-like—and the hyena's screams, night after night, used to have an extraordinary stereo effect."

In April, with the monsoon two months away, she asked the village tailor how it was in the monsoon. Were there snakes? "Oh, yes," he said, "lots of them, cobras and kraits and vipers, and boa constrictors." The monsoon floats them out of their holes, and they come into houses through any chink or crack, or up the drainpipes which, luckily, she didn't have. He told her that the snakes really weren't any problem, but she shouldn't walk around in the dark, indoors or out.

"Finally, after months of blistering blue days, there was a lovely earth-shaking thunderstorm one night, and everything was suddenly drenched and fresh. Everyone in the Tibetan settlement of Clement Town came out to sit on their back porches and sing to themselves. Even after the rains came, the days were muggy, so the nights were when things came alive. People sat around their porches telling stories and the little girls showed off their songs while the little boys chased the frogs away, and the snakes who eat the frogs and bugs." Her neighbors, who saw them all the time, told her there were lots of cobras, but she didn't see any. At first, she had been afraid, but having begun reading Kipling's *Jungle Book*, and having pondered a while, she started to think that cobras couldn't be all that bad. "After all, they are sacred to the Indians, and who would make a nasty animal sacred?" So with that sort of rationalizing, she held her breath and kept her eyes open when she was picking wildflowers for her altar. "One day, a big old snake did come into my house. It didn't look like a viper and, in fact, I thought it looked very sweet and lovable with its round eyes and pink tongue. It was a gray-green snake with brown diamonds on its back and was about a yard long. I figured it was a rat snake, probably after the Mummy rat and her babies who lived behind my clothes chest. Anyway, it seemed quite unafraid of me and determined to visit, so I decided to leave for a couple of days, and when I got back, it had gone."

There were a lot of crows and vultures, too, during the monsoon, but there were wild roses everywhere and kingfishers on the telephone wires, and at the beginning of September when the weather changes from moist and balmy to crisp and dry, as the sunny skies break through, sometimes, there are earth tremors in the early morning. "Strange to feel the big, old unmoveable earth wriggle like that, like a belly dancer's tummy. Actually, it really feels like a loose spring surfacing from somewhere down deep." She has never experienced any real earthquakes in Manali, "just tremors."

September is also flea and bug and bird season, and lammergeiers, white with black-edged wings and a wingspan that looks close to six feet, fly by her porch where the apples are drying for her winter muesli. For a while she can see the snow falling on the mountaintops. The local people cut the monsoon grass in the orchards, literally making hay while the sun shines. There is a welcome-to-autumn festival. "There," she says, "that's the way it is in Manali the year round. Now you know everything."

Do I? It has grown dark as Veronica has been talking, and it is cold in the car. I have been listening attentively to what she has been telling me. And yet, somehow, I feel myself a child again, looking up at my mother doing her crewel work from a wing chair, the confusion of colored thread I see on the "wrong" side of her tapestry seeming to have no relation at all with the intricate precision of the flowers and birds and trees I see when I stand up and look at the square on her lap.

I fall asleep, waking when Veronica tells me we are about to pass the Vashisht baths in Koshla which are fed by hot-water springs. "Just like those in Iceland," she says. And then around midnight, we are in Manali.

Twenty-Four

Being in Manali, where the Kulu Valley narrows and the snow-peaked mountains close in, you are never far from the rushing of waterfalls pouring from cuts in a twelve-thousand-foot-high rock face into the rising Beas. In Manali, the air is scented with the dusty fragrance of the dark, towering deodar forest at the foot of the mountains. Before them are the lawns of a few guest houses, comfortable old buildings where princes used to lodge in the spring when the best hunting could be expected, and venturesome British families stayed to enjoy the bracing climate and the restful atmosphere of a bounteous Himalayan outpost. Away in a valley of low hills to the west, in a clearing of deodars and tall timber trees, the old village of Manali is the color of wood-ash tipped with apricot and flecks of gold, with the melancholy charm of long-lost vitality. Few people are seen there except after sundown, when most of its small population returns from the valley's fields and orchards to sleep.

From the entrance gate of our guest house, it is less than a

516 ~ LEILA HADLEY

fifteen-minute walk past the ramshackle tents of the bazaar concealed among the tiered, pungent branches of deodars to the "new town." This accretion, this graceless mix of dilapidated old wooden buildings with gabled windows and overhanging eaves and shoddy new concrete structures (more are being flung up with much dust and hammering), this tawdry display of cafés, food shops, camping and mountaineering supply shops, clothing shops, tailor shops: *this* is *Manali*? The place seems as utilitarian as a mining camp, as flimsy as the structures in a carnival, and as filled with joyless bustle as a bus station.

"But that's what it *is*, Mummy, a sort of open-air bus station when the roads are passable." Veronica directs a long look at me and smiles with perceptible condescension. I turn away, jostled by the hippies who throng the street. They clamber with their gear from arriving buses, loiter about with babies on their backs and black umbrellas against the sun.

"They come for the Manali grass," Veronica explains. "This is the tourist season." She speaks in the tone of someone apologizing that a garden is not being seen at its best, that an infestation of cut-worms or beetles has taken the bloom from the peonies and pelargoniums. Granny used to speak in just such a tone when the starlings got at the strawberries.

The main street writhes with vendors of fried potato patties, vendors of florid shawls, fruit *wallahs*, hawkers of earthenware pots and jars. Stout Indian matrons descend from a newly arrived bus in a flutter of seasonal pink and green saris clutched onto by small travel-worn children. *Paharis* and men with Burmese, Thai, and Mongolian characteristics offload crates, tin trunks, knobbly jute sacks. Veronica says they are Tibetan refugees, that Tibetans are "awfully strong," that even old grannies, bent double beneath loads of firewood, jog down the path next to where she lives with the ease of raindrops sliding down a windowpane.

A blond-bearded boy in blue jeans, wearing a red velvet Kulu pillbox hat, silver toe-rings, and an Afghani embroidered waistcoat walks by arm-in-arm with a brown-eyed girl in a Rajasthani *ghagra*, embroidered Punjabi slippers, and an orange body stocking appliquéd with hearts and flowers. Over this she has knotted a Spanish shawl in which she totes a blond infant with a gold nose stud who clasps the handle of a tattered umbrella the man holds to shade them all. As I watch, the man calls out, "Fuck! Shit! Fucksucker! Yippee!" and executes a sort of dancing step.

"He's just stoned," Veronica says dispassionately. "Sometimes people like that make for amusing cups of tea." I don't have to worry, she adds. Her friends are much more serious, much more rewarding, much nicer. "You'll meet them at Abo Rinpoche's Gompa—that is, if you don't get emphysema climbing there."

Chogyam Trungpa Rinpoche, who escaped from Tibet to India, left India to live in Colorado, and has returned from Colorado to Manali where he teaches Buddhist philosophy, may also be at the Gompa. "He has his students learning ballroom dancing," Veronica informs me. She pauses. When I say nothing, she goes on explaining: Tibetan Buddhist sects emphasize different methods of coming to awareness. None is seen as better than another. Perhaps ballroom dancing is a dignified expression of man and woman at play. Perhaps Chogyam Trungpa Rinpoche sees something special about its rhythms.

Chogyam Trungpa Rinpoche isn't at the Gompa when we

get there. Instead, gathered in the cement temple high up in the hills near the Rohtang Pass, waiting for their class to begin, are dozens of hippies. Veronica's arm squeezes mine close to her. It's such fun, she says, so wonderful to see all her friends again. Often she has too little time. Often she gets "flushed and dizzy in the dash for achievement, all dizzy and speedy."

"You? I thought *I* was the speedy, aggressive one."

Veronica shrugs. The way every minute of *her* day is filled with activity is *different*. It's a *challenge* to study Tibetan and Sanskrit, to teach English, wash clothes, feed the dogs and cats, to make tea, memorize philosophy, chitchat, say prayers, and run across town or up and down the mountain all in the same morning, or in the same afternoon, not to mention eating, going to the loo in the bushes, reading books and letters, writing letters and meditating. "Sometimes I sit on the old cushion coping with thoughts that rise and disappear, trying to empty my mind of all images, and it can be pretty boring, like a regular job, with just enough time to eat and devour a book or two." She adds that she enjoys tumult in small doses. "Potentially high with enthusiasm or low with anxiety, tumult can reveal one's equanimity as well as one's vulnerability," she says, smiling angelically. Her teachers teach her not to get caught up in the superficialities of hope and fear, enthusiasm, anxiety. "And yet, I do, of course, every day, no matter where, and then simply have to abide the confusion that ensues."

Confusion ensues for me when she introduces me to her friends. Here are Helge, a Buddhist nun who was once a German rock singer; Mac-the-Monk, a former Marine; Dolly, who has separated from Mac and married Piet whom she met in Holland and with whom she now has two children, a son named

Tenzing Dorje and a daughter named Jenny Lhamo, both born in Dharamsala; Mary, who wants me to telephone her grandmother and her mother, who live in Klamath Falls, Oregon; Ernie from Vancouver, who is traveling through India with a Danish girl who is "in retreat" somewhere near Bodhgaya; Larry, the son of a Jewish clothing designer, who wanted to get away from "the unrewarding glitz" of Southampton and Palm Beach, and his girlfriend from Pennsylvania who has the air of one carried away by whatever company she finds herself in to profess opinions at one with theirs. "Oh, yes," she says, sighing. "Lordy me, yes," and speaks of the joys of the simple life. She has scabs and needle marks on her arms. So do Guy, a professional logger from Canada; and Luis, an optometrist-saxophonist from Argentina; so do Danny, an American who "made a fortune" doing live sex acts for Japanese businessmen in Tokyo; Sylvia, an Australian travel writer; Karen, in a bottle-green Guatemalan *huipil* and blue jeans; and Isabella, an Italian girl whose face is puckered the way skin forms on a cooling, fatty consommé.

There are nomadic hippies and junkies who appear clean, or grubby, or laid back—individuals until they speak, when their outpour of spiritualism, slushy mysticism, and inconsequential chatter seems merely a terrible wish to be interesting. There are some with boastful confidence, some who look lost and bewildered; some who are expiating guilt, punishing themselves by going down and out in India in search of some greater sustenance in nature than they have found in society, submerging themselves, testing their own limits and endurance. Some are dressed in monastic garb, and seeing them I think of T. E. Lawrence. "In my case," he wrote in *Seven Pillars of Wisdom*, "the effort to live in the dress of Arabs, and to imitate their mental foundation, quitted me of my English self, and let me look at the West and its conventions with new eyes. They destroyed it all for me. At the same time, I could not sincerely take on the Arab skin. It was an affectation only. . . . Easily was a man made an infidel, but hardly might he be converted to another faith."

Veronica says her friends are all finding themselves by finding other selves within themselves. To me, she seems set apart, fresh, with a well-cared-for look, beautiful, radiant, marked in some indefinable way by a mind charged with intelligence. I watch her being bubbly and sociable with the gathering. They appear to want her to approve of them, and I think she is making an effort to be for them what they want her to be, trying to please in company, the way one does when seated next to boring dinner guests.

After a while, we fall in behind the others and start filing up the stairs into the concrete hall. A monk, seated up front— Veronica whispers that it's Abo Rinpoche—says something in a deep, resonant voice. At once, Veronica, with the others, sits in the lotus position, steeples her hands at the top of her head, then in front of her face, then in front of her throat, then in front of her chest, and then touches her steepled hands to the ground, her head resting on them. She and they sit up. Then they repeat the performance.

The gesture on top of the head signifies the aspiration that one will have wisdom. ("You know, Mummy, Lord Buddha had that *ushnisha* bump on top of his head which means he was super bright.") The hands steepled before the face, touching the forehead, signify that one's body will only be involved in actions that will be beneficial to others. Touching the throat is for speech or voice, to still the mind so that love and appropriate thoughts can arise, to give advice, to tell the truth, to sing, to help other people. The Truth Mantra.

Then the gesture in front of the heart. In Tibetan, the word for the heart is the same as for the mind, and the gesture signifies the aspirations that the heart and mind will be pure and devoid of defilements such as anger, craving, ignorance.

All this I have yet to learn. Now I sit watching the completion of the prostration, watching Veronica, watching Billy from Santo Domingo beside us, watching Larry, Helge, Mac, Dolly, Piet, Mary, Ernie, Isabella—why don't they ever give you their last name, these strange people?—and all the others, *poseurs* and *poseuses* prostrating themselves. One of them is my *daughter.* I am appalled; aghast, disbelieving. Resounding in my Presbyterian mind, as Veronica sometimes chaffingly calls it, is the archaic verse of a hymn I used to sing:

> From Greenland's icy mountains,
> To India's coral strand,
> Where Afric's sunny fountains
> Roll down their golden sand
> *The heathen in his blindness*
> *Bows down to wood and stone.*

Like water coming to a boil, my mind bubbles with outrage. Now the group is half-singing, half-chanting, and swaying in preparation for meditation. Wrapped in his maroon robe with a bit of orange blouse showing over his right shoulder, the Rinpoche sits quietly fingering the hundred and eight beads of his *mala*, telling mantras.

A student comes forward. Bowing, he places a book in the hands of the Rinpoche.

A spoken prayer is now chanted. The group sways as they chant. *Om mani padme hum.* For thirty minutes by my wristwatch, this mantra is repeated over and over. I hear it as *Oh, MONEY pared may hum. Oh, MONEY pared my hum.* I look around the room and count the people there. Counting, I've read, is a defense against something. I've forgot what. Forty-three men and women, including three infants.

Finally, the class is over. Now everyone who wants to will circumambulate the Gompa. *Circumambulate the Gompa?* Yes, Veronica says. The Gompa is a sacred place, like a temple. Circumambulating is an exercise of purification, of symbolic progress which relaxes the mind. It is an elimination of mental and physical obstacles. It stills and relaxes the mind, a physical manifestation of overcoming defilements, an active form of meditation. Most of the group picks up a handful of pebbles. After each go-round, they place a pebble on a windowsill of the Gompa to mark the completed circumambulation. "That's fine," I say. "I'll just sit here in the shade."

Is my Christian conscience outraged at the sight of heathens bowing down to wood and stone? Of course not. I am not a nineteenth-century missionary or hymn-writer. I don't think of Buddhists as "heathens." I don't think of anyone not professing the Christian faith as a "heathen." In Muslim countries I have felt myself regarded as an "infidel." In the more tolerant eyes of Buddhists, I (in my present incarnation) am someone who has fallen just a little short of success. Many acts of merit in previous existences have saved me from rebirth as a fly or a dog, and all that is now required to achieve complete humanity is the enlightenment attained by following the noble Eightfold path. The ritual of prostration is not what outrages me. It is seeing *Veronica* perform the ritual of prostration. *My daughter prostrating herself.* That is what makes me feel withered, sere, dead. All the satisfaction, the pleasures, the shared jokes of our travels together seem here no more than sun-whitened bones, picked bare of substance. Persephone has gone where I am not, and I cannot follow.

Veronica completes whatever number of circumambulations she has determined to make around the Gompa. I trudge behind her down the mountain trail, down the road back to the main street of "town."

I have been waiting for Veronica to take me to see her house "up the goat path," but she hasn't offered to do so. Finally, I ask her to let me go with her, to help her carry and store some of the things she's brought from Delhi which she wants to leave there. "Oh no," she says, "coolies can do that. It's much too steep and high a climb for you to make."

Why couldn't the coolies carry me, too, in a palanquin, in a stretcher, drag me up there, if necessary, in a sledge? Oh no, Veronica says. Oh no. Her mouth tightens, thins. Demeter cannot follow Persephone into the underworld. Does she think I will defile her sanctuary, just as by touching something to do with food or its preparation I could render it inedible? She suggests we make a day's excursion to Naggar instead, to the village where Nicholas Roerich once lived. A Russian emigrant, Roerich painted Himalayan landscapes as a background to the teachings of Buddha while studying archaeology and compiling a Russian-Tibetan dictionary. Parvin says that lots of people think Roerich was a Russian spy. As he speaks, he reminds me of a businessman who told me once that what Kipling's *Kim* was really all about was British counter-intelligence.

In the early morning sunlight and at twilight, blue shadows are thrown on the Himalayas; "blue like the sky and blue like the mountain poppies, just like Roerich's paintings," Veronica says as we set off after breakfast for Naggar.

The former capital of Kulu State, Naggar is a village perched on a wide spur almost six thousand feet above the Kulu valley and the Beas river. The village consists of a dozen or so houses that look like Swiss chalets, uniformly built of dark wood which has been decoratively scalloped and carved, with fretwork-like dark lace runners on shutters, bordering doorways, and hanging from lintels and cornices. "I told you, Mummy," Veronica says. "Hill people always have to do something like weaving or carving to keep themselves busy during the long winter nights. I'll bet that Granny would have liked it here. She used to say that the Devil found work for idle hands." Granny? Oh yes, *her* Granny, my mother, and *my* Granny, my mother's mother, used to say the same thing in a different way. "How doth the busy little bee improve each shining hour?" both of them would ask if they saw me sitting still, daydreaming, staring into space. And I would feel at once that I should be *doing* something, reading, or even playing Solitaire. But I was no good at Solitaire or Patience. I was only good at games like Concentration, played with a partner, where you had to remember where cards had been laid face down. "And here face down beneath the sun / And here upon earth's noonward height / To feel the always coming on / The always rising of the night." Bryce liked to read Archibald MacLeish's poems to me. My grandmother used to quote Boswell's observation that he had no fanners in his head, "least no good ones to separate wheat from chaff," whenever she disapproved of something I had said or done. It was a legacy I had obviously received from him, she would tell me.

Naggar has a palace, a timber and stone building with an upstairs verandah on all four sides. "A Raja lived here once," Parvin says. Now, it is a deserted government rest-house, still littered inside with remnants of Victorian furniture. Parvin says that it is haunted, which is why it has been closed. No one likes staying here, he says. There are evil spirits.

In the courtyard of the castle is a small square structure built of stone. A dog kennel? A duck house? No, Parvin says. A temple. It contains a stone slab some six feet square and four feet thick, a site where legal disputes used to be settled by two goats, one the property of the plaintiff, the other, the property of the defendant. The Brahmin priest in charge would sprinkle water on each goat, and the first to shake off the water was the loser. Nearby, propped against a grassy ridge, are suttee stones, slabs of gray rock carved with figures silently shrieking out the primal power of the impassioned theme of love and death. I stare at them transfixed, and shiver in the sun. I stoop to pick a red flower. Is the plucked flower also screaming?

Wearing my field glasses around her neck, Veronica peers at two tiny specks in the valley, describing them as people she thinks she knows, wheeling their bicycles across a swaying suspension bridge toward the road leading up to Naggar. Yes, it's Mary and Ernie. She says she likes to be with people who have "put out their feelers." Sometimes, she says, she tries to urge others to be the way she wants them to be instead of putting out *her* feelers. "I shouldn't do that," she says. "It's best to be thoughtful of others' sensibilities." She drops the field glasses. Mary and Ernie are having a picnic. They aren't going to come up to Naggar after all. Now she glances upward. "Look how the sky is patched with clouds," she says.

I wonder if she is telling me that she remembers the *Gaddis* and a song of theirs. I don't ask her. She has begun to breathe deeply and is moving her lips silently, saying a mantra.

If the sky is torn, how can you mend it? If my daughter is lost to me, what hope is there? I force myself to look again at the row of monstrous suttee stones. Mr. Eliot returns to mind. "The ragged rock in the restless waters is what it always was."

Twenty-Five

Standing outside the hotel in a garden edged by upended beer bottles, I sweep the sky with my field glasses. I am tired of watching yellow finches flying among the apricot and plum trees. Maybe there will be a lammergeier.

The narrow, wedge-shaped cut of the Rohtang Pass is partially obscured with tatters of mist, and overhead is a cloud I can see for a moment as a grand and ghost-like Alexander riding on Bucephalus, that "noble steed who aged until he died without a wound" and fell to the ground beneath his master. I never tired of quoting that to myself as a child and, seeing Alexander in the sky, of whistling or singing the song that began, "Some talk of Alexander . . ." One has to go back in order to go forward. I remind myself to look for lammergeiers and see one sailing majestically over the Himalayas. Enormous. Rusty white belly, not buff, and yes, as it wheels, a black goatee on its chin. I am startled when I hear Veronica's voice.

"Bird-watching, Mum?" She has come up silently behind me and pulls a hook through the eye at the top of the zipper of my dress. "Daddoo used to say you needed a lady's maid. Granny

527

said her mother had one who was the illegitimate daughter of Edward the Seventh. Or sixth. Something like that."

"Seventh. Thanks for fixing my dress. I'll leave it with you when I go back to New York."

"Thanks. Look, *there's* a pretty little bird with a forked tail. See it?"

I catch a glimpse of a rose-colored bird, then lose sight of it.

"Do you suppose bird-watching is some form of sublimated sex? Voyeurism?" Veronica asks.

"Possibly. The Spanish call a man's cock *la paloma*, the dove. Oh, yes," I say, hearing myself sound like Gurdip, "Oh, yes, there's bound to be some connection."

They call the Holy Ghost *le pigeon* in France, and talk about putting their bird in your nest to make love. We endow with wings all that is superior, and the male organ is obviously high on the list. But there's a lot more to the symbolism of birds than sex. Solar birds and birds symbolic of souls. The birds who bear celestial messages, the birds which are symbolic of spiritualization. Birds that stand for trance-like states. Fire birds. The phoenix rising from the fire's ashes. The American eagle. Aristophanes. And as for the Holy Ghost, he can be represented both by the dove and by an image of Pentecostal fire.

I say that there's always more to everything, as a rule, than what you first hear, think, see, read, want—"more about penguins than I wanted to know," as the little boy said to the librarian.

"There's more to Manali than the international hippie brigade," Veronica says to show me that if I can't see Manali through her eyes, she can see it through mine.

Can she? We walk from the hotel garden to the new town to pick up her mail in a grocery store-cum-post office where the *poste-restante* is a worm-eaten box on a wooden bench. That my letters to her have never gone astray is a minor miracle, I reflect, as we go next door to a *chai* shop for a biscuit and a cup of tea. Wobbly legged kids and baby lambs have been parked at the entrance, with one of their owner's children left outside to keep an eye on them. We watch as *pahari* children triturate tops of marijuana plants beneath their palms, then rub off the residual hashish carefully on squares of newspaper.

"People cut holes in magazines and make little pockets, roll up the magazines and sometimes manage to smuggle out some of the stuff," Veronica says.

She cautions me against visiting a nearby Tibetan refugee transit camp. It's not like Byllakuppe, she says. "That's a *settlement*. This is a *transit* camp." But Jhamchoe has given me a letter for Dilgo Rinpoche, a holy man in attendance there. I have promised Jhamchoe I will give this lama some money to help buy supplies and medicines. I *must* go to the camp.

Well, all right, Veronica says. If you really feel you *have* to. She produces a map for Parvin to follow, and off we go, arriving at our destination in less than an hour.

From a distance, the camp's prayer flags, some square, some triangular as nautical pennants sun-bleached to pale pastel colors, can be seen fluttering and flapping in the wind, the semiotic expression of the worshipful heart of Tibetan life and devotional practice. The great wheel of Dharma, the Universal Law, set in motion by Lord Buddha, must be kept in motion by means of mechanistic and repeated invocations to the four cardinal points of the universe. This idea, once so alien, has caught deep in my mind like a grain of sand that has penetrated a mollusk to mature in concentric layers and become a pearl.

As we come closer, sloshing across the mucky, spongy ground along the bank of the Beas, I can see dozens of Tibetan men, women, and children moving among a huddle of burlap and tarpaper and board shacks, corrugated iron lean-tos, patched yak-hair tents. Then, welcomed by a smiling crowd, we step inside another world, a world of ugliness and the smell of poverty and disease, yet giving off an unexpectedly rich sense of calm, dignity, composure, friendliness. No one is whining. No one is begging. Above a cairn of stones with prayers in Tibetan on them is a poster with a picture of the Dalai Lama and a message which Veronica translates as "No madness, no suicide, no violence."

"You can see how astonishingly durable the Tibetans are, just like their clothes," Veronica says softly. She tells me that they are all suffering from TB, hepatitis, heat rashes, malnutrition, malaria, dysentery, yet they go on working on the roads until they collapse, die, or get transferred to a settlement like Clement Town in Dehra Dun. "Clement Town is much nicer than Byllakuppe, because it's got the Nindroling Gompa, which is Nyingmapa, and the Tashi Goman Gompa, which is Gelugpa, and the small Kargyupa Gompa." She says that the Tibetans are "incredibly adaptable and cheerful," that they have "paranormal energies," that their medicine is "remarkable," and "even though most Westerners think it's ghastly how casual Tibetans are about corpses, the Tibetans are probably the most civilized people in the world when it comes to dying." She says they don't bury their dead, but leave the corpses above ground for the hyenas and vultures to deal with. "If you think about it," she says, "it's nice to be laid out beneath the sun and the stars to be picked neat and clean and made one with Nature so promptly. The Tibetans make ceremonial bowls out of skulls to remind one of the impermanence of the material universe—" She breaks off as Dilgo Rinpoche, who has been summoned to receive me, appears, an old man with a shy smile full of crooked teeth.

I give him Jhamchoe's letter in its hand-made rough paper envelope and my own envelope stuffed with a wad of dollars and rupee notes, which he slips unopened into the folds of his maroon *chuba*. His nose is broad and snub. His smooth skull is covered with thin, silvery stubble. His almond-shaped eyes have an intent look of concentration, intelligence. He has come to the transit camp today to share in the act of dying, to "accompany" a woman who has died earlier in the day on her journey, assisting her through meditation to travel into the unknown without fear. She was an old woman, he tells Veronica, who was skilled in developing *tum-mo*, inner heat, psychic fire. She could raise her bodily heat as much as fifteen degrees Fahrenheit, and sustain it, which made it possible for her to survive her flight from Tibet during the winter months.

Internal temperature doesn't rise, Veronica explains to me, just the surface temperature of the body, enough so that neophytes in the practice of *tum-mo* yoga drape cold, wet sheets over their naked bodies and have contests to see who can dry them the fastest. Heat meditation combines powers of concentration, breathing exercises, and yogic exercises to acquire deeper knowledge of paranormal energies—untapped forces that lie within all human beings.

Dilgo Rinpoche says that these exceptional but existing energies, when properly directed, could lead humanity away from destruction toward liberation and self-realization. They can correct misperceptions of reality by producing heat in the body to burn away the emotional defilements that interfere with a proper outlook on life. Moral exercise is more important than physical exercise, he says.

But physically, heat-meditation is very useful and beneficial, Veronica interjects. How else could Buddhist monks survive swimming in icy water? Meditate for months in freezing cold mountain caves? If the old woman hadn't been an adept in the meditational practices of *tum-mo*, her fingers, nose, and toes would have frozen, and probably would have developed gangrene and required amputation. Instead, given the mind's ability to influence the body, she was able to dilate the blood vessels in her extremities and raise the temperature in them by eight degrees Centigrade. Nothing all that special about that, Veronica says. Lots of people can do *that*. I scribble in my notebook and pass it behind Dilgo Rinpoche's back to Veronica:

> Here I sit in a self-kindled glow
> Thinking about the practice of *tum-mo*.

Veronica says that some Tibetan Buddhists can sit in a cross-legged position and then, keeping the same position, leap *six feet* into the air. I tell her that I'm not interested in what seems to me to be the total impossibility of leaping into the air while in the lotus position, but I would like to know more about dying without fear.

Dilgo Rinpoche seats himself on a bench beneath a *pipal* tree, and gestures to us to sit beside him. He speaks no English.

Veronica enjoys showing off her skills as an interpreter as she translates what Dilgo Rinpoche says.

"There is a ritual meaning and significance to man's last hours on earth, and Tibetans place special emphasis on the conditions of consciousness at the time of death. In the Tantric system of Buddhism, death is a cessation of breath, of coarse winds and energies; the heart is no longer beating, and there is a vague indication that appears near the time of death as to the nature of one's rebirth.

"The hours preceding death and the hours after death affect the journey to Bardo, a dreamlike state that is the transitional stage between life and death. A dying person's emotional and mental state will influence and, to some degree, control, his afterlife and rebirth pattern." I like this thought. It seems natural and basic. Why shouldn't people, like some fruit, attain their best after they have been harvested, like pears and apples plucked from their branches, hard, sour, no longer able to grow, but alive, taking in oxygen, giving off carbon dioxide, respiring until they reach a sweet, soft, mellow climax before their tegument rots and their seeds are released? This analogy seems too simple to broach, and I don't want to interrupt the flow of Dilgo Rinpoche's speech. Yet I feel he knows what I am thinking, for as he continues to speak, I sense my mind set in the ground like a healthy plant, upright and firmly earthed.

Dilgo Rinpoche goes on. The nature of the Bardo experience is influenced not only by the degree of enlightenment attained by the dying person, but by the supportive services of the attendant family members, friends, and lamas as well. The rites of passage are very important. In the act of dying, the departing spirit must have peace and time to leave its physical house, its physical habitation, and the dying are urged to make a mindful effort to assure that this is so, to meditate so that their individual consciousness is better able to let go its hold on that forever in-flux state of human life and to experience the clear light of the void. A person who dies without much physical deterioration will remain in the state of the subtlest mind, the mind of clear light, for about three days. Some people can identify with the deep nature of their mind and are able to realize it or recognize it, and remain in it for a week or even a month. The living and the dead are divided by only the most diaphanous of veils. All living things are perfectible. Just as life begins slowly in the womb there must be the balancing state of Bardo at the end of life.

"All life is suffering," Veronica goes on, translating. "All life is filled with a sense of pervasive unsatisfactoriness. Everyone's mind suffers an ongoing tension between negative emotions of hatred, pride, envy, greed, and positive qualities of awareness, generosity, and love. The purpose of *tum-mo* is to help the mind escape such afflictive emotions. Disease can block or disrupt the passage of *prana*, the vital force of energy."

Dilgo Rinpoche turns his head toward me to smile. His crooked-toothed smile is one of the sweetest I have ever seen. He closes his eyes. The look is familiar, perceptibly different from napping upright. He is meditating. There is an aura of concentrated mindfulness about him, quite different from sleep.

The *act* of dying, not just passively letting life ebb away like water draining from a bathtub, but actively participating in one's own death, is a new idea to me, and I find it strangely comforting. I visualize *prana* as an underground river rising to meet a rainbow in a rush of blue energy and sparkling colors, a marvelous circle with myself as its vertical diameter. Diameter, Demeter. I long for the energy to charge through me. I feel only a pulse, a spark, a tremor through a breach in the withered husk of myself, but even that is enough to lift me from the bench.

Suddenly I am assailed again by the moldy smell of dysentery and sick bodies, a smell like decaying bulbs and old mushrooms, of damp earth under old stones. I remember being enveloped in just such a smell as a small child, sitting beneath a forsythia bush in a webby world of minute crawling, wriggling, darting things: maggots writhing in the body of a dead field mouse. An inchworm hunched like a green horseshoe on a forked twig above it suddenly dropped on a silken thread to swing above the dead mouse. The silken thread lengthened, prismatic in the dappled cool, thin as the longest thread of spit I could string between my thumb and first finger, a translucent thread of life. It is one thing to sever that thread when one is old, to perform the act of dying full of years and dignity. It is another to suffer as the people I see around us suffer. How can they experience *prana*, which is blocked by disease? How *can* meditation be enough? *Om MONEY pared may hum*. I wish I had hundreds more dollars, thousands more to provide food and comfort for these suffering, gentle-faced men, women, and children. "Have they got any pain-killers, any antibiotics here?" I ask Veronica. "Isn't there a hospital somewhere, isn't there a surgeon who could be called in?"

"You're such a Westerner, Mummy," she snaps. "You're such a Westerner. Tibetan medicine treats the whole problem, not just the symptoms as Western medicine does." Then she mutters, "Oh, gosh, now look what you've done." Dilgo Rinpoche has quietly disappeared. My blue energy with its sparkling colors dries up midstream. I must have driven him away. But no, he is coming back, accompanied by a man in a white shirt and khaki pants. It is the *emchi*, a Tibetan doctor. Veronica tells me that an *emchi* is invaluable, "a sort of peripatetic paramedic." The *emchi* is here on a visit, filling in for the regular *emchi* who has been called away to Mongod down south where his father has just died. This *emchi* speaks English. This *emchi* is a colleague of Dr. Yeshi Donden, the personal physician of His Holiness the Dalai Lama. This *emchi* has just returned from a medical seminar at Harvard and is glad to talk with me about Tibetan medicine during the afternoon lull before most of the roadworkers return. A dribble of new energy; a tentative scribble.

Western medicine acts quickly and is helpful in relieving acute symptoms, says the *emchi*, while Tibetan medicine acts gradually over a longer period of time. A Tibetan physician sees health as a state depending on diet, behavior (speech, thoughts, and acts) seasonal influences, psychological and social factors. Qualified practitioners of spiritual medicine and materialistic medicine often work together in treating a patient and, from ancient times, Tibetan physicians have emphasized the importance of preventive medicine. Records from the eighth century show that vaccines for smallpox were prepared from "a bovine extract" and injected into a patient's skin by means of a sharp sliver of bamboo.

For diagnostic purposes, Tibetan medicine relies upon a cup of the patient's urine, which "reflects his state of health as clearly as a mirror"; also, by feeling the radial arteries of both the patient's wrists, a physician can tell from the interplay of subtle pulses the condition of the patient's stomach, liver, intestines, heart, kidneys—a technique which takes five years of study and ten years of practice to master. "They are like voices shouting across an open field in summer," the *emchi* says. Illness, he adds, is a loss of "oneness" inside oneself. The disharmony a patient experiences makes him weak and receptive to all kinds of diseases. Since all parts of one's being interact, any one pain or problem has to be considered within the context of a person's total condition so that a sense of inner harmony and outer calm can be restored.

The *emchi* has used Western antibiotics, such as penicillin and tetracycline. And yes, he has dispensed Lomotil, Metamucil, Novocain, codeine, morphine, cortisone, aspirin, Tylenol, and other Western medicines donated by various relief organizations. He admires the techniques of Western surgery. However, he says, the role of karma can never be underestimated. The quality of the next lifetime depends upon this lifetime, in which it is to be hoped an adverse balance of merit acquired in previous existences has been righted. All sicknesses are karmas, and there is a definite connection between moral life and physical well-being.

Tibetans, he says, are more participatory than Westerners in their healing process. They make an effort to "be there" in full consciousness while they are sick and while they are recuperating. "If they have a fever, they will not sleep it off, but let themselves experience the fever by staying awake. They will do *puja*, and attend purification rituals performed by lamas. Curing and enlightening are often the same process." Ceremony and correct practice are important to the success of remedies by which even sicknesses brought on by karma can be overcome. Healthiness has to do with being pure, diminishing the physical

and demonic forces of the self in favor of spiritual dominance.
In cases of chronic ailments, such as epilepsy, diabetes, digestive
problems, leukemia, breast cancer, throat cancer, and schizo-
phrenia, Tibetan medicine has been "very successful."

The most common complaint among Tibetan refugees is
loong, a disease relating to the excess of wind in the body, a
problem of the mind, a physical weakness derived from an unhappy, problematic, unsettled existence, and often not enough
food. If they suffer too long from *loong*, they often become
tubercular.

As the *emchi* has been speaking, several refugees have gathered around us. A woman with a goiter as big as an orange
beneath her chin says that black mushrooms clean the hairs of
the intestines. She has come from Bhutan, where she was injected with iodized oil which has caused her goiter to shrink
from the size of "a small coconut" the *emchi* tells me, holding
out his hands to show how much larger the goiter had been
before it was treated. He says that in some Himalayan regions
the soil and water are so lacking in natural iodine that even the
goats and sheep develop goiters; the enlargement of the thyroid
gland is the way a person's body adapts to the deficiency. Goiters
are not life-threatening, but iodine deficiency can cause many
more serious problems: mental retardation, stunted growth,
impaired motor performance, deafness and mutism. The Indian
government's new iodization plants and monitoring laborato-
ries should solve the problem in time, he says. The woman tells
me that *ghee* heals cracking and dry skin on the soles of the feet,
that goat's meat cooked with butter can heal severe wounds,
that *tsampa* (roasted barley flour) mixed with butter can be applied to cuts to keep them clean and clot the blood, that rubbing

tsampa on the afflicted member can cure aches and pains. It is a long time, she adds, since she tried doing that, because she had no *tsampa* left over after she escaped from Tibet. Eating raw sugar prevents grass poisoning, she says, and so does eating roasted radishes. Pomegranates are good for indigestion and stomach trouble. Apricot kernels prevent baldness, but should not be eaten by pregnant women. *Chang* (rice beer) can cure kidney disease and also is helpful if you have *loong*. Wearing furs or extra layers of cloth and shawls around your waist protects you from colds. Other informants volunteer that a red string on which a lama has breathed mantras will provide protection against impurities and pollution, that amulets composed of the preserved relics of a lama's body will protect the wearer against sickness, that an amulet endowed with a blessing of Dilgo Rinpoche saved the life of a baby. A young boy points to scabs on his arms and says that he has applied stamps printed with special mantras to heal the open sores that had caused him great pain the week before. An old man opens his mouth and shows me a gold-capped tooth he says is a protection against poison.

As I listen to this mixture of common sense, faith and placebos, I remember Veronica at the age of two, stricken during a polio epidemic in Johannesburg, after having received only one shot of Jonas Salk's recently marketed vaccine. Our doctor recommended that she be taken to the local Fever Hospital. "Only her legs will be paralyzed," he said, trying to comfort me. I insisted on keeping her at home, moving her legs night and day, telling her when she was awake and asleep that she was going to be all right, that she must keep her legs moving and let me exercise them, that she was going to be all right, that she must stand up and try to walk, that she was going to be all right, all right, all right, all right. And so she was. Within a week, she was walking, a bit stiff-legged, with me holding her, but walking, up and down the corridor from our bedroom to the living room and back. Our doctor said he had never seen anything like her recovery, that maybe it had been an aborted case of polio, that maybe it had been a miracle.

The *emchi* tells me that many more refugees would have died if they had not been treated with Tibetan therapies, with herbal remedies and blood-letting ("No more leeches," he says, smiling. "We use syringes now."), with massage, with acupuncture, with moxibustion (the practice of burning herbs on or near the skin as a form of cautery). Of course. Didn't my grandmother believe in the burning of St. John's Wort to exorcise evil spirits and disease in the Eliott estate's barns and byres? Everywhere on the property there was smoke from leaping bonfires. Great bundles of the yellow flower with "the blood" dripping from its stems were smoked, the glandular dots on the vulnerary leaves shining, translucent. This plant called *hypericon* by the Greeks and *herba Sancti Johannis* by the medieval monks of Canterbury, this plant which had to be picked on the morning of the twenty-third of June before sunrise, and burned that evening, the Eve of St. John, the night before St. John's Day when the dried, smoked flowers would be carried inside the house so that "there shall come no wicked spirit within."

The *emchi* tells me that the Four Tantras delineate some eighty-four thousand diseases grouped into eleven hundred and four separate categories, for which two thousand mixtures of herbs and minerals are prescribed as remedies and preventive medicine. Dr. Yeshi Donden, he says, also emphasizes the heal-

ing aspects of compassion. Folk medicine, he says, places particular emphasis on diet, which is more affordable than herbal
remedies and is often the only form of treatment available in
areas where refugees can afford neither to make a journey to
visit an *emchi* nor to buy the various pills and liquids he might
prescribe.

All medicinal plants, he tells me, should be collected in the
right season, when their power and properties are at their peak.
Roots, trunks, and branches in the autumn. Leaves, shoots, and
sap in the monsoon season. Flowers and fruits in the late autumn or when the fruits are not fully ripe. Bark, inner bark, and
resins in the spring. All medicines should be collected in the
waxing of the moon.

Giving me the Tibetan names, and then the Latin nomencla-
ture, and a few common English terms with which he is familiar,
the *emchi* describes the major medicinal herbs found in the Kulu
valley and on Triund mountain in Dharamsala in the Kangra
valley.

Achillea sibirica is effective for back-aches and blood disorder.
Achillea millefolium, the common yarrow, is used to cure ulcers,
piles, skin wounds. Datura is good for neuralgia and as a vermi-
fuge. Artemisia is good for rheumatism. Motherwort, or *Leonu-
rus Artemisia*, is a contraceptive. *Artemisia vulgaris*, or Mugwort,
when boiled as a drink, aids in curing dysentery and diarrhea,
prevents colds and rheumatism and coughing blood, is soothing
during pregnancy. The root of the periwinkle is good for heart
diseases, its leaves and twigs can be beneficially chewed for
stomach cramps. *Pictorhiza* and *Chiretta* are good for jaundice
and fever. *Ts'ersgnon*, or *mecanopsis*, the Himalayan blue poppy,

and *Achillea sibirica* are not only effective for back-aches and heart disorders, but may also have the rejuvenating qualities some *emchis* attribute as well to powdered amber and camphor.

Now the *emchi* ticks off a few of the hundreds of useful plants that can also be found in Sikkim and Ladakh and near the border of Tibet, areas mostly in the mountains above nine thousand feet. There are *Astor Flaccidus*, *Corydalis*, *Pictorhiza*, *Achillea Sibirica*, Meadow crane's bill, *Artemisia*, *Chiretta*, *Paraquillegia Microphylla*, and the Himalayan silver fir which the Tibetans call *Balu*. Near the border of Tibet, there is much *Gentian*: here, and also in Sikkim, there is the Utpal flower; *Ephedra* from Sikkim and La-dakh is ground into powder, blended by hand, and formed into little round balls at the dispensary of the Tibetan Medical Centre in Dharamsala.

I am enthralled. I have always believed in the power of plants. Veronica once sent me a packet of *Mehn Drub*, a sacred herbal medicine, and a star-shaped seed pod, writing that the seeds it contained were an all-purpose remedy for maintaining good health and controlling anger. She suggested I find someone to analyze the ingredients and market them commercially so we could make "lots of money for the Tibetans." I had approached a few pharmaceutical companies and been discouraged by their skepticism and negativity.

The *emchi* smiles. The East could learn a lot from the West about medical practices and surgical techniques, he says, and the West could learn a lot from the East. Maybe some day they will work together, share their knowledge, and develop new techniques. Tibetan herbal medicines, he says, can be safely used by anyone because they have no side effects. He quotes from the Root Tantra that is the basis of all Tibetan medical knowledge: "Touching [reading the pulses], seeing [examining the urine], and questioning, all is known."

A ridiculous memory springs to mind. My mother is pouring tea from a large round silver teapot into my cup, and then adding milk and a lump of sugar. When bubbles appear on the tea's silky tan surface, she exclaims with the excess of enthusiasm that marks her social manner, "Aha, good fortune for you, my treasure. Money!" Later, looking down at my unflushed pee in the toilet bowl, I exclaim to my nanny who has to be shown all results of Number One and Number Two before they can be flushed away, "Oh, look, look, Nanny! Look at all the money!" Inexplicably, Nanny is as disapproving as my mother was enthusiastic. Tea in a cup was fine, but suffered a change in color and acceptability after it filtered through my body. Money was nice, tea was nice. My body was not nice. Pee was not nice. Was that why as a child I sometimes thought of myself as little peewee Leelee? I recall the man who styled himself a "one-man piss mission," that naturopath at a New Delhi cocktail party who believed drinking one's own urine was healthful. Urine for a treat. Urine for a surprise.

I am to think of the *emchi* again when I am back in America, reading a book called *Mortal Lessons: Notes on the Art of Surgery* by Dr. Richard Selzer. He records the examination of a female patient by the Dalai Lama's personal physician who is holding the pulsating wrist of the woman beneath his fingers.

He speaks of winds coursing through the body of the woman, currents that break against barriers, eddying. These vortices are in her blood, he says. The last spendings of an imperfect heart. Between the chambers of her heart, long, long before she was born, a wind had come and blown open a deep gate that must never be opened. Through it charge the full waters of her river, as the mountain stream cascades in the springtime, battering, knocking loose the land, and flooding her breath. Thus he speaks, and is silent.

"May we now have the diagnosis?" a professor asks.

The host of these rounds, the doctor who knows, answers. "Congenital heart disease," he says. "Interventricular septal defect, with resultant heart failure."

A gateway in the heart, I think, that must not be opened. Through it charge the full waters that flood her breath. Here, then, is a Tibetan doctor listening to the sounds of her body to which Western doctors are deaf.

"Not to be satisfied in this life is a big sin," the *emchi* says. He himself makes daily offerings to reduce his "desire, malicious thoughts, hatred" and reflects that his belief in deed and consequence helps him to avoid sin. I scribble all this in my notebook with a catechumen's energy.

> By oneself alone is evil done,
> By oneself is one defiled,
> By oneself is evil avoided:
> By oneself is one purified.
> No one can purify another.

I like the thought of death as the end of one life and the beginning of another in a spiritual form. All my life, to me, has been a succession of the killing of old selves and the struggle and release of changed "new-selves," not completely new and not completely changed, but somewhat altered and renewed. All my life I have been conscious of a feeling of continual education; of continual rebirth, with death, perhaps, the ultimate rebirth. Every day like a little life, every sleep like a little death, then waking into life again.

How extraordinary that I should have thought Veronica has gone somewhere I cannot follow. I've been with her all the time in the underworld of my unconscious.

The *emchi* is looking at me. The *emchi*, the M.D. I hear an actor in a film singing a tune in a parody of an Indian accent:

> From New Delhi to Darjeeling,
> I've done my share of healing.
> I remember how with one jab
> Of my needle in the Punjab
> How I stopped the beriberi
> And the dreaded dysentery.

"You'll be the death of me, Miss Leila," says Holloway, Granny's Cockney lady's maid, in a similar voice. "You'll be the death of me," she says, laughing, laughing, over forty years ago, this illegitimate daughter of Edward VII, who kneels to buckle Granny's evening slippers. She answers every summons with, "Yes, Milady, I'm coming, Milady, I'll do it, I'll mend it, I'll fix it, right away, Milady." That nice, kind Holloway, how could I make her die laughing? And then Bryce, quoting Fiddler Jones in *Spoon River Anthology*, who wanted to die with a thousand laughs and not a single regret. I guess I did, too, in a way, but death always scared me: the feeling of losing control, of being at the mercy of terrible, immutable forces, of leaving everything and everyone one loves. Now something Dilgo Rinpoche has said about dying has lifted the fear, has made me feel less worried about Veronica lost in an underworld, and all of my world dying with her departure. Sometimes if I stand still and let all my thoughts run around me, their circumference narrows with their circumambulation—yes, circumambulation—and finally, they all join together in one spot. I see this revelation as I see Veronica's and my interior journeys, journeys within journeys, like concentric circles, our journeys together ever-diminishing while the distance between us becomes less and less, our closeness gathering in on itself, closer and closer, becoming like the *bindu* mark, the *tika*, the eye of knowledge that Hindu women place in the center of their forehead.

Dilgo Rinpoche has returned. He speaks again about the act of dying, and Bardo state, the knowledge that if one conducts this lifetime in a mindful way, it will be beneficial in the next. He looks at me. The *emchi* looks at me. I look back at each of them, then at Veronica. The four of us, a quarternary, tetramorphs, symbolic of the earth, terrestrial space, the human situation, the natural limits of our awareness of totality. Four, half of eight, the symbol of regeneration.

From New Delhi to Darjeeling, I've done my share of healing. I look at the *emchi* with affection. I look at Dilgo Rinpoche with affection. I look at Veronica with love. A space seems to fill my mind, giving me a feeling of peace. Somehow things are going to be all right.

"You have a worm on your sleeve," Veronica says. We are sitting with our legs stretched before us in lawn chairs in the hotel garden. She leans toward me to slide the crescent moon of her fingernail beneath what—an inchworm? No, a silkworm. We are sitting beneath the shade of a mulberry tree. "There," Veronica says, placing the silkworm back on a branch of the mulberry tree. "Its front end is backward," she says. "It has horns on its tail."

Extraordinary that such lovely stuff as silk should come from the excretions of worms feeding from mulberry trees, understandable that so perfect a fabric should be venerated, a fabric as paradoxical as love and religion, its silken threads clues to the beauty which rustles like leaves in our hearts.

"Just think, each little worm spins a cocoon made of a half-mile of filament," my Aunt Vera once said to me, flourishing a wreath of flowers she had fashioned from cocoons. The wreath was a present for my mother. My mother had no idea what to do with it. She wrapped it in tissue paper, put it in a box labeled "Vera's wreath," and stowed it away in the attic.

I adored my Aunt Vera. She taught me how to draw and garden, and gave me a white leather-bound book of fairytales illustrated by Edmund Dulac on pages edged with gold. She was often spoken of disparagingly by family members for marrying Uncle Jack, a journalist and entrepreneur who was always going broke in "hare-brained ventures," as my mother referred to them. Aunt Vera's and Uncle Jack's final fling before they died within a month of each other, was a silkworm farm in the Bahamas. By then, her life and his had become an interchangeable larva and cocoon, each encasing and encased by the other.

Now I see Veronica and myself as chrysalides emerging from separate cocoons, side by side, "putting out our feelers."

Twenty-Six

Between Manali and Dharamsala, blue and white prayer flags printed with images and Tibetan script fly from poles stuck in cairns along the narrow asphalt road, and line each side of the suspension bridges across the Beas. They are homage to the gods of rivers and mountains, an aid to travelers to help secure their safety. "What works for the Buddhists, works for the Hindus," Parvin says, smiling.

The Tibetans, like the vanished Aryans of the Vedas, revere the white wind and the blue sky. Blue and white are the celestial colors of the ancient Bon sky god, who is an embodiment of space and light according to the indigenous religion of Tibet that was absorbed by Buddhist traditions. The reversed swastikas roughly inscribed on many of the cairn stones are images from the Bon religion, too—as well as being an emblem of Thor and Troy, Veronica tells me, recalling the research she did for her book on talismans. "Variously considered to bring good luck, to reverse time, to be associated with magic, and an archaic symbol of creation that occurs everywhere in the world except south of the Sahara and Australia, quote unquote," she explains.

A boat shaped like a crescent moon with a huge patched sail drifts along the Beas. Veronica says that when the monsoon comes, the river is filled with fishing boats like these.

As she speaks, I listen to the windbells attached to the prayer flags. The bells confide spiritual longings to the winds, to the creatures of the upper air, the garudas, griffins, and dragons revered by followers of Bon.

Dharamsala, Dharamsala, Dharamsala. Ever nearer, ever closer.

What will I say to the Dalai Lama in my interview with him? I picture myself showing him the copy of his book which Jhamchoe gave me. I hear myself asking him about its great themes of love and compassion, but will that be enough? What else should I ask him? What else should I say? Can I ask him to tell me the story of his being discovered at the age of two as the reincarnation of his predecessor, the thirteenth Dalai Lama? Can I ask him about the high-ranking lamas who visited the farmhouse in Takster in the province of Amdo where he was born? Can I ask him about the tests in which he was asked to remember objects and people from his previous lives? (No, no, I want the little drum, not the big one with the golden straps, *this mala*, not *that* one . . . *that* walking stick.)

Can I talk with him about the striking parallels between the birth of Christ and his own reincarnation? "The star, which they saw in the east went before them, 'til it came and stood over where the young child was." When the search for the fourteenth Dalai Lama began, there were many indications that he would also be found in the east. Clouds with auspicious shapes appeared in that direction; flowers grew unexpectedly from the base of a pillar. The body of the thirteenth Dalai Lama, which had been seated on a throne facing south, soon turned its face toward the east. On a wooden pillar on the northeastern side of the shrine where the body sat, "a great star-shaped fungus appeared," the fourteenth Dalai Lama recounts in his memoirs *My Land and My People*. High lamas and dignitaries, "wise men," searched for the fourteenth Dalai Lama just as wise men searched for the child who was born King of the Jews. Both children were born of peasant parents. Both children grew up to be great teachers who preached a gospel of love and compassion.

Can I ask him how he felt at the age of four-and-a-half when he was installed on the Lion Throne in Lhasa as the supreme temporal and spiritual ruler of Tibet? Or would these questions be gross impertinences? Would it be more appropriate to ask him about his present role as a political figure and religious leader? Suppose I disgrace myself, trip over one of his Lhasa Apsos, sit down or stand up at the wrong time, what then? And the ceremonial white silk *kathak*, however am I supposed to present him with that? Mummy and Granny were unfailingly correct in matters of social behavior and protocol. When Granny saw that I had addressed a Christmas card to the Earl and Earless of Minto, she remarked dourly that she despaired of my ever mastering the art of decorum. There was no way I was going to get by with mere good intentions, she said.

The stunning beauty of the approach to Dharamsala blows away all thought specks and no new crystal forms. *Dharamsala*, a resting place, the site of an ancient Hindu sanctuary sloped along a spur of the Dhauladar range, is of such peculiar intensity that nothing will do but to have Parvin stop the car and release me from it. Ours is the only car in sight for miles around. It is the hour of cow dust, and delicate shudders spiral through my body. "It's like the marriage bed. It's like making love with the world!" I say to Veronica.

All around us the fields of the Kangra plain are bathed in a honey-yellow light. The sweet-smelling air is festive with the confetti of orange, white, and pale blue butterflies. Beyond the fields, the water courses in the lower hills shine silver in the sun, and above the hills, three pinnacles of the colossal Dhauladar glittering with perpetual snow soar into the sky above Dharamsala.

A lone *pahari* heading toward us strides barefoot along the road. His *kurta* is white, his vest black, his white breeches reaching just below his knees, a costume at once magpie and magical, with a red, white, and yellow turban, gold earrings, silver wrist bangles. He stops abreast of us. His eyes, so dark that they appear chipped from onyx or ebony, come alive. He gives the dusty car and our three faces a quick, sharp glance, nods his head in greeting, and moves on. A truly beautiful male face, so stunning that I see it only as an abstraction, as if it were a proofread, punctuated text.

Tibetan faces are so different, Veronica says as we get back into the car. When she first arrived in Dharamsala and saw the Tibetan coolies with their faces smeared with *ghee* and ocher as a protection against cold and insects, "so buttery, so flat," she had been unfavorably impressed. But then she saw how open their expressions were, without defense, so free, so generous, so accepting of the large and small events of every day, the faces of the monks so wise and calm. "Just don't expect stunning beauty as an everyday occurrence," she warns.

Beauty *can* be stunning. But beauty is best when it is not anesthetizing, when it allows you to feel, to think. Beauty is best when it is like a tree, a symbol of ever-renewing growth and self-unfoldment, like Swinburne's many-rooted tree that "swells in the sky," declaring "that life-tree am I, in the buds of your lives is the sap of my leaves; ye shall live and not die." Robert is buried beneath a pine tree, and I think of him now as the air cools and we begin our ascent to Dharamsala.

We pass the depot where buses are parked, their sides painted in florid patterns and hues, and printed with names which seem wonderfully evocative to me: HILL QUEEN, SNOW VALLEY VIEW, SNOW VIEW TRANSPORT, ZAMANA BUD. They are parked every which way, forming a sort of starburst pattern around a large signboard with a hodgepodge handwritten listing of their destinations: Simla, Kulu, Manali, Jammu, Patiala, Kalimpong, Pathancot, Nagrota, Orissa, Hoshiarpur, Mussoorie, Dehra Dun, Chandigarh, Chamba, Amritsar, Delhi. A troop of rhesus monkeys lopes around the buses, some heading toward the trees around the depot and the forests ahead. The variety of trees here is extraordinary. Tree rhododendrons, deodars, oaks, cedars, blue spruce, alders, a few maples, limes, apple trees around the low village, kamela trees with orange-red bark, long-leafed pines. Mythical trees, Biblical trees, and fruit-laden trees, bending, stretching, sky-tickling trees. I want to leap out of the car and run from one to the next, hug them all and be a tree myself. My mother's name was Beatrice, but I want to be a tree, be a tree, be a tree.

I think of the linden tree where my tree house was, where I

imagined I was Kim and the Holy Man when I was a child. I remember climbing trees. The Japanese peach tree by my bedroom window was too small and fragile to climb, but the maple tree beyond, *that* was a tree to climb. Scholars say that climbing a tree is a variant of the initiatory journey, a deliberately induced altered state in which, like a shaman, one can explore other realms of consciousness. Climbing trees, scholars say, is like ascending stairs or ladders, symbolic of a magical flight to celestial realms.

I am still carrying on this mental "blither tangent," as Veronica would say, as we offload our luggage at the Dhauladar Hotel. An Indian government establishment, it is the tallest building in Dharamsala. We are shown to a ground-floor reception room which opens onto a balcony shaded by a banyan tree.

The banyan tree, the *pipal* tree, the Bodhi tree, the Bo tree— Veronica says she didn't realize they were all names for the same tree until she went to Buddhagaya or Bodhgaya, the holiest of holy places, the first sacred pilgrimage place where the original Bodhi tree stood, the one which Buddha sat beneath when he attained enlightenment.

The banyan, the Bo tree, the mythical cosmic tree of the Vedas, the upside-down-tree rooted in the heavens, with branches of ether, air, fire, water and earth, extending below. I like the idea of our being rooted in the Divine, in the higher planes of consciousness in which the good-evil opposites of conditioned existence don't obtain. I love the idea of the Tree of Life and the Tree of Knowledge and the Jesse Tree in the Old and New Testaments. Odin was hung on a tree. Christ was crucified. Siddhartha sat under the Bo Tree until he attained Nirvana and realized supreme enlightenment. The Bo tree, whose roots are in the awakening matter of the physical body, whose trunk is the development of enlightening transformation, whose branches are the creative self-extensions of our being, and whose fruit is the spiritual food of immortality.

The presence of the banyan tree pulls at me like a tidal current, and I run my fingers across the rippling bark of its trunk. I think of birds eating the fruit of the banyan and dropping the seeds which germinate and grow, nourished by nothing more than rain and air. Jung wrote that if a *mandala* may be described as a symbol of the Self seen in cross section, "then the tree would represent a profile view of the Self depicted as a process of growth." I like the idea of the miracle of the tiny seed, the potential of both the tree and the fertilized ovum, trees and people unfolding. Veronica told me once of a Buddhist Tantric text about the seed of pure compassion which grows into a wish-fulfilling tree of the openness of Being from which the fruit of pure spirituality will grow. Blake wrote a poem about a tree growing in the human brain. Yeats wrote about a tree growing in the heart. Rilke wrote about a tree that Orpheus sang to, "O tall tree in the ear! And all was silent. Yet even in the silence there was new beginning, beckoning, change."

Parvin returns from his tireless erranding about arrival forms and the disposition of our luggage. He has arranged for tea to be brought to us on the balcony and served beneath the banyan, where we can also enjoy a view of the valley beneath us. The balcony is built above rocks that fall steeply away to tree-tops below. With their peculiar rocking, pitching gait, rhesus monkeys lope along the balcony's edge. A flock of parakeets, in swift flashes of green-yellow, is shrilling, rocketing through the trees, twisting and turning, trying to settle in for the night. They have purplish-bluish-reddish heads and are called blossom-headed parakeets, the early morning robbers of all gardens up to an altitude of five thousand feet. Now they give back to the air what they have looted during the day: color—the green-yellow of sun-washed foliage, and the occasional white splash of their droppings on the balcony's polished tile.

The valley below is flat and pale in the fading light. Veronica says that the fields will dry to a uniform gold in the furnace heat of summer, and that the distant ribbon of a river will turn into a rust-colored torrent in the monsoon. But now it is a spring evening, and the scene which stretches beneath us is peaceful, pastoral, and pale as a leaf of iceberg lettuce. A tiny train comes into view, chuffing up white smoke and hooting mournfully as it makes its way across the valley.

Not far from the hotel, off to the right, Veronica points out the Kotwali Bazaar in the lower village of Dharamsala, "the Indian part." Then, up the rising hill, the Library of Tibetan Works and Archives, and the Kashag, the seat of the Tibetan government in exile; McLeod Ganj where the Tibetan bazaar is; the Tsuglakhang Gompa where Tibetan monks are quartered around the largest Buddhist temple in India and, opposite, the residence of His Holiness, the Dalai Lama. Lower down, and off to the left, is Forsyth Ganj, the road leading to the Tibetan Refugee Children's Village, the hospital and dispensary, and the Gurkha cantonment.

Using the Gurkhas in my lead sentence, I have already begun an article about Dharamsala. "Descendants of Rajput nobles driven by the Moguls in the fourteenth century into Gurkha, a village northwest of Khatmandu in the hill country of what is now Nepal, the Gurkhas raised an army of tribals from the Himalayan foothills, became renowned as the best foot soldiers in Asia, and marched as mercenaries with impeccable courage in campaign after campaign, war after war. It was to house a battalion of Gurkhas that Dharamsala became a cantonment in 1849. The civil authorities, attracted by the climate and scenery, built themselves houses in the neighborhood of the cantonment and in March 1855, the new station was formally recognized as the headquarters of the Kangra District. Sir Donald McLeod, a Lieutenant Governor of the Punjab, was honored by having the bazaar of the upper station and the settlement around it named after him. . . ."

"What a yawn, Mum," Veronica says. "Who wants to know all that?"

Well, I counter, I thought it was an interesting coincidence that James Boswell, her antecedent and mine, had been entertained by and written much about the MacLeods of Dunvegan in Skye, and that one of their clan—his name a spelling variant like the Eliotts, Elliots, and Elliotts—had come from Scotland to India to defend the British Empire, and to lend a hand in quelling the Mutiny of 1847. I thought it intriguing that McLeod had a settlement named after him in which Tibetan refugees are now living, an unlikely but *interesting* connection which links Scotland, India, the Tibetans, and Boswell in my mind.

"*Chut! Hai mai!*" she exclaims, mimicking to perfection Parvin's exasperation when anything is not to his liking. "You've just arrived, and already it's like old home week with the ancestors! Don't you ever see things just as they are, *now*? Why does everything always remind you of something else?"

"Not always, just sometimes."

Her frown, so like my mother's, uncreases. She looks at me with amused tolerance. We both smile. I push back my chair, get up, give her a hug, kiss her on both of her cool pink cheeks. The Dhauladar kisses my mind.

Veronica says that there is a tantalizing sensation on the apparent periphery of understanding that there is still so much unknown, so much to be delved into. Just as one is getting the picture into focus, one's gaze is being drawn into "the limitless unfocusable universe." The lamas have taught her that in order to quench her thirst, she must first pacify that thirst. "And then they laugh! Even if I don't understand how that works. I see how they are examples of wisdom and happiness, effortlessly virtuous, and so I try to follow their directions, lazily, grudgingly . . ." It's not much fun, she says, but wisdom and understanding do arise, "an ultimate hat trick." Loneliness ("the unquenchable kind") and restlessness do diminish, but confronting these emotions is painful. It is difficult to let them be, rather than "to seek their appeasement." Sometimes, she says, when life radiates excitement and beauty, there can be terrible loneliness in that, too. She says she doesn't really know where peace and happiness exist. "The whole deal seems like an impossible-to-bear existence, sometimes, but I try to be energetic in the path I have chosen, investigating my own dissatisfactions and fascinations in the illusion-like nature of the world, where other people can be symbolic of our yearning and our quests, which can only be understood in our own hearts and minds."

Quests and requests. By oneself is one purified. Like a dog padding around and around on a carpet, haunted by ancestral memories of making itself a bed in leaves and twigs, this thought stirs in my mind. I imagine *Canis major*, the dog in the sky, chasing clouds as though they were motorcars, or guarding and guiding flocks of sheep-like clouds. Cirlot says that dogs are associated with the symbolism of the mother and resurrection. I reach for my notebook to scribble about "the love of our singularity and our desire to be singularly loved," and think of the unity of mother and child that we pursue like a phantom throughout all our loves and lives. I add a rhyming line about "the mothering mountains and hills from which our strength derives," then close the notebook, put it back on the table, and give Veronica another hug.

Veronica says that Parvin has taken the car back to his uncle's tea estate in Palampur, and that she has arranged for us to have a Jeep for our transport during our stay. When it's time for us to go to Delhi for me to get the plane back to New York, Parvin will come to fetch us. She and he have worked out all the logistics while I was asleep. "The Jeep will be here soon, Mummy," she says. "You shouldn't walk much until you get used to the altitude." And so begins my first morning in Dharamsala.

The lower station of Dharamsala is across the spur to the right of the Dhauladar Hotel. Its main street is lined with the one-storey shops and a few two-storey buildings in the Kotwali Bazaar: a branch of the State Bank of India, a branch of the Punjab Bank, a post-office, police headquarters, a court-house, a library filled with Victorian and Edwardian books and records, a printing shop, a telephone exchange, a cinema that is closed for repairs, a photography shop with a limited supply of black-and-white film, a bicycle shop with an interior radio jabbering and

twanging noisily; a shop selling pads of paper, notebooks, pencils, pens, ink; several jewelry stores; a shop showing a variety
of fabrics, with a sign saying that it specializes in tailoring uniforms for the local boys' and girls' high-school. An Ayurvedic
dispensary displays a pharmacopoeia which consists largely of
cinnamon, ginger, mercury, arsenic, croton seeds by the sackful,
turmeric, asafoetida, fenugreek. The Indian proprietor of the
perfume and cosmetics shop next door obligingly unstoppers
vials of floral essences for us to sniff. His wife, in a spangled pink
sari and pink *choli*, tells me that the skin of boiled milk would
be good to rub on my face where it is sunburned, and that
yoghurt would also be good as a skin food. She heats a small
dish of mustard oil over a candle, soaks a wad of raw cotton in
the oil, lights it, lets it burn until only the soot is left, and shows
me how she applies this *kajal* on the outside of her eyelids and
inside the lower rims of her magnificent eyes. Not only will *kajal*
enhance the beauty of my eyes but she guarantees it will also
repel gnats and cut down on the glare of the sun. I let her spread
samples of face masks—turmeric soaked in water and ground
to a paste, ground lentils mixed with milk into a paste—on my
arm. When the patches are dry, she wipes them off with a rag
dipped in safflower oil, then wets a stick of sandalwood and
rubs it gently on my skin.

Yes, I can see the difference. I notice beneath the counter a
mound of soapnuts from a *dodan* tree. Their external rinds are
peeled and can be used as an effective cleanser for almost anything, and their heavy kernels are discarded. The small son of
the shopkeeper holds out a soapnut to me in his right hand,
while he clasps a walking stick in his left. As he stands there,
legs apart, he reminds me of a pottery image of Kamara, the

eternal divine child of Shiva, holding a lance in one hand, a piece of fruit in another, and sitting astride a peacock. There is an eighth-century hymn to Kamara:

> When all eternal props fail me
> Be thou my refuge.
> Come with thy lance, mounted on the peacock.
> Bid me, fear not, when the messenger of Death faces me.

The shopkeeper's wife smiles broadly as she looks fondly at her son. "He is a good boy," she says, as he exchanges the soapnut for the coins I give him.

"*Ciao!*" a passing hippie on a bicycle shouts to Veronica as she and I stand in the shop's doorway, looking out on the main street. Horse-drawn carts slowly make their way up and down the street, along with bicycles, motorcycles, a *gaddi* with a flock of sheep and goats, schoolgirls in green jumpers and shirts, schoolboys in green blazers, a few Sikhs, a few hippies, a Tibetan monk in a maroon robe. Stocky Tibetan coolies supporting sacks and tin trunks on their backs by means of a tump line on their foreheads jog to and from the bus depot. Veronica sings out *Tashidelek* to them, and they return the greeting as they swivel their heads to smile at her. Veronica says they have helped her move so many times that they are all old friends.

Circuitous switchback routing connects the lower and upper stations of Dharamsala. The shortest switchback route is accessible by foot, by horse—a few stretches are negotiable by bicycle and motorcycle—and by Jeep, our new mode of transportation, with an official Indian driver provided by the hotel. He sits in front. We sit in back. Raising her voice to be heard above the grinding gears and the stertorous engine of the Jeep, Veronica says that ascending the mountain from the lower station to the upper station is like going from one world to another, from India to Tibet, from Delhi to "little Lhasa. One step at a time," she says. "*Festina lente.*"

We reach the area of Gangchen Kyishong (Abode of Snow, Happy Valley), a community where everything has been built since the arrival of His Holiness, the Dalai Lama in Dharamsala in 1960—the Delek Hospital, the Dispensary, the schools, the *Kashag* or Secretariat of the Tibetan government-in-exile, the living quarters for some of the government officials and lamas who are employed by the Library of Tibetan Works and Archives, and the Library itself. All the buildings are two-storeyed with flat or gently slanting roofs, all are white, all are trimmed with turquoise or rust-red paint. "But the temple in McLeod Ganj and the Library are the prettiest," Veronica says. All are mounted on platforms raised above ground level, to which they are connected with many steps. When we are out of the Jeep, I stop to photograph the steps, and hear myself talk-talk-talking about them. Steps which lead from the first platform to a second narrower platform, steps which lead from the second platform to the entranceway, steps which ascend like a ladder or a spiraling staircase heighten the effect of progression, steps which are a humbling reminder that nothing worth having is easy of access, steps which hint of rewards concealed at their summit.

"Really?" Veronica's tone is quizzical. She says she doesn't think there's anything symbolical about steps, although, admittedly, the Tibetans seem very big on them. She says they are just a protective measure against dust, snakes, the torrential rains and dampness of the monsoon, the winter snows and slush.

Gangchen Kyishong has a somewhat raw, unfinished look, a

look of newness with construction still underway. There is also a pleasingly tranquil and durable aspect about this place enfolded by the Dhauladar and its forested ridges, tall deodars always in sight in the spaces between the buildings. Prayer flags are strung from deodar to deodar, and from rooftop to rooftop, their bannered mantras ever a reminder that all that is or was or will ever be is here right now, ever changing.

At the Information Office of the *Kashag*, the Central Tibetan Secretariat, there is a plaque bearing the governmental seal of Tibet: two snow lions holding the wheel of the Buddhist dharma, standing on a scroll printed with Tibetan script, with the sun, moon, trees and mountains in the background. We are ushered to the reception room, where there are banquettes covered with dark red and green rugs, cushioned with yellow bolsters. The Deputy Director and the Deputy Secretary, the Director in Western dress, the Secretary in a monk's robe receive us as we stand facing a framed photograph of the Potala, the Dalai Lama's palace in Lhasa, its vast, inward-sloping walls containing more than a thousand rooms, and some ten thousand altars, as well as the gilded tombs of eight Dalai Lamas. Dharamsala is now called Little Lhasa, not that there is any comparison in terms of splendor, of course, but, as the Director says, "Wherever Yeshi Norbu, the Precious One, the Wish-Fulfilling Gem, resides, there is the Holy City."

"If His Holiness sees with his own eyes and hears with his own ears that the Tibetans are happy under Chinese rule, he will give up the demand for a free Tibet. He will accept it as our destiny," the Secretary says.

"A big 'if,'" says the Director. "The policies of the Chinese are changeable. The white cat may become black. The black cat may become white. It does not matter whether the cat is black or white as long as it catches mice."

His Holiness is in retreat at this very moment, praying for the problem's harmonious resolution and, unfortunately, all interviews for the next fortnight have been canceled, including the appointment Veronica scheduled for me long ago. The Director regrets this disappointing news but, he says, perhaps I may be able to see His Holiness during one of his informal audiences at the Tsuglakhang Gompa, the Thekchen Choeling, the great Buddhist temple-cum-university, while preparations are in progress for the Kalachakra ceremony. When Veronica explains that we will be unable to stay in Dharamsala to see this ceremony performed, the Director suggests that perhaps, when His Holiness travels to America, I will be able to see the ceremony performed there. While the Director has been speaking, I have felt my anxiety and apprehension about my interview with the Dalai Lama being replaced with regret, the sense of losing an opportunity that I hadn't even realized I had hoped for.

The Secretary says that Padma Sambhava, the eighth-century guru who brought Buddhism to Tibet from India, had prophesied:

> When the iron bird flies in the sky,
> And horses are on wheels,
> The Dharma will move to the West, to the land of
> the Red Man.

Have I not heard the Hopi prophecy that a true spiritual being whose name is derived from "salt water," would come from the East? He is the Sun Clan brother, whose return will mark the completion of a millenium-long ritual, the Hopi Indians say. The name Dalai Lama means "teacher who is an ocean of wisdom."

I was brought up hearing that God is Love. The Dalai Lama is known to his followers, among many of his attributes, as Avalokiteshvara, the Bodhisattva of Mercy and Compassion. Now, hearing that he is considered to be an ocean of wisdom, I think of the symbolism of water as the giver and preserver of life; of its mother-image; of the fluid body of Man, symbolic of the unconscious, of the dynamic, motivating, female side of the personality; of water as the transitional element between fire and the ethereal element of air and the solid element of earth; of water condensed, returning from heaven to earth in the rain of Elsa Cloud. What I am really trying to get at is the connection in my mind between the Dalai Lama as an avatar of mercy and compassion, the ocean of wisdom, and the unconscious,[*] as the "immortal sea which brought us hither; intimations of which are given in moments of 'oceanic feeling': one sea of energy or instinct; embracing all mankind, without distinction of race, language or culture; and embracing all the generations of Adam, past, present, and future, in one phylogenetic heritage; in one mystical or symbolical body."

The Director and the Secretary regard me with expressions of amiability. They tell me that the Hopi word for "sun" is the word for "moon" in Tibetan, and that the Tibetan word for "sun" is the Hopi word for "moon." The Hopi Indians and some of the Tibetans have similar facial features, which would seem

---

[*] As Norman Brown interpreted Freud's thinking in *Civilization and Its Discontents* in *Love's Body*, pp. 88−89.

to bear out the theory that American Indians came across the Bering Strait to North America thousands of years ago. The Tibetans and the Hopis both believe that religion is a way of life, both are concerned with the interconnectedness between man and nature, both prize the turquoise. The Hopi's *kachina* icons are like primitive versions of certain Bon icons. Hopi Indians once used dry-sand painting in their ceremonies, the only culture outside of Tibet to do so, but the Secretary says he understands that the Hopi taught the Navajo the technique, and now the Navajo excel in sand painting and the Hopi seldom make sand paintings any more. Have I seen such sand paintings?

Yes, I tell him. I have seen Hopi sand paintings. I once wrote an article about the Red Ant pathway. Has the Secretary heard this Navajo chant of Hopi derivation?

> The herbs, the fir tree,
> I become part of it.
> The morning mists,
> The clouds, the gathering waters,
> I become part of it.
> The wilderness, the dew drops, the pollen
> I become part of it.

No, he has not heard it, but of course Bon was also a pantheistic religion.

I don't think prizing the turquoise is a reason to link the Tibetans with the Hopis, since the color blue was discovered later than earth colors in all cultures, and is prized by many. But similarity of features, the strength to endure, introspective personalities not given to chattering, dry-sand painting as a religious and medicinal ceremonial, well, there must be some connection. Tibetan Buddhism accommodates Bon, and Bon is not unlike the shamanistic practices of the Hopis.

"The clouds . . . I become part of it." "I'd like to be the sea, the jungle, or else a cloud." Love of nature and the identification with it. I am glad that this primal instinct co-exists in Veronica along with her search for spiritual values. I make the corollary comparison of Bon and Buddhism. The Secretary nods and smiles at me as we take our leave.

"Tibetan monks radiate mildness and yet have wills of iron," Veronica says. "They have the power to breed happiness and contentment, and the art of unlocking your mind and lighting it with peace and uncommon sense." Their "aura," she goes on, comes from years of preoccupation with spiritual matters and deep meditation. "I love the way they seem certain and assured in coping with the world."

It is the monks who traditionally have guarded the treasury of Tibet's accumulated knowledge, recorded in the books that filled the great monastery libraries at Ganden, Drepung, and Sera, as well as the libraries of smaller monasteries. These books embody the spirit of the Tibetans in a way that books have never done more vividly and poignantly with the exception, perhaps, of the books of Maya, which were also destroyed by foreign invaders. Thankfully, the Tibetans were able to save a greater quantity from the hands of Chinese Communists.

The Library of Tibetan Works and Archives—Veronica has spent so much time there that it is like "home" to her, she says—is not far from the *Kashag*. When we get there, Tibetan workmen are watering crotons in a trough-like brick planter fronting the second platform on which the Library is set. Another work force is chipping gravel for road work along the lanes on either side of the long, white two-storeyed building. The structure's severity is relieved with corbeling beneath the flat slate roof and over the twenty-four wide, tall windows, and above the triple-arched portico of the entranceway where fluted red columns support archivolts decorated with floral cartouches. The entrance door is bordered, as is the wainscoting of the entranceway, with traditional Tibetan patterns painted in brilliant greens, blues, reds, yellows. Close up, the carved, painted flowers and the Tibetan inscriptions above the Library's entranceways have the stylized clarity and reverent celebration of a *thangka*.

As soon as we open the heavy door of the Library and step inside, we are surrounded by Veronica's Tibetan friends. I am confused at first by all the introductions because "Tenzing," which is both masculine and feminine, is a very popular given name. Tenzing means holder of fate, holder of confidence. Half the members of the Tibetan cabinet and secretariat are named Tenzing. Most of the Tibetan and European babies born in Dharamsala are taken to the Dalai Lama to be named Tenzing. In print, the only way you can tell if Tenzing is a man's or woman's name is by the following given name. Tara and Lhama are the names of goddesses; Chime, meaning one who doesn't die, and Tashi, meaning good luck, are also women's names.

Veronica has arranged with two monks to give me a guided tour. Like a magnetic field, ions of calm and tranquillity flow from the two men, embracing me with gentle authority. They lead me through rooms with collections of Tibetan texts (more than fifty thousand, they tell me), ancient bronzes, *thangkas*, and ritual objects that have been brought from Tibet by the refugees. Brass, copper, and silver prayer wheel cylinders are inscribed in Tibetan script with *Om Mani Padme Hum*, a phrase so familiar to me now that I can "read" it. Inside some of the cylinders, prayer scrolls are furled around wands on which the mantra is carved. When the taller of the two monks holds a prayer wheel by its handle and makes it revolve from left to right, around and around, you can hear the little rattle of these prayer wands, or *soshings*. In other cylinders, the mantra is written on pieces of handmade paper, and these cylinders revolve silently. *Om Mani Padme Hum*.

The monks remove yellow and red silk wrappings from sheaves of handmade paper sandwiched between carved wooden covers to show me proclamations, marriage and land contracts, letters of high-ranking officials, revenue transactions, court cases that date back to the tenth and eleventh centuries. Across a hallway is a room set up with video-recording equipment as part of the Library's Oral History Documentation program. A plaque on the door states that funds for the program have come from the Smithsonian Institution and from the John D. Rockefeller III Foundation—to film and record Tibetan ceremonials, the gentle monks explain, to film religious and social festivals, the traditional skills of woodblock printing, wood carving, rug weaving, chants, dances, songs. But mostly, they say, the Library is supported by His Holiness and the Cultural Affairs Department of the Indian government.

There is a room in which more than five thousand photographs of Tibet are filed.

There is a room in which rare manuscripts are being catalogued and indexed. On a table are the rectangular, buff, fibrous pages of manuscripts made centuries ago from the leaves and inner bark of birch and aloe trees. The pages are written in Sanskrit, incised with a pointed stylus with the grooves then inked in.

The Vedic tradition of Sanskrit traces the origin of language to the cognitions of seers whose phonology meshed with the physics of creation in such a way that word and form are so intimately connected that they may be called equivalent. Like Sanskrit, Tibetan is a "natural language" in which the structure of speech reflects the structure of the Universe. Veronica tells me that Tibetan, the language of the teachings, the philosophy, the practices, is flawless, a language that really helps one to understand the world, because the words themselves, each one, point to the outstanding characteristics of the object. It is the epitome of onomatopoeia, a very simple idea, actually, and very practical. For example, the word for attachment is *dev-chak*. *Dev* means desire, and *chak* means clinging or holding tight. Clinging-desire, what better word for attachment? Or the word for firefly which translates as mind's fire glow? The written language is like no other she has come across because there are so many letters that have to be written that are not pronounced and, often as not, the orthography gives no clue to the pronunciation.

Om mani padme hum is a Sanskrit mantra, not a Tibetan one, but since it is dedicated to Chen-Resigs, the Divine Protector of Tibet, the Great Compassionate One, the mantra is essential to Tibetan Buddhism. OM is the sound and silence throughout all time, the sound of eternity that invokes all that is otherwise inexpressible. MANI is the essence of all existence, beyond all matter, all phenomena, all change and all becoming, the jewel of the world. PADME means "in the lotus," the world, like a lotus, unfolding its petals of spiritual progress, revealing beneath the leaves of delusion the adamantine diamond of MANI, the jewel of nirvana. HUM is a declaration of being, of a sense of the fullness of life, of Isness, Nowness. At rest in the very center of the universe, part of things, in the present, vibrantly aware as though it were your last moment on earth.

I write as softly and carefully as I can. This is the room in which Veronica has worked, where lamas are working now. The connection the Tibetans have with their past, their feeling that their past is part of their present, their devotion to maintaining relics and memories, their belief in the preservation of knowledge and tradition is so admirable and endearing that the warmth and sympathy I felt in Byllakuppe deepen. Veronica may be enamored of Buddhism. I am falling in love with the Tibetans.

In an alcove outside the room, a master-carver has constructed a large three-dimensional icon of Mahakaruna, an avatar of Avalokiteshvara, the Great Compassionate One. The deity has one head, two legs and four arms. One hand holds a lotus, another a *mala*, or prayer beads, and two hands are poised in the *mudra* of prayer. The craftsmanship and iconographical details of the sculpture sing out as sweetly as any bulbul in the concentrated silence of the scholarly lamas. Their silence, like a heavy blanket, is denser than the quietness in another room where monks, lay Tibetans, and European students are working on various library publications, including an illustrated English-language quarterly called the *Tibet Journal*. The shorter of the two monks escorting me whispers that the Imperial Printing Press of His Holiness, the Dalai Lama, is located further up the mountain. I buy several books and publications. The crackling of the paper in which an attendant wraps them for me is as sharp a sound as the Holi bonfire I still hear in my memory.

Another room nearby is bare except for trays of round loaves of bread aligned on the floor. The loaves smell like the small oval biscuits my grandmother's Scottish cook used to make from barley flour, butter, and water. I remember watching her stir the dough for these bannocks with a wooden spoon in a large ocher bowl with brown and white stripes around its middle. According to an old druidic belief, she always stirred the dough in a clockwise direction. Counterclockwise, or "Withershins," she said, "would nae bring guid luck."

The shorter and rounder of my escorts says that the loaves of barley bread are baked daily "for everyone to eat." And then, silently as paper drawn up by a flue in the draught of flames, the monks vanish, leaving me to read in a room where sunlight casts amber rugs on a polished wooden floor. The quiet is extraordinary. An active silence seems to be operative in the Library, a silence having to do with the pain which has caused its being. Memory is the treasure and guardian of all things, I have said many times before, but now as I say it to myself, Cicero's epigram, a worn stencil in my mind, takes on new meaning. The Tibetans, threatened by oblivion, bearers of traditions that could pass away with them, face a death that surpasses a normal separation from life. The extraordinary struggle to retain their history and transmit it, to preserve and pass on the knowledge of their lives and existence, to recall the past so that it can be re-lived in its original freshness, unaltered by intervening changes, seems to be expressed in the intensity of the silence. As a Tibetan explains to me later, outliving historical enemies is a personal accomplishment, a bittersweet triumph, a sense of the past that is never truly lost; and the brutalities the Tibetans have suffered have deepened their understanding, made them more loving of each other and their heritage.

I re-visit the room where the rare books are stored, and Veronica leaves her friends to join me. A monk who is reading an auspicious wedding song that is a recent contribution to the Library, asks an interpreter to explain to me (in answer to one of my questions) that while most Tibetans are monogamous, polygamy was once commonly practiced to keep property in one family, or because the first wife proved barren. Polyandry was also common. The custom was for sisters to share one husband, or for two or three brothers to share one wife. The children of such unions always looked on the eldest brother as the father. Veronica is not interested in such facts. She prefers to instruct me about the doctrine based on the Eightfold Path: Right Understanding (to be free from superstition and delusion); Right Thought (high and worthy of human intelligence); Right Speech (kindly and truthful); Right Action (peaceful, honest, and pure); Right Livelihood (bringing hurt or danger to no living thing); Right Effort (in self-training and control); Right Mindfulness (to keep an active, watchful mind); Right Concentration (in deep meditation on the realities of life). The monk, on the other hand, tells me about the great Jokhang temple in Lhasa where twenty thousand monks were served tea three times daily during *Monlan*, a festival celebrating Lord Buddha's victory over the malicious spirits who tempted him during his meditation. The festival began on the third or fourth day of the New Year and lasted for twenty-one days, with a Butter Festival celebrated on the fifteenth day of the first month of the New Year. For offerings at that time, butter was colored with powdered dyes and sculptured in figures that could be as tall as forty feet. His father, one of the chief monks at Sera, he says, was very talented at sculpting butter. He laughs like the child he was when he first saw the figure of a huge, laughing fat man his father carved. Veronica tugs me away, telling me I mustn't interrupt the monks, that they have serious work to do and can't be bothered with "frivolous trivia." She is cross that I haven't shown myself to better advantage. Why hadn't I asked them about the poetry of Milarepa or something of "more consequence"?

I retort that she's the intellectual catechumen, not I.

"Well," she says, sounding doubtful, but looking mollified. "Well, anyway, I hope you get along well with Geshe-la."

Three or four dozen hippies and students of Buddhism are massed about the steps of the Library waiting for the appearance of Geshe-la, who is scheduled to arrive soon to speak in one of the Library's classrooms. Veronica says that there's an old Tibetan proverb that a guru is like a fire: if you get too close, you get burned; if you stay too far away, you don't get enough heat. "But a guru or a spiritual friend is always there burning for you, a life-fire," she says. Her words are wrapped with sincerity, carefully and durably packaged as the presents she used to send me in flour-sacking stitched and sealed with red sealing wax. If it hadn't been for all the hippies around, I would have hugged her, but I didn't want to embarrass her in front of them.

Veronica tells me that the Lord Buddha said one should be like a goldsmith, rubbing, scorching, cutting, not taking something from your teacher just because you have respect for him, but investigating his teachings and analyzing them as your own.

"Geshe-la says, 'Don't take the words for gospel truth, because you have a brain of your own.' " I wonder now what the hippies expect from Geshe-la. Are they heuristic, bleakly hungry for revelation? Are they like actors, finding themselves by finding other people inside themselves?

An American Buddhist nun with a shaved head tells me it's "nice" being in Dharamsala "because no one expects you to be more than what you are." A young German photographer wearing chamois shorts and suspenders embroidered with edelweiss tells me that he had stalked what he was certain was the Abominable Snowman, the Himalayan *Yeti*, following huge footprints in the snow, only to find that they were the footprints of a *pahari*. When it gets warm, he says, the edges of an animal or human footprint crumble inward so that they assume a larger size; then they re-freeze, and become bigger and bigger as the process is repeated, "thus fostering a myth which encourages pranksters to play hoaxes, and the gullible to imagine sightings of a monster." Several others disagree. They know *yetis* exist. One tells me he thinks Geshe-la is "a neat guy, very simpatico." Like Veronica, a few have dug and planted their own vegetable and flower gardens. No one has ever volunteered to help the Tibetan work forces chip gravel for road repairs. Most have no interest in Tibetan politics. A majority, however, tell me how wonderful the monks have been to them—teaching them Tibetan, helping them with their problems. Monks and lay Tibetans have cared for them when they were sick, helped deliver and baptize their babies, provided them with food and shelter when they were broke, counseled them, advised them, and even baby-sat for them occasionally, free of charge.

"What a bunch of freeloaders," I grumble to Veronica. "A bunch of spongers."

"They're not *all* freeloaders," she says. "Some work very hard in the Library. Some help put together documentary films and stuff like that. They don't *mean* to sponge off anyone. They just don't have any money and aren't used to the climate and the altitude and that sort of thing. They mean well, Mummy." She folds her arms firmly around the kilo bags of dried fruit and nuts we bought at the Mohan Singh market in New Delhi to give to Geshe-la. "I hope he likes these," she says. "They don't sell them here."

I scribble in my notebook that some people dominate with their generosity. My mother? Myself? Others, like Veronica, have the gift of the truly giving heart. Veronica, seeing what I have written, says this is a "sickeningly sentimental" observation. "You always said it was better to give than to receive. Why give me more credit than I deserve?" she asks in a mild and reasonable voice. She says that in the code of the Bodhisattva, the meaning of life is to bring happiness to others, that later, when meditation has made one understand that the world as one sees it is one's own fabrication, the purpose of living to be good for another also dissolves. "One is naturally, appropriately good, with no motive for it." Then, in a rush of confiding honesty mixed with the gobble-de-guru that comes as naturally to her as psychobabble does to me, she says that perhaps with age and experience comes an understanding of why people act the way they do and "glimpses, through one's own fears and uptightness, of why one acts as one does."

Everyone rises when Geshe-la appears. Elderly, kind-faced,

his eyes twinkling behind his spectacles, he rustles past us. We troop after him to a white-walled, high-ceilinged room. There are orange poppies set about in bowls on the windowsills, and many flat cushions arranged on the floor to sit on. Geshe-la settles himself on a chair in front of a *thangka* mounted on brocade. He fingers the hundred and eight wooden beads of his *mala* in his right hand, while his followers prostrate themselves and then chant in preparation for meditation.

Finally, Geshe-la begins to speak. A lay Tibetan serves as his English-speaking translator. Linguistic signals are unpacked and their conceptual messages are spread before an audience of which I am the only one with open eyes, not sitting with my hands clasped and my thumbs pressed together. I am sitting with my notebook on my lap, scribbling away, and Geshe-la's ideas seem redemptive to me, coruscating as the sunlight pouring in through the open window that lets in with it the sound of boulders being chipped into gravel.

"Anger," Geshe-la says, "is no way to be happy. If you are angry, you can't sleep on a comfortable bed, and food is tasteless." But anger is our best friend, he says. "You should rejoice when someone makes you angry. How else can you practice tolerance and compassion?"

Now, that to me, is an exceptionally interesting thought to pin on my mind's bulletin board. Geshe-la goes on. "Through compassion, through love, many problems can be solved. Compassion and love are precious, not complicated, simple but difficult to practice. His Holiness the Dalai Lama believes that it is helpful to have many different religions, just as with food. Each person has different tastes, and each eats food that accords with his own taste. The Christian religion is more applicable, more useful to people who believe there is a god, a creator, and that everything depends on God's will. If thinking that, believing that, gives you greater security, that is the best philosophy to have. Certain people say our Buddhist belief, that there is no creator and that everything depends on your self, is preferable. You see, if you are master, then everything depends on you. For certain people, that way of seeing is much more preferable, much more suitable. Each great faith, each great teaching serves mankind, so that it is much better to make friends and understand one another and make an effort to serve humankind than to criticize or argue. What is important is that non-believers and believers respect each other. All religions have the same basic aim, the goal of creating inner peace."

My mind goes back to the sermon my Presbyterian minister preached one Sunday not long before I left for India. The man or woman who ignores God is apt to live in a dull, restricted, monochromatic world, while the believer delights in a rainbow world filled with the varied glories of creation and is open to the radiant world of the Spirit, the dimension of eternity. The non-religious live with the pallor of mortality. . . . In a Christian church no one is to say that the green in the rainbow is better than the red, the yellow more important than the blue. As no color is superior to another, all work is equal in God's eye. In each of us that Spirit is manifested in one particular way, for some useful purpose. "I love the picture that Zachariah gives us of the heavenly Zion," the minister said. "Here is the Rainbow community as he sees it through God's eyes, not a sleek, solemn gathering of almost identical saints, but this: 'Once again shall old men and old women sit in the streets of Jerusalem, each leaning on a stick because of their great age; and the streets of

the city shall be full of boys and girls playing in the streets. . . .
They shall be my people and I will be their God.' There is room
for everyone in this Rainbow church and every single gift is of
value in God's sight."

Now Geshe-la is speaking about attachment. "Attachment
concerns a selfish, aggressive, narrow-minded approach to living, and non-attachment brings compassion, patience, and
awareness. Non-attachment in its grossest form means renun-
ciation of that which leads to suffering. In its subtler form, it
means a real openness of relationships, every kind of relationship, oneself and the world. In its subtlest sense, non-attachment means not clinging to the creative arisings such as
thoughts, emotions, memories, perceptions. Selflessness does
not mean not accepting an 'I' or Self. This would be an extreme
of nihilism, and Buddhist doctrine holds that self-realization is
the finest contribution you can make in order to help other
people. Non-attachment is the sublimation of the ego so that
even though you are surrounded by chaos, you can still maintain
detachment and an all-calm inner self, not only freed from
worldly attachments to people and things, but also in a state
where you have true knowledge of yourself and are in total
contact with yourself. You can achieve this state best by the
mind-emptying process of meditation. Meditation helps you
attain the state where everything is at rest, everything is free, so
that you can let your mind open outward in life the way a
lotus—or a poppy on a windowsill—opens to the sun."

Geshe-la is rolling the beads of his *mala* between his fingers.
The interpreter says to the class that Geshe-la hopes his words
have been helpful and that we will put them into practice. If
they aren't helpful, then we have no need for them. The audi-

ence stirs; begins to chant a prayer. Sunlight streams into the room. Veronica, bathed in light, looks like an angel, all the promise of her father without his destructive flaws (or mine), all the promise of a heart and mind annealed in the conflicts of an experimental adolescence. Her search for a way of life and a way of being that will suit her contemplative temperament, her love of nature, her idealism, her expectations of herself may let her "mount up with wings as eagles." The philosophy of Buddhism is for her what Christianity and Deist belief are for me, an image of purity and hope and comfort for herself and the world, a force of good, an affirmation of an inward presence of divinity, visible, perhaps, only to her inward eye and my own, but there, always there, a force of good within, God within.

The chanting prayers end, and we leave the classroom, walk downstairs and out into the clarity of the pine-scented air.

Twenty-Seven

On the morning that we are to set off by Jeep for McLeod Ganj, Veronica says that my being with her in India has been like a healing talisman. "You've had to be awfully patient, haven't you, Mum? When I see grown-up friends of mine with their teenage kids, it seems so obvious all the stages we human beings have to go through, and that all mothers have to be so patient."

As the Jeep joltingly makes its way upward, I look at the white crown of the Dhauladar, a giant presence under heaven, glinting and flashing in the sunlight through scarves of wind-blown clouds. I listen for the beat of hooves on the macadam as a rider spurs his horse before us . . . alongside of us . . . behind us. I can feel my heart beating. I can hear my interior voice thanking God for this moment. Oh, Elsa Cloud, you condense the vapors of my mind into such fine droplets of joy that they seem to float suspended about me, misting my vision with in-finities like the Blakean particles of sand I seem to hold when your cool thoughts flow from your fingers into mine. As I say this to myself, I wonder if I am going crazy, hallucinating, seeing things. The building we are approaching appears to be a church—gray stone in the solitude of a glade surrounded by deodars. It has no steeple, but there is a sense of repose about it. Am I dreaming with open eyes?

No, I am not. When we arrive at the gate of the building, I climb out of the Jeep. I hoist the stirrup-shaped latch over and back from the gatepost, and shoulder open the iron gate. The hinges caterwaul resistance.

It is a Presbyterian church. Like the medieval traveler who made a complete circuit of the world without knowing it, I feel I have come back to the place I started from. "The wheel has come full circle. I am here." I visualize Shakespeare's lines above my head like a wreathed, candle-lit wheel, an Advent chandelier.

"But how do you know it's Presbyterian?" Veronica asks.

How could I not know? I grew up seeing small, country churches like these. I spent summer Sunday mornings in Scotland with my grandmother in a village kirk so much like the one before me that in the quietness, the solitude, my grandmother is here, breathing next to me. I *see* her. I kneel or sit beside her, listening to the cadence of hymns, stirred by the language of the liturgy.

The sun dapples the churchyard through the branches of deodars, weaving patterns of sunlight on the grass. Shining, shimmering patterns of light, and in my mind John Donne is saying, "Batter my heart, three person'd God: for you but knock, breathe, shine, and seek to mend. Take me to you, imprison me, for I, except you enthrall me, never shall be free, nor ever chaste, except you ravish me."

I want to embrace this church, have the sunlight amber it

forever in my mind, this church with its blunt Gothic towers, its dark gray stone durable and grave as the Scottish hills and the Scottish character.

The earthquake of 1905, which devastated the Kangra Valley, apparently toppled the church steeple, and the bell which hung suspended within it is now anchored to the ground. Stained glass in the windows has fallen away from its moldings, been broken, shattered, and only two windows on the lee side of the church remain. In one, two figures, one male, one female, are identified with scrolls as Justice and Sacrifice. In the two panels of the other are Jesus and St. John, St. John and a kneeling figure. Their finely etched faces remind me of the paintings of Frederic Leighton, of his Persephone poised before Demeter, who stands in a cave with her arms outstretched. "Yes, very pre-Raphaelite," Veronica agrees, "like Edward Burne-Jones. I think he did the windows in the cathedral in Calcutta, so maybe he did these, too."

Our musings are broken by the arrival of a *chaukidar* and his agitated shrilling. This is a Scottish temple, a Scottish temple, a Scottish temple, he cries. We must not go inside unless we take our shoes off. We cannot go inside because he has the key. We cannot go inside because the key he has is broken and is being repaired. Oh woe, woe, woe! In all these years there have been no visitors and now that we are here, the key to the door is broken. His wail raises to a jagged pitch, then lowers slightly as I reach for my purse. An exceptionally large tip produces a pleasing tone, a smile to show that he has put in his false teeth for our benefit. They hurt him and fall out when he eats, he says. Now that he has money, he can buy glue for them, and *chapattis* and vegetables he can chew. May all the gods and the Lord bless us! *Ram, ram.*

I listen to his dentured lisp, mourning the missing key, until I can bear it no longer. See? I say. If we just walk to the other side of the church where all the windows are gone, and we pile up these stones, and he is careful not to let them slip, and I am careful to hold tightly to the sill, I will be able to see inside. We won't need the *chabji*, the *kunjii*. All is well. And so it is.

Standing on a pile of stones, I can see the sun beaming through the stained glass panel of Jesus and St. John, casting pools of blue and red and gold that dance on the stone floor. Light filtering through holes in the roof illumines brass oil lamps fixed to stone walls and a bronze eagle gleaming on the lectern. The pews are gone, probably chopped up for firewood long ago, but the bare interior of the church is lovely as it is. I can see a baptismal font with an octagonal basin, a symbol of regeneration and resurrection. "Do you remember the little octagonal metal bolt with a brass keyhole glued on top of it that you gave me when you were a little girl? I loved it so," I say. When you looked through the keyhole, you could see a scrap of paper on which she had printed "I love you."

Veronica smiles and nods, and, smiling, the *chaukidar* performs a final *mudra*. I see him slipping his teeth into his pocket as he goes out the gate.

In the back of the church, there is a memorial, and a graveyard. The memorial, of gray stone, is all little turreted towers and spires, fenced about with wrought iron and small turreted bollards, a fanciful mix of fortress, cathedral, and castle in miniature. I begin to read the inscription aloud and then stop, and start again. "James Bruce, Earl of Elgin and Kincardine, Viceroy and Governor General of India, Governor of Jamaica, Governor General of Canada, High Commissioner and Ambassador to

China. Died at Dharamsala in the Discharge of His Duties on the 20th of November, 1863. Aged 52 years, four months. 'He being dead, yet speaketh.' This monument was erected by his widow Mary Louisa, Countess of Elgin and Kincardine." James Bruce, the son of Thomas Bruce, whose great-grandmother was also Boswell's great-grandmother and, therefore, a distant collateral antecedent of Veronica's and of mine.

I recall a drawing of James Bruce, 8th Earl of Elgin and 12th Earl of Kincardine, the frontispiece of his biography which my grandmother had shown me.

"Granny, how could he be two kinds of Earls at the same time?"

"Because he was, darling. Just look at his superb, almost saintly face."

Educated at Eton and at Christ Church, Oxford, a contemporary of William Gladstone, James Bruce was an intellectual and, according to his biographer, a man of great physical bravery who sat calmly on the deck of a sinking ship during a terrible storm in order to prevent panic among the passengers and the crew.

"A very brave man, my precious," Granny said. A man to my grandmother's liking, I gathered, because his rock-hard conscience and moral fiber were like her own.

After his first wife died in the shipwreck, when he was on his way to his first governorship in Jamaica, his life seemed doomed to personal tragedy. His children and kinfolk died one after the other at his family house at Broomhall, Dumfermline, in Scotland.

" 'I fancy the monks have won over the simple Indians'—he is referring to the American Indians, my treasure," Granny remarked, as she read selected passages of his letters included in his biography—" 'to a great extent by gentle methods.' " Granny told me that his mind and faith were above mere ecclesiology, that he was a true Christian, a true man of God, that he had even thought once of entering a monastery. She showed me a silver-backed mirror which she kept wrapped in tissue paper in a felt bag. It had belonged to Veronica, the Countess of Kincardine, his and Boswell's great-grandmother. From Boswell, it had passed to his granddaughter who married my great-grandfather who willed it to her. ("Not a mirror, precious, Lady Kincardine's looking-glass.")

I reach out my head to clasp Veronica's, and with my other I touch the name of Elgin on the memorial. My eyes delight in reading what they know, as when the name of a place you've been to is suddenly found on a map or in a book where you would least expect to find it. I touch the name carved in stone to form a magical connection, to bridge the generations, to link Elgin's name with my mother's and grandmother's, to link dear old Bozzy to Elgin, and to Veronica and myself by a silken line, fragile yet durable.

Oh, Elsa Cloud, you are part of me and part of your father, and I am part of you, you my link to Robert, you my link to life with him, you who are like me and not like me, an extension of myself reaching out into another world, proof of the immortality of the spirit of life, ever new, ever green, ever fragrant as the deodars around us.

Back in the Jeep, we continue our journey upward. Suddenly, we round a corner and are in McLeod Ganj, the place or way or road of McLeod, with nothing but its name reminiscent of the ancestral home of the MacLeods in the Isle of Skye in the New Hebrides. McLeod Ganj is also known as Little Lhasa. But it seems as removed from the thousand-room Potala as it is from the MacLeods' Dunvegan Castle. And yet, as I stand there on this dusty road, I see that the grandeur of both palaces is evoked by the grandeur of the setting. Below, on forested slopes scattered with the faded reds of corrugated iron roofs of houses with garden clearings around them, prayer flags catch the wind, fluttering their invocations in tireless reverence. Above, there are mountain slopes on three sides, a perspective of ridges, spurs, and rolling hills forested with virgin pines, their dark green dissolving into the teal blue and lavender of bare rock and scrub—and then the incredible, breathtaking vista of the snow-peaked Dhauladar, mother mountain, magic mountain, God mountain.

In the village, one-room marts are filled with objects brought from Tibet by refugees who carried them more than a thousand miles across the Himalayas to begin a new life. Most of the objects have religious significance: ceremonial bowls made from trepanned skulls aged to the patina of ocher kidskin and lined with silver; prayer beads carved from wood, bone, and gem stones; *damarus*, prayer drums, made from two human skulls; flutes made from femur bones; trumpets made from thigh bones. There is a strange allure about these objects, which seem far more beautiful than macabre. Veronica says the Tibetans feel that sorrow at death or parting is allayed by the prospect of rebirth, that the skull is just one of the many houses inhabited by the spirit on its journey of rebirths. Tibetans transform parts of the skeleton into utilitarian and decorative objects to symbolize the unity of the opposites of life and death.

The multitude of objects continues: *gaus*, silver and copper amulet boxes, inset with glass doors so that you can see the deity housed inside. Copper and silver prayer wheels; ego-stabbing ceremonial daggers, and daggers to exorcise demons. *Thangkas* painted with powdered gold, silver, and other mineral pigments, mounted on brocade. Butter lamps like chalices with the smell of *dri* butter still inside them. Ceremonial conch shell trumpets, bone-white, tipped with silver. Brass and silver bells capped with an emblematic *dorje* (thunderbolt) and the chopper-like, bird-shaped objects that are sacred to Tantric initiations. Heavy silver seals, like weighted *mandorlas*, each incised with one of the eight auspicious Buddhist symbols: arabesque, banner, twin fish, umbrella, vase, wheel, lotus, conch shell—I remember Veronica drawing these for me on the road past Byllakuppe. I like the feel of these stamps for sealing wax. My grandmother gave me one she always used, mother-of-pearl and gold, with the Eliott coat of arms carved on an amethyst. *Soyez sage*, it reminded me, "be good." The seal originally had belonged to my grandfather, and Granny said that holding the seal in her hand, sealing envelopes with his stamp of approval, gave her the tangible sense of his continuing presence in her life. "Here, my treasure," she said, the last year I saw her alive. "Here, my precious, 'When this you see, please think of me,' as we used to say when I was a girl." I upend a Tibetan seal with a particularly appealing shape. I see it is marked with an arabesque, the sign of longevity, and I think of placing it on the right-hand side of my desk in New York, with my grandmother's long-handled repoussé silver magnifying glass on the left-hand side, uniting Scotland and McLeod Ganj, Veronica, my grandmother, and myself. The arabesque. No marlinespike can separate us.

I look for wooden book covers for the Dalai Lama's book

about love and compassion which Jhamchoe gave me in Ooty, and which I carry as carefully as a diplomatic courier in my LV tote bag. I ask around at all the shops but there are no covers the right size, and the master carver who could make a set to fit is now working at a monastery in Nepal.

Veronica wants me to buy a roll of the hand-woven, grosgrain ribbon-like material Tibetan women cut and sew together to make their striped, ornamental aprons, called *pangdens*. By tradition, a woman's *pangden* is associated with her husband's life, and it is only taken off as a sign of mourning when a Dalai Lama dies. If a woman loses her *pangden*, she must perform rites in order to protect her husband from any illness or bad luck that this loss might cause. I listen to Veronica translating what an old Tibetan woman is telling her, and think of the *pangdens* Jhamchoe gave me in Ooty. What did he intend when he gave them to me?

The *pangden*'s durable colors—"the rainbow threads," Veronica calls them—and its varied combinations of woven stripes sing out to me. The fabric has what garment manufacturers call a good "hand," a good feel. Hand: the word conflates the feel of the product and the hand on the shuttle of the loom. Great Mother, Maya, Weaver of the World. I remember lines from William Blake's *The Keys of the Gates* (of Paradise):

> Thou'rt my mother, from the womb:
> Wife, sister, daughter, to the tomb;
> Weaving to dreams the sexual strife,
> And weeping over the web of life.

Veronica says that threads woven and spun are Tantric in their significance, that Tantrism—from the Sanskrit word *tantra*, which means the warp of threads on which the weft is woven—is a "teaching that stresses the interwovenness of things and actions." Tantrism teaches that everything in the world is inter-related, interconnected, spun, woven, threaded together like tapestries, like the fabrics and rugs the Tibetans are "so talented" at weaving.

I think of the symbolism of weaving in other cultures, how the woman is associated with the loom and sometimes even inseparable from it, like the Mayan women of Guatemala with their looms attached to themselves and to trees, so that woman, tree, and loom are one. I think of how the long twisted strands of deoxyribonucleic acid, that master chemical of heredity, require both men and women to pleach their lives together to weave new lives, new worlds.

In *All's Well that Ends Well*, Shakespeare says that "The web of life is of a mingled yarn, good and ill together." As a schoolgirl, I asked a teacher how bad things like war could happen if God was Love. "It is as though you were sitting under a tapestry and seeing the tangled threads on the wrong side," she said. "Only God can see the real picture."

Is that what Buddhism is all about, seeing things as they are?

The sweet smell of *kupsi*, freshly fried bread twists, sold from carts in the street, mingles with the aroma of old brass, old copper, woodsmoke, and pine. Walking out of earshot of the clattering looms of cottage industry rug factories, Veronica and I stop to rest on a bench by the settlement's *chorten* and the thirteen prayer wheels beside it. The white *chorten*, fenced about with concrete and wrought-iron, is a sacred Buddhist monument which contains religious relics and commemorates the heart of Buddha. It has a square base surmounted with three discs of diminishing circumferences that spiral to a dome-like extrusion. The top is capped by a golden finial beribboned with streamers in rainbow colors. The prayer wheels—tall, cylindrical copper containers inscribed with Tibetan calligraphy—are secured to a roofed-over frame in such a way that a finger's touch can set them rotating, releasing their substance and solidity, and transfiguring each into a spinning blur.

Tibetans come and go, setting the prayer wheels in motion. The cylinders are always set spinning clockwise, in the direction of the earth's orbit around the sun and the moon's orbit around the earth. As I watch the copper cylinders revolving, hear them humming, whirring, rustling the mystical mantra, I see the copper turning to blue the way it does on the spires of cathedrals. I see Veronica as the Mermaid Princess on a float rumbling down the main street of Digby and Nova Scotia; I think of the word *dig*. I think of the word *bee*. How doth the busy little bee improve each shining hour? I remember myself sitting next to a Scottish governess at the breakfast table. I slice the top off my boiled egg—neatly, as I have been taught. The eggcup is white with flowers on it, not like the silver ones my grandmother had as a child, their interiors washed with "pure gold," as she used to say (and said again later when she presented me with the silver stand holding the six eggcups she had grown up seeing daily at the center of the breakfast table). Suddenly, I am impelled to turn to my right and lay my head like a unicorn in the lap of my virgin governess, my right ear pressed against her corseted middle where, for a moment, I hear the abdominal gurglings of food being digested, feel a comforting warmth, smell the peppery, musty fragrance of her clothes, and see the boiled egg above my left eye on a plate.

I look up and am almost blinded by the whiteness of the snow on the peaks of the Dhauladar. The deep, resonating sound of a twelve-foot *dungchen*, a black-and-silver Tibetan trumpet, links what is outside with what is inside, deep as the chant of the monks at Byllakuppe, fills me with *awareness*, sets up a giant circle I am part of. God-consciousness, Buddha-consciousness. The herbs . . . the clouds . . . the wilderness, I am part of it. I remember Salinger's character Zooey saying, "Who in the whole Bible besides Jesus *knew*—actually knew that we're carrying the Kingdom around with us, inside, where we're really too stupid and sentimental and unimaginative to look." I don't know why Salinger used the word "sentimental" as a term of disapproval, because it exactly expresses the emotion aroused in me as an after-thought, as an echo of the sound of that extraordinarily long, black-and-silver *dungchen*.

Veronica is silent when I weep, tears filling my unblinking eyes, spilling over, sliding down my face. I have forgotten what it is I am weeping for, but our silence, hers and mine, is like glass that lets you see the other's thoughts. Tears slide into the corners of my mouth, tasting salty. I think of the white hands of the sea endlessly rearranging the waves as they roll into the shore, of a beach near a coral reef in the Caribbean where Robert and I and the children picnicked, of all the beaches where Veronica and I have been, together or apart, infinities of sand grains, the soft sift of sugar in a measuring cup or an hour glass. Children notice the shining sea first before they notice the sand. Robert's mother said that once when she visited us in Jamaica. We were sitting on the beach having a picnic—she, Robert, Sam, Allison, Veronica, Bryce, and I—and Veronica, looking at the sea, said that it looked just the way the sky does at night. And it did. Diamond-bright with the reflections of the sun, the white foam over the reef like a crescent moon.

A Tibetan woman is walking down the street with a Lhasa Apso sitting on her upturned palms, his forelegs upright on the palm of her right hand, his haunches resting on the palm of her left hand. I've never before seen a dog carried this way. It is an adaptive form of transport, a genetic trait of accommodation peculiar only to the Lhasa Apso, a legacy inherited from ancestors trained to seat themselves in this fashion to make their portage easier for their nomadic Tibetan owners who traveled on foot and on yak-back. The dog has a merry expression, bright-eyed as a Cairn terrier. The bearer of the dog tells me I can pat him. He won't bite. He's friendly, but a good watchdog, she says. These ancient guard dogs of Tibetan nobility are said to bring good luck into the lives of all who come in contact with them. "Good doggums," I say, hearing myself as my mother as she would affectionately greet one of her poodles. "*Tashidelek* doggums." I run my fingers lightly through his fluffy, lion-like mane before his owner proceeds triumphantly down the street, the Lhasa Apso perfectly balanced on her palms, like a birthday cake on a platter.

Veronica, linking her arm in mine, walks with me to the place where the dusty road narrows and leads to the Gompa, the Temple, and the Residence of the Dalai Lama. In front of the temple is a platform where monks are seated, chanting to the accompaniment of prayer drums and bells and little horns called *gyalings*. Over their heads are canopies garlanded with the perpetual knot, the arabesque.

"I love the sound of the monks. They sound like bull-frogs," Veronica says.

Frogs, bringers of rain, bringers of life, worshipped by the Maya. But to me the monks' chanting—this humming roar, this roaring hum—sounds more like the wind, the rumble of rocks, the thunder, an avalanche, a volcano, *fumaroles*, geysers, water-falls—like all, yet precisely like no one of these. The sound vibrates, pulses, contracts and expands in my mind as though I were part of the systole and diastole of the beginning of crea-tion. It is a pulsing, flooding darkness of sound—thick, deep, heavy, old, warm, profound—a sound that combines with the split of the voice into the light, high, thin, sound of whistling, a sustained note from some unknown instrument, like the pipes of Pan must have sounded. My ears take in the primal sound of the earth's body, its air and wind, and the cyclic, circadian beat of its rain and tides, until I hear the ringing of tierces, nones, vespers, Gregorian chants as they must have sounded in vaulted Gothic cathedrals. Veronica says that chanting heightens the sensitivity of thought inside the brain, while paradoxically it quiets and stills the mind. What meditation does by emptying the mind, chanting does by uncluttering it, drowning out the distractions of the world to make room for the mystery and miracles of dreams, the subconscious, the unconscious, the spiritual. Chanting permits both practitioners and listeners to enter into the world of the metaphysical.

Walking up the stairs behind the canopied platform, we en-ter into the glow of the temple's bronze and gilded images, the scented haze of incense and lamp-smoke. There is gold all around me—the gold of silk bindings around sacred scriptures, the gilt of images, the gleam of brass bowls for water offerings,

the eye-of-the-daisy yellow in *thangkas*, the yellow in small butter sculptures tinted also with green, blue, and pink. Everywhere my eyes travel, *ghee* burning in butter lamps casts reflections on the many faces of Buddha. I feel like a trespasser
admitted to a clandestine ceremony, an Orphic, Eleusinian mystery, a cabalistic rite.

Soon I am standing in front of a tented shrine, a glassed-in
baldachin, enclosing a *mandala* made of grains of sand, a dry-
sand painting. Looking at the *mandala*'s patterns of red, green,
blue, gold, I feel as one who stands outside a lighted church at
night in the lucency of the stained glass, aware of the worshipers
within but not one of them. In a niche above the *mandala* is an
image of Padma Sambhava, the Indian *siddha* who came to Tibet
in the eighth century to build the temple at Samye and subdue
all the enemies of the Dharma, the saint who brought the gift of
Tantric teaching to the land.

Veronica explains that *mandala* is the Sanskrit word for circle.
A *mandala*, a stage on which a divine drama can be visualized, is
an image to focus upon for meditation. "Like a *thangka*, but
more so," Veronica says. An artist who paints a *thangka* receives
merit for intent, but for those who compose a *mandala* of sand
for a religious ceremony, the merit is multiplied by the number
of grains of sand. Most painted sand *mandalas*, which may take
days or weeks to construct, are made for the joy of constructing
them, the joy of beholding them during the festival for which
they are made. Afterwards, with few exceptions, they are ritu-
ally destroyed in a rite that is symbolic of impermanence.

The *mandala* in the temple is a special one created as part of
the observance of the Kalachakra ceremony. Outside the tem-

ple, in the courtyard of the Gompa behind it, a new and much larger version of the *Kalachakra* mandala is on the way to completion. Four monks are seated on the ground before a low platform set on the stone paving. I watch them putting colored grains of sand in place with slender metal funnels, tapping the funnels to release a few grains at a time, working from the center of the design outward, working outward from their inner minds. It has taken five days for these four monks to construct this particular *mandala*, which is curtained to protect it from the wind and from "impurities." The monks wear masks to protect the grains of sand from their "impurities," and to keep their breath from disturbing the design as they bend over it.

The *Kalachakra*, or Circle of Time (*Kala* is the Sanskrit word for time, *chakra*, a wheel), is a Root Tantra which teaches adepts how to transcend time. "It is one of the Anuttra or Highest Yoga Tantras, which are divided into the father class of method and the mother class of wisdom," Veronica explains.

"Oh," I say, interested and grateful that my daughter is the teacher and that she regards me as a student who is capable of understanding.

"The *Kalachakra* Tantra belongs to the mother class." Veronica smiles at me as she says this, then turns, and with this fleeting smile renewed, greets Geshe-la who has appeared beside us with the suddenness of a bird. No, not sudden, Veronica says. Geshe-la was there all the time. He was standing at the entrance of the Gompa and saw us come out of the temple. *She* had seen *him. He* had seen *us*, but had not come forward to speak because he was glad to hear her telling me about the *Kalachakra mandala*. The Gelugpa sect, which belongs to the Mahayana tradition of

Buddhism, is particularly reverent about mothers. Geshe-la smiles and Veronica beams at me after he has remarked on this. Dear Geshe-la.

While Veronica and Geshe-la talk together, I look at the lovely image of the *Kalachakra mandala*, green and rose, blue, gold, and white, circles enclosed by a square, enclosing ever-diminishing squares, one within the other, along with many other shapes and patterns. For a moment, I think of the migrating birds on the Bharatpur *jheel*, containing, somewhere invisibly within, the landscape of Tibet and the knowledge of the air-routes that had brought them there. Had they seen in their tiny amber-button eyes an image of some larger world where they had once been, a space between two points that could be covered a second time? Had they seen the further point still visible, either in their heads or in the long memory of their kind? Could there be a genetic code, a map in my own head, which allowed me to find my way as Veronica would find hers?

The vision of the Kalachakra *mandala*, the Circle of Time, embraces me, the circle embracing the square, the square embracing the circle. OOO, the circles that stand for hugs in letters of children. Charles Sanders Peirce wrote in his *Scientific Metaphysics* that the movement of love is circular, "at one and the same impulse projecting creations into independency and drawing them into harmony." O the circle of the feminine principle that ensures birth and regeneration. O the monogram of God. Naught but O can save evolution from evil. O the rings and wreaths that celebrate the union of heavenly and earthly love! O the circle of Veronica's navel when the umbilical cord withered away. O the navel, the *omphalos* of the world, linking generation with generation. O the circle of breast and nipple,

the *mandala* of motherhood. O the way of circumlocution. O
the sound of OM, the sacred syllable that begins the mystical
mantra, the circular tool in the sound of the mantra, the primordial sound containing the energy present at the origin of
the universe, the Hindu belief that the creative power encapsu-
lated in the sound helped bring forth the world. The Oh of bliss
and exhaustion of the mother as the round crown of her infant's
head pushes through from darkness into light. O the sacred
syllable of the beginning of life, the sound of wonder, the first
shared sound of the mother and her newly born. O the sound
of creation. O the circle.

Drawn into the *Kalachakra mandala*, I haven't noticed that
Veronica has left Geshe-la and returned to stand beside me. She
quotes what Geshe-la has said: "From the heart of *Kalachakra*
are emitted Ones Gone to Bliss, in father and mother aspect."

Veronica says that Geshe-la is going over to the residence of His
Holiness, and that she is going to walk with him to the gate.
Would I like to come?

And see where the Dalai Lama lives? Is she sure that wouldn't
be an intrusion, an invasion of his privacy?

Veronica says that Geshe-la wouldn't suggest such a thing if
it weren't all right.

Has she told Geshe-la about Jhamchoe and the book written
by His Holiness that I have with me in my tote bag? Would
Geshe-la have any idea where I might get wooden covers made
for it?

Veronica confers with Geshe-la. Geshe-la holds out both his
hands. With both my hands I place the book wrapped in its
yellow towel in his. Geshe-la holds the book resting in his palms

and held steady with his thumbs. He takes it into the temple to find a proper place to unwrap it and have a look. We follow him. While Geshe-la is looking at the book, I go to stand beneath the platform where the monks are chanting. Each singer is simultaneously producing a deep fundamental tone, and two or three overtones. Sustained chords are punctuated occasionally by the sound of cymbals, bells, and horns. When Veronica joins me, she says that the chanting imparts subliminal blessings, listening to it is "beneficial to all sentient beings," that the monks control the muscles at their throat openings so they can produce two or more tones at the same time, that the monks are visualizing deities connected with the mantras they are chanting in preparation for the *Kalachakra* ceremony. "They sound like bullfrogs," she says again. She sounds the way she used to as a child, when she liked someone or something very much and, expecting to be criticized or laughed at for her thoughts, hid what she felt behind a screen of flippancy.

Veronica's birth was induced. I did not hear her first birth cry. And what happened to my own cry? Was I too drugged to cry out when Veronica was born?

Surprisingly, seemingly apropos of nothing, Veronica says that feeling guilty about the past does no one any good, that all of us make mistakes or do things we regret, and that we just have to learn to live in the present. As she speaks, I listen to the chanting—that humming roar, that roaring hum—and feel how extraordinary and beautiful, how comforting it is. "It's about method and wisdom, the father and mother principles," Veronica says softly. "The seeds of initiation take a long time to grow in one's mind."

Geshe-la joins us. Still holding the towel-wrapped book, he

says something in Tibetan. I hear the words Yeshe Norbu and Kundun, the Wish-Fulfilling Gem and The Presence, names by which the Dalai Lama is known. "He is happy that you have this wonderful book written by His Holiness, the Ocean of Wisdom," Veronica translates, as waves of sound roll over my head, drowning me in their blessings.

We follow Geshe-la toward an archway with trees and lawns beyond. Through the trees there is a glimpse of a building with a peaked and gabled portico. Two monks are walking along a path leading from the building to the archway. Their saffron undergarments look bright in the sunlight. Their right arms are bare. The shadow of hair on their shaved heads looks as if it has been penciled on. The metal rims of their glasses sparkle with points of light as they walk toward us. Their measured way of walking is so certain, so smooth that we are facing each other through the gate before I realize that the taller of the two monks is looking directly at us. Geshe-la and he are smiling, steepling their hands, bowing their heads in greeting. The other monk drops behind as the taller one passes through the gate to meet us. He has a lovely face, a sweet smile, and his eyes are twinkling behind his squarish glasses. He looks like . . . can he be? Geshe-la turns to me and introduces me to His Holiness, the Dalai Lama. My eyes meet his. He looks down as Geshe-la places the book, unwrapped, in his hands, and suddenly His Holiness has a pen in his right hand and is signing the first page of my book, the book he has written, Tenzing Gyatso, Gyalwa Rinpoche, Yeshe Norbu, Rundun, the Dalai Lama. Geshe-la gives me the towel so that I can receive the book back from His Holiness and re-wrap it, which Veronica helps me do.

This is one of six books which His Holiness has written,

Geshe-la says, three of them translated into English, which His Holiness speaks very well. Then the Dalai Lama speaks. His voice is melodious, and it bestows upon me a sense of peace, of being in harmony with myself and with the world, of being solidly grounded, yet light as a cloud. It is *darshan*, the blessing I'd felt in the presence of the Dalai Lama's junior tutor, Trijung Rinpoche, now magnified, and I accept it without questioning or wonder.

Geshe-la translates: "All religions can learn from each other; the ultimate goal of all religions is to produce better human beings. Better human beings would be more tolerant, more compassionate, less selfish. Love and compassion are the essence of all religions."

"Kindness," His Holiness says, speaking now in English. "This is something useful in our daily life whether you believe in God or Buddha." He rests his dark eyes on Veronica and me and laughs like a child, with pleasure, a wonderful, billowing laugh, joyful, soft, enfolding. He steeples his hands and nods and smiles to Veroncia. He holds out his right hand to me and I clasp it with my right hand. "Compassion and love are precious things in life," he says, "simple, but difficult to practice." And then he is gone. As I watch him walking toward the temple, I hear again the chanting of the monks. I feel free and light, disencumbered, as if the restrictive wrappings of worry, anxiety, depression, tiresome bindings of twentieth-century acedia, have been stripped away to reveal another self—not an entirely new self, but one that is better, more comfortable. Veronica puts her arm around my shoulder and leans her head toward mine, the wings of our hair nestling against each other without pressure, her ear cupped to my own like a whispering shell.